Pitt Latin American Series

The Expulsion of Mexico's Spaniards 1821–1836

Harold Dana Sims

University of Pittsburgh Press

Published by the University of Pittsburgh Press, Pittsburgh, Pa. 15260
Copyright © 1990, University of Pittsburgh Press
All rights reserved
Baker & Taylor International, London
Manufactured in the United States of America

Library of Congress Cataloging-in-Publication Data

Sims, Harold Dana, 1935–
    The expulsion of Mexico's Spaniards, 1821–1836 / Harold Dana Sims.
        p.   cm.—(Pitt Latin American series)
    Includes bibliographical references and index.
    ISBN 0-8229-3643-7
    1. Mexico—History—1821–1861   2. Spaniards—Government policy—
Mexico—History—19th century.   3. Deportation—Mexico—
History—19th century.   I. Title. II. Series.
F1232.S56   1990
972'.04—dc20   89-48351
                                                                    CIP

To my wife

Retsuko Hirasawa de Sims

Contents

Tables

Preface

THE INITIAL idea for this book was born in conversations with Dr. Lyle N. McAlister at the University of Florida, Gainesville, in 1964. He foresaw that it could become the work of nearly an entire career. Dr. Nettie Lee Benson of the University of Texas, Austin, guided me during several visits to the wondrous collection that now deservedly bears her name. She generously shared her profound knowledge of sources for nineteenth-century Mexican history. Retsuko, my wife, sustained me throughout and served as fellow notetaker in both Austin and Mexico, making it possible to accomplish the impossible during our two years of research. This book, then, is partly hers.

My helpers and advisers have been generous. In Mexico, the late José Ignacio Rubío Mañé was gracious and José Guzmán of the National Archives quite indispensable. At El Colegio de México, Josefina Z. Vázquez and Anne Staples provided encouragement. My former student, Francisco Uscanga, shared his insights with me. In the United States, Woodrow Borah, Charles Hale, and Friedrich Katz provided criticism during the early stages. I owe a special debt to Professor Katz for his willingness to read the work in several versions and his untiring encouragement over the years. David Quinlan was an invaluable colleague during the research in Austin. At formative stages of the writing in Pittsburgh, Bili Seddon helped clarify my intent by relentlessly demanding meaning from the prose. Gabriel Tortella read the manuscript at an intermediate stage and shared the peninsular perspective with me. Colleagues at Pitt helped by teaching me to appreciate social history and sharing their faith. George Reid Andrews, Walther L. Bernecker, Robert Doherty, Seymour Drescher, Van Beck Hall, Samuel P. Hays, the late Richard N. Hunt, Murdo MacLeod, Thomas J. McCormick, and Magnus Mörner—all are examples of what historians can be. Jane Flanders' creative editing made the results readable. Marge Yeager and Grace Tomcho were patient typists.

Much of the research was accomplished with generous support from the Foreign Area Fellowship Program of the SSRC/ACLS during 1964–66. In subsequent years, assistance was provided by the

Penrose Fund of the American Philosophical Society and by the University of Pittsburgh, especially the Faculty Grants Program, the Center for International Studies, and the Center for Latin American Studies.

The writing has passed through many stages over too many years to recount. Earlier monographs appeared on three occasions, in Spanish, edited by Fondo de Cultura Económica, based in Mexico City and Madrid. The first, *La expulsión de los españoles de México (1821–1828)*, published in 1974, treated the background and the first expulsion efforts, 1827–28. A second book, *Descolonización en México. El conflicto entre mexicanos y españoles (1821–1831)*, appeared in 1982. It reexamined the 1827–28 expulsion, then discussed in great detail the purge of Spaniards in 1829–31. A third study, *La reconquista de México. La historia de los atentados españoles, 1821–1830*, published in 1984, assessed each of Spain's efforts to regain her richest colony. None of my previous works has touched on developments after 1831, leaving for the present volume the analysis of the Spaniards' attempts to return to Mexico in 1829–32 and the subsequent expulsions of 1833–34. This book is both a summation of all my previous work and an attempt to carry the *gachupines* issue forward to 1836, the point at which differences were more or less resolved. It attempts to advance the analysis and pull together the whole story in a single volume.

The Expulsion
of Mexico's Spaniards

Introduction

HISTORIANS HAVE generally affirmed that the expulsion of the Spaniards from Mexico between 1821 and 1836 contributed to the political instability and grave economic decline that followed independence. Writing in the 1960s, Romeo Flores Caballero took issue with the economic argument, asserting that wealthy Spaniards departed prior to the expulsions and that since Mexican representatives were often left in charge of their investments, the loss to Mexico and to the *peninsulares* was not as severe as contemporary chroniclers contended.[1] But the seeds of doubt are present even in Flores Caballero's own work. My examination of the archival records of the expulsions of 1827–34 has led me to accept the interpretation of the era's liberals. It is no accident that Mexico's leading export in the 1820s–1830s was specie—its own money—as well as gold and silver bars and plate. With this capital went any possibility of restoring the "prosperity" of the late colonial silver and agricultural boom. Mexico could not hope to recover from stagnation induced by eleven years of warfare if capital flight could not be halted. Contemporaries such as Lucas Alamán, C. M. Bustamante, Lorenzo Zavala, J.M.L. Mora, and H. G. Ward saw, from differing perspectives, the disaster that awaited Mexico if a purge of European Spaniards should follow the emergence of the revolutionary "popular" party in 1824–27. While it is clear why Mexico suffered this turmoil, it is equally certain that the repressive atmosphere generated by nativist activity contributed to the post-1821 economic disaster.

I have tried to explore all aspects of the various expulsion efforts, emphasizing in detail the periods when state and national anti-Spanish laws were under discussion, as well as during subsequent periods of enforcement. I have attempted to tabulate the occupations of the Spanish population of Mexico on the eve of the first expulsion. The result indicates a more plebeian community than might have been expected, no doubt because of the importation of thousands of Spanish soldiers for the recent war. A theme that will interest us is how the conflict over the Spaniards, which seemed incapable of resolution, contributed to the deterioration of republican government. The rebellions of the era invariably utilized the anti-Spanish theme—often, it was the principal motive for insurgency.

The appeal of the late Jesús Reyes Heroles, to comprehend, first, why Mexico attempted to expel its Spaniards, must be borne in mind. Although he accepted the fact that expulsions are repugnant to "the present generation," and that the effort was "anti-economic," Don Jesús cautioned us to consider the political situation at the time. Mexico was torn between the two poles of its reality: the colonial order, of which the Spaniards were a visible reminder, and the new republican reality. The expulsion of the Spaniards, according to Reyes Heroles, had the objective of impeding the consolidation of an economic, political, and even racial oligarchy.[2]

Anti-*gachupín* sentiment (as the Mexicans called it) predated the formation of a popular nativist movement in independent Mexico. It had developed during 300 years of Spanish rule, in part, as a result of sociolegal discrimination, usually referred to as the system of *castas*, based on degrees of racial mixture. And, in part, it derived from a history of preferential treatment for *peninsular* Spaniards over Mexican-born "whites," or criollos. The hatred that many, perhaps most, Mexicans bore the *gachupines* was revealed in the Hidalgo revolt of 1810, which saw a popular mobilization of perhaps 80,000 persons march through the *bajío* region, north and west of Mexico City, killing hundreds of *peninsulares* and looting their property—a trend that frightened criollos nearly as much as it did Europeans. Social revolt took on the appearance of a vendetta against the Spaniards themselves, not just an effort toward independence. In the ensuing years of revolution, slaves were emancipated and the "caste system" abolished, only to be reinstituted as the colonial government regained control.

The nature of the independence movement of 1821, which succeeded in freeing Mexico from Spain's hegemony, differed from that of the rest of Latin America.[3] It witnessed an alliance of convenience between conservative criollos, like Agustín Iturbide, who feared Spanish liberalism, and popular republicans such as Vicente Guerrero and Guadalupe Victoria, survivors of the earlier social revolt. During the summer of 1821, the conflict took on the aspect of a domestic diplomatic offensive, as Iturbide convinced major Spanish commanders to change sides in exchange for the promise of union, a guarantee of future acceptance and personal security for *peninsulares* in an independent Mexico. The campaign was appealing to the anti-liberal church as well.

As a consequence, Spaniards played an important role in the final stages of the struggle and in Iturbide's short-lived empire thereafter. Even with the collapse of the imperial scheme and the birth of the republic in 1823–24, Spaniards continued to take part in political life, including some of the conspiracies of the era. But the Spanish community, like its criollo counterpart, was politically divided, as was Spain itself. Liberals supported the ideals of the Spanish constitution of 1812, particularly the political and economic liberties it promised. Conservatives, especially within the Catholic church, doggedly opposed the new ideas.

Spanish military men had introduced Freemasonry during the armed conflict, and liberal ideas were propagated through the new lodges and periodicals, such as *El Sol*, which they sponsored. Soon, Masons too were divided, over monarchy and republicanism, centralism and federalism. Just as in Europe, Freemasonry began as an elite activity with anticlerical overtones, then evolved into a form of mass organization. In Mexico, it commenced with the Scottish (Escocés) rite on the eve of independence, then witnessed the formation of the York (Yorkino) rite in the early days of the republic. The two camps became competing political clubs, sharply divided over the Spanish question. Scottish rite Masons defended the resident Spaniards, seeing their cause as a test of individual rights and guarantees; the Yorkists attacked the *gachupines* in a manner reminiscent of the Jacobins, as if to avenge Hidalgo and Morelos. Nativists desired a Mexico for the Mexicans, after centuries of *peninsular* discrimination. And yet, most nativists, like their liberal and conservative protagonists, found it difficult to conceive of government or public posts, whether clerical or civil, as anything other than personal property. Consequently, in their demands for the separation of Spaniards from such posts, and the expulsion of the *gachupines* from Mexico, they usually could not bring themselves to deny completely the "right" of the Spaniard to a major portion of the salary that went with his former position. The Mexican who replaced a *peninsular* could not look forward to enjoyment of the full salary associated with the post.

The question of expulsion itself proved to be fraught with complexity. If radicals expelled the hated *gachupín*, they injured, more often than not, his dependents, including a Mexican family—even orphaning Mexican children in many cases. This singular fact gave pause to many advocates, especially after they had witnessed the consequences of the early laws. Nonetheless, the movement would not die, so great was its appeal, especially as a political issue. Its survival was owing, in part, to the persistent Spanish threat of invasion. Ferdinand VII (who died in 1833) inflicted great harm on Mexico's *peninsu-*

lar community by refusing throughout his life to recognize Mexican independence. In 1829, a Spanish army landed near Tampico, and a stronger force prepared to follow in 1830. *Gachupines* were seen, then, as a likely fifth column, potentially loyal to the empire, and as monarchists. They were also held to be exploiters of Mexico's wealth, "coyotes" living among "lambs," as the pamphleteers portrayed it.

Expulsion laws were passed, at the state and national level, in 1827–28, in 1829, and, finally, in 1833–34. This study treats all of these efforts and attempts to assess their consequences. It was a relentless campaign, never wholly successful, from the nativists' perspective, but quite destructive. Compromises, personal friendships, family ties, intrigue, and bribery all played a role. Rich and poor departed or remained; married and single left or petitioned for time: the result varied with the law and the peculiar requirements of each measure and each administration. Some Spaniards learned, as we would say today, how to beat the system, but the majority departed in one or another of the expulsions. Those who remained in Mexico when recognition came in 1836, having survived all five national laws, as well as the state measures, were very few, at most a quarter of the *peninsular* population of 1827. In the process, Spaniards were virtually eliminated from the military, the bureaucracy, the mining industry, and the church. They managed to survive, to a degree, in commerce and as property owners.

All the weaknesses of this first republic are laid bare in the telling. One of the casualties was the revolutionary regime of Guerrero in 1829, the first attempt at popular government in Mexico. Another effect of the persecution was to demonstrate to conservatives that the restructuring of republicanism was necessary to forestall any such attacks on traditional privilege that might arise in the future. The final conflict that brought down the First Republic was focused on change versus tradition, with the church at the center of debate. The liberals were evolving, and conflict mounted in their wake. In 1834, conservatives sought to halt the social upheaval by resorting to dictatorship. The fate of the remaining Spaniards, until December 1836, depended upon the dictatorship's success.

1

The Origins of the Attempt at Expulsion

CLEARLY, THE anti-Spanish movement was critically important during independent Mexico's early years. Indeed, it can be asserted that the expulsion of the former colonial elite was the primary social issue that the governments of the First Federal Republic were constantly required to confront. Whether centralist or federalist, liberal or conservative, every ruling faction had to adjust its program to arrive at a compromise with the nativists who threatened disruption and rebellion if the "Spanish question" was not resolved, once and for all. In this chapter and the next, I shall examine the initial expulsion attempt (1827–28), its origins and impact on Mexico and on the *peninsulares*, or persons born in Spain.[1] The Spanish population living in Mexico on the eve of the first expulsion will be analyzed and an attempt made to assess the total effect of the state and national laws upon the *gachupines* (the term preferred by the Spaniards' enemies) in 1827–28. This will clarify the role of the anti-Spanish movement in weakening federal control over the states and in bringing about the collapse of authority suffered by the Victoria government during its final year.

In 1824–25 Masonic factions began to function as political parties in independent Mexico. Two such parties contested for authority during the first five years of the republic, the Yorkinos (York rite Masons) and the Escoceses (Scottish rite Masons). The Yorkinos were committed, from their founding in 1825, to a purge of the Spanish community. This implied the termination of the guarantees granted to *peninsulares* by the short-lived imperial regime of Agustín Iturbide (1822–23). Yorkinos would not acknowledge the Mexican citizenship of *peninsulares*, excepting only individual cases where citizenship had been granted by a specific act of a state congress. (Under the constitution of 1824, citizenship was vested in the states rather than in the nation.) The Escoceses, on the other hand, accepted the guarantees

7

extended to Spaniards during the Iturbide government as valid and binding, and rose to the defense of the *peninsulares* following the founding of York rite Masonry. This hardening of positions enabled the Yorkinos to win more recruits and to overtake their adversaries, the Escoceses, in the political realm.

The factions in conflict represented divergent tendencies within the framework of nineteenth-century liberalism. The Escoceses, attuned to the Spanish liberalism of 1812, were inclined to favor constitutional monarchy, placing great emphasis on civil liberties and social guarantees. In the main they were white paternalists, native-born criollos whose culture was European. They enjoyed social prestige, economic position, and dominance in the Senate throughout the First Federal Republic. The Yorkinos, on the other hand, appealed to all those who had been loyal to Iturbide, or were alienated by the Escoceses and unwelcome in the original branch of Masonry. The Yorkino was an early nationalist, a federalist, and often a mestizo (of mixed racial ancestry) or former *casta* (dark person) who, now that the system of legal discrimination against *castas* had been abolished, rose to compete with the criollos for political position in the republic. The Yorkinos dominated the Chamber of Deputies from the elections of 1826 until the flight into exile of many of their leaders in early 1830. They were the party of the nativists who demanded the removal of *peninsulares* from public office as early as 1824 and in 1827 pressed for the expulsion of Spaniards as threats to the peace and security of the new republic.

The political conflict occurred in a tense atmosphere heightened by the severe economic decline that inexorably followed the achievement of independence in 1821. In the popular press this economic collapse was attributed to the colonial legacy in the broadest sense, and that legacy, of course, was blamed on the Spaniards. *Gachupines*, or Spaniards who still lived in Mexico, were seen as the perpetuators of that malevolent inheritance. After an onslaught of Yorkino propaganda, by 1827 the extirpation of the *peninsulares* was viewed as a cathartic required for the restoration of health to the republic. In a symbolic sense, the Spaniards were to serve as expiatory offerings presented to a suffering public as evidence that the Yorkinos were attempting to remedy the ailments of the fledgling nation.

A type of action group called the Guadalupes was born in late 1826 within the Yorkino party. By means of overt acts aimed at heightening public indignation at the continued visibility of the *gachupines*, they sought to hasten the day when the Spaniards would depart. Their adversaries, the Spanish-born residents of Mexico, were a changed community from colonial times, however. In the first place, over 8,000 troops had arrived during the independence struggle, and many of these had settled in Mexico, replacing the thousands of colonial merchants, officials, and bureaucrats who had departed during and after Independence and after Iturbide's victory in 1821. In short, the *peninsular* community was neither as wealthy nor as uncompromisingly opposed to Mexican independence as their fellow countrymen had been prior to 1821. In fact, these *capitulados* (surrendered soldiers) may have comprised one-third of the *peninsular* population in 1827–28, as evidenced by the numerous appeals to the Mexican government for exception from the expulsion signed with the illiterate's "†". Unlike the colonial *peninsulares*, these men had roots in Mexico—many had founded families by 1827, and their Mexican wives had borne them children. A relentless expulsion in 1828 and again in 1829 threatened to widow thousands of Mexican women and reduce their children to poverty. This eventually did occur, and when it came to pass the spectacle gave pause even to the most vigorous enemies of the Spaniards.

But it would be an error to assert that the only motive for the expulsions was the Mexicans' desire for revenge or a confused notion of the cause of the economic ills besetting the new nation. For many, Spaniards did indeed represent a threat to Mexican independence. Not all of the opponents of the republic had joined those who voluntarily sought a remedy for their discontents in exile or emigration. *Gachupines* were involved in the fall of Iturbide in 1823 and they supported the Escocés regime that ordered his execution in 1824. Some *peninsulares* publicly scoffed at the democratic pretensions of the republic and openly denigrated the capacity of Mexicans to govern themselves without the "benevolent" assistance of the *gente decente* (people of quality) which, of course, included a number of *peninsulares*. It required the anti-Spanish sentiment of the day to reconcile republicans and Iturbidists and to make possible the cohesion of as diverse a group as comprised the Yorkinos. From 1827 through 1829, the Yorkinos were able to mobilize the heterogeneous Mexican public for a first experiment in "radicalism." When the Yorkino-dominated Congress created an extensive militia in the states in 1827 and consolidated its strength within the military itself in 1828, the way was prepared for an experiment in popular government in 1829. These developments spelled disaster for Mexico's Spaniards, whose fortunes remained bleak indeed until an empty treasury brought about the collapse of the Guerrero regime at the end of 1829. During the period of dominance of the Yorkino party, the Spaniards were reduced to second-class citizenship and thousands were driven from Mexico's shores.

The Position of the Spaniards in Independent Mexico

Peninsulares were a numerically insignificant minority, both before and after Independence. But clearly their importance was out of all proportion to their numbers. Even in Mexico City, which with 167,000 inhabitants in 1821 was the largest metropolis in the Western Hemisphere, Spaniards constituted only a tiny minority (around 3 percent). At the time of the first colonial census in 1793, there were only about 8,000 *peninsulares* in New Spain, rising to roughly 15,000 by 1810.[2] If the calculations made by Lucas Alamán are correct, the Hidalgo revolt of that same year reduced the Spanish community by 4,000 men.[3] The remaining 11,000 *peninsulares* would be considerably diminished by death and migration during the subsequent decade of insurgency. During this era of guerrilla activity, Spain poured 8,500 expeditionaries into New Spain, some of whom perished, and thousands more were transported from Mexican shores after 1821. Though it is arbitrary to attempt to estimate the size of a fluctuating population, perhaps a maximum figure of 10,000 might be reasonable for the *peninsular* community at Independence, when the national population had reached about 6,500,000.[4] I would estimate that at least one-third of these Spaniards emigrated during the next six years of somewhat strained coexistence. But, in spite of this migration over time, it must have appeared to the nativists—with the bulk of Mexico's commerce still resting in Spanish hands by means of the *peninsulares'* connections with the new foreign merchant houses, and with a number of prominent persons still visibly opulent—that the colonial social and economic system had survived virtually intact.

Initially, the politics of independent Mexico appeared to tolerate the Spanish presence. Neither Iturbide nor those closest to him were hostile to the Iberians. The successful independence movement of 1821 took on the character of a diplomatic triumph rather than a civil war. But deep resentment had survived the unsuccessful Hidalgo revolt of 1810 and the subsequent suppression of the guerrilla struggle of 1811–18. In general, republicans were anti-Spanish, while monarchists were not, and this alignment was altered after 1824 only by the addition of the Iturbidists to the republican camp. The failure of Ferdinand and the Spanish Cortes to send a member of the Bourbon house to rule over Mexico in 1821 effectively abandoned Mexico's Spaniards to the vengeance of the republicans who had suffered so much at the hands of their former colonial overlords.

The Spanish community was disunited: the liberal constitution of 1812 had divided priest from merchant, liberal from conservative. The coronation of Iturbide did nothing to heal that breach, in spite of his attempt to coopt the *peninsular* community, and the new emperor's change from constitutional monarch to absolutist thoroughly alienated what little support he had among liberal Spaniards. *Peninsulares* of this persuasion expressed their discontent through Scottish rite Masonry, and prominent criollos joined the movement to remove Iturbide. Tension grew between Iturbide and the Spaniards until the desperate emperor, who soon found himself presiding over an empty treasury, adopted a policy of encouraging the anti-Spanish elements in society.[5] The emperor needed new allies and hoped to weaken his enemies, who controlled a large part of the country's specie. The financial straits of the empire were the result of a large army inherited from the recent wars, a collapsed economy, and the disappearance of specie from circulation, as capitalists nervously awaited the return of a climate of security. The emperor repeatedly extracted forced loans from the cathedral chapters and the Spanish merchants, fortifying in each case the determination of these powerful groups to unseat him at the first opportunity.

The Spaniards failed to realize that the fall of Iturbide would also signal the collapse of the Third Guarantee—the plank in Iturbide's Plan of Independence, later incorporated into the Treaty of Córdoba, that gave the *peninsulares* legal security in Mexico. Liberal monarchists joined republicans in the Plan of Casa Mata, and the successful mutiny produced a ruling triumvirate, supported by the Escoceses, that included the Spanish General Pedro Celestino Negrete. But the resentment of nativists and the dissatisfactions of local elites in the provinces, who now demanded greater autonomy as states, made it difficult for the Escoceses to control events from Mexico City. The triumvirate acquiesced to the popular demand for a Constitutional Congress, which was federalist in the majority, and the *peninsulares* lost considerable influence in the process of transition to republican government. Moreover, the Spanish military, still ensconced in San Juan de Ulúa, an island fortress in Veracruz harbor, made matters worse by bombarding the port city intermittently from September 1823 until November 1825. This not only increased hispanophobia, it also disrupted commerce and decreased government revenue. The growing threat to Spanish citizenship rights became all

the more apparent when the constitution of 1824 failed to acknowledge the validity of the Treaty of Córdoba and Iturbide's earlier Plan
of Iguala. The Third Guarantee lost its constitutional validity.

Peninsulares were not encouraged by the composition of the first
federal Congress either, nor by the spread of anti-Spanish propaganda. Late in 1823, a series of local armed rebellions took place
in central and southern Mexico, demanding the purge of Spaniards
from all military, ecclesiastical, and bureaucratic posts. This resulted
in a popular revolt led by Brigadier José María Lobato in the capital
during January 1824. Although it failed, the uprising demonstrated
to republicans the popularity of the anti-Spanish cause. Riots and
"pronouncements" aimed at the removal of the Spaniards from their
posts, and indeed from all of Mexico, would become a frequent threat
to the lives and property of *peninsulares*, particularly in the south and
west of the nation.

Defenders of the Spaniards, therefore, threw their weight behind
Gen. Nicolás Bravo—a former insurgent known for his benevolent
acts toward *peninsulares* during the war—for the presidency in 1824.
But Bravo, grand master of Scottish rite Masonry, lost to another
former insurgent, Gen. Guadalupe Victoria, and had to settle for
the vice-presidency. Ex-insurgents were divided between the two Masonic camps by 1825, with those who had accepted pardons during
the war usually identifying with the Escoceses, and those who had
not with the Yorkinos. Victoria was neither openly friendly toward
the anti-Spanish camp nor a partisan of one Masonic house. But the
new government was suspicious of the plans of the Escoceses—upon
whose success or failure the ultimate fate of the *peninsulares* rested.
The Escoceses soon found that, initially, they were in a position to
dominate the Victoria regime, but would have to be content with positions of influence only. The new government was not strong, however,
despite its success in acquiring loans from Great Britain. Friends of
the administration, who included a number of ex-Iturbidists, were
resolved to create a party in support of the government and to oppose
Escocés "conspiracies."

The York rite party, which emerged in 1825 and rallied to the
support of the Victoria administration, held as its main goal the defense of Mexican independence against the Spanish threat and the
consolidation of federalism against the centralist tendencies of the
past. Yorkinos viewed virtually all Spaniards as potential internal enemies and all Escoceses as monarchists. The Yorkino party defended
the federalist provisions of the 1824 constitution, which the Escoceses
would have modified. For example, Escocés senators aggressively uti-

lized the right of the federal Congress to declare state laws unconstitutional, while Yorkinos in Congress attempted to obstruct use of the privilege. Yorkinos advocated the creation of state and local militias to defend local rights as opposed to those of Mexico City. Militias in the hands of Yorkinos were hostile to *peninsulares* and their armed role in the anti-Spanish campaign of 1827 was to be crucial. The Yorkino version of federalism, then, gave preeminence to state constitutions and state laws, and Yorkinos attributed to themselves alone the sacred right of defending the nation against its enemies, internal and external.

Born amid a rising tide of anti-Spanish feeling, the Yorkino party took up the cry, sounded in 1824 by Lobato, demanding the removal of *peninsulares* from all government posts. The urgency of the purge was attributed to the ongoing state of war with Spain and the internal threat represented by Mexico's Spaniards. The new political challenge was indeed serious, for the Yorkino lodges were spreading rapidly into all parts of the republic. By late 1826 they were present in at least fifteen of twenty-four federal entities, and the number of lodges soon reached a minimum of 130.[6] While the first expulsion was under way in April 1828, for example, at least 102 lodges were active throughout Mexico. The U.S. plenipotentiary Joel Roberts Poinsett, deeply involved with the Yorkinos from the outset, learned at the end of 1826 "that the leading members of the York party were about to organize a secret society on the plan of the Carbonari of Italy, of which some Italian emigrants who are here gave them the plan." In less than a year, "under the popular name of Guadalupes, this society . . . spread from Chihuahua to Chiapas, and [was] in possession of almost all of the strength of the country." As the ambassador noted, this type of organization was "peculiarly well adapted to engage the common people of these counties in promoting party views." In the capital, a "Chamber of Honor" was installed and a "Councils of Ancients" reported to it from the states and territories. Poinsett, impressed by the potential strength of the Guadalupes, concluded, "It is fortunate for the country that it is wielded by the friends of the existing institutions."[7]

Yorkinos swept the congressional elections of late 1826 and the "popular" party rode to power by virtue of carefully organized state and national victories. The new Congress that commenced on 1 January 1827 was more than half Yorkino, while very few of the remaining seats were occupied by Escoceses.[8] Yorkinos could not capture control of the Senate, however, since few senators were legally required to stand for election in 1826. The result was a Yorkino Chamber of

Deputies and an Escocés Senate, with the upper chamber clearly identified with the protection of *peninsulares*. In addition, a number of state legislatures were now Yorkino, the most important being those of Mexico and Jalisco. In the struggle for dominance of the Mexico State legislature, the governor resigned and the chief Yorkino organizer, Lorenzo Zavala, became governor of that vast and important domain surrounding the federal capital. Soon the Yorkino press began denouncing the ministry, excepting only the treasury minister Ignacio Esteva, friend of the president and a Yorkino founder.

But these efforts were soon lacking in interest, for a cause célèbre whose importance for the anti-Spanish crusade could hardly be exaggerated was about to become the daily fare of the capital's writers and periodicals. The pro-Spanish and reactionary Padre Arenas conspiracy, which appeared to involve a number of prominent Spaniards and criollos, was revealed in the capital on 19 January 1827. The two Masonic camps chose this ground on which to argue their political differences, with the Escoceses asserting that the Arenas affair had been arranged by their adversaries for the purpose of persecuting Spaniards. The Yorkinos insisted that the Spanish community represented a vast conspiratorial enclave and that the few who were directly implicated in Padre Joaquín Arenas's network of contacts were merely the tip of the iceberg. As a result of the discovery of the Arenas conspiracy and the arrest and imprisonment of the Spanish division generals Pedro Celestino Negrete and José Antonio Echávarri, a *peninsular* brigadier general, Gregorio Arana, and several friars, the Spaniards and the Escoceses found themselves in desperate straits in 1827. Minister of War Manuel Gómez Pedraza, who prosecuted the conspirators, later reflected in his mea culpa that had the Escoceses exercised sound judgment, they would not have defended the conspirators of 1827. They would thereby have avoided alienating public opinion—accomplished by the press—and would have lessened the chances of polarizing the political climate to the verge of civil war, a polarization that in the end produced the expulsion laws of 1827.[9]

Ultimately, about fifty *peninsulares* were linked to the plot whose reality, in retrospect, seems plausible enough. The church, undergoing serious economic decline following Independence, lacked influential representation in either of the major political parties, and no caudillo had thus far stepped forward to defend it against the tenets of liberalism. The friar Arenas and his friends were actively attempting to recruit for an armed insurrection on behalf of the church and its would-be protector, the Spanish monarchy. Since the church leadership was Spanish, they had their most extensive and safest contacts within the Spanish community. The Spanish division generals were found innocent, however, and General Arana was executed on circumstantial evidence while the Senate debated a reprieve. The trials dragged on for two years; ultimately, several friars were also executed. We may conclude that the conspiracy was not as serious as the Yorkinos asserted in 1827. Its major significance rests in the profound impact it had on the fate of the *peninsular* community. The Yorkinos, exercising their newly acquired political power, pressed the government to eliminate the Spanish threat. The hispanophobia generated in late 1826 and early 1827 by the popular party prepared the way for efforts to remove *peninsulares* from official posts and, ultimately, to drive the *gachupines* out of Mexico.

The administration was alternately active and passive toward these developments. While Minister Pedraza diligently pursued the Arenas conspirators, treating the Spanish military officers suspected of involvement with a heavy hand, President Victoria assumed an inactive, neutral position toward the party conflict that threatened his government. H. G. Ward, the British ambassador and an intimate of Victoria, reflected later that the president could have avoided the approaching disaster by either declaring himself an Escoces in 1826, thereby denying strength to the emerging Yorkino party, or by declaring himself a Yorkino and an expulsionist, making persecution "official" and eliminating all opposition based upon the conspiratorial, factional appearance of the anti-Spanish movement.[10] But the fact remains that by 1827 the Spaniards had lost any possibility of remaining in Mexico to reap the fruits of their former position as in the colony unmolested. Mexico was technically at war with Spain, and Ferdinand would not recognize the independence of his former colonies. In fact, at least since 1824 plans had been entertained in Cuba for the reconquest of his lost dominions. Ironically, the anti-Spanish movement of 1827 in Mexico increased Spain's hopes, since the unrest demonstrated the weakness of the Victoria government and, according to the king's advisors, signaled the imminent collapse of the republic. Ultimately, the intransigence of the Bourbon monarchy proved to be the greatest threat to the security of the *peninsulares* in Mexico.

A Collective Biography

In postindependence Mexico, the Spanish-born population often belonged to the social elite. Moreover, many apparently continued to be politically powerful, though they ceased to hold public office as of 10 May 1827. *Peninsulares* had always enjoyed social and economic advantages in Mexico, of course, by virtue of their undisputed *limpieza de sangre* (purity of blood). What was the new situation of the Spanish community after Independence, on the eve of persecution? We may examine the community's structure by using the extant records of the expulsions of 1827–28 and 1829. This will enable us to posit a general explanation of the economic origins of anti-Spanish sentiment.[11]

The majority of the Spanish *capitulados* of 1821 had melted into the civilian population, radically altering the social structure of the community of Iberian origin, giving it a more plebeian character than in colonial times. These thousands of former soldiers increased the ranks of the shopkeepers, small farmers, artisans, day laborers and, of course, the unemployed. No one knew how many Spanish males were living in Mexico in 1827. The most accurate public estimate was that of the Yorkino senator José María Alpuche, who asserted in the upper chamber that "the nation would neither suffer from the expulsion of 6,000 Spaniards, nor from the departure of their 12,000 Mexican allies."[12] In fact, however, there were more than 6,600 Spanish males in an estimated national population of 6,500,000. The *peninsulares* thus constituted little more than .1 percent of Mexican society. The diminishing efforts of *gachupines* to enter the republic, plus a government policy of turning away Spaniards and the fear-inspired migration of 1827, resulted in a decline of at least 200 Iberian males immediately before the official expulsion began. Over half those departing early were friars, while the remainder were often affluent entrepreneurs who took their families and servants with them. This contrasted sharply with subsequent migrations.

Although the Spanish population of the Federal District was decreasing throughout 1827, at least one-sixth of the *peninsulares* still resided in the capital. Several states had larger than average Iberian populations: particularly notable were Puebla, Oaxaca, Veracruz, and Yucatán, in that order. Puebla sheltered more than one-tenth of the Spaniards, while the total living in the four most important states amounted to one-third of the Spanish colony. The fact that only 8 percent of the *gachupines* resided in Veracruz reflects two developments: Spanish merchants from the port had been migrating to Havana since 1821, and under the republic Mexico City had replaced Veracruz as the principal commercial entrepôt.

The importance of Spaniards in Mexican society—a condition inherited from the colonial period—was reflected in their continued prominence in commercial enterprises, ecclesiastical sinecures, military positions, and bureaucratic posts. The *peninsulares'* occupational pursuits were by no means limited: Iberian males were engaged in over a hundred different occupations, and their social rank ranged from bishop to beggar. Fortunately, Yucatán and Guanajuato, among the large states, provided splendid occupational descriptions for over three-quarters of their Spaniards. Moreover, surviving occupational data is better than 50 percent complete for twelve federal entities.

From this data we can ascertain that commerce was the preponderant activity of Mexico's Spaniards, underlining the continuing importance of a former colonial elite. In Oaxaca State, one-third of the *peninsulares* were engaged in trade. In each of our sample states, between 40 and 60 percent of the Spaniards reported were in commerce, while the church attracted less than 10 percent, excepting only the missionary centers of the Californias (44 percent) and Querétaro (21 percent). Prior to the employees law of 10 May 1827, half the Spaniards in the army were officers, many of whom held high rank. The largest contingent of Spanish military appears to have been concentrated in Puebla—100 officers and men—contributing to our image of that state as a postindependence center of Spanish influence.

The pattern is similar in each region: Spaniards were found in positions of social and economic importance, but never occupying political office, even at the state and local level. For example, neither the Mexico State legislature elected in 1826 nor the Campeche and Veracruz municipal governments of 1827–28 contained a single *peninsular*, despite their economic importance in those regions. Let us contrast the Iberian occupational structure in a single city over time, using data for Guanajuato in 1793 as our base. By 1827, the Spanish population had declined 70 percent, but the decrease in its wealth was even more marked. The number of *peninsulares* in the commercial sector had fallen by nine-tenths, while Spanish mine owners had declined by three-quarters. The Hidalgo Revolt of 1810 and anti-Spanish violence since 1821 had undermined the Spaniards' position in the *bajío* region.

Variations within the Spanish occupational structure of the major states accurately reflect the pattern of local economic activity. Querétaro and Puebla contained large groups of friars, while Yucatán possessed the most secular clergy, though the number of parish priests was small everywhere. Oaxaca and Yucatán contained the largest groups of merchants and shopkeepers. Puebla had four-fifths of the farm administrators, while Oaxaca had proportionately more Spanish farmers than the other states. Yucatán possessed nine-tenths of the

Iberians engaged in marine occupations. Durango sheltered the largest number of mine owners and, though a frontier society, of servants as well, while owning real estate was characteristic of the *peninsulares* of Guanajuato. Most of the former government employees lived in Oaxaca. Unemployment among *peninsulares* seems to have been highest in Veracruz—a result, no doubt, of decolonization. Perhaps the most impressive characteristic of the official lists is the almost total absence of Spanish laborers in 1827. And yet U.S. customs officials recorded the arrival from Mexico of many *peninsular* "laborers" in 1829. It may be, however, that Spaniards had been reduced to performing manual labor in independent Mexico as a result of the declining economy and their demobilization in 1827.

In light of the Iberians' dominance of commerce, I would suggest that although the expulsions were the result of a broadly based, nationalistic anti-Spanish movement, a substantial source of criollo pro-expulsionist sentiment was mercantile rivalry between Mexicans and Spaniards during a period of severe economic decline. The thesis can be tested by examining occupations in Durango, where the *gente decente*, defined occupationally, consisted of only 3 percent of the male population in 1827. Less than 3 percent of the criollos belonged to that elite, while 70 percent of the *peninsulares* could claim membership. Though the Spaniards comprised only 1 percent of Durangan males, they accounted for 8 percent of the *gente decente*. The fact that one out of every seven persons engaging in commercial activity was a *gachupín* made this tiny minority highly visible to Durango's criollos.[13]

Though increasingly isolated politically by 1827, the *peninsulares* were yet powerful as a result of their capital accumulation, which took the form of scarce specie. The flight of this capital soon deepened the country's already serious depression. The continued visibility of the Spaniards and the opulence of a few in an era of stagnation excited the hostility of criollos and mestizos alike. Indicative of the source of the *peninsulares*' unpopularity was the epithet *pulpero* (grocer) so often applied to them during the expulsion era. When nationalistic criollos asked themselves who was to blame for conditions in the fatherland, they found in the Spaniards a satisfying target for blame. Nativists envisioned a splendid future to be realized when the hateful *gachupines* were expelled. Moreover, many Spaniards continued to occupy, on a proprietary basis, posts that were either no longer functional or should properly have been filled by Americans in an American republic—and certainly not by monarchists. In this case also, Spanish privilege was directly attributable to the advantages enjoyed in colonial times. The first goal of the Yorkinos was to put an end to this travesty.

The Federal Government Suspends Spanish Employees

The nationalists achieved their initial aim with the passage on 10 May 1827 of the Public Employees Law.[14] The surviving colonial concept of office as property was so strong, however, that the measure enabled the fired Spaniards to continue to draw their salaries, imposing on the treasury what now seems another unwarranted burden. Mexicans succeeded Spaniards almost universally in government and ecclesiastical posts. Exceptions were rare; Spaniards remained only in posts requiring technical knowledge, such as engineering or metallurgy.

The decree of 10 May prohibited any Spaniards from exercising any public, civil, or military post by federal appointment until Spain recognized Mexican independence. This included ecclesiastical positions of an economic, administrative, and judicial nature for both secular and regular clergy, excluding only bishops. The administration was authorized to separate priests and missionaries from their posts in the Federal District and in the territories until Spain recognized the new nation. Not only were employees to enjoy their full salaries, but, moreover, the time of their suspensions would be credited toward retirement. The posts vacated would be filled provisionally by those immediately below them in the chain of succession. Suspended priests were to enjoy their customary emoluments, while substitutes would be recompensed by the federal treasury. Only individuals born in Spain of Mexican parents were excepted from the provisions of the 10 May law. A presidential decree of 18 May extended coverage of the Public Employees Law to persons born in the islands adjacent to the Iberian Peninsula.[15]

Enforcement of the employees measure was thorough and, invariably, costly. It did more than increase the expense of government, it even contributed to a decline in government revenue.[16] A clerical historian has argued that when the law was finally enforced in the Californias in 1829 it brought into office the young men who "eventually ruined the missions."[17] Each suspension in the bureaucracy left a gap that had to be filled from below, which often meant that a functionary took on additional tasks with neither the title nor the salary commensurate to the position. As a result, efficiency was jeopardized in many departments without any savings in salaries. Fortunately, however, not all sectors of the military or bureaucracy were adversely affected by the employees law.

Under Mexican federalism, each state had to decide what should be done about nonfederal Spanish officeholding within its own domain. In May 1827, state legislatures began debating similar measures for the removal of *peninsular* employees, as well as how to maintain vigilance over the Spanish community. Oaxaca was the first state to pass an employees law, and between 26 May and late December at least seven other states did the same. The state laws were quite similar to the federal measure, with some notable exceptions. In Zacatecas suspended officials received two-thirds of their salaries, while in Michoacán the maximum salary was set at 1,000 pesos per annum. In Querétaro, suspended employees received only half salaries, and sons born in Spain of Mexican parents were required to demonstrate that they were "notoriously addicted to the federal system."[18] The "radical" congress in Querétaro even suspended Spanish employees of private companies, but with full pay, while their substitutes were to be subsidized by the state government for half their salaries! The Mexico State law was limited to authorizing the governor, in council, to remove or expel ecclesiastics. There were constitutional provisions passed at this time also, limiting the rights of Spanish nationals to exercise political office or prohibiting them from obtaining full citizenship in some states. In Yucatán only minor restrictions were placed upon *peninsulares* and none was removed from a nonfederal post. Everywhere in the states, Spanish military officials were suspended in conformity with the federal law of 10 May.

Before any anti-Spanish measures could emanate from Veracruz State, the dominant Escocés party first had to be removed from control over the legislature, the governorship, and the military. The Yorkinos were initially frustrated in their attempt to found a viable popular Masonic movement in Veracruz. An aggressive Escocés adversary was quick to use the state government to block the attempt and, coincidentally, to protect local Spaniards. Spanish merchants began to suspect that behind the Yorkino assault was a plot to rid the state of *peninsulares* in order to prepare the way for Yankee traders.[19] The Santa Anna brothers sided with Gen. Miguel Barragán and the Escoceses, while the Yorkinos received the support of the Rincón family, traditional rivals of the Santa Annas in local politics. This meant that Col. José Antonio Rincón would defy Jalapa from the port of Veracruz, which he commanded. When the Escoceses plotted to replace him with Gen. Antonio López de Santa Anna, he "rebelled" on behalf of the federal government against a "centralist" conspiracy.[20] While the men around the president were friendly to the Rincón "revolt" in Veracruz, Vice-President Nicolás Bravo was openly defiant of the administration's favorable attitude toward the Yorkino move. Recognizing the suspicion in Mexico City, the state legislature reaffirmed its fealty to the federal system and passed an employees law on 1 August which removed Spaniards and provided for their surveillance in the future. This step marked the gap that was developing between the more extreme Escocés leadership and the moderate legislature on the *peninsular* question. The federal government sided openly for the first time with the Yorkinos and decided to remove General Barragán from both the governorship and military command of the state. Bravo, incensed, informed the president of his willingness to defend the Escoceses should the administration continue to adopt the Yorkino party.[21]

President Victoria resolved the Veracruz affair by assigning Gen. Vicente Guerrero as military commander and introducing a number of prominent Yorkinos to fill other important posts. The federal law of employees was now enforced. Civil war in Veracruz was postponed by federal intervention, but party tension was heightened, and Escoceses everywhere became desperate following their loss of control over Veracruz. They now viewed the administration in Mexico City as a threat, while in its turn the government saw in these events proof of Yorkino charges that the republic had much to fear from Escocés plans.

The tribulations of the Escoceses and the *peninsulares* were only beginning, however, for these desperate allies would now be confronted with violent movements throughout Mexico for the expulsion of the *gachupines*. These "armed petitions" would be the method chosen by the Guadalupes and their Yorkino supporters for hastening the day of Spanish departure.

The selective use of violence seemed all the more appropriate to the Yorkinos when the "popular" party lost in seven important state legislative elections between May and July 1827. It was precisely in many of these areas that "armed petitions" would be necessary in order to enact local and national expulsion measures. Throughout these developments the Escoceses mounted an unrelenting attack on the minister of war, Manuel Gómez Pedraza, first for the arrest and ill-treatment of the Spanish generals and, subsequently, for the dilatory manner in which he reacted to the "armed petitions" of 1827. The Escocés party could not legitimately complain about the ex-Escocés minister's response to the less numerous centralist or monarchist "petitions": Pedraza proved to be most vigorous in these cases.[22] Anti-Spanish armed petitions produced a response from a government friendly to Yorkinos far different from that of 1824, when the pro-Escocés Executive Power had been confronted with similar demands. Inevitably, under the circumstances of 1827, these petitions met with only minimal resistance. In fact, such threats to stability would be cited by the administration as justification for hasty passage of expulsion legislation, in order to restore public peace and military subordination. Under this rationale, Minister Pedraza often restrained local commanders who offered resistance—a policy that gave Escoceses final "proof" that the government was now the creature of the Yorkinos. The correspondence between cabinet ministers, governors, and military commanders of the affected areas lends credence to Pedraza's assertion that the Victoria government could not have halted the revolt.[23] The movements definitely had a popular base: nowhere in the correspondence is there even a hint that the disturbances may have been Yorkino-inspired. Public and military reaction to their campaign was accurately foreseen by the Yorkinos.

The leader of the anti-Spanish rebellion was well known. During the wars of independence and afterward, Gen. Vicente Guerrero had suffered humiliation at the hands of Spaniards and criollos alike, as we can appreciate from the diary of the hostile Carlos María Bustamante. Neither President Victoria nor Governor Zavala could dissuade Guerrero from associating himself with the Yorkino cause, though the old insurgent did promise the U.S. ambassador in November 1827 that he would take no further part in anti-*peninsular* events.[24]

State governments varied in their receptivity to demands for expulsion in 1827. The extremes were represented by Jalisco on the anti-Spanish side and Tabasco on the anti-expulsion side. Jalisco passed the first law for the expulsion of Spaniards from Mexico on 31 August 1827.[25] Violent armed petitions had commenced at Acapulco on 27 August when Lt. José María Gallardo, in response to a plan published in Guadalajara, led a band of soldiers in the robbery and murder of some Spaniards in that port town.[26] Here also began the official policy of pardoning criminal acts in order to avoid a confrontation between rebellious elements in the armed forces, supported by popular wrath, and the government in Mexico City, now dependent upon the Yorkinos for survival.

As the armed petitions spread and more congresses took up the expulsion question, the necessity of a national law of expulsion became more obvious, at least to reconcile the diverse state laws, if for no other reason. All of these measures affected fundamental questions of civil rights—an area delegated to the federal authorities by the constitution of 1824.[27] Revolts accompanied the debates in Jalisco, Mexico, Michoacán, Oaxaca, Puebla, and Veracruz. In states where there were no disorders, local expulsion laws followed rather than preceded the national law—this was the case in Chihuahua and Durango. The pressure from armed bands was sufficient to the task: when a state legislature resisted, as many did, groups of armed men would directly confront the recalcitrant body, using intimidation to obtain the necessary majority. When a state military commander continued to resist these efforts, he would be arrested by officers around him and the legislature would find itself isolated with no help arriving from Mexico City. In the areas where armed petitions took place, "patriotic juntas" or "juntas of public security" sprang up to express the "popular will." The administration was convinced that the soldiers serving under rebellious officers had no idea of the illegality of their activities—a fact that, according to the intermediaries employed in each case in restoring peace, justified the offer of amnesty.

And, finally, the debate in the federal Congress late in 1827 was also accompanied by a campaign of armed petitions in and around the Federal District. The impatient civil militias of at least ten localities within the capital and surrounding towns in Mexico State took up arms in early December in order to force the debate in Congress. No official military steps were taken to free the Congress from this pressure. Pedraza, who was the dominant force in the cabinet, enjoyed the support of the president in his policy of appeasement toward anti-Spanish rebels. The Victoria government viewed the Spanish presence as more of an internal rather than an external threat. All the same, the nearly empty treasury in the capital may have contributed as much to the federal government's apparent weakness as its publicly repeated view that the rebels were "misguided patriots."

Expulsion Laws Appear in the States

The expulsion law passed in Jalisco on 31 August 1827 soon became a model for the other states.[28] The Spanish merchants, and their British allies, recognized the Jalisco law as a harbinger of future legislation in most of the states. The Jalisco measure raised fundamental constitutional questions and, as a result, precipitated an important debate in the Senate, which was charged with the responsibility of reviewing state legislation. The ministry felt that legal matters of this type should pertain exclusively to the federal Congress, because of their civil rights implications.[29] Congress would not accept the minister of government's thesis, however, since to do so would have created a furor in the federalist-dominated states. Moreover, Yorkinos in Congress desired laws that would rid Mexico of the *capitulados,* and the Jalisco decree did that and more. But the Senate, which had passed the 10 May employees law by a two-to-one majority, when confronted with the question of expulsions, found itself with a two-to-one majority on the side of the *peninsulares.* The Jalisco law was voted unconstitutional "in general," and the new majority was willing only to allow Jalisco to regulate Spanish immigration within the state in the future.

But the subsequent article-by-article debate produced some favorable votes on specific sections, resulting in a failure to negate the Jalisco law in toto. And while the Senate debated, the legislatures of Mexico and other states were acting. Congress was soon confronted with more than one law, and these were being enforced, regardless of opinion in Mexico City. Increasingly, the only solution appeared to be that suggested initially by Espinosa de los Monteros, the senior official of the Ministry of Government: passage of a federal law that would take precedence over all state laws. With the enactment of two laws in Mexico State, the congressional dilemma deepened, when only the second of these could be declared unconstitutional, due to the tenacity of the federalist minority within the Senate.

The passage of state laws proceeded apace: Michoacán, Tamaulipas, Guanajuato, Oaxaca, and Coahuila y Tejas all passed expulsion measures in November. In Oaxaca, when the state decree of 23 November proved too weak to satisfy the more militant, Col. Santiago García rebelled, seizing the state government by force and decreeing a severe law on the following day, to be enforced by a "junta of public security."[30] During December, additional laws were passed in San Luis Potosí, Veracruz, Zacatecas, Querétaro, Puebla, and Durango. The last noted came after passage of the federal law and granted *peninsulares* an opportunity to become citizens if they so desired, provided that they met congressional requirements (excluding regular clergy who were denied citizenship throughout Mexico, since their vows required them to renounce this world).

A comparison of the various state laws reveals striking similarities as well as contrasts.[31] While all twelve of the state laws that I have located sought to expel *capitulados,* only four offered to terminate the period of exile if Spain were to recognize Mexican independence. Seven states specifically sought to prevent entry by Spaniards in the future. Nine state laws were primarily aimed at the clergy, both regular and secular. Remarkably, only three state laws exempted *peninsula-*

res who had married and begun raising families in Mexico since 1821. By the end of 1827, a Spaniard who wished to remain in Mexico and who could not obtain an exception from the law of his state had only one recourse: to flee to Mexico City or to the federal territories where he might obtain the protection of the general government, in hopes that the enforcement of the law of 20 December might be more generous.

The General Congress Votes for Expulsion

The session of the federal Congress that was called upon to legislate the expulsion of Spaniards had been summoned originally to deal with the government's extraordinary financial plight. But the press, as well as opinion in the congressional districts, made it clear that the Spaniards were the most pressing issue.[32] While President Victoria was assuring foreign emissaries that Mexico would not expel its *peninsulares*, Congress was already debating a general law that would, to a degree, do just that. The new Yorkino periodical *El Amigo del Pueblo* (named for its French Revolution prototype), edited by the Yorkino deputies Colonel Tornel and José María Bocanegra, repeatedly demanded such a law and sharply criticized those who attempted to stand in the way. Escoceses fought back, without success, in *El Observador de la República Mexicana*, edited by the liberal ideologue Dr. José María Luis Mora and defenders of the Spaniards in the Senate. Opposition to these developments also came from all those involved with European interests in foreign trade and foreign relations. This stemmed from the links of the Spaniards with European— particularly British—merchants and the country's dependence, until late 1827, on Britain's belief in Mexico's stability in order to secure massive loans. The anti-Spanish movement terminated such confidence, however, and Mexico had to turn to local private speculators, the *agiotistas*, since declining port revenues could not support the army and the federal bureaucracy. Only in one sense was the federal law viewed as a relief by the twenty-three foreign "mercantile societies" of Veracruz: it would overrule the more arbitrary state laws that were forcing Spanish merchants to leave before they had time to settle their accounts properly. The British, German, and French houses were directly threatened by Spanish foreclosures resulting from hasty expulsion.[33]

The federal law began to take shape when a proposal signed by thirty-one deputies was introduced on 25 November. It was reported out of committee for debate on 5 December, in a form very similar

to the final law. The lower-house version was soon completed and
forwarded to the Senate.[34] By 19 December the Senate had approved
the measure under the watchful eyes of a belligerent gallery who
could only be controlled by the Yorkino senators. The final law called
for the expulsion of *capitulados*, the "disaffected," those arriving since
1821, the regular clergy, and unmarried *peninsulares* who had been
homeless during the past two years. Exceptions were reserved for
Spaniards over sixty years of age, the physically disabled, and those
who had served in the cause of Mexican independence and demonstrated "their affection for our institutions." Provision was made for
the expulsion of *peninsulares* who, in spite of meeting these criteria,
might still be viewed as dangerous by the administration (Article 9).
Financial aid was to be provided for the poor, bureaucrats, *capitulados*,
and regular clergy "to the nearest foreign port." Exile had to be endured until Spain recognized Mexican independence. Excepted *peninsulares* would have to renounce their allegiance to King Ferdinand
and pledge their support for the republic. Citizenship documents
were promised to all those legitimately excepted from the expulsion,
but *exceptuados* were denied the right to reside near the coasts. And,
finally, amnesty was declared for all who had participated in the
armed petitions for the expulsion of Spaniards.[35] The only modification which the Senate accomplished was exception for "professors
of a science, art, or industry useful [to the republic], who may not
be suspected by the government."

Publication of the measure was met with some skepticism, concerning both the law and the cabinet, by the revolutionaries in arms;
but they would have to be content with it for the moment. The accept-
ability of the expulsion would largely depend upon its enforcement.
To that end, the president issued instructions to accompany the decree
and prepared with his cabinet to oversee the compliance of state and
local governments. But before any serious steps could be taken in
this direction, the administration would have to confront the most
serious challenge to its authority since the formation of the Yorkino
lodges.

The Abortive Revolt of the Escoceses

In 1827 the Escoceses had resolved to increase their membership at
all costs, to meet the fateful challenge of the Yorkinos. To this end
Escocés leaders founded the *novenarios*—an attempt to recruit nine
new members for each existing member, ad infinitum. Seriously mis-
judging their weakness and spurred on by the federal law of expul-

sion of Spaniards, the Escoceses mounted a revolt in December 1827. The original plan seems to have contemplated the commencement of hostilities in Veracruz, where the Escoceses had recently dominated affairs. They assumed that the legislature and General Santa Anna would be friendly to the movement. After the success of the Rincón revolt and the establishment of Yorkino ascendancy there, an alternative plan was contrived in Mexico City in meetings with the vice-president beginning in October. According to members of the government, the conspiracy was well known in the capital.[36] Clearly, the Escocés party was encouraged to precipitous action by the Yorkinos' electoral losses of May–July 1827, and profoundly disturbed by the expulsion laws that followed.

The Escocés manifesto, the Plan of Montaño, became known in the capital on 19 December. It charged the administration to call for the abolition of all secret societies, the dismissal and replacement of the present cabinet, the expulsion of the U.S. emissary, Joel Roberts Poinsett, and "strict adherence to the Constitution and the laws." The rebels must have hoped to gain time, expecting the government to negotiate with them as it had with the proexpulsion petitioners of 1827. Poinsett saw the key to the plan in the final demand, which implied that, once the Escoceses were victorious, the present Congress and its decrees, including the laws of 10 May and 20 December, would be declared unconstitutional.[37] We may presume that Poinsett's interpretation was shared by the Yorkinos.

The *hombres de bien* (a self-designation of the *novenarios*) gathered at Tulancingo, some 140 kilometers northeast of the Federal District, where they were besieged and captured, following a brief skirmish, by a large force led by General Guerrero, the chief of Yorkino Masonry. The ultimate confrontation of the warring Masonic orders proved to be less cruel than expected, because the Escoceses were so few and lacked rank-and-file support within the armed forces. Vice-President Bravo was abandoned by a number of prominent persons whose cooperation had been justifiably anticipated. General Santa Anna changed sides, it seems, during the march toward Tulancingo, to cite only the most important defector. The conspirator Col. José Antonio Facio, who would emerge as minister of war in the more conservative government of 1830, noted that "others took part in the plan who would later manifest their opposition to what it had proposed."[38]

Because the fate of the Spaniards hung in the balance, they contributed financially to the rebellion.[39] Yorkino pamphleteers in the capital attempted to link the Bravo revolt with the Arenas conspiracy in the public mind and even suggested a connection between Havana and Bravo. British and French diplomats hoped for an Escocés victory, while Poinsett openly sided with the Yorkinos and the government.

The defeat and capture of the leaders of the Mexico City segment of the Escocés party isolated the important Veracruz sector of the revolt, which could now be dealt with more easily. While Santa Anna had changed sides, his family was still deeply committed to the revolt in Veracruz. Yorkino strength in the state was concentrated in the port city and among the military officers, while the civil administration belonged to the Escoceses. Governor Barragán and Lt. Col. Manuel López de Santa Anna were the leaders in Veracruz who adhered to the Montaño revolt, along with the state legislature.[40] The response of the port was to refuse, once again, to recognize the government at Jalapa. When the news of Bravo's capture arrived, the legislature was forced to recant, and Barragán and Santa Anna fled Jalapa for the Santa Anna estates, where they were later taken prisoner. In San Luis Potosí, Gen. Gabriel Armijo attempted to support the revolt, to no avail. By 13 January the government had terminated the rebellion and the Yorkinos were dominant throughout much of Mexico.

After a heated debate concerning the ultimate fate of the captured Escocés leadership—charged with "accepting command from outside the republic"—the government decided upon banishment rather than death. On 12 June at least forty-three *montañistas* were exiled through the west coast port of San Blas to Chiloé, Valparaíso, Guayaquil, and Lima.[41] The result of all this was apparent: the Spaniards would now be expelled in conformity with the law of 20 December, and their fate in the regions where the Escoceses had been dominant would be much harsher than it might have been. In the face of an even greater hispanophobia, the administration must now enforce the expulsion to the satisfaction of the confident Yorkinos or face a renewal of the violence and confrontation of 1827. And with elections approaching in 1828, the Yorkinos confronted an internal division between "Jacobins" who favored a thorough expulsion and supporters of the government who wished to put the Spanish question to rest once and for all.

2

The First Expulsion and Its Results

THE TENOR OF the enforcement of the expulsion law was determined, in part at least, by the attitude toward the Spanish question of the federal administration, who passed judgment on the acts of state governments and decided the appeals of Spaniards who petitioned to remain in Mexico. The long vacant post of minister of government—the cabinet member who was the day-by-day enforcer of the law—was finally occupied by Senator Juan de Dios Cañedo of Jalisco on 8 March 1828. The senior official, Espinosa de los Monteros, handled these matters in January and February when, as Luis G. Cuevas notes, "The government in the first months of enforcement conducted itself less generously than one could have hoped."[1] This changed, to a degree, with the arrival of Cañedo, who soon attracted the ire of the Yorkinos for his alleged attempts to soften the law's effects on individual Spaniards.

Instructions from the president concerning procedures for enforcement were circulated to state and local authorities.[2] State governors were ordered to see that *peninsulares* subject to expulsion departed within from fifteen to thirty days. A systematic round of correspondence was initiated telling Spaniards which routes to take and when to depart, while political authorities along the line of march and the supreme government were to be informed of each departure. Monthly reports had to be submitted to Mexico City, and port commanders were to be informed by all concerned of final departures. State governments would compile lists of persons affected and draw up appeals to be forwarded to the capital on behalf of those who might qualify for exemptions. The states were free to decide, in consultation with local federal commissaries, the amount of financial aid each indigent *expulso* might need. Ex-employees of the government were to receive their salaries, payable within Mexico, as long as they remained in a friendly nation. Those excepted were to take a formal oath of allegiance, and evidence of the act was to be sent to the capital. Those needing to settle commercial accounts would receive special treatment, including an extension of up to six months. And, finally, the president insisted that amnesty should be granted to all who lay down arms within three days of the law's publication in each locality.

There were problems of enforcement from the beginning, and the law contained clauses subject to varying interpretations. The principal dilemma resulted from the shortness of time specified for compliance. A second difficulty was that *peninsulares* often fled to the capital in hopes of appealing directly to the federal government for remedy. This so increased the burden on the Federal District that enforcing the law within the established time limits was impossible. Then there was the matter of the crews of the Spanish warships *Asia* and *Constante*, who had deserted to the Mexican cause in 1821. They could not return to Spanish territory or to any country having an extradition treaty with Spain, for fear of the gallows. At length, on 21 May President Victoria decided that the roughly 450 crew members should be allowed to remain in the republic.[3] Inevitably, the governors differed on a number of issues raised by the expulsion. Some governors were harsh, while others, such as Lorenzo Zavala of Mexico State, adopted lenient interpretations of the law, arrogating unto themselves broad powers of exemption favorable to the Spaniards' interest. Zavala insisted that the responsibility for a decision to *expel* rested with the federal administration, while the ministry maintained that, on the contrary, the decision to *except* rested with the federal authorities.[4]

The severity with which Governor Tornel—a proexpulsion deputy in Congress—enforced the law in the Federal District earned him the opprobrium of both Zavala and C. M. Bustamante.[5] Those few *peninsulares* who were Yorkinos had no difficulty in procuring rapid exceptions, but there were also many successful petitioners who had demonstrated no liking for existing political institutions. Twenty-five years later, Tornel insisted: "[Tornel] prescribed, with respect to the Spaniards, some seemingly severe measures for the purpose of gaining the liberty to do them some good, without causing alarm among the ultra-radicals."[6]

British merchants and mine owners were determined to minimize the damage of the expulsion to their investments. British agents worked to obtain exceptions, where possible, and time extensions for merchants and employees. In spite of President Victoria's friendship toward the British agents, there is no evidence to indicate that their appeals received other than the usual formal consideration.

The role of the federal Congress proved to be crucial whenever the expulsion law was strictly carried out. Clarifications were required to answer the many questions raised by the sweeping provisions of the law. For example, what was the status of an individual born in Spain to a Guatemalan father? Special cases were placed before Congress throughout the enforcement and were never really decided by that body. In virtually the only action taken to clarify the law, Congress voted to exempt from expulsion two Spaniards who had served in Congress since 1824.[7] State measures also required review by the Senate for their constitutionality. For example, a San Luis Potosí law of 14 February for preventing wives and children from accompanying *expulso* husbands and fathers was overturned.[8] Congress was finally forced by the expulsion to regulate the entry of foreigners. A passport law completed on 12 March required all future entrants to possess documents issued by the federal government.[9]

There were numerous conflicts between state and federal authorities as a result of the expulsion process. Public opinion was polarized by the enforcement in states where the Yorkinos were not everywhere dominant (such as Veracruz and Yucatán). The federal law took precedence over the state laws and, in some cases (for example, San Luis Potosí), this meant that a milder law was enforced, creating resentment among local Yorkinos. There were also instances in which the governor and vice-governor were at odds over the tenor of local enforcement. In some cases, a *peninsular* excepted by the federal measure had already been expelled by a state law. In practice this meant that the individual would be safe only in federal territory, though in some cases local authorities acknowledged that exception from the federal law constituted absolute exemption from future persecution. The states varied in their willingness to accept *expulsos* from other states, even temporarily. And some state decrees subsequently limited the freedom and the rights of excepted *peninsulares* (for example, Tamaulipas).

In spite of all these efforts to purge Mexico of Spaniards, unrest among the anti-*peninsular* populace began to plague federal and state governments once again in February and March. Gen. Isidro Montes de Oca in Oaxaca and Presbyter Jiménez del Río in the capital continued to agitate for the total expulsion of Spaniards. In March there were also said to be "seditious gatherings" in the capital of Escoseses who were sympathetic to the plight of the Spaniards, and these led to the transfer of some military officials to Guadalajara and San Luis Potosí.[10]

Expulsos received a sympathetic reception from Spanish officials in the Caribbean. As early as 14 September 1827, the Spanish crown had ordered that protection should be extended to emigres from "New Spain," and instructions to that effect were received in Havana in January 1828.[11] An official campaign of recruitment now commenced at New Orleans, and *expulso* volunteers were transported to Havana for the attempts at reconquest soon authorized by Madrid. In the Californias, the problem was different: *peninsulares* who wished to depart were prevented by local officials who feared the destruction of the missions.[12] The problem stemmed from the lack of qualified replacements; this evasion of the letter of the law was facilitated by the distance from Mexico City.

By late March, the machinery of enforcement was fully in operation, and *peninsulares* seeking exceptions were appearing before authorized medical authorities (*juntas facultativas*) to have their ailments verified. *Expulsos* were coping with the rigors of Veracruz—yellow fever, smallpox, a shortage of ships, elevated ticket prices, and fleecing by opportunists. Even after embarkation there yet remained the dangers of pirates, mistreatment, or even abandonment by an occasionally unscrupulous North American captain. For those who hoped to remain, a hasty marriage might help. The final lists of Spaniards in some states reveal an unusually large number of married *peninsulares*.

Civil authorities had jurisdiction over Spaniards who had served in the military, despite the tradition of military autonomy (*fuero militar*). But if a governor were to appear lax in the expulsion of ex-*militares*, a state military commander might seek to enforce the law on his own. In Puebla during April, for example, the military chief, convinced that the civil authorities were obstructing enforcement, attempted to force action through the minister of war. Finally, on 18 April 1828 the president declared that state governors had sole authority to enforce the expulsion law.[13] The new militias became involved in the enforcement by putting pressure upon recalcitrant civil authorities, such as Governor Zavala of Mexico State. The case of the new governor of Veracruz, Santa Anna, was apparently somewhat similar. Santa Anna was hesitant to expel *peninsulares* who enjoyed the military *fuero* and those he held in high personal esteem. More than once, the federal government found it necessary to demand that the governor carry out the instructions from Mexico City.[14]

Fear of Spanish invasion forced the administration to instruct the governors on 30 April to cease sending *expulsos* to the Gulf ports and to terminate voluntary departures. Henceforth, the unhappy Spaniards should be marched southward to Acapulco to be embarked, including those living in the state of Veracruz. Moreover, all able-bodied Spanish residents were now ordered removed to at least twenty leagues from the coast. Under the new policy, *expulsos* from the Federal District or the territories should depart through San Blas in the state of Jalisco.[15] This presented the *peninsulares* with the frustrating prospect of having to round Cape Horn in order to reach New Orleans! One of the side effects of this temporary withdrawal of Spaniards from the Gulf coast was to stimulate Santa Anna to hastily commence the expulsion of 205 *gachupines* previously ignored by the governor. Cañedo caught Santa Anna in the act and demanded that he follow normal procedure, documenting his actions with the appropriate reports. When the enigmatic Santa Anna caviled, the president was forced to order him to comply.[16] As this case illustrates, the administration would not surrender to the governors the special powers contained in Article 9 of the law, to expel "suspicious" Spaniards. The suspension of departures from the Gulf coast was terminated within a month, by an order of 31 May. The order removing *peninsulares* from the coasts had already been withdrawn in instructions to the governors of Veracruz and Yucatan on 24 May.[17]

As it became obvious that the expulsion law was not being enforced everywhere with the same attention to prior instructions, Cañedo began chiding the governors (excepting those of Chihuahua, Yucatán, and Mexico) on 28 May. Because of a continuing lack of reports, Cañedo repeated the action on 3 June.[18] The administration feared that, due to a lack of proper information at this late date, the "dangerous" among the *peninsulares* might escape expulsion at the hands of the federal government. But none was more distraught over this prospect than Governor Tornel of the Federal District. Tornel suddenly produced a list of forty-four "dangerous" Spaniards on 14 June, but without data to substantiate his claim that they constituted a threat to the republic. During the waning days of the enforcement in the capital, Tornel and Cañedo shuttled the list back and forth without expelling a single Spaniard contained therein, since the governor could not validate the charges against them. The original list of pernicious Spaniards, compiled by some members of the municipal government on 10 June, had contained 130 names.[19]

With the task of expulsion and exception incomplete, the major provisions of the 20 December 1827 law apparently expired in the Federal District on 22 June 1828. Tornel bitterly warned of the dire results of failing to enforce Article 9, charging that the requirements for evidence had been more stringent in June than previously.[20] By

2 July, Tornel was on trial before his Masonic brotherhood for his enforcement activities, but it is not certain whether this was because he had been accepting bribes or because he was too lenient in the eyes of the Yorkino leadership (or both).[21]

Probably as a result of the debate with Tornel, on 25 June the president reversed somewhat his earlier contention that the law had expired in the Federal District. Now it was argued that only the provision allocating to the federal government the right to arbitrarily grant exceptions or order expulsions had ceased: the routine provisions of the law were still in effect.[22] And decisions continued to be rendered, but apparently reluctantly, on individual appeals, some of which were still pending when the second expulsion law went into effect on 20 March 1829.

The federal Congress did little during the final months of enforcement to clarify the future status of Spaniards in the republic. A long-awaited citizenship law was passed on 14 April 1828 that continued the usual prohibition against immigration by Spaniards and denied certificates of naturalization to "subjects or citizens of the nation with which [Mexico] may find [itself] at war."[23] On 28 April the Chamber of Deputies approved a measure that would exempt "all persons born in any part of America dependent upon the Spanish government" from the category of Spaniards.[24] An often expressed urge to extend the life of the law, in order to more effectively carry out the expulsion, was overcome by the federalists' fear of any extension of presidential power.[25] By virtue of a measure that passed the lower house on 19 May, a Spaniard who wished to own property in Mexico in the future would have to overcome the provisions of the expulsion law and acquire citizenship through naturalization.[26]

As the enforcement flagged in the final months, public dissatisfaction with the slow progress made in removing the *gachupines* was manifest, especially in states such as Puebla, where Escosés influence in government was still dominant. From Oaxaca in June, General Montes de Oca's "Column of Liberty of the South," as he called it, still demanded a more thorough expulsion. A taste of the bitterness felt by Mexican hispanophobes can be sampled from a letter received by the activist Lt. Col. Manuel Reyes Veramendi:

In effect, the expulsion measure has been evaded by favors, or by intrigue, tied to interest; how many, many bad, dangerous ones still reside among us, still stir the tea of discord; how many, many others have swelled their fortunes, or formed their fortune in the shadow of this singular expulsion, interrupted according to influence and convenience.[27]

In many states, enforcement was moderated by sympathetic local administrations without arousing bitterness and resentment (as in Yucatán). This was possible, of course, only where violence was absent. The result was similar in the Californias. But in New Mexico, where many of the Spaniards were also friars, only two were allowed to remain, and this "by virtue of their extreme age, and by the payment of 500 pesos each."[28]

The Results of the First Expulsion

The effects of the expulsion law of 20 December 1827 fell in varying degrees upon Spaniards in every political division of Mexico. Surviving records indicate that 1,823 passports were issued by the governors, while the lists of departures forwarded by the port commanders named 1,771 exiles.[29] A number of individuals left voluntarily: the ministry reported that 885 *peninsulares* and 53 servants solicited passports in 1828. This could mean that roughly half the Spaniards departing did so "voluntarily," though, of course, their departure was a direct result of the expulsion movement. At least 4,831 *gachupines* remained in late 1828, or better than two-thirds of the estimated pre-expulsion community. The largest remaining Spanish populations appear to have been concentrated in the Federal District, Puebla, Veracruz, and Oaxaca. A number of state governments were more flexible on the Spanish question than they might have cared to admit. For example, only 5 percent of Mexico State's *peninsulares* departed under the Zavala regime.

An analysis of the occupational structure of excepted Spaniards will shed light on the first expulsion's impact. I was successful in compiling occupational data for seven states, and what I discovered suggests little change in the structure of the Spanish community for the nation as a whole. I estimate that commercial occupations attracted 45 percent of the Iberians surviving the first expulsion, while landowners made up one-quarter of the community, and these were principally farmers. Suspended military men equaled 8 percent, while clerics constituted barely 5 percent. Merchants and mine owners were hardly affected in these seven states, but the regular clergy was devastated, by and large. Querétaro lost half of its sizable monastic colony while losing none of its merchants. Yucatán issued passports to one-tenth of its merchants, but half the remaining Spaniards still engaged in commerce. It would appear, then, that the departure of rich merchants for France, as well as shopkeepers for New Orleans, was not so serious as to threaten the *peninsulares'* prominence in trade.

It is possible to analyze the occupational trend among the *expulsos* who departed through ports other than Veracruz. My tabulations reveal that merchants and shopkeepers made up half of the departures through the northern outlets, while clerics, particularly regulars, constituted one-third of the expulsions through these same ports. The bulk of the evidence indicates, therefore, that, as the more cosmopolitan criollos had warned, merchants and the regular clergy were the principal groups to be injured by the purge of 1827–28.

It is clear that few Spaniards took their families with them into exile, contrary to the expectation of Lucas Alamán, C. M. Bustamante, and others. This may have resulted from penury, or the *peninsulares'* expectation of either a rapid reconquest or recognition in the near future, which would have enabled them to return. The vast majority of the exiles journeyed to New Orleans. My final figures for the first expulsion indicate that a minimum of 1,779 expulsions and 4,555 exceptions were actualized, with roughly 276 cases still unresolved by late 1828 (see table 1). The states containing the largest number of excepted *peninsulares* in late 1828 were, in order: Puebla, Oaxaca, Veracruz, Mexico, and Zacatecas. Though the Federal District reported only 114 exceptions, it must have contained more Spaniards than any other entity. And, finally, by adding the cases pending to the total excepted, we obtain a reasonable estimate of 4,831 Spaniards still residing in Mexico prior to the second expulsion, or roughly 73 percent of the estimated pre-expulsion population of 6,610.

The data reveal some noteworthy trends in the enforcement of the first expulsion. The figures for the Federal District are probably misleading, since the ministry softened the hard line pursued by Tornel. Considering the role of Jalisco and Mexico in originally generating the expulsion movement, the results in those states appear quite moderate in retrospect. The federal entities least affected were Zacatecas, with only 3 percent of the *peninsulares* departing, and Mexico, followed by the Californias, with only 5 percent and 8 percent expelled, respectively. Clearly, a number of state governments were more generous with the *gachupines* than the Yorkinos desired. A Spanish middle economic group survived, still active in trade. Some Spanish capital yet remained in Mexico, but the majority of the great merchants had departed with their specie, together with many of the impoverished *capitulados*. A number of wealthy *peninsulares* avoided exile: merchants such as Manuel Terán of Jalapa or Francisco de Paula Herrera and Pablo del Paso y Troncoso of Veracruz escaped unscathed. Tomás Alamán of Guanajuato, father of Lucas Alamán, was excepted as easily as Juan Manuel García of Veracruz, the father-

TABLE 1
SPANIARDS EXPELLED UNDER THE LAW OF 20 DECEMBER 1827

	No. Ordered Expelled	No. Ordered Excepted	Unknown or Pending Cases	Total
Californias (Territories)	5	63	—	68
Chiapas	23	55	—	78
Chihuahua	57	140	3	200
Coahuila y Tejas	4	53	—	57
Colima (Territory)	4	5	—	9
Federal District	833	114	86	1,033
Durango	80	215	4	299
Guanajuato	34	246	46	326
Jalisco	29	280	4	313
Mexico	17	339	—	356
Michoacán	27	126	—	153
Nuevo León	10	77	—	87
Nuevo Mexico (Territory)	—	13	—	13
Oaxaca	107	423	19	549
Occidente (Sonora y Sinaloa)	45	145	—	190
Puebla	130	536	20	686
Querétaro	38	199	33	270
San Luis Potosí	110	214	—	324
Tabasco	11	80	—	91
Tamaulipas	33	124	6	163
Tlaxcala (Territory)	1	27	3	31
Veracruz	111	372	32	515
Yucatán	60	386	—	446
Zacatecas	10	323	20	353
Total	1,779	4,555	276	6,610

Sources: Federal and state lists located in AGN, Ramo de Expulsión, legs. 1–3, 5, 7–10, plus data from other contempoary sources as described in Sims, *La expulsión,* p. 230, table 24.

in-law of General Santa Anna. Spaniards who had demonstrated their loyalty by serving republican governments could also find favor with the Victoria administration. Two examples were former treasury minister Francisco de Arrillaga of Jalapa and Brigadier Juan Orbegoso.[30] Some two dozen wealthy merchants who remained soon "supported" the government as sources of funds (*agiotistas*), loaning money to the national treasury on a short-term basis at high interest.[31]

Spaniards who chose to stay on in Mexico still had to contend with a hostile public and the aggressive Yorkinos. It is not surprising, then, that so many entrepreneurs preferred to undertake the voyage to France. H. G. Ward reported that the principal capitalists of Mexico "established themselves at Bordeaux, and [had] given a great impulse to the trade of that town." While in 1827 only 34 passengers arrived in France from Mexico, the figure leaped to 616 in 1828, obviously reflecting the arrival of exiles that began on 26 April.[32]

The impact on the clergy was profound; the expulsion virtually destroyed the traditional system of hospitals and schools operated by the regular orders. Between 1826 and 1828, the regular clergy declined by 17 percent, or by a total of 325 friars. The expulsion was an especially serious blow to the Carmelites, who lost 57 percent of their membership, while the Franciscans suffered the largest numerical loss of any group—159 brothers. The apostolic colleges, or seminaries, were wiped out, with the departure of 83 Spaniards. Prior to the first expulsion, 21.8 percent of the regular clergy was Spanish-born. The loss suffered by the secular clergy, on the other hand, was just 8 percent during the 1826–28 period. The expulsion had little impact on parish priests.[33]

The economic consequences of the expulsion for Mexico are clearly visible if one reflects on the general decline that occurred in 1827–28, in trade, government revenue, and the circulation of specie. The new foreign merchant-importers who had arrived since Independence complained bitterly of the effect the expulsion was having on their commercial affairs. No one lamented these developments more than the English. However, one English merchant who traveled in five states in mid-1828 disagreed with his colleagues, concluding that "the law of expulsion [had] not caused the miseries and insecurity" reported to the merchants in Veracruz. As he saw it, the effects were insignificant, because the only persons dislocated were the "*capitulados* and those introduced since 1821; that is to say, . . . those who possessed nothing, or who used to possess very little."[34] Unfortunately, this traveler failed to detect the marked variations among states. The data reveal, for example, that virtually all the *expulsos* from Querétaro were regular clergy; the friars were also hard hit in Oaxaca, Jalisco, and Guanajuato. Merchants were most affected in Yucatán and Oaxaca, and Spanish servants were largely eliminated from Durango. Oaxaca also expelled many farmers and laborers, which resulted in a greater occupational balance among the exiles from that state than elsewhere. And if we reflect upon actual departures from ports other than Veracruz for which data is available, merchants constituted

TABLE 2

SPANIARDS REMAINING IN MEXICO IN 1828, BY OCCUPATION

(selected federal entities)

	Chihuahua	Durango	Guanajuato	Jalisco	Nuevo León	Querétaro	Yucatán	Total
Regular clergy	2	2	7	10	3	19	2	45
Secular clergy	1	3	1	1	2	4	12	24
Suspended military officers	3	—	26	29	—	2	10	70
Suspended soldiers	—	1	12	17	1	—	6	37
Merchants	45	58	49	119	27	101	152	551
Shopkeepers	—	8	3	1	—	—	29	41
Farmers	12	24	44	39	14	34	28	195
Mine owners	24	31	9	6	—	—	—	70
Real estate owners	—	—	50	1	1	—	—	51
Ex-government employees	3	5	7	8	1	—	11	35
Professionals	1	5	—	5	2	—	8	20
Artisans	2	2	10	2	2	—	14	32
Farm administrators	—	—	7	—	—	—	1	10
Maritime workers (fishermen, etc.)	—	—	—	1	—	—	88	89
Servants	14	10	4	4	2	—	2	36
Laborers	1	—	—	—	—	—	1	2
Others	—	2	—	—	—	—	—	2
Unemployed	—	3	6	7	2	—	6	24
Total Spaniards whose occupations are known	108	154	235	250	57	160	370	1,334
Total Spaniards	143	219	292	284	77	232	386	1,633

Sources: Lists preserved in AGN, Ramo de Expulsión, legs. 1–4, 8, 10, 13–15, 17, 22 3/4, 23, 26; Sims, La expulsión, p. 235, table 27.

roughly half the departures, in spite of the fact that clergy were the primary group receiving passports. An assessment of the occupations of excepted Spaniards may be seen in table 2.

The fiscal and economic repercussions for Mexico may be appreciated by an examination of three vital areas: revenue and expenses of the federal government, customs receipts, and imports and exports. The income of the federal government was higher on the eve of the first expulsion than at any time since the last year of the colony.[35] The treasury contained a surplus in 1827, but during the next fiscal year, government revenue fell off by approximately 3,350,000 pesos. This reflected a sharp decline in customs receipts, upon which the government depended for nearly half its income. The roughly 42 percent decline in customs revenue during the two years prior to June 1828 reflected the radical decrease in commercial activity that coincided with the anti-Spanish movement.[36] Imports fell by nearly one-third in 1828 from their 1827 level. Export activity fluctuated unpredictably in all but gold and silver. A leap of 112 percent occurred in the reported export of precious metals between 1826 and 1828. The withdrawal of specie from circulation by *peninsulares* mounted rapidly and would have severe repercussions for the Mexican economy. Local production of precious metals had declined since Independence, and foreign capital had failed to revive output significantly before 1828. In that year, gold and silver (fleeing capital) amounted to no less than 85.5 percent of the total exports recorded.

Little more than educated guesses have been offered as estimates of the outflow of specie. The French agent Alex Martin, for example, wrote before the passage of the expulsion law, "During the past three years, more than 40 million pesos had been shipped to Bordeaux by Spaniards." Or to choose another, C. M. Bustamante contended that by January 1829 *peninsulares* had exported 34 million pesos in specie.[37] But if we add the figures contained in the reports of Mexican consular agents in France, we find that the recorded arrival of specie from Mexico between October 1826 and March 1829 amounted to 4,027,487 *pesos fuertes*, plus 1,812 ounces of gold and considerable silver bars and silver plate. In any case, the shortage of specie in Mexico was so acute that a secret session of Congress was required to deal with the problem by summer 1828. Stepped-up production in the mines and a 50 percent increase in minting between 1826 and 1829 could only partially compensate for the severe loss.[38]

In the words of the British ambassador, "The credit of the Republic received a shock [as a result of the expulsion of 1828] from which it will not easily recover."[39] Mexico would now be forced to change its policy of relying upon British loans for solvency and begin to rely upon the notorious *agiotistas*, many of whom were *peninsulares*. But that was not all: in addition to eliminating foreign sources of loans and reducing internal sources of government revenue, the anti-Spanish movement also generated new expenses for the federal government. In 1827 alone, the law of 10 May may have cost the government over 1,300,000 pesos in salaries to former employees. And the church, like the government, suffered its own decline in income, amounting to about 20 percent in tithes in 1827–28, plunging to nearly an all-time low.[40]

A series of important political and social results of the first expulsion may also be detected. To a degree, exiling prominent Spanish liberals contributed to the growth of the incipient nineteenth-century conservative movement. A U.S. senator visiting Mexico, John Milton Niles, viewed the first expulsion as ending constitutional guarantees and commencing usurpations of authority by the military. The liberal Mora felt keenly the expulsion of the Spanish liberals of Iturbidist days, as well as the departure from constitutional guarantees. Looking back on the events of 1828 from the vantage point of 1833, Mora observed that after 1827 the Escoseses had supported the clergy, while the Yorkinos had relied upon the army.[41]

The impact of the expulsion on Mexico's social structure is more difficult to gauge, but certain visible changes had occurred by 1829. Public office and direct political power were no longer held by Spaniards, though the number of *peninsulares* on public pensions had increased markedly. The Iberian may have been humbled a bit by his new second-class citizen status, but his attitude toward the republic had not improved. All those with property to protect or status deriving from traditional considerations now rallied about him, forming a cluster of "white" families suspicious and resentful of the upwardly mobile, republican political elite of the Yorkino lodges who now governed. These families hoped for the eventual return of the *peninsulares*, in order to restore the urban culture they had known and even to maintain the somatic identity of the old elite. Liberals of 1812 vintage were disillusioned also: they had allotted to the Spaniards and their capital a crucial role in the construction of the new society.

In conclusion, we are compelled to recognize that the expulsion movement of 1827–28 failed in both of its principal purposes. It removed only about 27 percent of the *peninsulares* from Mexico, and it endangered Mexican independence by furnishing merchant capital and officers for the reconquest that was so dear to the heart of Ferdinand VII. This would become evident in the course of 1829. Moreover, it impelled conservatives and liberals alike to reexamine their differences and to begin the formation of what would soon become the movement for the defense of privileges. But the *jacobinas* of the Mexican Revolution were to have their day before the protracted struggle of nineteenth-century liberals and conservatives could commence in earnest. Before 1828 was over, the Spaniards would discover to their chagrin that they were not to be freed from nativist suspicion and resentment for some time to come.

3

Anti-Gachupinism and the Rebellion of 1828

BY LATE 1828 the anti-Spanish party intended to expose the duplicity of the *peninsulares* who had escaped expulsion in 1827–28 and to justify a second persecution much harsher than the first. The bitterness of the popular party at seeing their much desired expulsion frustrated in 1828 found expression in the founding of *El Cardillo*—which even abused the Mexican wives of Spaniards[1]—and in conspiracies surrounding the national elections of 1 September 1828. The result was the prevention of the Pedraza presidency, the revolt of Perote, and the collapse of the Victoria regime in early December in the wake of a popular uprising in Mexico City known as La Acordada.

The Spaniards' dilemma and near helplessness in the face of the Mexican nativist movement had several causes. Their party was destroyed in mock battle at Tulancingo in December 1827; their ranks had been diminished by the first series of expulsions and, to a lesser degree, by the Antimasonic movement which, though never wholly successful, obtained a federal law on 28 May 1828 abolishing Masonic organizations.[2] Escocés lodges declined in vitality throughout 1828 and the Spanish cause in Mexico found fewer supporters as the Yorkinos, now seemingly invincible, soon turned their ideological debates upon themselves and discovered sharp internal differences on a number of important questions.

As the September elections drew near and the Pedraza-Guerrero split in the Yorkino camp widened, the Spaniards were forced to choose sides in a conflict that offered no ideal candidate, from the *peninsular* perspective. One of the reasons for Pedraza's popularity was his vigorous prosecution of the Arenas affair—which earned him the animosity of the Spaniards and the adulation of the Yorkinos.

43

Vicente Guerrero presented the *peninsulares* with a dilemma: he was the recognized caudillo of the anti-Spanish forces, though he never publicly denounced the *peninsulares*. Yet Guerrero was the only leader in Mexico who had demonstrated that he was capable of suppressing violent movements aimed at the *gachupines*. That Spanish money and opinion ultimately supported Pedraza was due to fear of the "radicalism" of those surrounding Guerrero, as well as the decision by most moderate and conservative criollos to seek the stability that Pedraza seemed to offer.

The Yorkino camp lost control over its so-called moderates, who split off to support Pedraza. Pro-Guerrero Yorkinos were left, therefore, with a resort that had helped them in previous political struggles —the Mexican masses' real or assumed hostility toward the Spaniards. And while neither Zavala, who emerged as Guerrero's principal advisor, nor Santa Anna, who launched the initial military movement on behalf of the Guerrero presidency, had previously demonstrated marked anti-Spanish proclivities, their following would make antigachupinism the cardinal point of the popular Guerrerist movement. Though some Yorkinos did not use the Spanish question for political advantage, it is nonetheless true that the Yorkino party used the widespread antipathy toward the Iberians to enhance its own popularity.[3]

The intensity of the resulting hostility was not a function of the size of the Spanish community. Though Zavala believed that 6,000 Spaniards escaped expulsion in 1827–28—and more recent historians have accepted his estimate—the surviving records of the expulsion do not allow so large a figure.[4] As we have seen, a minimum of 4,831 remained in Mexico in late 1828.

On the very day of balloting for the presidency, there was pending in the Grand Jury Section of the Senate an accusation against the ministry for "lack of observance of the law for the expulsion of Spaniards."[5] Moreover, the vote of a plurality of state legislatures for Pedraza—who was now viewed, for better or worse, as the Spaniards' candidate—was intolerable to Mexicans who were vehemently anti-Spanish. The Pedraza victory, obtained in this manner, would not stand; for his enemies and opponents could utilize the anti-*gachupín* cause to justify their forthcoming attack on the legitimate succession. Pedraza, who knew the extent of anti-Spanish feeling, was in a position to counter popular suspicion with military force, since he was reputed to be a strong minister of war. But his opponents were quick to point out that a majority of the state legislatures voting for Pedraza had been elected before the establishment of Yorkino hegemony. This meant that they were "unpopular" in their own states and could not claim to democratically represent their constituents. This would be the reasoning of the federal Congress in January 1829, when called upon by events to legitimate the Guerrero presidency.

The election and subsequent revolt were acted out in the midst of a severe economic decline for both the private sector and the government. Specie was disappearing from circulation and government revenues were declining. Mexico was falling into arrears on interest payments on its newly acquired English debt, and many of its principal capitalists were emigrating. It suffered from the fiscal burden of a large army, which was now allotted 80 percent of the federal budget,[6] and duplication in federal posts—the result of the preservation of the Spanish concept of *empleo* as inalienable property. Foreign loans were no longer available to Mexico; disillusion had set in among London's financial houses.

National xenophobia was intensified not merely by Mexico's relations with foreign bankers, but also by its increasing contact with foreign merchants. Local entrepreneurs had depended for centuries upon Spanish monopolists, guild merchants, and wholesalers—an important source of anti-*peninsular* feeling. Now, with national independence and the persecution of Spaniards, which resulted in the loss and withdrawal of investments, Mexican merchants were increasingly dependent upon foreign houses for their goods and often were in direct competition with foreign merchants on the scene. As a result, by 1828 there was a developing hostility to foreigners in general; Spaniards were everywhere the symbol of alien exploitation, but in the west the British were mistrusted as well, and in the north hostility to North Americans was rising. Demands for restrictions on the activities of foreign merchants and on the entry of foreign merchandise, as well as for limits on the export of silver and gold, were common.[7]

The Spanish Question and Perote

Within a week of the elections, rumors reached the capital of a revolt in Veracruz, to be commanded by Santa Anna. Rumor became fact on 10 September, when Santa Anna and approximately 600 followers illegally assumed control of the fortress of Perote. In summary, Santa Anna's manifesto demanded the annulment of Pedraza's victory and supported the election of Guerrero, requiring the state legislatures to hold new elections in which they should respect the popular will. His plan called upon the chambers of Congress to pass a law that would expel all Spaniards as "the origin of our problems."[8] The expulsion demand flowed logically from his explanation of the alleged election betrayal. Spanish machinations had led to the Pedraza triumph, thereby rendering the results invalid. The call for expulsion was just and even necessary, according to Santa Anna, in order to preserve democracy and federalism.

President Victoria, who had played no visible role in the election, allowed the defense of his moribund administration and of the legal succession to be supervised by Pedraza, the minister of war and president-elect. Pedraza responded to Santa Anna's challenge by ordering Gen. Manuel Rincón with 3,000 men to Perote. The decision seemed wise, since the Rincón and Santa Anna families were rivals for dominance in Veracruz State. But Rincón, with government support, was no match for Santa Anna, who lacked assistance outside Perote. The rebels, after a lengthy siege, abandoned the fortress and undertook the arduous trek toward Oaxaca, with diminishing forces. The federal Congress then declared Santa Anna "outside the law unless he surrendered arms."[9]

A modicum of support accrued to the rebels on 27 September when an anti-Spanish supporter of Pedraza, Lt. Col. Manuel Reyes Veramendi, joined the rebellion in Mexico State.[10] In the south and west anti-*gachupín* bands stirred anew, but no generals overtly joined Santa Anna—an indication that his cause was considered lost. Pedraza and the moderates seemed the victors once again.

The question of whether the election had indeed been "bought by Spanish gold" was warmly debated in the final days of September, with public rebuttals voiced by legislatures who stood accused by the revolt's supporters.[11] Though the state legislature of Querétaro took legal action against the *Correo*, on 22 September judges of the Federal District ruled unanimously that there were no grounds for the suit.[12] Moderates were quick to point out that many of the judges were Yorkinos. It appeared that during the Victoria years the administration had no control over the courts.

For Zavala, the Perote movement presented an acute personal dilemma. He, like Santa Anna, saw in the Pedraza victory an intensification of the political persecution that he was already experiencing at the hands of the minister of war. And yet, he was perhaps the most lenient of Mexico's governors in enforcing the first expulsion of Spaniards. As one close to Guerrero and much admired by Santa Anna, Zavala was soon a refugee from justice, hiding in the Federal District. Zavala's eventual decision to conspire for the success of the revolt is understandable. The anti-Spanish line of the movement must have troubled him, though. An anonymous writer publicly accused Zavala as early as 30 September of drawing up the expulsion plan just issued by the violent hispanophobe, Loreto Cataño, and of being the force behind the Reyes Veramendi revolt. Zavala denied these charges and placed himself on the side of the administration.[13]

While both parties lacked funds for the contest, the government's desperation was more visible. In late September, according to Joel Poinsett, the secretary of the treasury assembled the merchants of Mexico in order to obtain a "voluntary" loan. He frightened the European Spaniards by telling them that "if the government had not the means of moving national forces against Santa Anna, they might expect to be stripped to their shirts, and to have their throats cut in the bargain." The foreign merchants pledged $2,000 each, while the Spaniards gave what they could.[14]

With the rebellion of Reyes Veramendi at Monte Alto and a second movement in southern Mexico State, the revolt became a purely anti-Spanish movement. Nothing was said by the Mexico State rebels about the outcome of the presidential elections. The pretext of Santa Anna's movement now became the goal of the rebellion. The moderates (*imparciales*) who edited *El Aguila* saw the hand of the Yorkinos in this and suspected that, should the revolt succeed, Guerrero would become president.[15] In response, the Yorkino *Correo*, which had so often accused the Escocés *El Sol* of being allied with the *gachupines*, now began to accuse the *imparciales* of an alliance with the Spaniards.[16]

The government remained firm through October and November, with Santa Anna besieged in Oaxaca and the anti-Spanish bands of Mexico State dispersed in the mountains. Then President Victoria announced on 25 October 1828 that Madrid and Havana were definitely preparing to attack Mexico.[17] In light of this, Santa Anna, whose plight in Oaxaca had grown increasingly desperate, adopted a new tactic on 20 November, seeking to delay events in hopes of new rebellions. Santa Anna's officers signed a document declaring the Spanish invasion of Mexico imminent; consequently, they contended, Mexicans should not be fighting each other.[18] Letters had arrived from Veracruz indicating "that the enemy squadron had been seen off Campeche, and that the coast of Yucatán was the intended destination." The document proposed that Santa Anna should convert his force into "the vanguard division which would march to Yucatán, or wherever convenient to attack the Spanish hosts." Santa Anna's conditions were that no member of his forces be separated under any pretext, and that his revolutionary demands be judged by the next general Congress, to which he was willing to submit. Santa Anna's warning, coupled with Victoria's official announcement of the Spanish threat, was unexpectedly favorable to the insurrection. General Guerrero's former collaborators in the south, Gen. Isidro Montes de Oca and Col. Juan Alvarez now adhered to Santa Anna's movement.[19] The Spanish threat—both internal and external—now clearly outweighed more ephemeral questions of electoral legitimacy.

Revolt in the Capital

The poet Guillermo Prieto—a keen observer of his times—recalled that "the masses" were basically ignorant of the causes of the Acordada revolt. All they knew was that Victoria had supported Pedraza while Zavala and Lobato had wished to be led by "*el negro* Guerrero." Witnesses and participants alike have all acknowledged the significance of popular antipathy toward the Spaniards in the mass appeal of the revolt. The Mexico City rebellion was organized by two prominent Yorkinos, Deputy Anastasio Zerecero and Governor Zavala.[20]

In the Federal District on the night of 30 November 1828, Col. Santiago García and an ex-marquis, Col. José María Cadena, suddenly extended the rebellion to Mexico City by seizing the fortified compound called the Acordada, with its strategically important artillery. General Montes de Oca was now in revolt, and the rebels of the Federal District announced their adherence to his plan for the expulsion of Spaniards. President Victoria erred in taking the expanding revolt lightly, merely fortifying the palace and calling Congress into extraordinary session.[21]

In the Acordada, the ex-marquis of Cadena—a Pedraza supporter —proposed that a note be addressed to the government "requiring the presence in the Citadel within twenty-four hours of all the Spaniards resident in the District, to be thence conducted under escort of our army to be obliged to embark." The document was signed by all present and by those who adhered to the revolt during the next three hours. Zavala later wrote that García and Cadena initially commanded only 200 soldiers and 300 civil militia in the Acordada, and there was division at first in the leadership: Cadena, Pedraza's man, desired only the expulsion of Spaniards, while García, linked to the southern forces, hoped to place Guerrero in the presidency. The ex-marquis suddenly withdrew from the movement, giving Victoria and Pedraza a genuine opportunity. But, in spite of congressional urgings, the moment was lost, and the Acordada was reinforced by the arrival of Gen. José María Lobato and Zavala. The government now attempted persuasion, sending the Yorkino Colonel Tornel and Ramón Rayon to reason with the rebels, but to no avail.[22]

Early the next morning—1 December—the rebels announced

their decision to adhere to the Santa Anna plan, calling for the expulsion of Spaniards and for new elections. Victoria then published a proclamation asserting that since García's faction was aligned with Santa Anna, they too should be punished. The president appeared before Congress to report that the cabinet wished him to have "extraordinary faculties," but his request was denied on the presumption that these powers would have been used to grant amnesty to the delinquents. The ministers of government, justice, and the treasury urged all authorities in the states to impede efforts to second the movement.[23]

Propagandists for both sides seized their pens, of course; but this was not to be a bloodless paper rebellion. The Yorkino *Correo* greeted the revolt with equanimity, claiming that 1,500 troops had entered the Acordada, three times the actual number. The *Correo* attacked the ministry, not Victoria, in accordance with the Yorkino strategy.[24]

The poor of the capital joined the revolution in large numbers on 1 December, either out of hostility to the Spaniards or in hopes of gaining the sack of the Parián's commercial establishments. A government bid for the support of Lobato failed and he assumed command of the troops in the Acordada. Sympathetic politicians, including Zavala, who had met in a pro-Guerrero junta the night before, now entered the fortress.

The administration rested its hopes on Gen. Vicente Filisola, a Neapolitan, royalist, and former supporter of Iturbide, who, though temporarily absent from the capital, was to return that evening. Guerrero had refused to obey government orders to report to the palace. Filisola arrived, disposed to fight, and Victoria promised that on the morrow his administration would "give an account of itself with happier results." But with rebel sympathizers sitting in Congress, the president's message could not fail to alert those of the Acordada.[25]

The Escocés *El Sol* suspended publication on 2 December, as hostilities commenced between loyalist forces and the rebels. The struggle was taking on the aspect of a contest between the regular army and Victoria's former comrades, the stalwarts of the independence wars. The congressional majority demanded action, in light of seizures of convents and the sacking of Spaniards' houses by the "outlaws." Some *peninsulares* were being held for ransom, and rebel ranks were growing. Finally Victoria resolved to commence hostilities, beginning at noon. Firing continued from both sides until nightfall and was renewed again the following morning, lasting most of 3 December. Rebel losses were significant, but noncombatant fatalities were apparently much greater.

The loyal forces held, but Victoria could not tolerate the tragedy that was unfolding, and he sought to end it by compromise. As a consequence, President-elect Pedraza departed the city on horseback, bound for Guadalajara to the west, where he hoped Gen. Joaquín Parres could offer protection. Victoria left the palace temporarily and met with Lobato in the church at Tepito, but a compromise was not reached. During the night, General Guerrero seized Chapultepec castle.

Firing was heavier on the morning of 4 December, until the rebels sent up a white flag at 8:00 A.M. and Victoria ordered a cease-fire. But loyal forces throughout the city were forced to defend their sectors against bands of pillagers who attempted to sack stores and houses. By 11:00 A.M. it was apparent that the cease-fire had enabled rebels to gain positions from which they could surprise principal points, capture cannon and move closer to the palace. Guerrero was now welcomed into the Acordada.[26]

Congress was beginning to disperse as Victoria went before a rump assembly to discuss his options. He was again urged to take energetic action. But loyal chiefs now began taking steps to save themselves and their troops from massacre; Victoria was indecisive to the last. As Lobato approached the palace, Victoria ordered a cease-fire, and again the rebels seized strategic points, this time around the plaza. Victoria went out to speak with Lobato from the balcony. Addressing the revolutionary following as "sons," Victoria asked, "Will I be safe if I come down?" The president then joined the multitude and abandoned his government, departing on horseback with Lobato for the Acordada, where he was greeted by Zavala and Guerrero. The poor sacked the storehouses of the national palace and invaded the congressional chambers.[27] But for the Spaniards and criollo merchants, the worst was yet to come.

The Sack of the Parián

The total collapse of the Victoria administration before a small military force and the poor of Mexico's barrios, bode ill for Spanish (and criollo) merchants. The wealthiest traders of Spanish birth sold their imported goods in the Parián, ancient symbol of European wealth, taste, and privilege. Zavala suggested later that for the masses it symbolized the survival of the colony; his friend Poinsett referred to the booty as "the goods of their enemies."[28]

To nineteenth-century historians, property was sacrosanct, and even a defender of the Guerrero presidency, Suárez y Navarro, vociferously condemned the sack of the Parián and adjacent shops. "But while points of the capitulation were being discussed," he said, over 5,000 *léperos* and a portion of the troops began to rob the Parián: "Large sums were invested here and the fortunes of thousands of families would disappear, the result of a sacking by an uncontrolled mob."[29] Forces sent from the Acordada to contain the looting stood by passively, pleased to see the Spaniards' stores sacked. And Zavala acknowledged later: "It may be true that [Lobato] failed to do all he could" to prevent the sacking, but Zavala insisted that noncompliance was not ordered. Zavala lauded the poor for their role in the revolt: they had carried munitions, hauled artillery, and cared for the wounded. In fact, on 4 December the movement numbered 30,000–40,000 persons,[30] reminiscent of the mass support achieved by Hidalgo in 1810.

Estimates of damage reached as high as 4 million pesos. British Consul General O'Gorman assessed the loss at "anywhere from two to three millions of dollars in merchandise and specie." By 30 July 1829 the *Correo* was admitting that 3 million pesos had been lost. Zavala, writing in 1830, accepted a maximum figure of 2 million pesos.[31] He asserted that the merchants' own demands, made subsequently before Congress, supported the smaller figure. Estimates of the death toll in the Acordada revolt vary also. The earliest report to the U.S. government suggested that 300 lives were lost; subsequent estimates went as high as 800 fatalities.[32]

The impact of the revolt on Mexico's political future has been exaggerated by conservatives. The fact that it broke the legitimate chain of succession and secured the presidency for Guerrero is significant. But the tendency to pardon unsuccessful as well as successful revolutionary "petitioners" had already been established. The men who carried out this revolt had gone unpunished for previous anti-Spanish plots, forgiven by Victoria himself. Suárez y Navarro asserted in defense of the outcome, and without citing proof, that Guerrero's coup prevented the launching of a Spanish conspiracy that was related to the frustrated Arenas affair.[33]

The reaction of foreign merchants varied according to nationality and politics. British merchants were stunned: O'Gorman's reports reveal the close links between Spanish and British mercantile interests. French property was also looted, which contributed to a brief war with France in 1838. The French representatives had cause to fear the rising tide of xenophobia in Mexico and concluded that the Spaniards would surely have to depart.[34]

The reaction of resident U.S. merchants may have been tempered by Poinsett's connections and opinions, which were consistently favorable to the popular party, though he was sympathetic toward the aggrieved Spaniards. Poinsett's actions during the revolt were at odds with his previous politics: he sheltered several Spaniards and monarchists in his residence, at some personal peril.[35] Perhaps the most serious result of these events for Mexico was the quickened flight of foreign capital after the sack of the Parián. The British minister, Pakenham, reported that "the merchants of Europe suspended their operations in Mexico."[36] Foreign trade was seriously affected by these events and by subsequent developments surrounding the second expulsion of Spaniards.

After the Acordada

The revolt that spread in the days following Victoria's submission was now official: because the president had joined the revolutionaries, all resistance could be viewed by the federal government as insubordination. State commanders who attempted to impede the activities of the anti-Spanish "armies" that sprung up in the south and in the *bajío* would be acting against the orders of Victoria. Understandably, there was confusion as to whether the government was at liberty to act. Partly because of this state of uncertainty, Lobato and his adviser, Zerecero, published an extraordinary justification on 8 December in which they failed even to mention the fall of Pedraza as a motive for the Acordada. Not the least remarkable of its claims was the charge that the Spaniards had "by their perverse maneuvers, obtained the expulsion of General Nicolás Bravo from the Republic."[37]

As the violence at the Acordada spread to other localities, the similarity between this uprising and that of Hidalgo in 1810 became even more striking. The rich sugar estates surrounding Cuernavaca and Cuaútla—Spanish-owned and managed—soon experienced anti-*gachupín* violence. Squads of bandits rose up under the command of Captain José María Larios, robbing and murdering Spaniards encountered along the way. They invaded haciendas, invoking Guerrero's name. Similar disturbances occurred in Puebla, where in December the populace rose up to the cry, "Long live the Virgin of Guadalupe and death to the Spaniards!" and sacked the majority of *peninsular* houses of commerce.[38]

These actions may have resulted from the "official" nature of the revolt following the Acordada, or from the widespread belief that the Mexico City government had fallen. The revolutionary army assembled in the capital on 14 December to halt the notion that the

Victoria administration was not free to act and, second, to remind Congress that it should pass a drastic expulsion law. The resulting document protested that the rebel army had never ceased to obey and even to sustain the government's deliberations; that it was prepared to depart for whatever point the government should direct, in order to remove the appearance of coercion; that it was appealing to Congress for "legislative measures, freely arrived at . . . [for] the expulsion of the Spaniards"; and that the government was free to designate the military units it desired to maintain public order.[39] The appointment of Guerrero to the ministry of war, following the Acordada, made the revolutionary occupation of the capital unnecessary.

Pedraza's failure to renounce the presidency and his support in Guadalajara threatened the revolutionary settlement. Troops in Guadalajara remained loyal, thanks to the influence of Parres. The states of Jalisco, Zacatecas, Vallodolid, and Guanajuato tried to put together a plan of defense, but their efforts depended upon the resolution of General Calderón at Puebla who had the most respectable force in the republic. Puebla rose in revolt in December and Calderón signed a convention with Santa Anna sanctioning the uprising of Mexico City.[40] Pedraza then renounced the presidency on 27 December and fled the country soon after.

The events in Puebla were very serious indeed. On Christmas Day, following the disturbances of 24 December, troops escorting a shipment of pesos became insubordinate and broke open the boxes. The poor of the city "shared" in the wealth of the Spanish and Mexican capitalists. Commerce in Puebla was greatly affected by the resulting loss of capital and by the eight days of disorders that followed. The city was at the mercy of a group of about 400 "bandits" until 1,500 soldiers arrived, sent by Colonel Alvarez. Mexico State also sent infantry, commanded by Governor Zavala and Col. Juan Domínguez.[41]

The *bajío* would not long escape the new era of anti-Spanish violence. According to C. M. Bustamante, an army of 1,400 unemployed men led by Colonel Codallos formed at Querétaro—a textile center ruined by cheap imports. Querétaro escaped sacking, as Codallos's army marched, like that of Hidalgo in 1810, toward San Miguel el Grande and Guanajuato. Codallos was soon joined by the president's brother, Lt. Col. Francisco Victoria. At Guanajuato, General Cortázar prepared to resist but on 28 December at Salamanca his infantry commander, the Yorkino Col. Domingo Chico, turned his entire force over to Colonel Codallos. This sizable army, now christened "Protector Division for the Expulsion of the Spaniards," was soon joined by a contingent from Valladolid. This enlarged force then set out for Guadalajara. Pedraza's renunciation at Guadalajara took place in the face of these developments.[42]

Commander Parres and Gov. José Justo Corro—later president of Mexico—attempted to aid General Cortázar, but Codallos's force of 2,000 men was too strong. Codallos protested to the people of Jalisco, "I left the state of Querétaro on orders from the Supreme General Government," having come "to guarantee peace." He warned that all opposition to the expulsion—which was now being debated in Congress—would be fruitless.[43]

The revolutionists signed an agreement with representatives of Governor Corro on 14 January allowing the "Protector Division" to enter Guadalajara and placing all local forces under the command of Codallos. The governor agreed to order resident Spaniards not to leave the confines of the capital, and expressed his conviction "that the supreme general powers operated with complete liberty, and for that reason, they would be obeyed." Furthermore, Governor Corro had to force his influence upon the local congress's Permanent Commission (which functioned when a congress was not in session), urging it to "make the same manifestation." The governor agreed to supply the needs of Codallos's troops, and the insurgent promised to maintain peace in the city and to respect the "persons and positions" of local authorities.[44]

Codallos forced the states of Guanajuato and Jalisco to pay his troops and, upon returning to Guanajuato, was named state military commander by Victoria, replacing Cortázar. It would seem that the president had ordered the state commanders not to resist. Veracruz remained uncertain until 27 December, when military leaders secured the state for Guerrero. Once the decision of a council of war was known, it was accepted. A similarly peaceful decision had been obtained in Tampico by the joint efforts of the town council and officer corps on 22 November.[45]

Disarming Mexico State proved to be far more difficult. There the civic militia of Toluca, commanded by Col. José Ignacio de Aguado, had insisted on remaining in arms until "the last Spaniard leaves the Republic." The president ordered the militiamen of Toluca to return to their homes on 1 December, but the directive did not get beyond Governor Zavala until 29 December, for obvious reasons. The anti-Spanish Toluca rebellion was in conformity with Santa Anna's revolt, of which Zavala was an important member. The militiamen were paid their daily subsistence while in revolt by a loan from the local administration and from private individuals. The officers and some troops met on the night of 1 January 1829 to consider the federal orders which, if obeyed, would force them to disarm before the passage of a new expulsion law. A resolution calling for total expulsion was approved unanimously, its backers protesting "that if the Supreme Government should fail to accede to this appeal, [this force] shall continue to be mobilized under arms even if it should receive no pay."[46] The government was powerless to prevent this defiance and Congress convened with the revolutionists still in arms.

And so it was decided that Guerrero and the popular party would take office in place of Pedraza and the "impartials." Santa Anna survived the law of proscription, and the Spaniards were to suffer a second round of expulsions. Petitions for the total expulsion of Spaniards began to be dictated immediately following the success of the Acordada.[47] It now remained to halt the panic that seized foreign capitalists. The *Correo* undertook the task, though its nationalistic spirit was not sacrificed in the least. It attacked the British consul general for his commercial connections: O'Gorman was accused of aiding their rivals, the Escoceses, by discrediting Mexico before his government and favoring aristocratic rule in Mexico.[48] The dilemma of the popular party was that while it needed European credit, it was confronted with a European community intimately connected with representatives of Mexico's traditional order.

Amid economic uncertainty and social tension, the Chamber of Deputies discounted the election of Pedraza and on 12 January 1829 declared Vicente Guerrero second president of the Federal Republic. Those who believed in popular sovereignty and favored social change looked forward to the inauguration. But for many Spaniards, who had good reason to fear popular sovereignty, the time had come to depart. On the night before the congressional decision, the violence spread to Zacatecas State. Around fifty military deserters entered Sombrerete in the evening, overcame the local garrison, rallied the poor to their cause, and sacked the houses of local Spaniards for more than six hours.[49] The impact of the revolution in Mexico City was remarkable: the flight of *peninsulares* was such that on 5 January Governor Tornel prohibited the Spaniards from leaving by the gates of Peralvillo and San Lázaro without passport, and ordered that documents be withheld until petitioners demonstrated that they owed nothing to the public treasury or to individuals, or until sufficient funds were deposited to cover such obligations.[50] By 18 January 1829 a minimum of 183 Spaniards, among whom were prominent merchants such as Antonio de Ugaldea, had voluntarily requested passports and licenses to leave the republic.[51] As the heated debate over expulsion dominated the attention of the federal Congress for the next three months, *peninsulares* continued to emigrate from a Mexico now dominated by the men who had despised them since at least 1810.

4

The Defeat of the "Impartial" Senators

JUAN RODRÍGUEZ PUEBLA was an Indian, born to poverty, who had the good fortune to be cared for and educated by a priest. In 1827 he joined the "India Azteca" Yorkino lodge at Chapultepec and rose rapidly to the position of Great Speaker. He was elected to the Chamber of Deputies and supported the expulsion of Spaniards in 1829. Carlos María Bustamante was a criollo, born white in a colonial society. But his prolific pen had supported Morelos as readily as his Catholic religion and Mexican independence. He was Antimasonic and a vocal defender of the rights of Mexico's Spaniards in 1829 in the Chamber of Deputies. These men represented opposite poles in the debate over the fate of the *peninsulares*, but on other fields of battle they would not have been so dissimilar in their views.

The Congress met on 1 January, poorly attended because of the recent violence at the Acordada, and with the capital occupied and the south and the *bajío* still at the mercy of armed bands. Bustamante tells us that the commissions formed that day were composed largely of Yorkinos.[1] Congress heard reports from the minister of government, Juan de Dios Cañedo, and the minister of justice, Juan José Espinosa de los Monteros, on the enforcement of the first expulsion in 1828. Cañedo insisted that the law had been thoroughly enforced, but with justice and humanity:

All individuals covered by the law with Mexican families that would be reduced to indigence by expulsion were excepted, as well as those engaged in some class of industry necessary to the subsistence of Mexicans, provided they had the required reports and assurances regarding their peaceful conduct and provided their remaining in the country did not represent a danger.[2]

Cañedo requested Congress to except natives of Cuba and Puerto Rico from the expulsion provisions of the 20 December 1827 law.

Concerning the demands made by the revolutionaries, the minister of government abstained from comment, leaving the matter to the legislature. The minister of justice discussed the departure of Spanish regular clergy as a result of the first law, noting that the administration had been most circumspect in granting exceptions.[3] The church was still numerically and materially strong, especially in convents and monasteries, but the hierarchy had been reduced to a single bishop by 1829. The ministerial reports, in essence, warned the deputies against complex expulsion laws, so difficult to enforce and readily eluded.

The first proposal for a new expulsion measure was introduced into the lower chamber on the following day, 2 January 1829, by a Yorkino, José Sixto Berduzco.[4] It called for the expulsion of all Spaniards within three months, excepting only Cubans and Puerto Ricans. It prescribed six months "in a military fortress" for *peninsulares* who evaded the law or returned to Mexico before Spain recognized Mexico's independence, or for persons concealing Spaniards. Wives could not be forced to accompany husbands "and it would suffice for these [women] to explain their will to any of the authorities to gain protection." A wife's goods could not be exported, but the *expulso* could take his own, "one-third in specie and two-thirds in products of the country"; *peninsulares* who possessed "pension, salary, or ecclesiastical sinecure" could enjoy their income so long as they did not settle in Spanish territory.

The Senate was forced by its Yorkino minority to consider anti-Spanish measures as early as 5 January—reluctantly, of course, as the Yorkinos were quick to point out. Several measures were submitted that, if approved, would restrict the rights of Spaniards. One provided that *peninsulares* "may not acquire property within the territory of this [nation]," while another would have conceded "to the government anew, for three months, the faculty . . . to expel Spaniards."[5] The latter proposal avoided the passage of a new decree while making it feasible to expel "dangerous" Spaniards under the unrestricted provisions contained in Article 9 of the 1827 law. Yorkino writers attacked the federal government for failing to prevent Spaniards expelled by the states in 1828 from taking refuge in the Federal District; for having revoked so many passports, and for excepting persons who had received passports from state governors. The *Correo* called for the new city council to act in order to clear the Federal District "of these harmful moths which the states could not tolerate."[6]

The deputies' Public Security Commission delivered its opinion on 9 January after modifying only slightly the original Berduzco-

Isidro Reyes plan. The commission declared, unconvincingly, that the resultant measure would actually restore commerce and lamented the fact that past experience had shown that exceptions were out of the question. The commission, therefore, proposed none. According to the revised project, all Spaniards were to meet the following schedule:

Those who reside in the interior states of the East and West, territories of upper and lower California and New Mexico, [must] leave their place of residence within one month of the law's publication, and depart the republic within three [months]. For residents of intermediate states and territories, within one month from their place of residence, and within two months from the republic. And inhabitants from the border states to the [Gulf of Mexico] shall leave the republic within one month, counting from the publication of this law.

The remaining provisions were virtually identical to those proposed by Berduzco, with an addition to the clause concerning the rights of wives; "and for those [wives] who may not enjoy rights, a third [of all wealth] shall be left for subsistence, and for the children's guardianship." The definition of Spaniard was broadened to include those born of Spanish parents at sea, while persons born to Spanish families in Cuba, Puerto Rico and the Philippines were specifically excluded.[7]

The plan was harsh—devoid of exceptions—and it was not to the liking of the Senate majority, though the Chamber of Deputies could accept it. Anti-Spanish rebellions were still in effect, and their vocal leaders demanded stern measures; from Puebla to Guadalajara, the cry was the same—a general law of expulsion, "but definitive in its generality and reduced to a peremptory term."[8] During this acrimonious period, lists of *galli-coyotes* (pro-Spanish Mexicans) were published in the capital by a Yorkino press. The more vociferous Yorkinos, such as Alpuche, contended that *galli-coyotes* should be expelled as well, but as for who should be included in this group, general agreement was lacking. The government responded to the growing nativism on 13 January by renewing the prohibition against Spaniards' entry into the republic.[9]

The debate over the commission's report took shape in the Chamber of Deputies on 14 January, and speeches by both sides were published verbatim by the major periodicals. The orations often reveal the impact the deputies believed the movement was having on the Spaniards. Deputy Matías Quintana of Yucatán, an opponent of the expulsion, remarked:

Fearing that between now and March not even half the splendid and a
thousand times unfortunate population of Mexico City would remain, as
a result of the great emigration that grows day by day, I approached the
ministry of government to verify my calculations and found that not even
a half, but only a third would remain . . . of the troubled federal city; and
if such depopulation may be foreseen before the law is passed, what will
be the case after it is published?[10]

Deputy Bustamante, equally opposed to an indiscriminate assault on
the *peninsulares* and no more concerned about exaggeration in the
cause of justice, asserted:

The great property owners who might have opened their treasures to us,
as they have done on other occasions, having emigrated, the amount
registered in France alone by the Mexican *expulsos* exceeds 34 million
pesos, not counting that smuggled out as contraband or remitted by
various means to Spain, Holland, England, the United States . . . as well
as [to] other countries. . . . This is going to cause our ruin and make us
prisoners of the first country that invades us.

Reinforcing the point made by Quintana, Bustamante exaggerated
the wealth of the mass of Spaniards and the tendency of Mexicans
to flee the nation:

Passports issued in recent days number 4,600 or so, which means . . . that
as many more individuals have departed with them. And how many
Americans of both sexes have accompanied them? Supposing that more
than half may have been married, we must concede roughly five persons
[per Spaniard] including women and children. . . . I know of one Spaniard
who has taken nineteen Americans, including servants and friends who
have joined him. Among the emigrants of 3 January there were 650
Americans and only 35 Spaniards; here you have horrifying depopulation
. . . that cannot be replaced with the foreigners who are drifting into our
country; they will not adopt our customs, they are only transients, do not
marry, and are only interested in milking us of our money and soon depart.[11]

Proexpulsion arguments lacked concrete estimates of the measure's impact, preferring to assert that the Spaniards were the root
cause of the nation's ills, that they deserved no better fate, or that
Mexican independence was threatened by their presence. The most
frequent assertion was that the expulsion was justified because public
opinion demanded it.

The Chamber of Deputies urged the government to attend the
debate and sought the administration's opinion of the commission's
report. The president limited his response, relayed by the minister
of government, to the following:

The government favors the expulsion of Spaniards in the manner that the general public demands it; but concerning its extent, timing, and the terms by which it should be verified, [the administration] will be guided by whatever the wisdom of the Congress shall determine.[12]

Victoria was still attempting to evade the very issue that had wrecked his administration.

On 14 January, without government representatives present, debate commenced on the report "in general." Deputy Quintana asserted that public opinion, as expressed in the recent riots, was directed at merchants and at persons of property, not at Spaniards as such. To demonstrate his point, he declared that only seventeen Spaniards, out of 200,000 residents of the capital, had suffered losses in the sacking of the Parián—all other victims were Mexicans and foreigners. Quintana predicted, correctly, that "a great number of men [were] going to find themselves in Veracruz without ships," and he assured the chamber that many would die there of "the black vomit" [yellow fever]. Deputy Reyes dismissed his concerns as irrelevant. Even a federalist argument would not succeed: Deputy Castañeda pointed out that the proposed decree violated the rights of states and of Mexican citizens, since some states had granted citizenship to certain Spaniards who would now be subject to expulsion. Castañeda appealed for exceptions, especially for the ill, demanding, "By what principle do you attempt to expel a bunch of sick, blind, septuagenarian Spaniards . . . for whom, evidently, by this law's lack of discrimination you are going to prescribe death before they can be embarked?" But Castañeda agreed that the power to except should not again be placed in the hands of the government "because it did not exercise it for the best during last year." Rather, he suggested the naming of a qualifying junta that could judge the justice of each case, once the exceptions were clearly set forth in the law.[13]

The caliber of argumentation revealed the humble origins of the anti-Spanish deputies: their reasoning was always general, with constant references to awareness of their own deficiencies, which they trusted would be compensated for by their "patriotism." Arguments such as that of Deputy Bermúdez were common: "Many [*peninsulares*] are innocent, are honorable, are men of good will . . . but when we speak of a certain case, we are not counting Spaniards, and here we are not examining Pedro or Juan but this popular voice which detests all members of the class."[14]

But the necessity of excepting some Spaniards could not be ignored; even anti-Spanish deputies such as Alpuche and Tornel spoke

openly of the need for some exceptions. Moderate deputies criticized
the commission for rushing to its verdict. Deputy Lanuzo, who favored a less harsh measure, charged on 17 January: "We don't even
know how many Spaniards there are in the republic, or the number
of their wives and children, or that of their relationship to the general
and particular interests of the nation." To such calls to reason the
hispanophobes could only retort that total expulsion or its denial
would determine "whether peace among Mexicans may be preserved
or the republic should be destroyed."[15] After three days, the concept
of total expulsion, contained in Article 1, was approved by a voting
ratio of three to two.

The call for mercy was not entirely in vain, however, for there
immediately followed an effort by a coalition of moderates and Yorkinos to add a provision to the initial article: "Exceptions to this law
shall be nominal, and decreed by the general Congress, after receiving reports from the government." The concept, when approved,
would free the legislative branch to protect *peninsulares* with friends
or intermediaries within its chambers.

Some Yorkino writers were willing by 18 January to concede exemptions to "those Spaniards . . . proscribed by King Ferdinand because of services . . . performed in America, or who have had some
member of their family sacrificed by the enemies of liberty and independence." But the same authors would include as Spaniards persons
born in the Caribbean "if since the year 1821 they have remained
subject to Spanish domination until this day." The Yorkino press attacked Minister Cañedo, who, having enforced the first expulsion,
was not anxious to become the archenforcer of another. Deputy Quintana Roo was also condemned, for founding an antiexpulsion periodical "with the object of going against nationalist opinions." And the
Correo persisted in its demand that the city council drive out of the
capital the *expulsos* who had recently arrived from the states. Though
such attacks continued, the ministry was not removed until April,
when Guerrero assumed the presidency.[16]

On 19 January the deputies representing Yucatán attempted,
without success, to exempt their state from the federal expulsion measure. Deputy Requena would have granted local legislatures the right
to decide the fate of Spaniards since, in Yucatán, none of the reasons
adduced by the commission to require the law existed: there had been
no clear assertion of public opinion, and Spaniards were in no danger,
nor was there any fear of new revolutions.[17] By abruptly rejecting
Requena's proposed addition to Article 1, the congressional majority
revealed that the commission's stated motives were not the only rea-

sons for desiring the expulsion, and that federalists could make exceptions to their own principles.

The departure requirements of Article 1 were debated next, with the commission's views prevailing by a vote of thirty-nine to fifteen. Opponents of the thirty-day time limit argued that the *peninsulares* would not "be able to arrange their commercial affairs, which are so complex, so as to be ready to depart with their families." But, the Yorkinos responded, "These [matters] could be left in the charge of representatives, as many others who left the republic in the year 1821 had done." On the following day, by similar voting margins, the deputies approved the requirement that *peninsulares* residing in "intermediate" regions leave their homes within one month and the republic within two months, while those in states bordering on the Gulf of Mexico should leave the republic within a month.[18]

It was now possible for the well informed among the Spaniards to recognize the inevitability of their departure, unless the Senate should act to block the harsh law. By 7 February, the deputies' measure had taken shape. Spaniards were flocking to Veracruz, where the backlog of passengers was becoming a problem. In fact, rumors of revolt in Veracruz led José Ignacio Esteva to urge Guerrero on 21 January to hasten the embarkation of Spanish officers with passports who were gathering in Jalapa and Veracruz.[19] The threat of an imminent Spanish invasion made his suggestion a practical one as well.

The deputies took up the matter of penalties for Spaniards who evaded the law and their Mexican accomplices, voting in conformity with the commission on 23 January. *Peninsulares* who failed to comply within the established time limits, or those returning to Mexico during the existing state of war, might be imprisoned for "six months in a fortress and, afterwards, embarked." The commission agreed to reconsider the matter of absentees with federal permission. The *Correo* attacked deputies who had spoken against the measure, denying that *peninsulares* had ever contributed to Mexican culture.[20]

British merchants soon impugned the expulsion measure, since its time stipulations dealt a blow to the foreign houses to whom the Spaniards had obligations. Pakenham demanded that the Mexican government protect British interests during the precipitous "expulsion of a number of individuals, through whose medium [our] commerce has been carried on." Cañedo assured Pakenham that it was within the government's constitutional powers, should the need arise, to make necessary recommendations in Congress to moderate the law in appropriate ways.[21] Cañedo's letter implied, however, that the administration was not anxious to become a party to the debate in Congress. Guerrero would have to confront this problem, with an eye to Mexico's foreign relations and deteriorating credit position, just as Victoria had in 1828.

The commission rendered its report concerning exceptions on 27 January and the principal clause was approved the same day. Article 9 of the law stated: "Those with well-known physical disabilities shall be excepted, while their impediment endures." The commission decided to retire, for the moment, its recommendation to except those with documents of citizenship in friendly nations. An attempt to introduce exceptions for Spaniards over fifty years of age who had lived in the republic for at least twenty-five years failed. Deputy Alpuche did manage to introduce the same provision for Spaniards over sixty-five years of age, however. And on the same day approval was obtained for Article 11, which stated: "The government shall undertake to replace those in charge of Indian missions opportunely with appropriate individuals," but Deputy Requena failed to gain provisional exceptions for those actually carrying out missionary tasks among the Indians.[22]

As January ended, the revolutionary army still occupied the capital, and Guerrero found it necessary to move from Puebla to Veracruz to cut short a rumored revolt in the port. Pro-Pedraza senators expressed concern about the "exalted spirits" of the soldiers from the south who occupied the capital, and *Correo* saw this as a "Pedrazist" ploy to cultivate the success of the Veracruz conspiracy. In the Chamber of Deputies, Berduzco proposed the destruction of the Parián —an act that would have deprived the Federal District of 40,000 pesos annually in needed revenue. Deputy Quintana Roo published the last of his rational appeals, *Apelación al Pueblo,* and for his efforts on behalf of the Spaniards received the opprobrium of the *Correo.* The editors of the Yorkino journal professed dismay at the planned departure of the sons of ex-Viceroy Iturrigaray and conceded that these men should be excepted from the forthcoming law, since in 1808 their father had been expelled by "the vagrants of the Parián." The editors also favored exceptions for Ramón and Juan José Ceruti, Yorkino Spaniards who had become citizens of Mexico State. The *Correo* renewed its attacks on the Senate, which would soon determine the fate of the expulsion proposal.[23]

The British ambassador summed up the state of affairs at the end of January by citing the unrest among the troops in the capital and dimming hopes that the Senate might dilute the expulsion measure. Pakenham was particularly disturbed by the fact that "a Regiment composed of men of colour, from the country about Acapulco, have been particularly refractory." And he informed his government:

In the Senate the [expulsion] measure will probably be considerably modified; for, putting aside all consideration of reason, humanity and policy, the law as proposed by the Deputies, is at first sight manifestly impracticable. The limited quantity of shipping which frequents the Mexican ports would not be sufficient to transport the number of individuals, affected by the measure (at the lowest computation amounting to 10,000 [*sic*], without taking into account the families and dependents of the richer class of Spaniards, who will naturally accompany them) within the term of three months.[24]

The deputies completed their measure on 4 February, voting on half of the bill's provisions. The result was forwarded to the Senate on 6 February. Opponents of the expulsion had exhausted their arguments; their only victory consisted in obtaining revocation of the law of 20 December 1827, except for its prohibition against Spanish immigration into Mexico.[25]

The Chamber of Deputies was not yet free of questions raised by the growing xenophobia within Mexico. On the day the Senate received the measure, Deputy Gil proposed that the government inform the chamber of "the number and circumstances of Spaniards presently resident in the republic." His request was buried in the Commission of Public Security. Once again, Congress was legislating social change without basic information at hand. With the *peninsulares'* fate to be determined by the Senate, the deputies began to consider the position of foreigners generally, at the insistence of Mexican retail merchants and some Yorkino representatives. On the same day, Deputy Col. Juan Nepomuceno Almonte introduced a proposed law on behalf of "various merchants of the interior," which provided that:

1. Foreigners may not open stores in any part of the United States of Mexico . . .
2. The stores of foreigners in which retail commerce currently takes place, shall close within one year . . .
3. Foreigners may take part in retail commerce only when married to Mexican women, or when they possess a letter of citizenship.
4. Nor may foreigners be commercial brokers or business agents.[26]

In addition to retail commerce, absentee ownership of farms and real property came under attack in the chamber. Deputy Alpuche introduced a proposal on 16 February that would have prohibited foreign ownership of real estate, unless the proprietor were naturalized or living in a Mexican state.[27] Though the measure did not provide for expropriation—merely public administration until the owner fulfilled the above requirements—it could have prevented departing Spaniards from making personal or private arrangements for the management of their properties. To assure ownership, the *peninsular*'s Mexican family remaining behind could have been forced to "expropriate" the exiled head of the family. Such measures were not enacted at the federal level, but some states did eventually pass analogous laws. The representatives had complied with the "popular will," as they understood that consensus; it now remained to counter the response of the Senate, to determine whether the resulting law would be as unyielding as the measure forged by the Yorkino deputies.

Pressure from the States

Though the Senate had demonstrated previously its sympathy for the *gachupines*, the will of the majority of deputies left little to hope for, and *peninsulares* were already conceding defeat. Even Spaniards whose criollo sons had political influence or the right party affiliation were not exempt. The father of Guerrero's collaborator, Mariano Arista, urged his son in early February to recommend him to the general "so that nothing [adverse] might happen to him while it was being decided to what place he should march." The father-in-law of Lucas Alamán, Juan José García Castrillo, was preparing to remove his entire family to Europe, including Don Lucas, who had agreed to the plan, when García suddenly died on 8 February and the scheme was abandoned.[28]

The fears of the elder Arista were justified; the slow pace of the legislative route provoked regional uprisings in February, resulting in local attempts to resolve the expulsion question. The impoverishment of civic militias contributed to insubordination. In Orizaba local Spaniards boycotted a forced loan for the support of the civil militia, and on 4 February the militia "pronounced" for the expulsion of all *peninsulares* from the city within eight days, refusing to lay down arms until this was accomplished and promising to enforce the abortive loan decree. The governor managed, with the aid of Santa Anna, to calm the local militia and avert illegal expulsions.[29] In Michoacán, the provincial deputation ordered extraordinary sessions of the Congress to commence on 5 February. The first item of business was to produce an expulsion law. The Michoacán congress promulgated an exceptionless decree on 17 February, expelling all *peninsulares* within thirty days but allowing former state employees to retain their salaries while residing in a friendly country. The legislature proved to be generous with the Mexican victims of its actions, decreeing on 3 March that the *expulsos'* families should be assigned a salary.[30] The state was also committed to pay the exile's transportation costs as far as the Federal District.

Meanwhile in Querétaro, Canalizo and his national troops published a manifesto on 14 February resisting the disarmament and dispersal order received by both Canalizo and Francisco Victoria on 10 February. They protested their fidelity "in all that does not contradict the 'pronouncement' made in December," and swore to remain under arms until the expulsion of Spaniards was accomplished. Canalizo agreed to retire a part of his troops "in order to avoid burdening the public treasury," but they would retain their arms. He insisted that the states that had resisted the revolt might yet attempt to obstruct the enforcement of expulsion.[31] The situation in the *bajío* illustrated the plight of the revolutionary government prior to passage of the expulsion measure. General Lobato had occupied the western portion with his Army of Operations, enforcing local loyalty, while Canalizo was in the eastern sector, with his "Protector Division of the General Expulsion of Spaniards," disobeying his superior.

The federal Senate considered the expulsion measure under these intimidating circumstances—as intended by the revolutionists—while proexpulsion petitions from civil authorities, especially provincial town councils, accumulated in Mexico City.[32] In the Federal District, as well, the authorities applied pressure. Governor Tornel issued passports to all who requested them and took steps to assure that no Spaniard departed the capital without appropriate documents. The majority of the city council's treasury commission chose this moment to issue a report favoring destruction of the Parián—an act that would have dealt a serious blow to Spanish trade in the capital.[33]

Division in the Senate

The senators could be expected to moderate the deputies' measure, thereby arousing a hostile public reaction. The Senate received the bill on 6 February and turned it over to the commission of government. The president of this commission, Pablo Franco Coronel, requested a report from the ministry of government on the number of passports that had been expedited to Spaniards by virtue of existing laws, as well as those requested voluntarily since December. Cañedo replied that reports were still outstanding from the Federal District and states such as Veracruz, Puebla, Mexico, and several others. The government had raised its count to 809 departures under the terms of the first law, and the ministry had issued 653 such documents to Spaniards who had requested them since the recent revolt (between 9 December 1828 and 31 January 1829).[34] Questioning of the government in this manner produced new interest in compliance with the first expulsion law. Minister of Justice Espinosa sent a list of forty-seven regular clergy—over half the total in Upper California—who had come to light for the first time, having failed to comply with the provisions of the 20 December 1827 decree. The president demanded an explanation from the political chief of the Californias and the governors of seven states.[35]

The Senate's Commission of Government rendered its report on 23 February, which departed in several important ways from the measure presented by the deputies.[36] The result was a proposal drawn up in moderate terms, appealing to *imparciales*. The measure called for the departure of the *peninsulares* lacking exceptions from their states within three months and from the republic within an additional month. It defined Spaniards narrowly, excluding persons born in the Philippines and the Caribbean. And it excepted from expulsion: (1) those who had fallen into decrepitude, (2) those notoriously impeded by physical incapacity, for so long as it lasts, (3) those who had served the cause of independence within Mexican territory between 1810 and 1821, (4) those living with Mexican wives or widowers with Mexican children. Within a month, men who qualified for these exceptions should present the justifing documents to their state governments, to be passed on to the ministry of government, and then, "reviewed in council of ministers, that which is convenient and just shall be resolved." The remaining articles of the deputies' measure were approved by the Senate commission, with an addition to Article 9, requiring the federal government to issue a document of exception to those so favored.

In a tense atmosphere, debate commenced in the Senate on 25 February 1829, with the hostility of that body evident from the outset. Following an initial statement of support on behalf of the commission, hardly a senator arose who would defend the measure. Opinion varied among the Spaniards' supporters: "*El indio*," Senator Paz, refused to approve any measure that expelled a single *peninsular*, while Senator Pacheco gave the measure his qualified approval, due to its broad exceptions.[37] Senator Rejón, a Yucatán liberal, suggested on 26 February that the secretaries of war and government should attend the expulsion debate. (It was not until the second day of the debate that a senator attacked the exceptions contained in the measure as too generous.) No one who peruses the Senate debates on this question can fail to marvel at the degree to which Franco-Spanish liberalism had permeated that body wherein even those inclined to favor "the popular will" were yet devoted to "the rights of man and the citizen." The liberals summoned the doctrines of Benjamin Constant "concerning the fact that arbitrary measures destroy social guarantees" to attack the political wisdom of the expulsion as advanced by the Yorkinos.

But the defenders of the measure could say in the heat of the moment:

Although the emigration of as many Mexicans as will depart the republic is regrettable, and even if these were to reach one million, still this evil should be endured as better than that which threatens those same Mexicans and all the republic, if the expulsion of Spaniards is not decreed.[38]

On 27 February, Espinosa repeated the government's position on expulsion, and Colonel Moctezuma, when pressed by Rejón, responded "that the government could affirm that [the chambers] were secure." Before the session ended, the Senate had rejected the measure, which was returned to the Commission of Government for restudy.[39] Zuñiga introduced an alternative measure designed to ease public tensions by expelling immediately only those *peninsulares* who might be a threat to national independence. The project was both simple and direct:

1. The government is authorized, for the term of four months, to expel . . . Spaniards who represent a threat to public tranquility.
2. This qualification shall be made by a junta of five individuals who shall be named by the government with the assistance and vote of the president-elect and the approval of the chambers.

In response, "various Mexicans" expressed their approval in the *Correo*, adding that the president should be empowered to overrule the junta, if he disagreed with a verdict. They desired a guarantee that the opinions of the governors and local authorities would prevail in the junta; Spaniards receiving passports should unfailingly depart, while those excepted could receive a document attesting to their good conduct. The writers insisted that junta members be sworn in before the president and that they be legally responsible in case of "conspiracy to bribe or actual bribery."[40] Zuñiga failed to gain the Senate's favor, since the executive would have exercised excessive freedom to tamper with individual rights, in the liberals' view.

The commission produced a revised bill, and debate resumed on 2 March. It was apparent from the outset that Senate opinion had not altered. The revised report was approved in general, though Article 1 was returned to the commission, since three months allowed for departure seemed inadequate.[41] The period was expanded to four months; the Senate accepted the expulsion on those terms, despite the fact that many Spaniards would perish in the ports during the deadly summer months, a point that Paz impressed upon his colleagues. The Senate agreed to the deputies' definition of Spaniard and also to the four types of exceptions outlined in the original measure. Several suggestions followed for revising portions already approved: Rejón wished to exempt the sons of Mexicans born in Spain, Canary Islanders, and Spaniards naturalized in friendly countries; Gonzales sought to except those who had contributed to the cause of independence between 1810 and 1821, and Acosta hoped to extend this period to 1828. Their proposed changes were considered by the commission and severely attacked by *Correo*.[42]

The matter was resolved, then, in its essence; there would be another expulsion, apparently more extensive than the first. Only the differences, great though they were, remained to be worked out between the chambers. The *Correo* was not pleased, referring to the Senate version as a law "which cannot be called of expulsion but rather of letters of security for all the natural enemies of Mexico who wish to live and conspire in the heart of the republic." But the fate of the Spaniards was obvious to the British minister who continued his official campaign to reduce the impact of the expulsion on British commercial interests. Pakenham described how Senate resistance had so alarmed the capital that the chamber was forced to concede to expulsion demands; he was reminded of the steps required in late 1827 to avoid sizable losses to British houses due to the precipitous expulsion of indebted Spanish merchants.[43]

The Senate approved most of the articles contained in the deputies' measure on 5 March. It accepted the penalties to be suffered by noncomplying *peninsulares*; the monthly federal reports to Congress; the payment of passage of poor *expulsos* to the nearest U.S. port; the right to draw their salaries in friendly republics; and the derogation of the first federal law of expulsion. The debate was no longer spirited, though efforts to amend the approved articles continued. Rejón hoped to make it possible for *expulsos* to draw their salaries in neutral nations and in friendly monarchies as well as in republics. Senator Paz sought exceptions for all clergy, secular and regular, from the expulsion, and several liberals sought to rescue the permanently settled Spaniards by excepting "those married or widowed with Mexican children, and those [lacking children] who may be married to

Mexican women and live a conjugal life."[44] In addition, a petition arrived from the state legislature of Jalisco, requesting "that Spaniards who have been excepted from expulsion under the laws passed by state legislatures, should also be excepted from the law of expulsion of Spaniards." The Jalisco congress asked that local congresses be allowed to decide which exceptions should be included in the general expulsion law. Jalisco's government, like that of Yucatán, now desired to minimize the local consequences that could be expected from a general expulsion. On 10 March, the Senate rejected Jalisco's petition.[45]

In Querétaro—the refuge of the "Protector Division for the Expulsion of the Spaniards"—a wholly different result was being arranged. The local legislature unanimously admitted and hastily elaborated a state expulsion measure proposed on 3 March. The decree granted *expulsos* thirty days to leave, or face six months' imprisonment, and it temporarily excepted the physically incapacitated.[46] The measure clearly paralleled the one produced by the federal Chamber of Deputies.

When the federal Senate's Commission of Government presented its report concerning additions on 9 March, all but one of its recommendations were acted upon. Exceptions were advocated for Spaniards who had contributed to independence since 1810, to sons born in Spain of Mexican parents, and to Spaniards who had been naturalized prior to 20 December 1827 in nations having "treaties of friendship, navigation and commerce" with Mexico.[47] The latter provision excluded U.S. citizens, voiding thereby the tactic used by many to evade the expulsion of 1828. Canary Islanders might be considered Spaniards in Mexico. On 10 March, the Senate agreed to except "those who are married to Mexican women and live in matrimony, or widowers with one or more Mexican children." Paz's proposal to except clergy gained Senate approval by limiting its exception to clergy "who were not suspicious," in the government's view. Rejón's proposal that Spaniards residing in friendly nations should be allowed to receive their pensions or salaries was also accepted. But an attempt to obtain exception for Spaniards "who may not live in matrimony" was rebuffed. The Senate approved the deputies' provision for financing the expulsion of regular clergy, but disapproved of the proposal that those in charge of the missions be replaced "opportunely, with corresponding" personnel.[48]

Senator Pacheco Leal appeared in the lower house on 12 March with the Senate version of the proposed law and spent more than an hour clarifying the reasoning behind the revisions. But the chamber was hostile to the Senate version, replete with exceptions, and the measure was sent to the Commission of Public Security to be revised. On the following day, the commission obstinately recommended that "the additions and reforms to the project of law made by the Senate should not be approved, and that Articles 1, 3, 4, 9 and 11 should be reproduced in the terms . . . approved by the chamber of representatives." And during the next five hours the chamber did just that: each addition was disallowed as the deputies reconstructed their original measure. When the result was handed to the Senate on 14 March, more than a month of conscientious consideration was annulled.[49]

The Senate sent the measure immediately to the Commission of Government. Rumors of an impending revolt of *léperos* was abroad in the capital, and these threats persisted until an agreement was reached on the expulsion issue. The Senate had resisted the Yorkino push for amnesty demanded by the victorious revolutionists.[50]

On 16 March, the Senate commission presented its new report. With only one dissenter, the commission attempted to equal the deputies' recalcitrance, reproducing the Senate accord. But the required two-thirds of the chamber could not be mustered in a number of cases—the result being that despite the plurality's disapproval, a compromise was effected with the deputies' version. The attempt to disapprove wholesale all the articles restored by the deputies could not be carried, and Article 1, which set the terms of the expulsion, was allowed to stand as the lower house had determined. Article 4, calling for congressional review of documents of exception, was suppressed, then restored to its Senate form. Article 9, which forbade Spaniards to live along the coast, was also restored to the Senate form. In addition, all sons born to *peninsulares* on the high seas were defined as Spaniards. Then, on 16–17 March, the Senate tenaciously reproduced all previous exceptions.[51] The challenge was thrown back to the deputies, who would decide, finally, which *peninsulares* could be excepted.

The inevitability of their expulsion had, by this time, led additional Spaniards to prepare to depart, while still others were being expelled by state laws. The result was a chaotic situation in the Federal District. Governor Tornel attempted to bring order to the exodus on 17 March, insisting that departing Spaniards obtain a passport, and that entering *peninsulares*, as well as owners of inns or houses, report arrivals to the authorities or risk a fine of 100 pesos.[52]

The law was completed in the Chamber of Deputies on 18 March, to the clamorous joy of the packed galleries. Deputy Berduzco had presented the report of the Commission of Public Security concerning the second Senate accord and, predictably, virtually all the Senate's exceptions were once again eliminated. The lower chamber accepted the Senate versions of Articles 9 and 10, then proceeded to negate each exception, with the single omission of "[Spanish-born] sons of Americans." In the end, Deputy Ortiz de León attempted to obtain exceptions for Spaniards who had served independence since 1810 by suggesting congressional review of these cases, but it was no use. The matter was closed, and only the ill and sons of Americans could remain in Mexico.[53]

The new law reached the ministry of government and the president on the same day. Cañedo circulated printed copies on 20–21 March to the ministers and governors, along with a set of presidential provisions that clarified enforcement procedures.[54]

The federal law did not appear soon enough to avoid violence in Celaya, Guanajuato, however. On the evening of 17 March, an anti-Spanish mob demanding the expulsion of *gachupines* began to sack the houses of Celaya's prominent Spaniards. With great effort, Col. Manuel de Llata and Lt. Col. Francisco Victoria managed to defend the *peninsulares* and their possessions. On the following day, Francisco Victoria wrote to Governor Montes de Oca, insisting that an expulsion law be drawn up by the local congress. The governor apprised the president of his brother's actions, and the state congress acted on the same day, drafting its law in the same terms as the federal decree. It gave the *peninsulares* one month to depart and excepted only the infirm. Cañedo replied to all inquiries from the states in the same manner: "The general Congress having passed the law, which is being circulated today, the matter . . . should be considered closed, and it only remains to comply exactly with its terms, in order to assure complete tranquility."[55]

The federal expulsion law of 1829 differed from that of 1827, primarily, by being less flexible and—seemingly—less subject to manipulation, since it only allowed for exceptions due to illness, and even these were intended to be temporary delays in departure. While the 1827 decree had been aimed at unmarried and dangerous Spaniards, plus those "illegally" in Mexico, the 1829 expulsion threatened *all* Spaniards, whatever their condition in life, political beliefs, or family ties. It remained to be seen whether such a sweeping law could in fact be enforced.

The presidential guidelines for implementation circulated on 20 March made state governments responsible for compliance in their own entities. Governors determined who should leave, prescribing an appropriate route and informing the governments of states and ports through which the Spaniards should pass of their impending arrival. Reports of these matters were sent regularly to Mexico City. At the conclusion of the periods specified in the first article—a maximum of four months in the northernmost territories, final reports would be expected of each governor. In addition, the administration insisted upon frequent reports "by every mail," in order to fulfill the monthly federal reporting requirement. The local commissary-generals or subcommissaries would determine the *expulsos'* financial requirements, ranging from 2 *reales* to a peso per league (three miles). Employees receiving under 1,500 pesos annually were eligible for financial aid. Governors of ports and the supreme government would need reports on financial disbursements, since federal funds were expended at the ports for fares to New Orleans. Friars received the maximum assistance—"twenty *reales* per day's journey of ten leagues" —if their convents could not assist them. And, finally, salaries of suspended government employees should be paid, pending evidence that the recipient resided in friendly territory.[56]

During the acrimonious debate, at least 647 Spaniards had requested passports, together with 743 Mexican members of their families.[57] Expelling the remaining Spaniards would prove more difficult than the Yorkinos had imagined.

In light of this fact, a fundamental question raised by the campaign for expulsion remains to be answered. Were the *peninsulares* as unpopular and the cry for expulsion as general as the Yorkinos insisted? I would answer both in the affirmative, though I suspect that Quintana was also correct in his assertion that mass feeling was aimed primarily at merchants per se, not merely at Spaniards. A modern observer, Jesús Reyes Heroles, has contended that "the Yorkinos encouraged and channeled existing sentiments that were general and possessed extended roots." Don Jesús believed the expulsion prevented the consolidation of a traditional oligarchy in Mexico, concluding that, all things considered, the expulsions had a positive impact.[58] Considering the evidence preserved in expulsion records on the nature of the *peninsular* community—which was far more plebeian than previous authors have realized—I am inclined to doubt that conclusion. The typical *expulso* was a former expeditionary who had established residence, taken up a trade, and fathered a Mexican family. The disruption of this developmental impulse and the resultant destitution of hundreds of such families, scattered throughout the republic, compensated no one for the past avarice of Spanish merchants, bureaucrats, and landlords.

What impact would the expulsions have upon liberals and persons of property? As Reyes Heroles has also suggested, it was a major factor in the rapid downfall of the Yorkinos. This, I contend, resulted from the consolidation of a conservative coalition that gained new impetus from two interrelated Yorkino "excesses": the introduction and perpetuation of political instability and destruction of social guarantees. As a result of these developments, the elite—now predominantly criollo—would gain in desperation what it had lost in numbers, and soon adopted the methods of its rivals in order to assure its dominance in political life. These *hombres de bien*, as they called themselves, would govern the country from 1830 until 1833.

5

The Second Federal Effort: From Expulsions to Exceptions

The favors that were conceded . . . were based on no other principle than consideration of respect for the men who spoke up for the Spaniards, [and] the result of this iniquity was that [the peninsulares] who were most unfortunate and wholly lacking in representation were often the least considered.

—*Luis Gonzaga Cuevas (1853)*

NINETEENTH-CENTURY liberals and conservatives alike acknowledged that in all the expulsions many Spaniards were excepted by special favor of the enforcers. During the life of the 20 March 1829 law, six ways to be excepted developed: (1) by the Chamber of Deputies (between 15 and 25 April 1829), (2) by the Senate (between 21 and 25 April 1829), (3) for permanent physical impediment, (4) for temporary physical impediment, (5) as the son of Americans, and (6) in presidential use of extraordinary faculties (during the invasion from 25 August until 31 December 1829). Since the law contained few exceptions, the destruction of the Spanish community seemed inevitable. In time, however, the practice of expanding the types of exceptions and the circumstances under which they were granted weakened the effect of the expulsion. This is not to say that such evasions seriously reduced the total impact of the second and most severe expulsion, for much economic uncertainty resulted from the revolutionary climate that surrounded the law as well as the rigor with which it was enforced during the first days.

The law circulated rapidly and was generally received with approbation by regional governments. The Mexico City council was delighted with the decree. It reached Oaxaca on 16 March "in the midst of the most beautiful emotion which has ever been seen among honorable people." It was published in Guadalajara four days later, where the governor personally assured Guerrero that though it caused a sensation among families with Spanish relatives, it would be enforced. The law was circulated to local authorities in Chihuahua on 7 April and in California on 6 July, long after its enforcement had been unofficially suspended in Mexico City.[1]

Governors added their own instructions, for the use of local officials, to those received from the Ministry of Government. Typically, departmental chiefs were to assure the effective circulation of the decree in their regions. The official in charge of each locality was to inform the Spaniards in his jurisdiction of the decree's contents, "stressing their punctual and exact observance." *Peninsulares* would leave Tamaulipas, for example, through Tampico, Matamoros, or Soto la Marina, "applying personally or in writing to the government for the corresponding passport." Local authorities were to assure that Spaniards did not forcibly take their families with them. *Peninsulares* applied for passports to local authorities, who would compile nominal lists of Spaniards for submission to the state government within three days of the law's publication. Those who claimed physical impediments should be examined by local officials within fifteen days, having forwarded their appeals through the chain of authority to the federal government. Evidence of inability to pay one's own way should also be submitted to the state government. And, finally, each week local authorities were to report on compliance, assuring that enforcement would be completed within one month.[2]

The Spaniards' Wives Respond

Mexican women waged a tenacious battle on behalf of the fathers of their children. Both Victoria and Guerrero were moved by the plight of the families, but Congress was deaf to their pleas, and the rather routine appeals emerging from the executive were rapidly shunted aside. Deputy Bustamante drew up an exposition that was presented to Guerrero by a delegation of families. The future president was affected by the plight of the Spaniards' dependents, but Congress ignored his representation. The legislators agreed to publish the expositions of Victoria and Guerrero, but this was never done, contends Bustamante, due to the efforts of anti-Spanish congressmen.[3]

Yorkino writers were quick to condemn the Mexican victims' campaign. Bustamante and the wives were viciously attacked in April by an anonymous writer who callously asserted that Don Carlos's alleged impotence led him to champion such an unworthy cause, for which

he himself should be invited to depart.[4] The women of the capital
were undaunted, however, and took their cause directly to the congressional chambers. Wives in the states also drew up petitions for
presentation to the Ministry of Government. A multitude of women
and children besieged the Chamber of Deputies on 9 April demanding the right to speak. They were rebuffed and sent to call upon
Guerrero, who professed to be unable to aid them. Dissatisfied with
his response, they marched to the Senate chambers where an extraordinary session was called to hear them and, subsequently, this body
agreed to extend until December the time allowed for the Spaniards'
departure. But the Chamber of Deputies rejected the Senate accord,
and the matter was thrown back into the lap of the administration.[5]

The federal government was, by now, receiving petitions from
wives in the states and, recognizing the difficult situation of the families and the unhealthful climate of the Gulf coast ports commencing
in April, it was inclined for the moment to support the extension
proposed in the Senate. Petitions arrived early in April from Veracruz, Alvarado, Morelia, Guadalajara, and Tepic. The largest and
most impressive of these was drawn up in May by 123 wives from
Campeche. They addressed themselves directly to the president and
each signatory claimed up to eight children, as well as siblings, as
dependents. The governor of Yucatán backed their petition, attesting
to the "general commotion upon receipt and publication of the law
in March." On 15 June their appeal was rejected, on grounds that
Congress was in recess.[6] Petitions from the more remote regions often
met this fate: the advantage rested with the Spaniard closer to the
center whose voice and influence could be exerted in time. Nonetheless, family efforts were instrumental in bringing relief to all those
in a position to obtain it.

Enforcement in the Federal District

Politics were always enmeshed in the Spanish question; enforcement
of the second federal law, like the first, was inescapably political and
selective. Once again, the most controversial figure was Colonel Tornel, governor of the Federal District. Tornel's conflict with Zavala
was also repeated, leading some Spaniards to seek refuge in Mexico
State from the rigorous compliance initiated in the capital. Tornel
now seized the opportunity he was denied in June 1828, to purge
the Federal District of "dangerous" *peninsulares*. Neither Congress nor
the authorized panel of doctors would allow him complete freedom
to purge at random, however. Immediately, Tornel began seeking

clarification of questions left obscure by the law or the instructions accompanying it. The regulations had failed to specify who should issue passports—federal or local authorities. The governor was also concerned that Spaniards currently residing in Mexico who had voluntarily requested passports for a limited period might escape permanent expulsion. He also inquired whether the obligation of 1828, requiring *peninsulares* to provide a bond guaranteeing that they would not disembark at the Spanish Antilles, remained in force. Tornel also noted that no regulations had been provided concerning how *peninsulares* were to cover their public and private debts. Should *expulsos* be required to provide documents demonstrating their solvency? What was to be done with those who could not do so? And, finally, he asked to whom documents of exception should be presented.[7]

President Victoria resolved on 24 March that the procedure would be that used in 1828; passports already distributed by federal authorities should not be collected; the law left *expulsos* free to go wherever they pleased; Congress should be consulted concerning Spanish debtors; and all documents of exception must be channeled through the Ministry of Government.[8] Tornel, besieged by families desirous of departing with their Spanish husbands and fathers, doubted that the names of Mexicans or of Spanish women should be placed on passports of expulsion. The president asserted that families should be free to depart and instructed the governor to comply with the passport regulations of 1 May 1828.[9] C. M. Bustamante took Tornel to task for prescribing a poor departure route that forced *expulsos* to pass through both Córdova and Orizaba so that they would leave some money in his hometown of Villa de Orizaba. This necessitated travel by horse, since there was no carriage road between the two towns.[10]

A Tornel *bando* of 8 April was attacked by both Zavala and Bustamante. With the 21 April deadline only two weeks away, the governor threatened the *expulsos* with prison should they fail to leave on the prescribed day. Bustamante charged that in this same edict Tornel "proposed an espionage plan in order to make all Mexicans into informers on the Spaniards." The governor's guards could prevent *peninsulares* from escaping to the state of Mexico, but they could not legally deny entry to documented *expulsos* from the states.[11] The daily arrival of Spaniards possessing passports valid only for the capital, but without funds for their departure, presented a serious problem to the treasury of the Federal District. The minister of government advised Tornel to issue the proper documents and aid these *expulsos* out of the general commissary. An individual would have to demonstrate that no such funds had previously been received and that he qualified for aid under the law.[12]

As the 21 April deadline approached, Tornel foresaw numerous difficulties in enforcement which would need federal resolution. A circular from the Ministry of Government reassured the governors on 18 April: Spaniards qualified for exceptions whose cases had not yet been resolved, as well as those who had applied directly to Congress, should not be forced to leave by the approaching deadline.[13] Tornel, impelled by the urgency of his situation, reported that many Spaniards had not been aided financially for their journey and that by 21 April still more would be in the same condition. Since the federal government decided appeals concerning temporary physical impediments, he wished to know whether these cases fell under that category. The president resolved that "they should be taken for impeded until such funds are administered, having to depart immediately when this is accomplished." Tornel forwarded his *bando*, which threatened Spaniards with arrest if they evaded the law, and inquired whether he should proceed with these arrests after 21 April. He also asked whether arrests should be made in the *peninsulares'* homes, despite the public commotion this might cause, since many Mexican families could be compromised. The ministry promised to answer before the deadline. The governor also urged resolution of the status of Spaniards naturalized in friendly countries, but the minister could only reply that Congress was considering the matter: in the meantime, these people too should not be molested. Tornel had learned that "various Spaniards were considering departing for villages in the state of Mexico in order to gain another month, since this state [was] not one of those bordering on the [Gulf of Mexico]." He was uncertain "whether permission could be granted, since it [was] not in the direction of Veracruz." To this the government simply replied: "Take care to comply with the law in the Federal District according to the tenor of the respective article." And, finally, Tornel urged the administration to request lists of Spaniards with appeals pending before Congress or already excepted by the chambers, so that their status would be clarified. Bocanegra responded that the Chamber of Deputies was currently considering whether "the terms of the law should apply to them," and that congressional resolution was required before the cases could be resolved.[14]

With only one day left for enforcement in the Federal District, Tornel expressed renewed concern about the handling of the inevitable cases of noncompliance: should the violators be processed by the government, in which case "it will be necessary to provide rules in order to determine the Spaniards who through no fault of their own may have failed to depart within the prescribed term," or by the courts "in conformity with the common principles of our law"? And what of *expulsos* from the states who now resided in the Federal District? They were not "residents" strictly speaking—or were they? Should they be expected to depart by the morrow? To these important questions the government had no answers and applied directly to Congress for resolution. But Congress failed to respond quickly, and on 23 April Tornel was again pressing the ministry, although he had received no notice of Spaniards being arrested in their homes. The president refused once again to preempt Congress's right to resolve these dilemmas, merely recommending that Tornel should proceed in conformity with the law, if such cases occurred. On the following day the first Spaniard was placed under house arrest for failing to leave the city by 21 April, and Tornel protested, "The law does not state under whose authority the Spaniards should remain." By 27 June several Spaniards had been imprisoned in the capital, but no resolution was forthcoming. As late as 2 July the administration was still unable to obtain a ruling from Congress concerning whether the prisoners were to be tried judicially or simply sent by the governor to a fortress for six months.[15] President Guerrero would ultimately favor a judicial process, once the Spanish invaders, who landed at Tampico in July 1829, had surrendered.

"The day of 21 April, . . . the day of tears, finally arrived," relates Bustamante, "the day of the departure of the Spaniards and their unhappy families." In the words of a *peninsular*, "They looked at [their families] and fell silent; and they looked yet again and were deeply touched." Guards were placed on the gates on the morning of 21 April, "so that no Spaniard might be permitted to leave in any direction other than Veracruz, and with this measure some were prevented from taking refuge in the state of Mexico where Zavala paid heed to one or another."[16]

Tornel anticipated that applications for financial assistance would continue to be received after the departure date had expired in the Federal District. In his judgment such appeals should be rejected since both the law and his own bando of 3 April specified a legitimate, limited time during which all such requests should have been received. His reading of the law would deny financial aid to Spaniards whose pending cases were resolved negatively after 21 April. The administration did not concur in Tornel's interpretation. A second pressing matter required resolution on the "day of tears": "In such anguished moments," reported Tornel, "I am receiving communications from the courts requesting that Spaniards who should leave in conformity with the law be detained for debts to individuals." The governor reiterated his early plea for resolution of the question, noting that on the previous day the matter of public debtors had been resolved in the chamber of deputies. The administration's resolution of the question is not apparent, but on the same day, Tornel issued an order, published in the capital's periodicals for four consecutive days, offering guarantees to all Spaniards "who may have appeals pending in the secretariat of government concerning exception from the law of 20 March," to avoid being molested.[17]

The departure of impoverished Spaniards on 21 April exhausted the financial resources of the federal treasury: insufficient specie remained even for the routine expenses of government. Yet the task of financing the departure of Spaniards was not completed—new demands were received daily. The minister of the treasury replied to an appeal from the commissary general that the president "has seen fit to order the administration of assistance suspended until further notice." Informed of the suspension, Tornel insisted:

Although I am fully aware of the urgencies of the treasury you will permit me [to point out] the grave prejudice to which these same Spaniards will be exposed, who have dispensed with their belongings in order to depart; some of these unfortunates no longer have even a home.

"These reasons," concluded Tornel, "deserve the same consideration as the judgment which the people will form believing that these [individuals] will no longer leave national territory." Bocanegra could only pass along Tornel's exhortation to the Ministry of the Treasury.[18]

By 23 April the government of the Federal District had compiled a statistical summary of its enforcement compliance and an index describing the fate of each individual who had appealed for exception. Tornel defended his enforcement in these words: "I have taken care with the most active effort to assure that the rights of humanity may be respected, and that [these] unfortunates . . . may not receive bad treatment of any kind." And he promised to substantiate his assertion with "copies of the providences dictated," as soon as possible.[19] Because the statistical summary included transient Spaniards as well as permanent residents, it cannot be taken as an exact indication of the fate of Spanish householders in the capital. Tornel had issued 1,341 passports to *peninsulares*. Only 426 applied for travel allowances, while 302 actually received money. Awaiting resolution of their appeals by the supreme government were 221 Spaniards; an unknown number still hoped for favorable treatment by Congress and sixty-eight awaited payments owed them by the federal treasury. Documents of protection had been issued to 165 *peninsulares* with appeals pending in the Ministry of Government. According to the guards at the gate of San Lázaro, 5,000 Spaniards (a figure that challenges credibility) had left since January 1829, with 401 departing on 20–21 April. The ministry's list, covering the period 8–21 April, indexes 563 applications for exceptions, of which 103 were rejected and 82 pending. Exceptions had been granted to 378 Spaniards; of these 194 were temporary, 114 perpetual, 68 for "physical impossibility" and, finally, there were two exceptions for sons born in Spain to Americans.[20] Lest the public develop the idea that the expulsion had been ineffective in the capital, the *Correo* published the names of those receiving passports contained in a list released by Tornel's secretary on 23 April.[21] The move was probably intended to offset the unfavorable effect produced by the sizable lists of exceptions being drawn up at this time by the medical juntas and the Senate.

The governor was apparently thorough and energetic—perhaps even impartial—in his enforcement of the expulsion law of 1829. Unlike the purge of 1827–28, this second expulsion measure was made less rigorous than its authors supposed by the medical boards and by Congress itself, rather than the governor. The experience of the first month of enforcement in the capital resembled that of the entire republic, at least in terms of the states' relations with the federal government and the legal and financial dilemmas posed by the law. While some states had their own laws to enforce, many did not. The weakness of the federal executive illustrated above, as well as the evasiveness of Congress, became more apparent in the months ahead, as the Guerrero regime lapsed into insolvency.

The Federal Executive

Vicente Guerrero assumed the presidency on 3 April only to be confronted, within three weeks, with an exhausted treasury. One of the earliest fiscal questions raised by the expulsion concerned *peninsulares* who owed money to the federal treasury. Due to financial stringency, Bocanegra recommended to Congress on 15 April that debtors who owed money to the government should not be expelled.[22]

Administering travel funds to *expulsos* was an onerous burden that eventually drained the scant remaining specie from the Veracruz federal commissaries. *Expulsos* appeared from other regions with empty purses, but were confronted with a time limit for departure. They bore certificates of poverty given to them by town councils, but which commissaries should provide their aid? And what of the Spaniards who arrived with passports dated before the publication of the law? Or those carrying passports valid for a limited time only? Guerrero resolved not to aid *peninsulares* who had voluntarily solicited passports, while qualified *expulsos* from other regions should receive assistance in Veracruz.[23] A number of Spanish servants of merchants who chose voluntary exile were abandoned by their masters at Jalapa. Other *peninsulares* attached themselves temporarily to the entourage of a wealthy Spaniard who assisted them as far as Jalapa. In this salubrious climate, the shipping at the port could be monitored. Guerrero agreed that these men should be aided, but with the utmost economy.[24] The shortage of funds for departing *peninsulares* was acute in Mexico State as well, but here the matter was complicated by a state legislative accord that prohibited dispensing any money, even federal funds, until all state employees were paid. And that had not been accomplished because of the exhausted state of the public treasury. Bocanegra could offer no solution; he merely passed Governor José Ignacio Sotomayor's inquiry on to the new treasury minister, Zavala. But by the 21 April deadline, Zavala had already compiled a list of sixty-eight former Spanish troops who could not depart for lack of funds.[25] The problem was not settled until July, when provisional funds were made available in Mexico City.

In addition to financial preoccupations, doubts arose concerning who should be responsible for individual appeals. Governor Zavala had raised the issue of states' rights in this context on 3 April, asserting that the federal system required appeals to be channeled through state administrations to the ministry of Government. But Bocanegra disagreed: "Since the law in question cites no other channel than that of this secretariat, state governments should be considered excluded by the [federal] legislature." But Zavala proved recalcitrant and continued to act as a channel of appeals to the ministry, although he obeyed orders in other respects—establishing the required medical juntas throughout the state, for example, as ordered on 8 April. Bocanegra asserted his authority over Zavala's successor, Sotomayor, in the strongest terms on 22 April, though he did not rule out the supreme government's right to use state authorities for handling appeals originally submitted to the ministry.[26] The law was so designed to eliminate regional variations in compliance—apparent in the first expulsion—and Zavala's effort here had been aimed at regaining some leverage for the governors in the selection of Spaniards to be excepted.

The ministry that enforced the law—composed of Bocanegra in Government, Herrera in Justice, Moctezuma in War and, after 17 April, Zavala in Treasury—was divided in opinion over enforcement. Bocanegra later wrote that the cabinet essentially attempted to solicit from Congress a retraction of the law of expulsion; "but, unfortunately," he concluded, "it was very difficult to obtain such a derogation." Exaggerating to a degree the liberality of the deputies, at least, Bocanegra attributed to the cabinet a direct role in persuading Congress to multiply the exceptions: "It could only be arranged that the exceptions—such as they were . . . might be softened and the severity with which they were dictated [made less harsh]." Deputy Bustamante remembered it differently, however. He charged that on 18 April "Minister Herrera had [Guerrero] complain about the exceptions, in an attempt to frustrate them." His motive was concern over the proliferation of exceptions, not the severity of the law. Bustamante attributed the change in ministerial policy to the hardening of party lines following the admission of Zavala to the cabinet on the previous day.[27]

Herrera may have attempted to toughen Guerrero's view of the expulsion, but a circular was issued by the minister of government granting Spaniards whose cases were as yet unresolved exemption from the departure deadlines imposed by the law.[28]

Routine measures of this kind, plus the rapid increase in exceptions in mid-April, produced some disenchantment among Guerrero's admirers. Rumors of his "softness on Spaniards" reached Oaxaca, where José Manuel de Micheltorina, who edited three periodicals friendly to the government, insisted on 22 April that the president rebut the charges. A pro-Yorkino editor wrote to him, "It is being said that your Excellency has been protecting the Spaniards, that you have requested from the chambers time extensions so that [*expulsos*] may remain six months more."[29] Guerrero's dilemma in these circumstances illustrates the political costs of an equitable enforcement carried out in the face of a bankrupt treasury.

Spaniards who were citizens of friendly nations constituted one such small but prominent group who had not departed as the law's expulsion provisions expired in the capital. Though the Senate provision establishing grounds for exception on that basis had been eliminated from the future law in the chamber of deputies, the federal government was determined to exempt them in any case. Bocanegra contacted the British chargé d'affaires, Richard Pakenham, the United States plenipotentiary, Joel Poinsett, and the French chargé

TABLE 3
FIRST REPORT OF CONGRESS, 25 APRIL 1829:
EXCEPTIONS GRANTED UNDER ARTICLE 3

State	Passports Expedited	Perpetual Illness	Temporary Illness	Sons Born in Spain to Americans
Mexico	12	—	—	—
Puebla[a]	463	25	17	—
Veracruz	9	2	17	—
Jalisco	8	5	1	—
Guanajuato	112	1	23	—
Michoacán[b]	9	—	3	—
San Luis Potosí	29	—	—	—
Yucatán	(?)	1	—	—
Zacatecas	35	1	2	—
Durango	14	—	—	—
Querétaro	46	5	15	—
Oaxaca	116	—	—	—
Tamaulipas	(?)	1	—	—
Tlaxcala (Territory)	(?)	—	1	—
Federal District[c]	1,341	100	202	5
Total	2,194	141	281	5

Sources: AGN, Ramo de Expulsión, leg. 18, tom. 18, exp. 2, fol. 4.

Note: No reports were received from states omitted above, nor in those marked with "(?)."

a. Passports issued by Puebla include all known Spaniards residing in that state; but since many of these may have lived elsewhere and may have been eligible for exception under the 20 March law, they are classified by date of receipt of the report.

b. The Michoacán government indicated that expulsion had been executed by a state law passed before the 20 March law, and that only seven Spaniards had been excepted for physical impairment. Hence only the passports noted above were expedited in compliance with the federal law.

c. According to official records, 5,000 Spaniards departed from the Federal District between January and 23 April 1829.

d'affaires, Celeste David, on 21 April requesting lists of Spaniards who were citizens of their respective countries. The president's orders were intended to protect these *peninsulares* until Congress should decide the fate of subjects of friendly nations. Pakenham replied that it would be impossible to submit a list immediately, since the place of birth of British subjects was unknown to him, but members of his community suspected of Spanish birth would be contacted so that they might apply for protective documents. Poinsett was more forthcoming: he submitted a list of thirteen United States citizens born in Spain and contacted all U.S. consuls requesting additional information. This policy was respected in the future and Pakenham successfully vouched for Pedro Mont, the Spanish-born Colombian consul in Guadalajara, among others.[30]

It was in this atmosphere of suspicion and internal division among Yorkinos that the Ministry of Government made its first formal report to Congress, as required by the law, on the state of enforcement. The detailed analysis was presented on 25 April, after the expulsion measure had run its course in the Federal District. (See table 3.)

Bocanegra's statistics were partial, at best, and his observations concerning the dilemmas of enforcement were brief and lacking in emotion. He could only provide adequate data on passports issued, since so many states were still complying with the law, and reports were delayed by distance. While noting that many inquiries had been necessary in order to clarify the decree, he did not criticize Congress for its failure to provide immediate interpretations. Bocanegra reported that medical juntas had been established throughout the republic and that "the government [had] deemed it necessary to resolve [questions] in light of congressional determinations." The administration had been swamped with appeals by Spaniards subject to examination by the juntas: "We have been forced to undertake a task so complicated and difficult that we have hardly been able to manage it in the short time fixed by the law," he observed. Nonetheless, the decree had been enforced "in major part." But all appeals had not been resolved as yet, partly because Spaniards were granted a month to present their petitions and, second, because Congress had not resolved the questions presented to it by the ministry. Bocanegra confessed that the scarcity of revenue had brought the payment of travel funds to a halt, resulting in a temporary suspension of departures by eligible Spaniards.[31]

Some characteristics of the statistical report merit examination. In Puebla, *every* Spanish resident of the state had been issued a passport and only 9 percent of these residents had since been excepted. In Michoacán the state law was enforced prior to the arrival of the federal decree, rendering the latter virtually irrelevant. In all, 2,194 passports were issued during the first month of enforcement and 427 exceptions granted. Though the number of exceptions reported for the Federal District, where passports outnumbered exceptions better than four to one, appears small, the figure was above average for the nation as a whole, at this juncture. In summary, according to the ministry's first report, the law appeared to be fulfilling the wishes of the more extreme hispanophobes.

Yorkino opinion had modified by late April, however, and any movement for strengthening the expulsion law was doomed from the outset, if we can generalize from the changed tone of the *Correo*'s writers. The editorial of 26 April referred to the Spanish question as closed.

> The public spectacle of so many suffering families created by the recent departure of the Spaniards has notably moderated the exaltation and popular hostility to them. It seems that those who remain are being forgiven in light of the suffering of those who have departed with their families. Outbursts are no longer heard in society, nor in the portals of markets, nor in corridors as it was before. Justice and moderation are being born anew. One or another extremist, failing to encounter support becomes embarrassed, fearing that he may appear ridiculous. In effect, who in good faith might fear the miserable residue of Spaniards which remains among us?[32]

This tolerant spirit would be somewhat shaken, however, as the "leniency" of the medical juntas and Congress became better known.

A survey of the day-to-day performance of the federal executive branch in administering the expulsion law is revealing. Decisions on individual appeals began in earnest on 12 April, and during the next thirty days at least 481 cases were resolved by the president in council of ministers—an average of 16 per day.[33] The most active single day was the first, when 151 cases were decided. During the thirty-day period noted above, appeals were resolved proportionally as follows: 54 percent "temporarily incapacitated," 24 percent "perpetually ill," and 22 percent without any impediment. In other words, of those who appealed, nearly four out of five could remain, at least temporarily. The executive branch was inclined to accept the opinion of the medical juntas.

The Ministries of War, Treasury, and Justice (the last including ecclesiastical affairs) played a minor role in the enforcement, and only with respect to those Spaniards who had been under their jurisdiction before the restrictive employment law of 10 May 1827. In addition, Minister of War Moctezuma began on 9 April to provide a daily military escort for Spaniards leaving the capital.[34] The Ministry of War accumulated appeals from sixty-two suspended Spanish military, and these provide insight into their fate during the enforcement period. Forty cases were handled prior to publication of the official lists of exceptions in late April: thirty former military men asked for aid to leave the republic, and seventeen requested overdue back pay. In most instances these appeals were directed to the governors of the states, who were the proper authorities to handle travel funds.

The majority had been soldiers but prominent Spanish officers such as Col. Francisco Palacio de Miranda of Jalisco, Col. Justo Huidobro and Lt. Col. José Manuel Ricoy of the capital, were included. Perhaps the most unusual case was that of surgeon José María Pages, friend and personal physician to Santa Anna. Pages was also a medical junta member in Veracruz. He was ordered by the colonel of his battalion to present his birth certificate and had failed to do so.[35] The appeals reveal the tendency of military personnel to look to the leaders of their guild for assistance, rather than to the civilians charged with enforcing the law.

The Ministry of Justice and Ecclesiastical Affairs was in communication with church authorities concerning the shortage of monastic clergy throughout Mexico. The clerics noted that the number of regular clergy had fallen from 1,300 to 400, and they pleaded for the exception of the thirty elderly friars who were subject to expulsion. Herrera responded that the government had decided not to grant exceptions for reasons of public policy but he urged them to appeal in any case, on the basis of age. Similar appeals soon arrived from the cathedral chapter of Puebla, with the same result.[36] The avid Yorkino Herrera did not appear so vindictive when dealing with high church functionaries. This does not mean that he dealt gently with the friars themselves, of course.

The Role of the Facultativos

In each city and state of the republic, wherever qualified medical practitioners were to be found, juntas were established to examine Spaniards who claimed illness. The result should have been foreseen; charges of corruption were soon heard and rightly so, it appears, for these *facultativos* were susceptible to temptation. One must concede that the financial opportunity presented to these men of none-too-secure economic status—who, by law, could grant the security desired by some of the wealthiest capitalists of Mexico—was extremely tempting. What remains uncertain, however, is how far they yielded to temptation. Deputy Bustamante believed that this was the norm rather than the exception:

The medical junta members were Yorkinos . . . ; they dubbed the healthy as ill, and the infirm as healthy; this depended upon the personal fortune of the Spaniards and how much they paid; he who paid generously, 10 or 12 ounces, could be judged useless, while he who was clearly in dire straits, though he might be paralytic, was judged a Hercules in health and robustness. The traffic that developed in these [documents] was scandalous in the extreme and was denounced in hushed tones within the Chamber of Deputies, as well as in the press.

"And not without reason," continued Don Carlos, "some sought the post of junta member with a zeal that might have been expended by aspirants for the canonate of Toledo."[37] The image is clouded, however, by the fact that this alleged corruption was never denounced in the *Correo,* which had so ardently sought the expulsion of rich and influential *peninsulares.* The Yorkino affiliation of the *facultativos* might have silenced the editors; but, as we shall see, there was considerable uncertainty concerning the extent of venality—though the juntas proved to be the most generous source of exceptions.

Guerrero established the medical junta of the capital on 7 April, naming eight members, of which five would constitute a quorum. Dr. José Manuel de Jesús Febles was named junta president by Guerrero. On the following day the general ordered the establishment of similar juntas in the states. He planned to submit all appeals pertaining to the illness exception allowed in Part 1 of Article 3 to the juntas for their immediate resolution, to be returned in the next mail. The administration would then resolve these cases on the basis of advice from the juntas. The *facultativos* of the capital were instructed to visit the homes of those who were too ill to appear in person, and in the Federal District all appeals forwarded by the government were to be returned within two days. Bocanegra sent the first fifty-seven appeals to Febles on 9 April; during the following three weeks the junta received 451 cases in 16 batches.[38] Within the first thirteen days Bocanegra forwarded 447 appeals, which, in conformity with Guerrero's rules, would be resolved within a fortnight—requiring an average of 28 examinations and reports per day. This demonstrates that the junta in the capital could have devoted little time to each case, especially in view of the difficulty of coordinating the examination of all *peninsulares* who were clamoring for exception and the delivery of their appeals to Febles's house at the appropriate time. On 27 April the junta sent Bocanegra a list of eighty-five Spaniards who had not yet appeared—though their appeals had been received. In view of this difficulty, Bocanegra extended the application deadline, which should have been 24 April, until six days from the list's publication. The list appeared in the *Correo* on 1 May; by 11 May the *facultativos* of the capital had completed these appeals, raising their total to 536 cases concluded during one month. By 25 April,

307 exceptions had been confirmed in the capital by Bocanegra.[39]

It is doubtful that the junta gave sufficient attention to each case. A careful review of the appeals and lists contained in the manuscript records of the expulsion inevitably reveals questionably resolved cases. For example, the treasury minister admitted that among the Spanish soldiers contained in Zavala's 21 April list of those awaiting travel funds were two invalids and a blind man.[40] In fact, the rumors and suspicions generated by the decisions of the Febles junta forced Guerrero to authorize a formal investigation in May.

The president declared on 25 April that *peninsulares* excepted "while their impediment shall persist" should undergo a new or second examination. Within two months, all temporarily excepted Spaniards in the capital were to appear before the district government for reexamination by a medical junta convened with at least five of its seven members present. The membership of the junta would be renewed on the first and fifteenth of each month from names, in order of appearance, on a list to be drawn up by the physicians' guild (*protomedicato*) and published by the government. Rulings would be made in one of three forms: the impediment is temporary, has become permanent, or has ceased. Those with temporary impediments would be examined every two months until their malady changed, for better or worse. The junta's decisions were to be forwarded to the Ministry of Government by the governor of the Federal District. Tornel ordered the medical guild to prepare a general list of *facultativos* by 28 June. Bocanegra's special instructions, included in the 25 April circular for state governments where *facultativos* were scarce, suggested using medical practitioners who enjoyed the confidence of the local government. Bocanegra urged the governors to specify whether the impediments were temporary or permanent—reports had been inconsistent in this respect—and to state in writing their opinion of the juntas' rulings.[41]

The executive branch and its instrument, the juntas of *facultativos*, thus set up a process that would inevitably produce injustices, venality, and impolitic decisions. And, in this, the president and his cabinet more than equaled Congress in "generosity," excepting at least 2,181 Spaniards from expulsion in 1829. As we shall see, deputies and senators—including many who had supported the law of expulsion—now found themselves obliged to accept the role of spokesmen for one or more *peninsulares*. The result would be several lists of excepted Spaniards produced by the two houses of Congress in mid-April, greeted by inevitable public resentment.

6

Two Distinct Modes of Compliance: Congress and the Governors

Shame passes, but the gold remains at home.
—*Deputy C. M. Bustamante (1829)*

EVEN BEFORE publication of the law, the federal Congress began to receive Spaniards' petitions for exception.[1] The Ministry of Government approached the chambers on at least ten occasions for clarification of the law, without obtaining the rulings needed to resolve pending appeals. Minister Bocanegra consulted Congress, mostly in April, about Spaniards who owed debts, Spanish-born subjects of friendly nations, the interpretation of Articles 1, 2, 4, and 9 of the law, various obstacles that could block compliance in the case of debtors to the public treasury, and Tornel's doubts about the law's interpretation.[2] Congressional reluctance to confront issues left unclarified by the expulsion law reflected the legislative branch's willingness to forego its constitutional authority in this case and to force the administration to resolve all difficulties—a task the government was hesitant to undertake. The definition of Spaniard remained unclear, especially with respect to citizens of friendly nations—a problem that would plague future governments as well, since *peninsulares* sometimes adopted alien citizenship to ensure readmission to Mexico.[3]

Other complex issues touched on the limits of state and federal authority where potential conflicts under the federal system required resolution. Since judicial authority was vested in the "sovereign" states, a governor could assert that neither prisoners in presidios nor persons involved in court cases could be expelled by federal law. Also, contradictions between two federal laws were possible—an example being the expulsion decree on the one hand and the law prohibiting

92

the departure of debtors to the federation on the other.[4] None of these issues received the necessary attention of Congress.

Initially, the Chamber of Deputies even attempted to evade its legal responsibility to consider appeals forwarded by the minister of government. Pursuant to a chamber accord, on 8 April the secretaries returned to the ministry appeals that Bocanegra had submitted on the previous day. The purpose was to have the minister "draw up the initiative which may seem convenient."[5] Bocanegra quickly returned the appeals, with five more, relaying the president's opinion on the issue:

The government does not judge it convenient to make an initiative, either concerning the suspensions of the law of 20 March which the interested parties solicit, nor concerning [the law's] repeal as requested by [their] families; and if cases were forwarded to the chambers . . . it was to avoid negating the legal channel from this secretariat to the General Congress concerning matters of this type.[6]

The administration also impeded enforcement by consistently refusing to initiate clarifying legislation.

The government's attitude was shared by a majority in the Chamber of Deputies, as was evident in the maneuvers that commenced on 9 April. The Senate, responding to an appeal from the Spaniards' wives, unanimously resolved to postpone departures until the end of December, due to the insalubrity of the Gulf ports during the summer months and the scarcity of travel funds. But the attempt was doomed from the start, since the government would not support it and the deputies could not accept a blanket postponement. The chamber's reluctance led to the illness and death of a number of proscribed persons at Veracruz. Because the deputies refused to admit the Spaniards' wives, it was besieged that evening by more than forty women with children.[7] Earlier in the day, Bocanegra had consulted the chamber concerning the impossibility of enforcing the law within one month: the distance from Mexico City to northern towns and cities made it impossible to process appeals and expel those whose petitions were denied within the time allotted. But rather than advocating an extension, the administration merely asked "whether, once the month was concluded, it could continue considering exceptions that may have been alleged during the month without prejudice to those interested persons whose cases had not been decided, or whether said term having expired, the matter should be considered terminated and they should be obliged to depart."[8]

The chamber now had a second reason, in addition to the Senate accord, to seriously consider postponing compliance with the law. Moreover, the *Correo*'s editors were prepared to support a postponement, now acknowledging that thirty days was not sufficient for a merchant to satisfy his accounts: four to six months would be more appropriate. They concluded that it was "unjust that besides the penalty of exile, they should be deprived of the goods with which they might support themselves outside the republic."[9]

The Senate accord reached the deputies on 10 April and was sent to the Commission on Public Security, which reported to the chamber on the next day. The majority report recommended rejection of the Senate accord, but it compromised on the matter of postponement by proposing that "the government should be empowered to extend the term of Article 1 of the 20 March law . . . for up to six months, for those Spaniards who need[ed] it." Berduzco of the commission dissented from its report on the grounds that the substitute proposal compromised the government.[10] In the following debate, the report was approved in general, but the Senate accord was rejected. A substitute motion authorizing a six-month extension, with presidential approval, was returned to the commission.[11] An attempt to return the original accord to the Senate as disapproved was blocked by a vote of thirty-five to twenty-six. Meanwhile, the Senate formally requested agreement by the deputies that "while the matter of the extension of the term prescribed by the 20 March law is pending in the general Congress . . . the time limit shall not be applied to those who are covered by [that law]."[12] The request emerged from the Commission of Public Security with majority approval (only Berduzco opposed it) and was overwhelmingly approved by the Senate. The decree met with a hostile reception from the government, which delayed publication until 20 April, after many *expulsos* had already departed.[13]

During the week beginning 15 April, "deserving" Spaniards were rapidly excepted by Congress. In the first instance, the deputies debated the fate of 105 Spaniards, rejecting only two, sending fourteen cases back to the commission charged with their selection, and excepting eighty-four on the first day. According to Deputy Bustamante, when the deputies' list was sent to the Senate, the upper chamber seized the opportunity to except many more and resolved that should its list be rejected, it would reject that of the deputies.[14]

Three days before the deadline in the Federal District, while exceptions increased, Bocanegra pressed the Senate to reverse itself on the suspension of the 20 March law's time limits.[15] He bluntly told the senators: "The decree of 15 April is not convenient, in the opinion of the government." After ritual protestations of generosity on the part of the administration, Bocanegra found two major problems with the decree:

1. It leaves the provisions of the 20 March law without any force, . . . since it does not indicate the time limits of the suspension, which remain undefined. . .
2. It will damage the public treasury, which has already spent nearly 8,000 pesos in travel funds for Spaniards . . . perhaps we shall have to distribute that much again.

Bocanegra wrote to the Senate president urging the chamber to gather for an extraordinary session that very afternoon.[16] Pacheco Leal complied with Guerrero's wish, but the Senate refused to reverse its stand. On 20 April the government took its case to the Chamber of Deputies, which by a vote of thirty to twenty-five invalidated the Senate's suspension of the departure date.[17] On the following day —the deadline for departures from the Federal District—the administration was able to publish a decree, signed by officers of both chambers, limiting the suspension of time limits to "Spaniards excepted by either of the chambers until today, 21 April."[18] As a result, the law would continue in force for those unable to obtain exceptions, while *peninsulares* who could find favor in either chamber would not be expelled.

Both houses of Congress were hastily producing their lists of excepted persons during the last days prior to the expiration of enforcement in the capital. After 21 April, several attempts were made to submit complete and accurate rosters to Bocanegra. A secret session of the Senate had been required on 20 April to resolve protests by some senators concerning alleged omissions in previous lists. As late as 25 April, forty-three new names, "missed" earlier, were sent to the ministry.[19] Pakenham reported this conflict over exceptions to London, providing a glimpse of what occurred outside the halls of Congress.[20] He noted that the controversy had to some extent reopened the Spanish question politically. Before the deadline for departure from the Federal District, he wrote, "great exertions were made to excite a feeling of commiseration . . . at least on behalf of the numerous Mexican families with whom so many [Spaniards] are connected." These efforts resulted not in any relaxation of the law but in a willingness to consider the merits of each case, some by deputies and others by senators, "as the Individuals concerned have happened to possess interest in either of the chambers." The result was the separate lists. But a conflict soon materialized, Pakenham reported. "Many of those who have found favor with the Deputies have been objected to by the Senate, and vice versa; each chamber holding out against the Resolution of the other, in order, by that means, to effect the exemption of the individuals whom they respectively protect."

The congressional disagreement over the law had been translated into a conflict over specific exceptions, not easily resolved:

> In the meantime a system of private intrigue and negotiation has been carried on, and means resorted to for the purpose of obtaining the votes of many members of both chambers, little consistent with the dignity and integrity of the legislative body and calculated greatly to diminish the respect, in which . . . the acts of the Sovereign Congress should be held.

It was therefore necessary to suspend the law for anyone on either list until a compromise could be effected. Though no joint list was ever produced, these *peninsulares* were in no danger, since the separate lists themselves were subsequently accepted as valid indicators of exception. When the governor of Chiapas inquired whether those named on the lists "were simply excepted from the time limits of the 20 March law, as the law of 21 April says, or if they are excepted from the expulsion,"[21] Bocanegra replied:

> The Spaniards of whom we speak are not definitively exempted from the expulsion, since until now there has been only an accord from each of the houses of Congress (which in itself constitutes neither law or decree), lacking the necessary revision of each respective chamber, and also, finally, sanction by the executive; but, nevertheless, you may not force [Spaniards] to leave the republic, nor the state where they reside, so long as the matter of their exception, initiated in the accord of one or another chamber, is not definitively resolved, the decree of 21 April having provided that the time limits of the law of expulsion should not be applied until [such resolution shall be achieved].[22]

The manuscript list contained 503 names, but the published official list attributed 518 of 2,699 exceptions to Congress, 445 excepted by the Senate and 73 by the Chamber of Deputies.[23] The *Correo* observed on 24 April that each senator and deputy seemed to have *peninsular* godsons. In radical quarters the response threatened to be more violent, as the title of a pamphlet of 25 April revealed: "The Congress's Treasons Shall be Avenged in Blood."

Enforcement in the States

State officials were bound by the federal law, but in the current atmosphere of state sovereignty, they could not be expected to be wholly subservient to Mexico City. Moreover, the states passed their own laws and, despite the constitution of 1824, it was difficult to prevent state law from superseding federal decrees, where the two conflicted.

In Oaxaca, for example, while Governor Miguel Ignacio Iturribarría required Spaniards to depart within twenty-four hours, in many cases, he filed the normal reports with Mexico City, which made it appear that the *expulsos* were allotted the thirty days allowed by law.[24] *El Oaxaqueño Libre* published a list of forty-six *expulsos* on 31 March who, it said, were to leave within twenty-four days—a period which, while more generous, did not conform to the law either, since it measured the thirty days from the date of publication in Mexico City, not Oaxaca.[25] Enforcement in San Luis Potosí—a bastion of anti-Spanish sentiment and the birthplace of harsh laws—was strict and thorough, according to local historians. A state law was in force when the federal measure arrived and, in the words of Muro:

Governor [Vicente] Romero was one of those who took pride in applying the [expulsion] law with the greatest rigor. He gave orders that the prefect, through his agents, should with all scrupulousness search for Spaniards who might be hidden in the city, in villages, haciendas, and ranches; that those who might be found should be brought in as prisoners, and placed in the public jail until they could be conducted with military escort to some point along the coast.[26]

Of course, the governor was merely complying with Article 5 of the law. Muro noted that the Spanish capitalist, with only ninety days to leave the country, found it impossible "to recover his capital . . .; as a result, most of them departed . . . leaving their fortunes in the charge of friends or relatives."[27]

In Guanajuato legislators resented the large number of exceptions obtained by *peninsulares*. In effect, the state expulsion law was being undermined by criollos who were writing "certifications" for local Spaniards and by the ease with which exceptions were obtained for physical impediments. A group of state legislators proposed, on 27 April, that the Guanajuato law be modified to prevent a recurrence of the revolution of December. Though their suggestion apparently did not become law, the method advocated illustrates the frustration felt by late April among anti-Spanish forces. They recommended that "only Spaniards who are to be found in bed should be considered physically impeded, [as well as] those who suffer a severe illness which impedes their natural movements or functions, or that places them in immediate danger of dying, in the judgment of the expert *facultativos* named by the government."[28] Reports of such moves in the states must have increased the anxieties of Bocanegra and Guerrero con-

cerning the dangers of lax enforcement of the law—which, to their
eyes, seemed to prevail.

The states, like the federal government, were inclined to continue
the salaries of former state employees, so long as they resided in
friendly or non-Spanish lands. Legal sanction for these payments was
usually written into the laws of expulsion themselves, though separate
measures were occasionally passed, such as that of Puebla on 27
March.[29] In sum, we may conclude that local enforcement conformed
less to the whims of governors than was the case in 1828. But the
law's effects varied widely in 1829, as earlier, with the *peninsulares*
receiving harsher treatment in San Luis Potosí and Oaxaca.

Illustrative or Unusual Cases

Conservative Mexican writers have always maintained that the crews
of the *Asia* and *Constante*, which had mutinied and handed over their
ships to the Mexican authorities after Independence, were not excepted from the expulsion of 1829.[30] A petition to exempt them was
in Congress in early April, and Bustamente editorialized on their
behalf in the *Voz de la Patria*. But it was already too late for many,
since state governors were precipitously expelling them. In Oaxaca,
for example, by 24 April, the five former crew members living there
had received passports and travel funds from Governor Iturribarría
and were heading for Central America. As mutineers they could not
risk embarking for the United States, whose treaty obligations with
Spain could have led to their deportation and possible execution.
Some relief came on 2 May when the administration informed the
governors that the *Asia's* former crew should not be forced to leave,
pending congressional resolution. Unfortunately, the circular was
prepared after the Federal District's departure deadline; moreover,
it failed to include the crew of the smaller *Constante*. Iturribarría replied, of course, that he would conform to the act if any additional
members of the crew appeared in Oaxaca. The circular was everywhere too late to save the majority of the *Asia* crew, if Arrangoiz
is correct. Not until 25 May did the government learn that the crew
had consisted of 450 men, including officers, gunners, sailors, and
infantry. By 20 July one expelled crew member was prepared to return to Mexico from Bordeaux. As late as August, with the Spanish
invasion under way, Congress had not resolved the question and the
remaining crew members were still protected from expulsion by documents received in May.

Conservative Mexican writers of the nineteenth century listed names of prominent Spaniards who were expelled in 1829 in order to illustrate the injustice of the measure. Alamán especially was angered by the departure of men such as Canon Monteagudo, a leader of the junta of the Profesa (which had supported independence), or José María Fagoaga, a member of the first Congress. On the other hand, conservatives were no doubt incensed over the exception of the Spanish Yorkino and editor of the *Correo*, Ramón Ceruti. This writer of proexpulsion articles and pamphlets had escaped the law of 1827 with the aid of Zavala, and was excepted in 1829 by the Chamber of Deputies.[31]

It was also possible for the relatives of prominent or influential Mexicans to obtain special consideration. Mariano Arista appealed personally to Tornel, Bocanegra, and Guerrero on behalf of his aging father, who eventually received an exception for perpetual physical impediment.[32] A biographer of Guerrero claims that the president "exempted the former archroyalist, Gabriel de Yermo . . . since he had once been the employer of his father."[33] Though this cannot be substantiated in the official lists, it is true that during the period of "extraordinary faculties," initiated with the 1829 Spanish invasion, Guerrero did grant special exceptions to the sons of Viceroy Iturrigaray, José and Vicente; to Joaquín Rea, the exiled son-in-law of General Bravo; to Ramón de Parres, the father of Gen. Joaquín Parres, who would become minister of war in the Liberal government of 1833; and to ten other prominent *peninsulares*. Illustrating the political differences between the two chambers of Congress, Tomás Alamán, the father of Lucas, was excepted by the Senate, while Domingo Busce, husband of Ignacio Allende's sister, was excepted by the deputies, with the assistance of his wife.[34]

Spaniards who had served in postindependence governments were, in practice, also excepted. Francisco Arrillaga, who had protected Guadalupe Victoria in Veracruz before 1821 and served as finance minister thereafter, documented his services and was excepted by the deputies. Deputy Cipriano Blanco, the only *peninsular* in Congress, was excepted by his colleagues in the first list.[35] An exiled Spanish liberal such as Domingo Lopes de Somosa could also receive special treatment. He was recommended to Bocanegra and to Guerrero on 9 April by nine representatives from Yucatán in both houses of Congress. Bocanegra ordered Governor Tiburcio Lopes of Yucatán to delay Somosa's expulsion while he appealed, successfully, on grounds of illness—a tactic recommended by the congressmen.[36]

The fact that proexpulsion congressmen often served as advocates of Spaniards in appeals for exception gave some credence to the con-

servatives' oft repeated charge that the anti-Spanish laws were favored as a form of "speculation." To find Deputy Reyes or Senator
Alpuche assisting a Spaniard would not necessarily validate the
charge, but it demonstrated inconsistency on the part of Yorkinos.
Alpuche, for example, represented several individuals, including the
wealthy *peninsular* Martín Rafael de Michelena, who received a temporary exception.[37]

Many a Spaniard excepted from the expulsion of 1828 also escaped the 1829 purge. Ironically, often the same governor issued
a second passport to the same individual and on an identical form,
printed during the first expulsion. Benito de la Serna provides a case
in point: while he received passports in both instances from Governor
Romero of San Luis Potosí, he probably did not depart, since both
passports remained in Mexico and he was not listed among those
arriving in either France or the United States.[38] What kind of recommendation was needed to persuade the government and Congress
that one was not a threat to national independence? A passage from
a letter of recommendation used on two occasions to gain an exception for Luis Villamil illustrates the ideal type. Joaquín Ladrón de
Guevara, third mayor (*alcalde*) of Jalapa, wrote on behalf of Villamil:
"In the various rebellions that have broken out, he has never succumbed to the antinational party; united with the federalists he has
performed various distinguished services that have earned him the
hatred and persecution of his own countrymen and those addicted
to the Plan of Montaño, which he opposed by force of arms."[39]

Congress could be persuaded to grant exceptions despite the
wishes of a state governor. Genaro Cabañes, for example, was excepted by the Senate even after the supreme government found him
to be without physical impediment. When Gov. Patricio Furlong of
Puebla protested and Bocanegra sent his complaints to the Senate,
Cabanes answered that the *facultativos* in Puebla were not distinguished in medicine and, moreover, were "out to get him."[40] Disagree-
ments were common between different branches and levels of government.

Enforcement was made more complicated by the sheer volume
of cases before Congress. On May 11, for example, fifty appeals arrived; some were from debtors to the public treasury, others appealed
for a variety of exceptions, and still others requested time extensions.[41] In the meantime, the first report of a Spaniard successfully
hiding to avoid compliance with the 1827 expulsion law occured on
19 May 1829, in Chiapas.[42] Though the deputies had resisted granting exceptions to sons born of Americans in Spanish territory, the

Senate forced the matter during the debate and continued to demonstrate concern for such persons, as the exception of Cuban-born Col. Santiago de Menocal demonstrates.[43]

Sometimes an entire community attempted to influence the outcome of appeals. Presbyter Diego Díaz de Mendivil of Monte Morelos, Nuevo León, obtained a temporal exception with the aid of a petition signed by sixty men in his parish. In Panuco, Veracruz, seventy-two community members petitioned for the expulsion of Domingo Lucas Rivas, their parish priest.[44]

The uncertainty of the appeal process can be seen in the letters Col. José Sánchez Espinosa of Jalapa penned in April. He gave his wife and business associates alternate sets of instructions: he wished to dispose of his properties, yet provide for his ailing wife, if he had to leave alone. Some of his tenants might have to move if his land were sold in parts. He might take a loss, but everything had to go —furniture, equipment, everything. If his wife's health improved and she followed him into exile, the land should be rented out instead, though it would only bring in about 200 pesos annually. Sánchez Espinosa saw no way out of his dilemma.[45] Moreover, a Spaniard's departure for Veracruz exposed him to new dangers and greater uncertainties. José Severo de Arana described his experience to his relative Pedro Arana, writing from Puebla on 24 April and six days later from Jalapa. He had found the troops insubordinate and prone to mistreat "people of [his] skin." It was unsafe to go out at night, due to the menacing attitude of the military officers. Arriving at Veracruz on 16 May, he found that he had missed his ship and that he would have to pay again to embark on 20 May. On that day, he wrote of strong rumors in the port about the approach of a Spanish expeditionary force. In reply, Pedro Arana spoke of his concern at receiving merely a temporal exception and assured José that he should have tried again, since others in his condition had received exceptions. He had heard about the "sickness, . . . scarcity of ships, and rising costs of food" in Veracruz and that "intimates in [Mexico City] had the kindness to help the poor Spaniards at the gates, seeing to it that they left for Veracruz with money and other things."[46] But these lines never reached José: Pedro Arana was poisoned in an inn in the Federal District with the letter still in his possession.

An Investigation of Facultativos in the Capital

Colonel Sánchez Espinosa wrote to Guerrero on 26 April concerning abuses commonly attributed to the *facultativos* and Congress. His letter set off an investigation of the practices of the *facultativos* of the Federal District which, though it changed nothing, was nonetheless revealing. Sánchez charged that the law was being "flouted entirely" in the capital, where Spaniards obtained exceptions "either by means of declaring physically incapacitated those who were not, or by acquiring through the chamber of Congress one's exclusion from the general law." Healthy *peninsulares* were flaunting their papers of exceptions, according to the colonel, and often these were the most dangerous of Spaniards. Concerning the role of Congress in this scandal, Sánchez declared:

In the majority of these exceptions, no explanation may be found other than caprice and arbitrariness, or favor, friendships, and relations with the favored. In the Senate; . . . it was also said that many were artfully inserted into the approved lists whose fraudulence it is not possible to determine. And it appears that this chamber continues to augment the number of dispensations, without any knowledge . . . whether this favor was granted as a result of merit . . . or simply from the personal whim of deputies or senators, because they are their friends, or owe favors, or share other relations. And this arbitrariness has [created a] . . . source of peculation that would cover even the most barbarous of peoples with shame.

Nor did the *facultativos* escape his judgment:

The sums of money with which the certifications of impediment have been bought are spoken of with as much publicity. Lately, the price has reached 60 ounces up front [and] we have seen . . . unfortunates . . . whose illness is visible even to those who are not physicians, and whose poverty was equally evident to all, ordered to leave the republic since they lack the wherewithal to satisfy the greed of the [*facultativos*]. Although this infamous maneuver may not be attributed to all those named by the government, I can assure you that some are taking advantage, making the law a source of enrichment for four prostituted men rather than for what it was intended.

The law had not contributed to national security, observed Sánchez: "[As a result] of the rich Spaniards who are truly pernicious, and even of the remainder who are not to be found in extreme insolvency, only those have left who did not wish to remain, because they justifiably feared the people's vengeance—and because they had not forgotten . . . the echoes that resounded so recently in the Acordada."[47] *Correo* attacked Sánchez's "furious declarations" on 29 April, choosing to see in them "a tactic adopted by the enemies of our prosperity to discredit the actual administration." To the Yorkinos the colonel was a voice of the recently defeated aristocratic party.[48]

The president took the matter more seriously, especially with re-spect to the activities of the *facultativos*, and Bocanegra ordered Tor-nel to begin an investigation of the charges. The governor was able to report that Judge Pedro Galindo had begun his investigation on 8 May and would be reporting the results every three days.[49] Colonel Sánchez was the first witness called. He told of instances related to him by Deputy José Domínguez of excessive fees charged by *faculta-tivos*. The deputy, having intervened on behalf of an ill Spaniard, was told by the *facultativos* that sixty ounces of gold would be required for the certificate. Domínguez had then consulted two other physi-cians, the first of whom requested eight ounces and the second noth-ing for the certificate.[50]

Judge Galindo heard "an infinity of witnesses" during the follow-ing three days, but was forced to report that, although many con-firmed the sale of certificates, "an effective case had not been estab-lished." Further investigation of the specific case referred to by Domínguez proved negative also, at least in the opinion of the judge. The fee charged was justified, Galindo said, because the physician in question was not a member of the junta of *facultativos* and was acting as a lawyer in obtaining the papers. Finally, on 17 June, Ga-lindo concluded his investigation and submitted information result-ing from the hearings, amounting to four notebooks, which were passed on to the supreme government.[51] The most impressive case cited in the thick file was that of Col. José María Michaus, a merchant, who was asked for 200 ounces and actually paid 120, though he natu-rally denied it, as did the *facultativo* responsible.[52] These measures produced neither convictions in the courts nor material changes in the "practical" requirements for obtaining certificates.

Governor Tornel Concludes His Enforcement

The expiration of the law in the Federal District and the publication of the lists of exceptions did not end Tornel's problems. In late April, Spaniards continued to enter the capital, perhaps in the belief that the exception of so many would somehow shield them from compli-ance with the law. The governor's request for instructions concerning the handling of these cases resulted in a reaffirmation of all previous "decrees, regulations and circulars."[53] By this time Tornel had numer-ous *peninsulares* incarcerated for noncompliance but still lacked in-structions concerning what should be done with them. It would ap-pear that the question was never resolved by competent authority, and consequently the fate of imprisoned Spaniards was subject only to the decision of local officials: some were sent to serve in a fortification, while others were marched to the ports for expulsion.

During the month of April, Tornel had authorized financial aid, totaling 8,705 pesos, for 352 *expulsos*;[54] but some recipients of travel funds failed to leave, while others could not depart for lack of aid. The governor sought to unscramble this situation, noting:

> Among the Spaniards excepted by the chamber there are some who have
> been aided for departure from the Federal District and are still on the
> road to their port of embarkation; but since the lists have been published,
> their families have applied to this government for the appropriate
> documents, the result being that those who have not left remain in this city,
> and those who had already departed are returning here, under [shelter] of
> the congressional declaration suspending the terms of the law, believing
> that they have no obligations to remain in a fixed place.[55]

Guerrero resolved that Spaniards entering the Federal District could stay there, and as a general rule *peninsulares* included in the chambers' lists could remain in their homes. Guerrero thought it wise to clarify the sense of the order of 2 May: it was quite proper for *expulsos* who had begun their journeys toward Veracruz, for example, to return to the Federal District if they so wished; they should not be compelled to remain in the towns where they first received the release from earlier expulsion orders.[56]

Tornel reported that other Spaniards who received financial aid remained in the capital awaiting payments owed them by the general treasury. And the governor asked:

> Should the funds distributed to Spaniards who have not left for the
> reasons indicated be recovered? Because if these are left in their power,
> they will use them; and if departure is verified, they will again request
> assistance, or they will not be able to return [funds] already dispensed, to
> the harm of the treasury.

Guerrero suggested that the money should be recovered "if it cannot be guaranteed to the satisfaction of this government," and he renewed his earlier directive that those requiring federal assistance to leave could not be expelled until funds were again available.[57] The visible delay in departure of numerous *peninsulares* in the Federal District had a predictable effect upon the more virulent anti-Spanish writers. On 7 May the most extreme of the diatribes criticizing the alleged duplicity of the authorities appeared in the capital. The pamphlet, entitled "Signal Agreed to for a General Riot and Massacre of Coyotes," forced the governing Yorkinos to seek suppression in the courts, which they themselves had dominated in the past to the disadvantage of the Escoceses.[58]

The remarkable change brought about by the passing of the departure deadline in the Federal District and by the exhaustion of the treasury was reflected in the enforcement statistics for the following month. Tornel expedited only twenty-seven passports for Spaniards who because of illness or by voluntary request had failed to pick them up before 21 April.[59] In fact, the district government's principal activity consisted of handing out 375 "security guarantees" to "those with appeals pending before the supreme government or excepted by the chambers, or those who have not received aid, were naturalized in friendly countries, or [the crew] of the ship *Congreso* [formerly the *Asia*]." During the month only 44 *peninsulares* had entered the Federal District, while 108 had departed.

Mexico City authorities remained vigilant throughout June, watching for *peninsulares* with faulty documentation and hoping for funds with which to expel those whose appeals had been rejected by the federal government. The city council resolved on 22 June "that verifying which Spaniards lacking documents of exception are in the city, or those who cannot document [their stay], they shall be apprehended quietly, without scandal, and remitted to the Deputation's prison, under the same rigorous responsibility." Neither Tornel nor the supreme government objected to this procedure adopted by the council.[60] The position of many Spaniards awaiting funds for departure was indeed difficult. On behalf of several who wished to end the uncertainty, Tornel appealed to the general commissary of the treasury for financial assistance, despite the order of 22 April suspending the distribution of travel funds. The treasury refused to violate the order, however, noting that its revenue "had not improved." The administration was still unwilling to reopen the state's coffers for this purpose.[61] Among those awaiting assistance were a number of Spanish soldiers whose departure was advocated by both Tornel and Moctezuma.[62] So critical was the condition of the treasury by July that military units loyal to Guerrero went unpaid and officers who were personally close to the president were writing to Doña Guadalupe de Guerrero for funds.[63]

Tornel launched the process of "new examination" in July for those with temporal exceptions, using the list of *facultativos* provided by the Protomedicato.[64] New juntas were appointed each month thereafter and the same name never appeared twice among the membership.

In August Tornel made his last inquiries and compiled his final report on the enforcement. The Spanish invasion near Tampico in July had led to the evacuation of Spaniards from the ports, and some of these individuals soon arrived in the Federal District. The governor wished to determine whether their presence in the country at that late date was legal. The ministry found it impossible to answer his questions, due to the sheer volume and chaos of its own records, and admonished Tornel to learn from the migrants themselves how they came to be in Mexico.[65] On 21 August Tornel submitted to Bocanegra his final report covering activities of the past two months. Only fourteen passports had been expedited, and on "second examination" 159 *peninsulares* were granted "perpetual" exceptions, illustrating that the advancement from temporary to perpetual status was fairly common during the summer, despite the Spanish invasion.[66] The military conflict, in fact, appears to have had little effect upon the enforcement process in the capital.

Congress Under Attack

Perhaps it was inevitable that Congress, rather than the juntas of *facultativos*, should become the primary target of popular wrath when the extent of the exceptions granted became evident. The public well knew the sentiments of the Senate, the source of most of the congressional exceptions. Even after the formal lists of exceptions were submitted to the ministry, the Senate met again to "correct" its lists, and in a secret session of 23 April added the names of forty-three *expulsos* who had already departed. Bocanegra, in order to place complete lists in the hands of the enforcing authorities, was required to send revised lists to the governors on 27 April.[67] In spite of the popular outcry, the various lists prepared by Congress were respected in practice by this as well as subsequent administrations.

The congressional exceptions had split the Yorkinos, however, as seen in the conflict between the pamphleteers and the *Correo*. Berduzco took exception to the *Correo*'s statement that "each deputy has had his godson," since he had neither supported a Spaniard nor voted for a single exception.[68] The same could be said for a number of Yorkino deputies. But the pamphleteers were now attempting to discredit the very majority in the lower house that had appeared so harsh during the expulsion debates—in hopes of reversing the exceptions approved by Congress. Pamphlets appeared in the Federal District with titles such as "Either the Gachupines Go or Guerrero Will Fall," and "Now There Is No Remedy but to Put the Gachupines to the Knife," attacking the congressional lists. On 25 April a pamphlet circulated entitled "The Congress's Treasons Will be Avenged in Blood," and the officialist *Yorkinos*, recognizing the seriousness of the threat to public peace, attempted to attribute its publication to an alleged "conspiracy of Spanish agents and anarchists in combination to destroy the republic in favor of dictatorship or monarchy."[69]

Criticism also came from Veracruz concerning some of the exceptions. Bocanegra received a critical "Exposition" from the Council of Government of Veracruz, published 1 May. The minister replied, on behalf of Guerrero, that all exceptions made by the federal government had been merited, in accord with the law of 20 March—no personal sentiments were involved. If exceptions appeared unjustified, they were the result of the law itself. As for the congressional exceptions, the president hoped that the legislative branch would take this exposition into consideration and decide "what was just and appropriate."[70] The concern of the council and of Governor Santa Anna was public tranquility, which Guerrero felt could be assured by the proper measures.

Rumors circulated of possible uprisings and new violence. A sequel to the "Treasons of the Congress" pamphlet appeared on 4 May attacking the editors of the *Correo*. They returned the abuse, belittling the "libelists of the Portal" as well as the rumors they spread.[71] In early May the civil militia of San Juan del Río petitioned the legislature of Querétaro State, concluding, "Neither the Spaniards who were residents of this village nor any others may locate here even if they are legally excepted."[72] The federal Congress was distracted at this time by the issue of compensation for the victims of the sacking of the Parián the previous December. The matter was debated in an unrealistic atmosphere, considering the state of the national treasury, yet it was nonetheless hotly contended, with officialist *Yorkinos* joining the opposition against more radical voices and in favor of federal indemnity.[73]

The debate appears even more quixotic when one considers the pressing questions raised by expulsion consultations that were going unattended in Congress. The administration beseeched the Chamber of Deputies on 16 May to resolve these issues with the utmost haste, lest the law remain unfulfilled, threatening public peace.[74] None of the many consultations made since 24 March had been resolved, and Congress's closing session was not far off. In addition, Bocanegra submitted four new questions to the chamber:

1. Should we admit the appeals of the Spaniards who allege a physical impediment and who claim that they did not present themselves before

the month prescribed by the law had passed due to a grave illness which prevented them from personally seeing to their affairs, or from having no notice of the law because they were on a ranch or in some depopulated place, or some other such cause?

2. Should we admit [the appeals] of those who residing in some state or territory might come personally to this capital to present their exception [*sic*], and due to mishaps on the road arrived after the month had expired in the Federal District?

3. Should we admit those who arriving in Mexico City (during the second or third month in which they could do so) allege a physical impediment . . . claiming to have contracted it in transit?

4. Should we concede exceptions . . . to those who are to be found in their residence after the month has expired, but who truly have a physical impediment that impedes their departure from the republic?[75]

It is clear that the Guerrero regime was now exceedingly legalistic, or cautious, in its expulsion decision making—desiring to avoid responsibility for unpopular interpretations of the law. Congress's hesitation even to debate these questions was, in effect, a tacit refusal by the Chamber of Deputies to lift that burden from the shoulders of Guerrero, whose government had come to power on the strength of public feeling concerning the expulsion question.

Congress closed its sessions on 23 May without facing up to either the expulsion consultations or the appeals of hundreds of Spaniards. As if to resolve all pending questions and to hand Guerrero total responsibility, during the last days of the session Congress debated a measure that could have allowed the president to expel any excepted Spaniard considered politically dangerous. Deputies opposed to expulsion opposed this measure on the grounds that a judicial process was more appropriate to such cases than giving the president such arbitrary power.[76] Petitions were arriving from states that wished to see the expulsion law absolutely enforced, whatever the cost. But the legislative branch, which had failed to produce mutually agreed upon lists of exceptions, finally left the matter in the hands of a government debilitated by penury. Congress had done nothing to relieve that problem, either. Future compliance would be characterized by the government's determination to adhere to a narrow view of the law, while leaving major interpretive decisions in the hands of a dispersed Congress. Guerrero said at the closing session: "I can assure you that in grand part [the expulsion] is executed, and it will be in its totality as soon as Congress resolves the consultations we have submitted." The president obviously meant that the government would await resolution of these matters during the next normal sessions of

Congress. While Deputy Gondra must have sensed the implicit threat broadcast by the pamphleteers, he responded hopefully, "The law of 20 March will calm once and for all the machinations of our astute enemies, sanctioning the general opinion unequivocally expressed from Dolores to Iguala, from Juchi to Perote."[77]

7

From Exceptions to Coexistence

So I'm just awaiting the final reply, the document of my exception . . . in order to return and plunge into that volcano, perhaps to be consumed by its flames.

—Ex-Count of Peñasco (May 1829)

ONE OF THE crucial questions unresolved by Congress was the matter of citizens of friendly nations who were born in Spain. In a circular of 2 May, the president declared that unless and until Congress ruled otherwise, these individuals were to be covered by the law, but they should not be forced to depart by the approaching deadlines, prior to a congressional ruling. The secretary of government instructed affected *peninsulares* to apply to their governors for documents of immunity, presenting proof accredited by the consul or agent of their nations. Bocanegra, following a Pakenham proposal, instructed the governors to determine which Spaniards were British subjects, and he informed the Chamber of Deputies of his procedure.[1] Pakenham's earlier denial of knowledge concerning which British subjects were born in Spain had been partly a manuever to prevent the Mexican government from distinguishing among Spaniards. Pakenham reported that, while believing the government sincere in its desire to protect British subjects, he had thought it best to let Bocanegra discover for himself which British subjects were Spanish-born. The British emissary concluded that the 2 May circular had resulted from pressure brought by the U.S. minister and the French consul, who had allegedly "demanded that Spaniards possessed of the rights of citizenship or naturalization in [their] countries should be exempted from the operation of the measure." Pakenham made no such demand, since he felt that the treaty in force between Mexico and Great Britain would effectively protect any who held British citizenship. He set about informing all those he believed to be Spanish-born British subjects of the government's intentions, so that they might apply for documents of exception as additional protection.

A second motive for Pakenham's exchange with Bocanegra was the ambassador's desire to plant firmly in the minds of Mexican authorities the distinction between British subjects born in Spain and those intrinsically Spanish who had acquired British citizenship. This distinction was clearly accepted by the Mexican government.[2] The sensitivity of British and foreign representatives merely added to the burden of enforcement.

By May, financial considerations were increasingly a matter of concern for the federal executive, as travel funds for *expulsos* dried up and officials could no longer look forward to payday with any certainty. Spaniards bearing passports for their expulsion were demanding back pay prior to departure, while the secretary of government attempted to obtain the refund of financial aid given to *peninsulares* who had subsequently obtained exceptions or protective documents. Instructions were circulated by Bocanegra to recover funds paid to any of the persons mentioned in the lists published by the chambers, or anyone remaining because of money owed to them by the treasury. The president insisted in this circular that "Spaniards excepted by the chambers may not enter the Federal District." The effort produced meager revenue; as late as 22 August only 280 pesos had been returned by those excepted.[3]

There were also cases in which a Spaniard was subjected to arrest and imprisonment for having remained in the republic beyond the departure deadline, though he was owed back pay by the treasury. When José de Argüelles y Velarde of Yucatán, a naval captain, refused to leave without being paid the 1,500 pesos owed him, Governor Lopes ordered his arrest. Argüelles languished in prison until the governor acknowledged the applicability of Bocanegra's order on 25 November; even then, the captain was expelled with travel funds but without back pay, due to Yucatán's empty treasury.[4] Argüelles knew of Bocanegra's directive, but Lopes apparently did not until the order was reiterated in November.

The financial obstruction to Spanish departures had become the major deterrent to the law's enforcement. Governor Sotomayor of Mexico State had twice urged the government in April and May to resolve the problem, but Bocanegra could only respond that these consultations were being sent to Zavala at the treasury for resolution. No initiative was made to Congress to solve the financial problem exacerbated by the aid requirement. Rather, as the secretary of state for Chiapas reported to a local periodical on 20 May, the supreme government itself was said to be working "to procure resources to cover the travel costs for [poor] Spaniards." Bocanegra urged Zavala once again, on 27 May to resolve the problem, but no solution was forthcoming. Moctezuma's instruction of 18 June, that the salaries of Spanish ex-military men should continue to be paid in their former units, appears quixotic in view of the fact that few active soldiers were being regularly remunerated by this time.[5] Finally, on 6 July, Zavala reported that, by order of the president, he had transferred the consultations concerning travel funds to the provisional general commissary in the capital. The message was passed on to Sotomayor, but little or nothing came of it, for future governors of Mexico State —where numerous Spaniards in this condition resided—repeated these inquiries in 1831 and even in 1834, indicating that money was never provided.[6]

Peninsulares in the states confronted greater difficulties than federal financial uncertainties. As late as May, the governor of Jalisco still entertained the notion that women might be subject to expulsion under the law. And, once again, a Spaniard excepted from the federal measure often had to cope with a state law as well. Jalisco provides a case in point: there excepted *peninsulares* who could not qualify for exemption from the state decree of 24 April had to depart, since they could not remain within the bounds of that state.[7] This illustrates the dilemma presented by discrepancies in the various expulsion measures for federalists who desired a national expulsion but dreaded the inevitable conflict between the supreme government and the states. The case of José Gregorio Gómez Humarán, the Spanish-born son of the Colombian vice-consul at Guadalajara, brought out the conflict, and the resulting solution neither established federal supremacy nor injured federalist pretentions. Bocanegra insisted that Gov. José Ignacio Cañedo apply the circular of 2 May concerning citizens of friendly nations, but Cañedo refused to violate the strict terms of the state expulsion law of 1827 until he discovered that it was possible to except young Gómez Humarán under a provision of the law of 22 May 1829.[8] He could thus satisfy Mexico City without surrendering Jaliscan sovereignty.

Guerrero was willing to concede to the states, after 9 May, the right to decide which Spaniards had submitted their appeals late with adequate justification and which could produce only inadequate evidence of justifiable tardiness. The president believed it impossible in these cases to establish rules that could be applied uniformly throughout the republic, and the governors were granted discretion either to forward or to reject future appeals, based on the merits of each case. The justification for these instructions was that only local authorities could fully appreciate the conditions that might force a Spaniard to present a late appeal.[9] The performance of the governors on this point, as on so many others, was uneven, and the ministry received numerous appeals lacking comments or observations justifying the tardiness.

Bocanegra explained these procedures to Congress in his second required report of 22 May. According to the minister, "The difficulties and obstacles presented to the government have been [too] many for the precise enforcement that was desired." Now the closing of congressional sessions would be a new source of obstacles. He reminded the deputies that on 16 May he had appealed urgently for resolution of pending questions that were obstructing enforcement; yet "not a single resolution [had] been received." Bocanegra described the circulars of 2 and 9 May, including in the former the protection of a group of Spaniards who, intentionally or not, had been left out —the crew of the *Constante*. (Their fate is unclear.) Steps were being taken to ensure that temporally excepted Spaniards would be reexamined and expelled, should they fail to satisfy the *facultativos*. He also explained why local officials should decide which Spaniards had appealed in time, but he accurately predicted future problems: "In this measure the business will be interminable and the law shall remain without effect in the many cases of difficult classification."[10]

Enforcement statistics compiled by the Ministry of Government revealed that during the second month, 856 passports had been issued to Spaniards, while exceptions totaled 533, the majority only temporary. More than a quarter of the passports were issued in the state of Puebla, while exceptions outnumbered expulsions in Veracruz, the Federal District, Mexico State, and Jalisco. Most of the expulsions took place in Puebla, Zacatecas, Chihuahua, and San Luis Potosí. For harshness, Chihuahua and San Luis Potosí were unequaled—only nine of their *peninsulares* escaped expulsion. Comparing the first and second months, we discover that, logically enough, exceptions increased with time, and the issue of passports had slowed considerably. After two months of enforcement, 3,501 Spaniards had received passports and 959 were excepted, of whom 62 percent were *temporales*. Passport recipients and *exceptuados* were sometimes the same, of course, and we cannot assume that either or both constituted the sum of the group that remained or departed as a result of the law of 1829. Within two months, the fate of nearly 4,000 Spaniards had been decided, at least as far as the regime was concerned. Because of transportation and enforcement difficulties, only three-quarters of the federal entities had as yet reported to the ministry.

Following Bocanegra's report, the editors of the *Correo* renewed their attacks upon rabidly anti-Spanish pamphleteers and enemies of the regime. The officialist organ challenged the reasoning of one writer who wished to seize Spanish wealth in order to create agricultural and commercial banks in each state. When a pamphlet entitled "Down With the Deputies and Death to the Gachupines" appeared on 30 May, the *Correo* found itself attacking opponents on both the left and the right in the same editorial. A new periodical, *El Zurriago*, had become the voice of expulsion, while the periodicals of C. M. Bustamante and Ibar continued their criticism of both the expulsion and the government. In addition, *El Sol*, the traditional liberal opponent of the Yorkinos, was reborn on 30 June.[11]

Congress, responsible for decisions concerning individual appeals, went into recess in June, while a number of legitimate requests for exception were still being received by the ministry. From Veracruz and Jalisco came numerous applications, none of which was considered in Mexico City during the congressional recess, though the subjects had appealed in time. Governor Santa Anna requested a presidential decision "concerning whether the appeals no longer have any place, whether they may have in the future, and whether these persons may remain while awaiting the resulting decision." Bocanegra responded cruelly on 17 June that to take these cases under advisement would be tantamount to "extending the term set by the law," the authority for which did not rest with the administration. In fact, the minister now asserted that authority was lacking even to grant these Spaniards the right to remain in the republic until Congress ruled on their appeals.[12] In practice, however, a favorable resolution could result if the *peninsular* in question had a friend on the executive committee of the recessed Congress. Vicente Pumarejo of Jalisco employed Pacheco Leal, the secretary of the Senate, as his legal representative in June, in order to secure an exception. Pacheco successfully overcame the resistance of both the federal and state governments, arguing that Pumarejo was ill and owed money to the general commissary. The governor of Jalisco insisted that Pumarejo be expelled from his state after having appealed too late, but upon learning that the *peninsular* was "a debtor to the federal treasury," the governor requested instructions. Though Pumarejo was en route to Veracruz, Bocanegra twice insisted that nothing could be done until Congress acted on the general question of debtors to the treasury. Finally, Bocanegra reported on 18 July that the president had granted a temporal exception to Pumarejo, whose case was deftly handled by Pacheco. The Spaniard's indebtedness was not used as a reason for the favorable decision.[13]

Congressional hesitation had resulted in a hampered enforcement, as reflected in Bocanegra's third and final report to the chambers, delivered on 21 August, during the Spanish occupation of Tampico. The data covered three months, from 23 May, and revealed that over 1,000 additional Spaniards had been excepted—nearly three times the number of passports issued. In addition, 234 *peninsulares* had "passed" second examinations. Total passports issued now stood at 3,411, and exceptions at 1,966. However, since many Spaniards who received passports were subsequently excepted, the sum of these two figures probably exceeded the actual size of the *peninsular* community of 1829.[14] Some regions had still failed to submit reports in time; this third accounting was incomplete due to the absence of data from Michoacán, Tabasco, the Californias, and Colima. Taken as indicative of the results of the second expulsion, the three reports would lead us to conclude that by late August 1829 there were only 1,966 legal Spanish residents of the republic, of whom just 1,299 were permanently excepted from expulsion. Recall, however, that the final list of exceptions, published in 1833, included 2,699 names, or 732 more *peninsulares* than in the three ministerial reports of 1829. Bocanegra's figures for exceptions are probably much too low, though the lists of the excepted published in 1833 represented more than the number who remained, since many Spaniards departed before their exceptions were officially approved.

Three characteristics of the final report are particularly noteworthy. First, Governor Santa Anna of Veracruz issued nearly half the passports for the period—his lateness caused, no doubt, by his customary hesitation in enforcing expulsion laws (ironic indeed in light of his anti-Spanish posture at Perote). Second, the states that had opposed the law in Congress exiled few Spaniards: Yucatán expelled only three, obtaining perpetual exceptions for most of its *peninsulares*. Jalisco also demonstrated a new inclination toward leniency, excepting 60 percent of its Spaniards during this final period. And, last, to a substantial degree second examination was occurring in the Federal District; three-quarters of the "perpetuals" granted in the republic had been expended in the capital. This striking fact was both the result of migration from the states by those seeking to obtain federal exceptions and an indication, perhaps, that the expense, as well as the opportunity, were beyond the reach of most Spaniards outside the capital. In addition, the figures reveal that by 21 August only slightly over one-quarter of the 887 "temporals" had received favorable consideration during second examination. Though we might assume that the remainder had been judged fit to depart, I believe the majority simply had not appeared for reexamination because of the apparent laxity of the system.

The last *peninsulares* to escape the expulsion during the Guerrero regime did so after 25 August, while the president could exercise the "extraordinary powers" granted in response to the Spanish invasion. Fourteen Spaniards were excepted by the president using this prerogative, and in several cases the reason is clear.[15] Included were the two sons of ex-Viceroy Iturrigaray, as well as Joaquín Rea, the son-in-law of General Bravo, plus the fathers of Yorkino governor Agustín Viesca, and of Joaquín Parres, who would become minister of war in 1833. The exceptions granted to Escoceses were consonant with the president's policy, adopted during the national emergency, of amnesty for the Yorkinos' former enemies.

Implementation in the States

The governments of the states and territories were under orders to present the results of their decisions in periodicals published in both the federal capital and their own localities. The attitudes of the state governments with respect to the law's enforcement were as diverse as during the first expulsion. In Michoacán, for example, local authorities considered it appropriate to provide a pension for the Mexican families of the *expulsos*, a decision that had cost the state 2,508 pesos by 7 August 1829.[16] Such generosity was not found in Oaxaca, where the government demonstrated great hostility toward the Spaniards. The cruelty of Oaxaca's Governor Iturribarría, as well as the generosity of Vice-Governor Argüelles of Veracruz, may be appreciated in a report from the chief of Orizaba Department. Argüelles wrote during the final days of November that many of the *expulsos'* accusations were undoubtedly true, "since some [who arrived from Oaxaca] were blind, cripples on crutches, and men near death who gained their exceptions [in Veracruz State] because they were justly heard."[17]

Arbitrary acts committed by state governments occasionally produced protests by the *expulsos*. In Tabasco, for example, a group of thirty-eight departing Spaniards signed a vigorous protest before boarding ship, because their passports said "they requested it" when this was not the case. The Tabasco *expulsos* desired that the law be modified in the future, so that they might return to enjoy the fruits of their efforts in Mexico.[18]

Although the expulsion provisions of the federal law were suspended by the circular of 2 May, the government of Chihuahua authorized further expulsions by virtue of a new state law. In May 1829, for the third time, the special commission on public security of the local congress proposed an expulsion law. The decree of 19 May allowed Spanish residents of any Mexican state at the time of publication of the 20 March law who might be eligible for the exceptions under Article 3 to remain in Chihuahua. Some Spaniards whose departure had been suspended by the circular of 2 May were permitted to remain until the federal Congress should resolve questions of interpretation.[19] In effect, Spaniards who were citizens of friendly countries were simply considered transients.

California, once again, was a special case in which the fate of the missions and the ultimate destiny of a great part of the national territory were affected. During 1828 the governor of the territory, José María Echeandía, had refused to expel any Spaniards—even those who had refused to swear allegiance to the federal constitution —in order to avoid the destruction of the missions. There was no one to replace the Spanish friars. In June 1829, one month before the arrival of the March law, Echeandía sent to the capital an annotated list of friars—all but three of whom were *peninsulares*. Once again, he urgently requested that they be allowed to remain. Within days, the new expulsion decree arrived; the governor had no choice but to publish it. The measure specifically demanded the expulsion of Spaniards from the northern territories within a month of publication. The decree circulated on 6 July with provisions for issuing passports to all friars who had refused the oath and providing a month's delay for those who wished to appeal on grounds of infirmity. In practice, however, the only men processed for exile were nine sailors, none of whom actually left. The governor and several town councils appealed to Mexico City for nullification of the law; the village of San José appears to have been unanimous in its opposition.[20] There were no more directives from Mexico City during 1829; the matter continued unresolved, and the law was unenforced in the Californias for the remainder of the Guerrero regime.

The Spaniards Embark

The embarkations for New Orleans, Havana, and Bordeaux commenced at Veracruz on 2 March and ended on 15 August, with no departures in July because of the Spanish invasion. More *expulsos* arrived at Bordeaux toward the end of July, having embarked, presumably, from New Orleans and Havana. The brigs and schooners that sailed between Veracruz and New Orleans between March and June each carried an average of thirty-one Spaniards accompanied by family members and, occasionally, servants. The costs incurred by the general commissary at Veracruz, were burdensome: just three ships, carrying a total of 160 *expulsos* and their families (who in turn also received aid), collected 6,400 pesos in passages. By 5 June the commissary had exhausted its reserve of specie, and ships' captains were paid with "certificates of credit" only.[21]

For many *expulsos* the road to Veracruz was difficult, although the Yorkist press pointed with satisfaction to the "passivity" of the populace encountered by the exiles en route. But the *peninsulares* occasionally faced poor treatment by a North American captain during the voyage to New Orleans. When the frigate *La Belle* arrived at New Orleans on 17 July carrying 180 Spaniards, "the captain, to excuse himself for the bad treatment he had meted out, accused them of mutiny." Zamaçois (apparently writing of this same group) reports that the captain had attempted to rob them, and all that stopped him was an uprising by the intended victims. Although these *expulsos* lost all their baggage, they had the satisfaction of seeing the captain hanged at New Orleans by order of the local authorities. Earlier, on the night of 20 June, more than 138 Spaniards and their families had been abandoned by the ship in question at Río Lagartos, Yucatán. The governor and the ministry agreed in July that the victims should be taken to the port of Sisal for transport to New Orleans. The minister of war dispatched a detachment to the area to prevent the victims from reentering the interior. Many of these *expulsos* preferred to return to Veracruz "to recover their health" and depart from there for New Orleans. The federal government eventually approved this petition and the majority embarked for Veracruz on 28 July, with the help of yet another investment of government funds, together with private donations collected in Sisal. As late as 3 September some *expulsos* were still in Sisal, due to lack of funds—the treasury in Yucatán was also empty. By late September the president had decided that the remaining victims need not depart so long as funds were lacking. During this episode, four Spaniards learned that Congress had excepted them from expulsion, and they were permitted to return to the Federal District.[22]

Thus ended the second expulsion under the Yorkinos; with treasuries empty, various Spaniards abandoned in different towns and ports, Spanish invaders besieged at Tampico, hundreds of Mexican wives and children in New Orleans and in France, and the federal government about to confront a new internal enemy—an emerging military-ecclesiastical alliance determined to destroy the Yorkinos and Guerrero. As if to signal the termination of yet another only partially successful attempt to expel the *gachupines*, on 10 October the *Correo* announced:

> The great allegorical painting of the expulsion of the Spaniards, done by professors Mr. Franck and F. Waldek, which the public has seen adorning this city's float on days of national celebrations, is to be raffled off. The drawing will take place very soon, from one hundred tickets at six pesos each, which are on sale at the shop of Sr. Ackerman.[23]

Mexico had acquired a new colony of industrious foreign merchants, with names and customs less familiar than those of the unfortunate *expulsos*.

The Collapse of the Guerrero Government

In the words of Lucas Alamán—the guiding light of the new regime —the coalition that undermined the Guerrero presidency consisted of "the remaining Escoceses and all the respectable people who had been Yorkinos, who began to refer to themselves as 'men of good will' [*hombres de bien*], and to whom rallied the clergy, the army, and all of the propertied class."[24] Here began the tacit alliance of clergy, army, and property that would bring so much grief to Mexican Liberals for the remainder of the nineteenth century. In the bloody civil war that lay ahead, consuming much of 1830, the opposition consisted of the Yorkino remnants, supported by Guerrero in the south. The authors of the rebellion at Jalapa were Lic. Sebastián Camacho, former representative to Great Britain and governor of the state of Veracruz; Col. José Antonio Facio, the Spanish-educated secretary to Vice-President Bustamante; and a Spaniard, Juan Grambi.

Zavala declared, concerning the Plan of Jalapa, "The Spanish party managed to divide those who could give impetus to public matters, and everything unraveled as a result." In an open letter to the Mexican people, the deposed president proclaimed on 12 December 1830 that the new rulers were "fed with the milk of the Spaniards, and determined to follow in the footsteps of the ancient tyrants in order to govern under these auspices." It should be noted that, although General Bustamante had become vice-president with Yorkino votes, he belonged to a faction that had abandoned them.[25]

Since the new government would institute a cautious but sympathetic policy toward Mexico's *peninsulares*, it is useful to observe the trends that led up to the rebellion of December 1829. As early as 15 September the danger signs were described in a letter from Santa Anna, personally delivered by General Garza, in which Santa Anna called for the resignation of the ministry as well as increased military aid. The latter theme would be repeated countless times in the waning months of 1829 by all the commanders involved in the defense against Spanish invasion. Guerrero retained the support of the anti-Spanish faction in the capital, but was rapidly losing the loyalty of military officials generally, due to fiscal bankruptcy.[26] With the defeat of the Spaniards under General Barradas, Escoceses could legitimately claim the role of defenders of the republic, giving the lie to the "monarchist" label attached to them by the Yorkinos. Pamphlets soon appeared denouncing the expulsion of the Spaniards and the exiling of Escoceses as a cruel Yorkino plot. General Mier y Terán detected, by 19 October 1829, serious signs of discontent and conspiracy in the northern army. And complaints were loudest in the state of Veracruz, since the federal government regularly drained off about 50 percent of state revenues in the form of contingency payments. Santa Anna wrote to Guerrero on 29 October, "It has been several months since [Veracruz] has met its civil payroll, [and should nothing change] offices will have to be closed and employees of all divisions will disperse to seek out a living for themselves and their families, many perhaps at public expense."[27] The president was also forewarned by Bustamante's many dispatches—which usually dealt with the state of the external threat—of the restlessness within the reserve army under his command and its possible consequences.

The beginning of the end was a centralist proclamation in Campeche on 6 November that spread to Mérida three days later. Bustamante's reserve army was agitated at the news, and some officials apparently favored joining the movement with Santa Anna in command. But the victor of Tampico retired to Manga del Clavo, as he so often did during crises. Abandoning his post as commanding general of Veracruz, Santa Anna professed agreement with the plan but not the means suggested. Before his departure, he pleaded with Guerrero for financial assistance, observing in a postscript:

The misery here is incredible: the troops are groaning from hunger; the officers are five months behind in their pay, and all are quarrelsome. I have written repeatedly to the minister about the situation, but without result; and I am mortified at hearing so many laments because in the end it reflects badly on the government. I hope that this will impress upon you the importance of this matter.[28]

The president learned of the Campeche rebellion on 20 November and issued a proclamation in which he declared, "What the Spanish government could not effect by the folly of reconquest, the rebels wish to put in practice, placing factional interests above the common good of the sovereign people." General Bustamante made a final attempt on 27 November to impress upon Guerrero the gravity of the situation, his message containing an implicit threat:

I send word that the evil is progressing, as I said officially to the minister. Spirits are high, and on all sides revolutionary efforts are mounting. I consider it of the highest importance that assistance be sent to these troops in order to assure that desperation and misery will not force them to depart from the path of duty.[29]

Ultimately, the Veracruz State legislature forced Santa Anna out of retirement by placing him in charge of the loyalist forces. Upon his arrival in Jalapa, Santa Anna discovered that Bustamante had ordered the reserve army to march on Mexico City. The conflict could no longer be evaded; Santa Anna announced his support for Guerrero, securing the state for the Yorkino regime. The matter would now be decided in the capital. As if to symbolize the collapse of Yorkino authority, U.S. Minister Poinsett received his letter of recall from President Jackson on 9 December (the Mexican government had requested it long before), and the meddlesome emissary took formal leave of the new government on 25 December 1829—departing, like so many other Yorkinos, in January 1830.[30] The capital had fallen on 22–23 December, when Gen. Luis Quintanar deposed Acting President Bocanegra, with the assistance of an ex-Yorkino, Ignacio Mora —the officer who had uncovered the Arenas conspiracy in 1827. Affairs of government ultimately fell into Alamán's able hands, supported by General Quintanar, until the arrival of Bustamante, and only Veracruz seemed determined to resist the change. But when the Jalapa legislature failed to meet and act, Santa Anna again resigned, and Veracruz State was brought under the new regime.[31] Henceforth, armed resistance took on the familiar aspect of guerrilla warfare focused in the south.

Severely weakened by the anti-*gachupín* conflict, the Yorkino regime, despite its unquestionable popular support, collapsed almost without a struggle. In addition to the ever present opposition of conservative interests, the government faced growing hostility from former Yorkinos who had withdrawn their support in part because they believed that the hispanophobes were undermining the Federal Republic. Ex-Yorkinos who lost faith in the Guerrero regime would reappear later in the reform government created by Liberals in 1833–34. The moderate Mexican National Rite, about which we know very little, had been operating since 1828, competing effectively with the Yorkinos. It was not that the new Masonic clubs would remove themselves from politics (they would not), but rather that they no longer focused on the Spanish question. Yorkino leaders such as Zavala and Alpuche fled into exile in January 1830, while many of those who remained at Guerrero's side died in guerrilla encounters or before a firing squad during the protracted civil war of 1830.

Conservatives Complete the Expulsion

From the northeastern frontier, General Mier y Terán recommended to Minister Alamán that "one of the reforms that should be made to the constitutional code . . . is to organize the executive power in another manner, and get rid of this presidency, an all too seductive object for [ambitious] aspirants."[32] In the capital, proponents of the new regime produced pamphlets "legitimizing" the coup d'état. C. M. Bustamante, an admirer of both Alamán and Mier y Terán, attacked the previous republican regimes, reiterating his old charge: "From this very presidential palace orders were issued to certain local chiefs to sound the alarm and raise gangs, using it as an excuse to carry out the expulsion of the Spaniards." Don Carlos favored a conspiracy theory of the origins of the anti-Spanish movement: the Yorkinos, in his view, needed the movement to perpetuate themselves in power; impetus for the expulsions did not spring from the popular will. An anonymous Escocés went even further in examining the "constitutional infractions that not only [could] justify but ostensibly legitimize this necessary and healthful uprising." The revolt was justified; the law expelling the Spanish violated the constitution "because this measure was taken as the most efficacious means of destroying the republic, break the national pact, and aggrandize lawbreakers, imagining crimes that existed only in the seditious heads of the Yorkinos."[33]

In his first ministerial report to Congress, delivered soon after assuming office, Alamán observed that despite the expulsions, peace had not returned to Mexico. He stressed the previous government's difficulty in enforcing the expulsion law and noted that damage to the treasury had been great, because of Congress's failure to clarify the status of persons owing money to the federation. Contrary to rumors promoted by the opposition, no return passports had been issued to *expulsos* by the new government, Alamán insisted. He confessed that "many unfortunate families" had approached the ministry, "urging that their fathers and husbands be restored to their homes." But since the law of 20 March 1829 was still in force, the administration was not permitted to make exceptions. Eventually, Alamán extracted from Congress a decree enabling the Mexican families of exiles at New Orleans to return with government assistance.[34]

Immediately, the Bustamante administration faced the specter of the incompleted expulsion, and placed its own stamp on the matter without departing from the legal norms established by the the Guerrero regime. Though their enemies would accuse them of "patronizing the Spaniards," the new government did not consider itself free to override earlier precedents.[35] Numerous sacked employees, inherited from previous governments, also constituted a problem, particularly in view of the empty treasury. Most of these were Spaniards, and the government was obliged to renew salary payments once revenue could be generated. By 13 January 1830 the secretary of the treasury was taking steps to meet the payroll, including salaries pertaining to suspended employees. In response to a petition initiated by the peninsular ex-employees of the Mint (Casa de Moneda), the vice-president decided "that employees who were not retired should consider themselves as 'effectives' with the guarantee of their salaries, in accordance with the [law of 10 May 1827] and be rewarded the same as employees in actual service." A directive from the secretary of the treasury on 5 February declared that "Spaniards suspended from the exercise of their positions . . . should not be considered to have resigned but, rather, [seen] as effectives with their respective salaries guaranteed."[36] The concept of "job ownership" was thus reinforced.

Inevitably, questions concerning ex-employees forced the cabinet to decide matters pertaining to individual *peninsulares*, some of whom improved their lot under the new regime. It was decided in late March that a Spanish ex-employee excepted from expulsion could live where he pleased and change his residence at will. When a *peninsular* was suddenly discovered who had evaded the employees law, Bustamante faced a new issue. An official of the fourth regiment petitioned the federal government on 15 May requesting that Franciso Urriza, whom knowledgeable persons had identified as a *gallego*, be removed from the army "without rights to promotion," in conformity with the 10 May law. The new regime would resume salary payments to expelled ex-employees in New Orleans, in compliance with previous commitments, once it was determined which of them had helped to plan the Spanish invasion. The renewal of salaries, understandably, elicited petitions from military men who were reputed collaborators. The measure of their loyalty would ultimately be "permanence in New Orleans throughout 1829."[37]

The Ministry of Government sought to clear up all pending matters concerning the expulsion law and its victims, but too many questions had gone unanswered in 1829 for that to be accomplished immediately. The ministry's Department of Internal Relations began by closing all appeals cases outstanding since 1828, on grounds that "the law of 20 March [1829] accepts only Spaniards with a physical impediment."[38] It seemed obvious that their fate had already been decided by the harsher second law. Minister of War Facio began collecting data on excepted *militares* who had failed to return funds received from either the treasury or customs following the favorable resolution of their appeals. The previous government had decided in September 1829 that appropriate amounts should be deducted from their retirement pay. In addition, Congress had to resolve the question of the Spanish *militares* who had defected to the Mexicans at Tampico in 1829. When one such individual, Andrés Pompillón, requested permission to travel within the republic, Alamán decided that the defector's case was similar to that of the *Asia* crew, and Pompillón was forced to remain in the capital. When a defector, Antonio Puchet, left Mexico City in July, he was arrested in the state of Mexico and returned to the Federal District. He was ordered to Veracruz for expulsion in October 1830 because his claim to have defected was not believed. Finally, six months later, the governor of Veracruz reported that Santa Anna and others had testified that Puchet did defect at Tampico, and he was given a security document on 8 April 1831 allowing him to remain in Veracruz.[39]

The position of the *peninsulares* was sometimes better outside the capital. In Jalisco the legislature repealed the law prohibiting Spaniards from residing less than 60 leagues from the coast, and, on 4 September 1830, it resolved the conflicts between the state expulsion law and that of 20 March, as requested by Bocanegra in June 1829.[40] Conflicts between state and federal authority persisted, however. When Ygnacio Avila, who had been excepted by the Senate, attempted to enter Michoacán with a passport issued in the Federal District, he was threatened with imprisonment. Alamán informed Gov. Agustín Pérez de Lebrija that, since the list of those excepted by Congress had been forwarded to the states, in order to prevent legal residents from being molested, no further proof of Avila's exception was required: he should be permitted to reside in Michoacán.[41] But Alamán was sensitive to charges that his administration granted illegal exceptions or was unjustifiably tolerant of those desiring to return from exile. When Governor Montes de Oca of Guanajunato expelled Agustín Salgado on six hours' notice for stating publicly that since the government was bankrupt, Spaniards no longer had to depart (which was essentially correct), the minister approved the governor's arbitrary act.[42] The reprisal was all the more surprising because Salgado was linked by marriage to prominent families in Alamán's own state. Continuing enforcement of the law in 1830, with federal approval, was demonstrated by the imprisonment in Guanajuato (with Alamán's endorsement) of Lorenzo Paya, who had evaded expulsion in 1829. Paya appealed from prison in Apaseo on 3 May 1830. Having received no response from Mexico City, the Spaniard's family was still beseeching local authorities in July for his release, on the grounds of poverty. Paya signed a new appeal in October. Finally, in February 1831, the vice-president decreed that "if he [could claim] no legal exception allowing him to remain in the Republic," Paya should suffer the penalty under the law.[43]

These cases aside, one can detect a softening of attitudes and restrictions in the course of 1830, particularly in the northern states. In Tamaulipas, a congressional decree of 23 March *excluded* Cubans and Puerto Ricans—clearly former subjects of Spain—from the restriction of 9 November 1826: "Subjects of the state who originated in foreign nations that have not recognized the independence of the republic may not be named to municipal offices." Moreover, Spaniards were not covered in a Tamaulipas law of 19 April requiring most foreigners to pay a tax of 1 percent on all commercial capital.[44] The new attitude was also reflected in the annual report of the local secretary of state to the Chihuahua legislature on 3 July 1830. Secretary José Pascual García attempted to assess the harm done to commerce in Chihuahua by the expulsions of 1828 and 1829, noting that he had not been free to do so before the legislature in 1829 because of the Yorkinos' dominance. According to this proponent of the new political order, the expulsion laws

were undoubtedly exterminators; because in addition to diminishing our population by expelling the proscribed Spaniards, [including] innumerable Mexicans who made up their families, it gave rise to a shocking drain of capital, not only that of the unfortunate victims . . . but of many others as well, Europeans and Mexicans alike, who having shown more or less

support for the [*peninsulares*], became the object of the most atrocious . . .
persecution by the fanatics of the Yorkino party.[45]

García's new freedom of opinion suggests that by the summer of 1830
the supporters of the Bustamante regime had succeeded, according
to plan, in challenging the credentials of enough deputies in state
congresses to assure a more conservative majority.

The question of the mission friars in the Californias remained
for the Bustamante government to confront in 1830. Alamán learned
from the military commander of disturbances caused by "the bad
example and bad teachings of the Spaniards and Spanish missionaries." Both the public and local troops had opposed an attempt to
expel Padre Francisco Vicente de Sarría, allegedly the chief trouble-
maker. Moreover, since the expulsion law "had not been enforced,"
Spaniards in the Californias had been joined by seventy-one *expulsos*
from Sonora and even from Jalisco. As a consequence, Alamán ordered Gov. Manuel Victoria to investigate the matter, take action,
and report on the exact state of affairs.[46] Both factions in the Californias had recommended that troops and new missionaries would be
needed to carry out the expulsions. Vice-President Bustamante approved the assignment of ten friars from Zacatecas to the Californias,
but the move required two years because of financial problems at
the Franciscan College of Guadalupe. Since there were still not
enough Mexicans to fulfill the friar's tasks, as under the Victoria and
Guerrero regimes, Spaniards in the Californias were not molested
during the Alamán ministry. Hittel suggests, in addition, that the soli-
darity of all foreigners, including non-Spaniards, prevented acts of
violence against the *peninsulares*.[47]

Governor Victoria launched a defense of the friars in 1831 and
an attack on his opponents, the Echeandía-Padres faction, which he
now accused of responsibility for troubles previously blamed on the
Spaniards. The governor issued a circular in October professing his
intention to enforce the expulsion, but expressly excluding the friars.
In the end, only the sole Spaniard residing in San Francisco was expelled. Victoria stood accused on this account in 1832, but his successor, José Figueroa, did little better, simply recommending the expulsion of two friars who had refused the oath. Nothing more was
required of him by Mexico City.[48] By this time, at least for the moment, the laws of expulsion were viewed as having expired in all
of Mexico's regions.

8

The Impact of the 1829–1831 Expulsion

THE REBELLION OF the Acordada resulted in the hasty flight of many *peninsulares*, usually merchants, and, at times, their families. Judging by the embarkation reports in the *Correo* from 1 January until 20 March, early departures totaled at least 251 Spaniards and 196 dependents.[1] The commercial crisis and capital flight of 1829 thus began before 20 March and persisted throughout the enforcement period (see table 4).

We cannot provide a wholly accurate total for those who departed or were expelled (see table 5). The ministry reported expediting 3,411 passports to Spaniards, of whom at least 1,200 actually departed, judging by our data on arrivals in New Orleans and France. Illness, either temporary or permanent, exempted 1,960 from expulsion, according to the Ministry of Government (see table 6). Many but not all excepted Spaniards had previously received passports; the total number of passports and exceptions (5,377) is too high to represent the size of the Spanish community in early 1829. Reconciling all the responses of 1829 produces an even higher total: 5,684 Spaniards (table 5), which is surely too high and for the same reason —passport recipients did not always become *expulsos*. My previous estimate for December 1828 of approximately 4,831 *peninsulares* appears more reasonable. The final *reconciled* totals, compiled from all responses of 1829, reach 3,411 passports issued (see table 7) and 2,699 exceptions granted (the published lists), while 31 cases were never resolved (table 8).[2]

The extraordinary discrepancy, now revealed, between earlier and later figures for Mexico City, Puebla, and Guadalajara, comparing December 1828 and March 1829, no doubt results from the flight of Spaniards to those bastions of security in response to the first expulsion (see table 9). During the second purge, the regions with the largest *peninsular* communities were, in rank order, the Federal Dis-

trict, Puebla, Veracruz, Jalisco, and Yucatán. The congruity between
the earlier and later estimates for the states of Chihuahua, Nuevo
León, and Yucatán is remarkable, while there was wide disparity between the two for Durango, Mexico, Oaxaca, Querétaro, San Luis
Potosí, Sonora y Sinaloa, Tabasco, Tamaulipas, and Zacatecas. Apparently, reports are incomplete for these nine states.

The pace of enforcement varied: a hasty initial compliance, then
an extraordinary slowdown, occasioned largely by the terms of the
law. The bulk of the passports were issued in April, followed by a
marked decline during the next four months. Nearly half of all cases
were resolved within the first month and only one-sixth of these favorably. Consequently, exceptions mounted steadily with each report,
outnumbering passports from June through August by a ratio of
three to one (see table 5). If we accepted the ministry's word concerning exceptions, we would be led to acknowledge the existence of
slightly fewer than 2,000 *peninsular* residents by the time of the Spanish capitulation at Tampico (which would mean that there were more
invaders than residents). But the final list of 2,699 exceptions,
published in 1833, provides a more realistic though somewhat over-
stated total for late 1829, before the gradual return of surviving
expulsos that commenced in 1830. It constituted the final word on
exceptions.

The law was not enforced equally. The Federal District issued
40 percent of the passports for the republic as a whole, followed
distantly by Puebla with 21 percent. No other state approached these
numbers. Concerning exceptions, both Veracruz and Yucatán rivaled
the Federal District, with Jalisco a near fourth in ranking (see table

TABLE 4
DEPENDENTS LEAVING WITH SPANIARDS AT VERACRUZ,
28 MARCH–1 APRIL 1829

| | Destination | | |
	Bordeaux	New Orleans	Total
Individuals	9	21	30
Spaniards with family	10	15	25
Wives with children	58	54	112
Total	77	90	167

Sources: AGN, Ramo de Expulsión, leg. 15, tom. 33, exp. 17.

8). This is eloquent proof of the rigidity of enforcement in the capital, as well as in Puebla, compared with the leniency of Yucatán and, to a lesser degree, of Jalisco and Veracruz. However, the most thorough enforcement (that is, the severest ratio of passports issued compared to Spaniards excepted) was achieved in San Luis Potosí (nearly 8.6:1) and in Chihuahua (about 6.5:1). Perhaps we can best appreciate the potential total impact of enforcement at the local level by observing an (apparently) extreme case—Chihuahua—where the issue of only 98 passports led a total of 160 people to choose exile, despite the fact that 80 percent of the *expulsos* claimed no dependents.[3] The reality of this impact—again, in the extreme—may be appreciated by noting the extent of actual departures through Veracruz in the final days of March 1829 (table 4). The twenty-five probably wealthy Spanish fathers who embarked at Veracruz between 28 March and 1 April took with them 112 dependents. The number of children and wives accompanying *expulsos* decreased rapidly, however, as the less affluent made their way to the ports.

The federal government attempted to rectify its figures and to assess the extent of the expulsion by means of a circular of 10 October 1829 calling for "final reports." Unfortunately, the responses of only fourteen federal entities are preserved, making final estimates difficult (see table 10). But in virtually every case the data from October is clearly superior to that provided by the earlier reports to Congress (table 5). In the states controlled by "radical Yorkinos"—notably, Michoacán and Oaxaca—all *expulsos* owed their fate to the state law, while all exceptions resulted from the federal decree. In the fourteen

TABLE 5

RECAPITULATION OF THE 1829 REPORTS TO CONGRESS
ON ENFORCEMENT OF THE EXPULSION LAW

| Date of Report | Passports | Exceptions | | | | Total Cases |
		Perpetual	Temporary	Sons of Americans	Total	
25 April	2,194	141	281	5	427	2,621
22 May	857	219	313	0	532	1,389
21 August	360	713	293	1	1,007	1,367
Total	3,411	1,073	887	6	1,966	5,377

Sources: AGN, Ramo de Expulsión, leg. 18, tom. 29, exp. 2, fols. 4, 14–15, 21.

TABLE 6
SPANIARDS AFFECTED BY THE 1829 EXPULSION
(estimates)

	December 1828	March 1829	Difference
Californias (Territories)	63	63[a]	—
Chiapas	55	40	−15
Chihuahua	143	149	+6
Coahuila y Tejas	53	45	−8
Colima	5	4	−1
Durango	219	115	−104
Federal District	200[b]	1,746[c]	+1,546
Guanajuato	292	226	−66
Jalisco	284[b]	367	+83
Mexico	339	201	−138
Michoacán	126	94	−32
Nuevo León	77	84	+7
Nuevo Mexico	13	13	—
Oaxaca	442	220	−222
Puebla	556[b]	852	+296
Querétaro	232	83	−149
San Luis Potosí	214	172	−42
Sonora y Sinaloa	145	23	−122
Tabasco	80	46[a]	−34
Tamaulipas	130	27	−103
Tlaxcala	30	22	−8
Veracruz	404	528	+124
Yucatán	386	339	−47
Zacatecas	343	225	−118
Total	4,831	5,684[c]	790

Sources: Sims, La Expulsión, table 26, pp. 232–33; AGN, Ramo de Expulsión, legs. 1–5, 7–10, 13–15, 17, 22 3/4–23, 26.
   a. Figures reflect the addition of Spaniards noted in sources other than the reports of 1829.
   b. Notoriously understated figures.
   c. The results of heavy in-migration from the states.

federal entities reporting in October, expulsions were nearly double the number of exceptions, revealing a more severe enforcement than indicated by earlier figures (table 10).

Nearly one-third of the resolutions affected Spaniards living in the Federal District; two-thirds of resolved cases pertained, in fact, only to residents of the Federal District, Puebla, Veracruz, Jalisco, and Yucatán. The remaining one-third of the petitioners were dis-

TABLE 7
SUMMARY OF ALL 1829 REPORTS

		Exceptions			Second Examination Exceptions		
	Pass-ports	Per-petual	Tempo-rary	Ameri-cans	Per-petual	Tempo-rary	Total
Californias (Territories)	—	—	—	—	—	—	—
Chiapas	5	7	4	—	—	—	11
Chihuahua	129	9	11	—	—	—	20
Coahuila y Tejas	17	3	12	—	—	—	15
Colima	—	—	—	—	—	—	—
Durango	67	18	28	—	—	—	46
Federal District	1,382[a]	112	247	5	159	2	364
Guanajuato	156	6	43	1	—	—	50
Jalisco	64	236	67	—	22	1	303
Mexico	82	94	25	—	—	—	119
Michoacán	10	—	3	—	—	—	3
Nuevo León	58	10	11	—	—	—	21
Nuevo Mexico	2	3	—	—	—	—	3
Oaxaca	177	31	29	—	6	1	60
Puebla	724	66	62	—	33	10	128
Querétaro	49	8	17	—	—	—	25
San Luis Potosi	120	9	5	—	—	—	14
Sonora y Sinaloa	12	7	4	—	—	—	11
Tabasco	—	5	3	—	—	—	8
Tamaulipas	—	12	15	—	—	—	27
Tlaxcala	6	3	3	—	—	—	6
Veracruz	192	102	234	—	—	—	336
Yucatán	3	305	31	—	—	—	336
Zacatecas	158	27	33	—	—	—	60
Total	3,411	1,073	887	6	220	14	1,965

Sources: AGN, Ramo de Expulsión, leg. 18, tom. 29, exp. 2, fols. 4, 14–15, 21.

  a. Sentries reported, apparently without foundation, that about 5,000 Spaniards left the Federal District between 6 January and 23 April 1829.

persed among nineteen entities, none of which contained more than 226 *peninsulares*.

As table 9 shows, I found only 2,181 documented cases of exceptions or pending exemptions among archival records. The largest decline among *peninsulares* during 1829 occurred in Puebla, followed by Oaxaca and Zacatecas. By year's end, the Spanish community in Mexico City was apparently larger than it was the previous December —obviously, because of migration from the states. Following the first general expulsion, the federal entities with the largest *peninsular* populations were Puebla, Oaxaca, Veracruz, Yucatán, Zacatecas, and Mexico. By December 1829, however, most *peninsulares* were in the Federal District, Veracruz, Yucatán, and Jalisco, or 61.4 percent of the total—up from 26.4 percent in December 1828. The Federal District now harbored about 16.7 percent of the Spaniards, while Veracruz and Yucatán each contained 15.4 and Jalisco 13.9 percent, respectively.

Closer observation of the groups affected by the expulsion suggests what was actually occurring at the local level. Most passports issued in the states went to Spaniards residing in the capitals—nearly two-thirds in the cases of Puebla and Zacatecas, for example.[4] This fact helps account for the distribution of occupations among passport recipients. Roughly half of the fifty-five *expulsos* who departed through Veracruz during the first five days of enforcement had been engaged in commerce. During June in Tabasco fifteen of the twenty-two passport recipients were merchants. Spaniards did not dominate a less visible profession: medicine and surgery. In the Federal District, among seventy-four such specialists, only three were Spaniards.[5] *Peninsular* merchants and grocers (*pulperos*) were numerous and highly objectionable in unsettled times. The case of the clergy, both regular and secular, was quite different. Whereas the expulsion of 1828 had a marked effect upon mendicants (although much less on parish priests), the 1829 purge apparently dealt more lightly with the clergy. Reports revealed that up to 28 percent of the 151 Spanish friars were expelled; this would account for the entire numerical decline in regular clergy (thirty-eight) for 1829–30. The number of secular clergy fell by 160 during the same period.[6]

The cost of the second expulsion was troublesome, given the fact that requests for travel funds were honored, until the federal treasury ran dry, during a period of increasing discontent among the ranks of an unpaid army and bureaucracy. Though it is uncertain how much was spent, or how many *peninsulares* received aid, the result can be assessed in terms of the five entities for which reports were reasonably complete. Tamaulipas probably spent the least—375 pesos —and the Federal District the most—8,705 pesos. It cost Mexico about 38 silver pesos in travel funds to expel each Spaniard, not counting the rich, of course, who normally received no aid. It seems

TABLE 8
SUMMARY OF ACTIONS TAKEN WITH RESPECT TO THE LAW OF 1829

	Passports Issued	Exceptions Granted	Resolution Pending	Total Cases
Californias (Territories)	—	—	—	63[a]
Chiapas	14	11	15	40
Chihuahua	129	20	—	149
Coahuila y Tejas	24	21	—	45
Colima	—	4	—	4
Durango	46	61	8	115
Federal District	1,382	364	—	1,746
Guanajuato	153	6	94	226
Jalisco	64	303	—	367
Mexico	82	119	—	201
Michoacán	82	9	3	94
Nuevo León	58	26	—	84
Nuevo Mexico	9	3	1	13
Oaxaca	150	70	—	220
Puebla	724	128	—	852
Querétaro	63	20	—	83
San Luis Potosí	107	65	—	172
Sonora y Sinaloa	12	11	—	23
Tabasco	38[a]	8	—	46[a]
Tamaulipas	—	27	—	27
Tlaxcala	14	8	—	22
Veracruz	192	336	—	528
Yucatán	3	336	—	339
Zacatecas	154	71	—	225
TOTAL	3,500	2,090	31	5,684[a]

Sources: Reports of 1829, adjusted by responses to the circular of 10 October (AGN: Ramo de Expulsión, leg. 18, tom. 29, exp. 2; ibid., leg. 23 3/4, tom. 55, exps. 54–56, 87–94, 106).
   a. Results from adding Spaniards noted in sources.

that government directives urging frugality meant more in states where the Spanish were most detested by local officials than in entities with less hostile governments. Ironically, the greatest generosity was shown by Coahuila y Tejas, the state closest to New Orleans and most in need of retaining immigrants.[7]

In fact, the entire northern periphery of Mexico was adversely affected by the law of 20 March. Colonization remained no more than an idea, so long as the *peninsular* threat and internal political divisions distracted the republican government. Alamán called the

TABLE 9
DECLINE IN SPANISH MALES IN MEXICO DURING 1829
(estimates)

	Dec. 1828	Dec. 1829	Decline in Number	Decline in %
Californias (Territories)	63	60ª	3	4.8
Chiapas	55	26	29	52.7
Chihuahua	143	20	123	86.0
Coahuila y Tejas	53	21	32	60.4
Colima	5	4	1	20.0
Durango	219	69	150	68.5
Federal District	200ᵇ	364	+ 164ᶜ	+ 82.0ᶜ
Guanajuato	292	73	219	75.0
Jalisco	284	303	+ 19ᶜ	+ 6.7ᶜ
Mexico	339	119	220	64.9
Michoacán	126	12	114	90.5
Nuevo León	77	26	51	66.2
Nuevo Mexico	13	4	9	69.2
Oaxaca	442	70	372	84.2
Puebla	556ᵇ	128	428	77.0
Querétaro	232	20	212	91.4
San Luis Potosí	214	65	149	69.6
Sonora y Sinaloa	145	11	134	92.4
Tabasco	80	8	72	90.0
Tamaulipas	130	27	103	79.2
Tlaxcala	30	8	22	73.3
Veracruz	404	336	68	16.8
Yucatán	386	336	50	13.0
Zacatecas	343	71	272	79.3
Total	4,831	2,181	2,650	100.0

Sources: December 1828 data from Sims, Expulsión, pp. 232–33, table 26; December 1829
estimates result from adding "exception granted" to "resolution pending" figures from table 8.
    a. Author's estimate; reports lacking in AGN, Ramo de Expulsión and Ramo de Gobernación.
    b. Notoriously underrepresented figures.
    c. Represents a gain in population.

attention of Congress to the problem in early 1830, after the fall
of the Yorkinos, and sought to facilitate the return of Mexican families exiled to New Orleans. The expulsion itself did lead to some settlement on the frontier, but the number expelled from those regions
far exceeded this incidental influx.[8]
    The greatest cost of the expulsion, of course, was the loss of the

TABLE 10
RESPONSES TO THE CIRCULAR OF 10 OCTOBER 1829
IN FOURTEEN FEDERAL ENTITIES

	Expelled by			Excepted by					
	State Law	Fed. Law	Total	Congress	Temporary	Perpetual	Total	Pending Resolution	Totals
Chiapas	—	14	14	—	3	8	11	15	40
Chihuahua[a]	—	31	31	9	7	15	31	—	62
Coahuila y Tejas	—	24	24	16	—	—	21[b]	—	45
Colima	—	—	—	3	—	1	4	—	4
Durango	—	46	46	—	31	30	61	8	115
Guanajuato	—	153	153	6	5	58	69	4	226
Michoacán	82	—	82	—	3	6	9	3	94
Nuevo León	—	29	29	11	6	9	26	—	55
Nuevo Mexico	—	9	9	—	—	3	3	1[b]	13
Oaxaca	150	—	150	8	8	54	70	—	220
Querétaro	13[c]	50	63	—	—	20	20	—	83
San Luis Potosi	—	107	107	2	26	37	65	—	172
Tlaxcala	—	14	14	—	2	6	8	—	22
Zacatecas	—	154	154	3	35	33	71	—	225
Total	245	631	876	58	126	280	469	31	1,376

Sources: AGN, Ramo de Expulsión, leg. 22 3/4, tom. 55, exps. 54–56, 87–94, 106.
  a. Apparently incomplete figures.
  b. Includes Spaniards from other states.
  c. Six were excepted by federal law but not by state law. They were consequently denied residence in Querétaro (exp. 87, fol. 4).

Spaniards themselves, although nativists were loath to recognize the fact. While one purpose of the expulsion was to rid Mexico of internal threats to its security, the result, ironically, was to strengthen the power of the Spaniards at Havana and to hasten the day of the Spanish invasion.[9] The significance of the loss may also be appreciated from the occupations of forty Spaniards who registered with the Mexican consul at Bordeaux between 20 March and 14 September 1829: these included fourteen military officers, ten government employees, eight merchants, five clerics, a landlord, and a student.[10] Among the military were an editor of *El Sol* (Codorniu), a colonel, and five lieutenant colonels. Others included a former general treasurer of customs, an administrator of customs, and a general commissioner of war.

Capital drain was a serious problem in 1829, as it had been the previous year. While the final amount of bullion and specie shipped to New Orleans is uncertain, we can reconstruct the arrival of a portion of the gold and silver shipped to Bordeaux, the principal European haven for the exiles. Alamán contended that 12 million pesos in specie left Mexico with Spanish capitalists during the first and second expulsions, and Britain's Minister Ward attempted in vain to assess the critical situation in view of capital flight and declining production in the mines.[11] Receipts at Bordeaux between 27 February and 14 September 1829 totaled 2,075,353 *pesos fuertes*, plus fourteen sacks of uncounted pesos; 4,350 ounces, two ingots, and one bag of gold; and eleven ingots, four bars, a barrel and 542 marks of silver, plus forty-three ingots of mixed gold and silver. And smuggling precious metals may have been common. A part of the capital may have belonged to *peninsular* exiles in New Orleans, such as merchant Pedro de León y Collantes.[12] Juan de Dios Cañedo had observed in December 1828 that *expulso* merchants at Bordeaux "converted themselves into proprietors of Franco-Mexican commerce, inciting the Spanish government to reconquest."[13] In sum, a considerable amount of bullion and specie, representing only a part of the total export (that recorded by the Mexican consul), left Mexico.

Owing to the flight of specie, production in Mexican mints, which had declined to 8 million pesos by 1826, was stepped up to over 10 million pesos by 1827–28, and, finally, to better than 12 million during 1829. This exceeded the previous high attained in 1819, and was the greatest minting of the First Federal Republic.[14] The stimulus was clearly the export of specie by *peninsulares*, which meant not only a scarcity of circulating medium but also a bankrupt treasury.

The persecution of Spaniards is also reflected, in complex ways, in the volume of foreign trade. While 1828 witnessed a sudden collapse of imports, 1829 offered an even gloomier picture, with the exception of a roughly 20 percent gain in imports from Great Britain. Recovery came suddenly, even remarkably, with the establishment of the Bustamante regime in 1830. It is equally clear, however, that the expulsions of 1828 and 1829 had a "positive" effect on the volume and value of Mexican exports, which enjoyed their best year of the First Federal Republic in 1829.[15] This is explained by the fact that the principal export of the period was bullion, which ranked far ahead of dyewoods, the only other important export. The flight of specie was hardly a positive sign.

Since the federal government's income was derived largely from revenues produced by fees levied on goods passing through the ports, Mexico suffered a radical decline in funds accruing to the federal treasury. A roughly 10 percent gain at Veracruz, and 13 percent for all ports, occurred between the cessation of enforcement of the 1828 expulsion and the exhaustion of the treasury in 1829. But this was followed by an extraordinary collapse during the July 1829–June 1830 fiscal year, occasioned in part by the Spanish invasion at Tampico. This decline was more than 28 percent overall and almost 40 percent at Veracruz—a development worth stressing, in light of the bankruptcy of the Guerrero government in late 1829.[16] Indeed, the collapse of the treasury was partly the result of the expulsion, which caused a drain on the federal commissaries throughout the republic by the payment of suspended employees and travel funds and led to a disruption in imports, thereby rendering European merchants at Veracruz unable to pay their duties to the treasury. These problems are stressed in the correspondence between Pakenham and Bocanegra and the petitions of British, French, and German merchants at Veracruz. Matters improved in the summer of 1830, once the second expulsion was ended.[17] The recovery of trade in the early 1830s, and the resulting influx of revenue into the federal treasury, were crucial to the survival of the Bustamante regime.

An undetermined proportion of Mexico's commerce continued to be controlled by foreign merchants, who had gained in power since Independence, although their numbers had declined because of the expulsions. Spanish middlemen, who served as links between the large English merchants and European and Mexican retailers, still remained. North American, French, Spanish, and German merchants continued to be overshadowed by their British rivals.[18] In fact, the second expulsion had an unforeseen negative effect on U.S. trade with Mexico. The ships that transported *peninsulares* produced an increase in U.S. tonnage, of course, but many were attracted from European ports and arrived laden with European goods, so that, in the words of Consul Taylor, "The commerce of the merchants of the United States with this port [Veracruz], exclusive of tonnage, is now reduced to almost Zero."[19] It seems logical that the arrival of so many *peninsular* merchants in New Orleans, carrying at least a portion of their capital and experienced in Mexican commerce, should revive "United States" trade, and, indeed, it was soon rejuvenated. One need only recall the impact, noted earlier, on Bordeaux following the first expulsion. However, the principal goal of the exiles in New Orleans was to return to Mexico, either as conquerors—should Spanish plans bear fruit—or as chastised husbands and fathers, should Ferdinand's imperial ambitions fail.

9

Spain Attempts Reconquest, 1829–1830

M E X I C O ' S   E C O N O M I C decline and political tumult led the Spanish monarchy to believe that the reconquest of "New Spain" might be easily accomplished. The resulting Spanish invasion at Tampico in July 1829 has been considered quixotic, without possibility of success, and essentially unrelated to events in Mexico. And yet it was a logical consequence of the expulsions of 1827–29. The armed conflict disrupted enforcement of the second expulsion and hastened the fiscal and political destruction of the Guerrero regime and the collapse of the Yorkino party.

Armed clashes between Spain and Mexico commenced anew in December 1826, when the Mexican navy began an effective campaign along the coast of Cuba and in the Atlantic Ocean against Spanish trade. Spain countered by ordering warships to Mexican waters where in December 1827 they captured the *Guerrero*, killing its North American captain, David Porter. Hostilities continued, and along with a severe decline in the number of Spanish-born residents of Mexico during the anti-Spanish campaign, contributed in 1827 to Madrid's decision to invade the "rebel kingdom." Invasion plans were delayed by rebellions in Spain's own provinces, following the French withdrawal from the peninsula. Frequent reports in 1827–28 that Spanish troops were about to attack Mexico all proved to be false alarms.[1] Mexico's agents in Europe observed the activities of wealthy Spanish and criollo exiles in Bordeaux and Paris. Such a group, including ex-nobles, had tried unsuccessfully to return to Mexico in January 1828, during Bravo's brief rebellion. Minister Cañedo noted in December 1828 that exiled Spaniards had gained control of Franco-Mexican trade and were attempting to convince the Spanish government to undertake the reconquest of Mexico. And, in fact, Mexico's agent in London, Vicente Rocafuerte, reported in March

1829 that Ferdinand VII had promised 8,000 soldiers for an expedition against "New Spain."[2]

Wealthy merchants were the principal financial supporters of such plans. The Spanish established duty-free trade at the port of Cádiz in part to win over the exiled merchants. But Mexico's ports were closed to Spanish commerce and on 7 July 1828 the president of the Federal Republic of Central America declared that all trade with Spain was prohibited and all ports closed to Spanish ships because of Ferdinand's hostile plans. Nor would agents from Spain be permitted to enter Central America.[3] The Spanish government, backed by the merchants, saw with the closing of every port between New Orleans and Colombia that a portion of their mercantile interests would be irretrievably lost unless military action was taken.

Planning the Reconquest

The expulsion of Spaniards in 1829 both inhibited and assisted the *peninsular* cause. It is a fact that some Spaniards communicated with Havana; at least seventy-seven persons were compromised by intercepted correspondence, and there were connections between *peninsulares* in Mexico and exiles in New Orleans. While the departure of so many weakened the Spanish network throughout Mexico, it also provided potential investors for the reconquest as well as experienced and knowledgeable military veterans among the *capitulados*. Some of the latter were soon planning an expedition into Texas, and at least one worked on a plan for the reconquest of Yucatán, even suggesting its independence.[4]

Eugenio Aviraneta—in the view of the novelist Pío Baroja the archetypal Spanish conspirator of the period—became a principal source of plans for reconquest. In October 1827, on the eve of the first expulsion, he, together with the monarchist Padre Bringas and some wealthy Spanish merchants, left "voluntarily" for New Orleans and began to plot with local and New York Spanish merchants. They hoped to exploit existing social and ethnic cleavages in Mexico and to sow discord between criollo generals and those of Indian or mestizo origins. Since this distinction resembled differences between Escoceses and Yorkinos, there was a possibility, they thought, that the Yorkinos would go over to the reactionary cause.[5] Aviraneta's first plan proposed to act in accord with the third article of the Treaty of Córdoba—rejected by the Spanish Cortes in 1821—placing a Spanish prince on the Mexican throne. The governor of Cuba did not forward this proposal to Spain, knowing the crown's past hostility to separatist solutions. Though no approved plan existed as yet, by April 1828 efforts were already under way to recruit the recent exiles in New Orleans.[6]

The reconquest was discussed by the Spanish Council of State from the end of 1827 until 29 May 1828 before a definite decision could be taken. Exiles in Spain advised the king that 15,000 men would be needed, with 6,000 held in reserve, and another division based in Cuba. They considered six months sufficient time for a successful campaign. Brigadier generals Angel Laborde and Isidro Barradas were named on 21 August to head the expedition. The Council of Ministers resolved on 28 October to proceed with the reconquest and authorized the ministers of war and finance to draw up a plan. And, finally, on 7 April 1829 a royal order sanctioned the expedition to Mexico and named Barradas to lead it.[7] In reality, the Spanish plan was being formed in Cuba, though the island's government was none too keen on the enterprise. The original plan, authored by Captain General Vives and Aviraneta, called for a rapid attack on the fortress of San Juan de Ulúa in Veracruz harbor, using Spanish troops and mulattos, followed by an attack on the city of Veracruz. But this plan had to be abandoned due to the efficiency of Mexican espionage agents who intercepted letters between Aviraneta and his Veracruz contact "Montiel."[8]

As planning progressed, the regent at Havana, Pinillos, was guaranteed troops and full financial authority. Aviraneta developed a second plan that called for bribing those within Rincón's Veracruz battalion who were inclined to the Spanish side. After 3,000 men had disembarked at Mocabo and Antón Lizardo, just south of Veracruz, these bribed men were to betray their commanders and seize San Juan de Ulúa while the Spanish took Veracruz.[9] Aviraneta believed that even if the troops failed to capture the fort, the Spaniards would soon be able to affect its surrender. Propaganda was stressed by the plotters. In New Orleans liberal *expulsos* launched the newspaper *El Español*, supporting a constitutional monarch "to rid Mexico of the evils which were destroying it." The Spanish government paid thirty pesos a month to this periodical, while monarchist exiles in New York published three others.[10]

Barradas's arrival at Havana on 2 June 1829 with the royal order of invasion was met with little enthusiasm. Following initial discussion, the general inclination was "to obey but not comply" in time-honored fashion. According to Aviraneta, when Barradas threatened to appeal directly to the king, the principal officials of Cuba reluctantly agreed to carry out the order. The brigadier had spoken primarily to exiles

who assured him that the people of Mexico, under the influence of
the clergy, would join royalist ranks as soon as troops were landed.
Aviraneta claimed to have attempted to convince Barradas that the
only support would come from Indians who hated their masters, but
to no avail.[11] Madrid was determined to implement its plan for the
"pacification" of "New Spain," despite the adverse opinion of officials
in Havana. Field Marshal Juan Sanllorente and Col. José Osorio were
sent to Havana on 20 July to discuss the royal intentions with Vives
and to ascertain the measures the governor had taken.[12]

Mexican Prewar Policy

By January 1829 Victoria's weakened government recognized all too
well the intentions of the *gachupines*. Governor Lopes of Yucatán had
learned that two expeditions from Cuba were planned for March–
April—the first to consist of 20,000 soldiers under General Morales
and a second of 3,000–4,000 men with Barradas in command. Victoria ordered the military commanders of Yucatán and Tamaulipas to
prepare their defenses, though it was unclear where funds might be
found.[13] As evidence mounted that the Spaniards actually would invade, pressure grew in April and May for a complete expulsion of
peninsulares. The federal government resisted, however, and chose to
abide by the law of 20 March, continuing to grant exceptions when
merited.[14] The more radical Yorkinos concluded that the grand master
of their rite treated internal enemies with excessive moderation.

In June Guerrero was informed by a Mexican agent at New Orleans—a former Spanish officer, Col. Feliciano Montenegro—of new
preparations under way in Cuba. The exiles were active in New Orleans, he reported, and an expelled officer named Boado was in
charge of recruiting *expulsos* for Havana. Three regiments of Spanish
troops, consisting of 5,000 men, with four months' supplies, were
said to be ready for departure from Cuba, and three or four other
regiments were expected to join them. Barradas's contingent was
bound for Yucatán. Montenegro urged an assault on Cuba to forestall
the plot.[15] Despite overwhelming evidence of an imminent invasion,
internal conflict in Mexico did not cease. Even a 16 June report in
El Español to the effect that an expedition would leave Havana on
24 August for Campeche, and a second contingent, of 6,000 men,
would leave later did not convince some skeptics. The Escoceses were
claiming as late as 20 July that the Spaniards would not invade. After
21 July, when the reality of the Spanish attack became clear, Yorkinos
and Escoceses were finally able to work together. The government

used men of both parties in the defense effort without discrimination. The conservative Luis Cuevas later claimed that during the days of the invasion, "even the name they had called the enemies of the popular party [Bourbonists] disappeared" in the common effort to expel the invader.[16]

As the expedition sailed for Mexico, the governors of coastal states, particularly Veracruz, organized patriotic juntas in each municipality to gather funds for the defense effort. Yucatán's governor collected over 100,000 pesos in this manner. These governors were also concerned about concentrations of Spaniards in their states. *Peninsulares* who had escaped expulsion in 1829 were placed in a difficult situation, since anti-*gachupín* sentiment was certain to grow as blood was spilled. The governors of Yucatán and Veracruz reacted differently to resident Spaniards. Santa Anna in Veracruz requested permission to arrest *gachupines* in the event of war, and authority was granted. The port was closed to avoid the flight of large sums of money, and additional *peninsulares* were prohibited from entering Veracruz. But in Campeche, when the order was given to arrest the Spaniards, the military commander demurred, protesting that he would vouch for the security of the local *peninsulares*.[17]

By 4 July, there was speculation that Tampico would be the site of the invasion, as a result of the sudden abandonment of the town by many of its Spanish residents. Curiously, not even Barradas knew his final destination until the expedition was on the high seas. Forty ships carrying up to 3,556 men left Havana on 5 July to rendezvous at Cabo Rojo, near Tampico.[18] Reports reached Mexico City on 1 August that Spanish ships were off Pueblo Viejo, near Tampico, and, in response, Mexicans hastened to enlist in the civic militia. Anti-Spanish violence broke out in the capital, but was ended quickly. In Tampico, the remaining *peninsulares* were less fortunate, partly because the federal government was not fully aware of events there.[19]

Policy in Response to War

Guerrero publicly acknowledged the Spanish invasion on 21 August 1829, cautioning that the Barradas expedition was only the vanguard of a larger army yet to arrive. The Spanish general had promised "that the people would retain their positions, have their seniority recognized and, in addition, a half ounce of gold would be given to those who presented themselves with a gun." The president ridiculed the "generosity" of the Spanish offer. Guerrero explained his plan of defense. Permanent troops, plus both the active and local militia,

would form the army of operations. The forces would be divided
into five large sections under the command of Generals Santa Anna,
Garza, Herrera, Valdivieso, and Velázquez. Permanent troops would
be augmented by the militia as circumstances required, so as not
to leave "art and agriculture" unattended, nor to disturb the citizenry
more than necessary. This, in outline form, was the official strategy
that led to the defeat of the Spanish at Tampico. Correspondence
between Santa Anna and Guerrero reveals that, contrary to most his-
tories of these events, the general's actions were known to and approved by the government.[20]

The leaders of the expeditionary force placed undue hopes in
the efficacy of propaganda. Both Vives and Barradas had statements
prepared for circulation in Mexico. According to Minister Zavala,
the Spaniards expected to form an army of volunteers when they
landed, and they believed their rhetoric would help obtain supplies
and recruit men unhappy with the current regime. Barradas denied
that the Spaniards meant to avenge old injuries: "All would be forgotten because that is the royal will." He urged Mexicans to leave the
"banner of anarchy" and to have faith in royalist forces. Barradas
sent out proclamations aimed at Mexican soldiers to encourage desertion, inviting them to join the army of the crown, and claiming
that they would be "well uniformed, well paid, and better fed." Soldiers who joined him would not be used by the leaders of political
parties, "nor would they support the temples of Scottish rite or York
rite Freemasons." Padre Bringas, who had preached vociferously
against the forces of Independence, justified the invasion on religious
grounds. During the invasion, his influence was limited, if not coun-
terproductive.[21]

The Spaniards disembarked at Cabo Rojo, twelve leagues (40.9
miles) south of Tampico on 27 July 1829. The 3,000 troops had to
march north along the beach without water and with little food, having lost a major portion of their supplies during landing. After an
arduous trek, they occupied Pueblo Viejo and a small fort near the
sandbar, meeting no resistance. They were fortunate that the inhabitants had not destroyed the town as ordered. The only support Barradas received was provided by a small group of monarchists in the
capital who, according to Poinsett, tried to sabotage government activities. And even though exile periodicals supported the invasion
with exaggerated reports of anarchy in Mexico, predictably, opposition publications such as Bustamante's *Voz de la Patria* and the Escocés
El Sol were united behind the government.[22]

The administration's response was stalled by a lack of funds, as a result of two expulsions of Spaniards and, particularly, the closing of the port of Veracruz in July. To raise the necessary revenue, state governments ordered forced loans from both the remaining Spanish residents and those who had fled or been expelled. The model law of this type was passed in Zacatecas on 6 August. It stated that "the goods of all expelled foreigners were hereby seized; unmarried Spaniards were to surrender one-third of their capital as a loan; married couples without children a fifth; and widowers or widows without children one-third." All capital belonging to Spaniards who arrived with the invasion forces or residing in enemy territory would immediately be transferred to the state treasury. The property of expelled residents exiled in the United States or France, including cash, personal objects, and real estate, was seized and held on deposit. Exceptions were granted for Spaniards whose wives or children remained in Mexico. Traitors would receive the death penalty. Governor García of Zacatecas instructed local authorities: "The [treasurer] of each municipality will make a sworn manifest of all capital that the person possessed or administered and, in accordance with this measure, the officials will assure that the correct loan is made within two months."[23]

The federal government had reason to be especially concerned. Mexican troops had not been paid, and the president wished to order payment of salaries to all government employees and retirees as well, but he lacked sufficient funds. The Chamber of Deputies' response was to suspend salary payments to Spanish ex-employees and to retirees who resided outside the republic, until Mexican agents could establish the nature of their conduct during the invasion. A small group of Spaniards made voluntary donations—Cayetano Rubio, a merchant of San Luis Potosí, gave generously and even constructed fortifications.[24] But these financial measures were deemed insufficient and the federal government had to resort to forced loans.

In August, the Chamber of Deputies took more concrete steps, requiring the seizure of goods that belonged to Spaniards residing in enemy territory. Their Mexican families were to be given shelter. A more severe proposal was approved on 19 August: all goods belonging to *peninsulares* who lacked "obligatory heirs" were to be seized. In addition, the goods of Mexicans, Spaniards, and foreigners who took part in the expedition would be confiscated. The national law had the same provisions as its Zacatecas counterpart concerning the proportions of an individual's capital that must be loaned to the state. In addition, a forced loan of 2,395,849 pesos, exclusively for use during the war, was authorized, and a quota was apportioned to each state.[25]

Emergency funds were actively sought by the state governments. In Veracruz, Santa Anna received money from *peninsulares* in exchange for guarantees of personal safety. In Coahuila y Tejas, the loans described above were required, plus one-eighth of all goods owned by Spaniards with more than one child, and one-fifth of the goods of widowers or widows with only one child. In San Luis Potosí, Romero confiscated the material wealth not only of those who fought on the Spanish side, but also of all *peninsulares* residing outside the republic, and the governor decreed a forced loan of 100,000 pesos more than assessed by federal law.[26] As a result of federal and state measures, the stakes were very high for Spaniards, whether they supported the invasion or not.

In addition to attempts to put its financial house in order, the federal government also tried to neutralize the threat from resident *peninsulares* and military deserters. A September decree effectively disarmed all *gachupines*. To ensure that Mexican soldiers did not desert to the Spanish side, double pay was authorized for those who saw battle. But fulfilling this promise would not be easy, given the financial straits of the treasury. All deserters since 1821 could be pardoned if they reported for duty within fifteen days of the law's publication. To facilitate desertion by Spanish troops, Guerrero promised indulgence, and a few took advantage of the offer, including several black militiamen from Havana.[27]

The government acted decisively on the military front. On 7 August Santa Anna sailed with his army of 800 men from Veracruz northward to Tecolutla, where he was joined by cavalry and soon had a force of roughly 4,000. General Valdivieso recruited more than 4,000 soldiers in San Luis Potosí, while General Velázquez took command of 2,000 men from the capital. Mexico would soon have at least 10,000 poorly trained, irregularly equipped, and unpaid troops to face 3,000 veteran Spanish soldiers. Yorkinos and Escoceses were united in this action, and both were represented on the beaches of Tampico. As Santa Anna, Valdivieso, and Velázquez marched on Pueblo Viejo, Mexican militiamen watched the Spanish troops push northward along the beach, denying them access to higher and more traversable ground.[28]

Appeals were sent to the United States to halt the recruitment of *expulsos* in New Orleans, from which point a certain Lara was said to have transported 400 to Havana for the Spanish cause. Poinsett rather disingenuously denied that this was occurring.[29] The administration feared that additional Spanish units might be sent to attack

Veracruz or Coatzacoalcos. The minister of war reported on 19 August that another expedition might have left Havana on the fifteenth in support of the enemy forces at Tampico. Zavala briefed Congress, revealing that the Spaniards possessed contacts inside Mexico, they had been able to buy supplies for cash, Tampico had not been burned as ordered, and the Spaniards had settled in without resistance on 4 August. In order to meet this force, he contended, 1 million pesos would be needed to pay the troops currently proceeding to the war zone.[30]

While federal authorities wrestled with the fiscal crisis, some states took still stronger measures against resident Spaniards. In Jalisco *peninsulares* were prohibited from living within sixty leagues (204.5 miles) of the coast, on pain of a 2,000-peso fine or two years in the presidio at Mescala. But it proved to be impossible to enforce this law. Many expulsions had not been carried out because the government lacked funds to transport individuals to New Orleans, and state governments had to watch for suspicious activity among them. Despite difficulties, some governors still attempted to carry out expulsions. When the governor of San Luis Potosí ordered the Carmelites and Franciscans to depart, Friar Bartolomé de la Madre de Diós "began to gather people to help the Spanish expedition" while being held at Horcasitas.[31]

A motion was introduced into the Chamber of Deputies on 7 August to expel all *gachupines* not previously excepted, including those allowed to remain because they had "accounts pending." The measure did not prosper. Instead, on 30 August the government ordered a census of resident Spaniards who had not been excepted. Also, all *peninsulares* who entered the capital had to report to the authorities within two days of arrival or face a fine of twenty pesos.[32] But more important, very much against its wishes, on 25 August, Congress conceded extraordinary powers to the executive branch. In the process, it demonstrated the lack of confidence that people of property had in Guerrero and Zavala. Since Congress was unable to find a viable solution to the fiscal problem, it was compelled to take this dangerous step. The grant of extraordinary powers was modified to safeguard civil liberties: the president could not expel or take the life of a Mexican. Having granted such powers, Congress then adjourned, following assurances by Guerrero that they should not be unduly concerned about his exercise of this new authority.[33]

Extraordinary powers were in effect between 25 August and 18 December 1829, or until the Yorkino government collapsed. Guerrero neither violated his oath nor the 25 August law by arbitrary acts against civil liberties. Only two actions against Spaniards were ordered; the first involved the merchant Francisco de Paula Tamariz, who was sent back to Jalapa from the capital in late August, and the other concerned the polemicist Ibar. This Spaniard's *Muerte Política de la República Mexicana* was known for its diatribes that drew angry responses from the *Correo*. His arrest was provoked by a pamphlet of 2 September attacking the president, ministers, and other officials, and declaring that the exiled Bravo was "the only worthy man in the entire country." The president intended to expel Ibar quickly, as a Spaniard, through the port of Acapulco, but this was never done, and his pamphlets continued to appear intermittently. As a result of Ibar's attacks, Guerrero issued a controversial decree on 4 September requiring the media to support the federal and state governments during the emergency.[34]

Among the president's actions under extraordinary powers were fourteen grants of exception to *peninsulares*. Taken together, they reveal that Guerrero did not attempt to use his authority to further reduce the Spanish community in Mexico. On the contrary, the more conservative administration that followed charged that Guerrero and the Yorkinos had granted, indeed, "sold" federal passports liberally during extraordinary powers, resulting in a veritable exodus of returnees from New Orleans during 1830–31. Representatives of the exiles' Mexican families pressed the ministry of government for passports and were sometimes successful. Of the 147 *peninsulares* arriving at Veracruz between September 1829 and July 1830, however, only ten bore these documents.[35] Ironically, federal authorities were denounced by Yorkinos if they acceded in the admission of such individuals, who had often obtained their documentation with Yorkino mediation.

The anger of the Spaniards' defenders was severely provoked, however, by a presidential decree of 2 September that carried a step further a measure passed by Congress in early August. The law was aimed at raising revenue for the war. In summary, its four provisions authorized the federal government to claim the properties of all persons who had settled in enemy territory, half the income of Spaniards residing outside Mexico during the war, all estates seized by state governments through acts of their legislatures, and one-third of the Duke of Monteleone's profits as a loan. (The latter was the Italian heir of the conquistador Cortés.) This meant that the federation would now usurp what had been seized by the states, in many cases. Commissions were established in each federal entity to oversee compliance with the decree and to submit regular reports to the federal government.[36]

The law was only partially implemented and additional measures would be required. The governor of Michoacán reported as late as 18 December that he was still trying to determine which expelled Spaniards resided in enemy territory. The president soon ordered half salaries for *peninsulares* separated from their posts, and he clarified on 14 September how the forced loans were to be collected in the Federal District. Guerrero established a defense fund to be supplied by specific taxes, donations, and loans. The directors would receive no salaries. The most important tax designated to supply the fund was a 10 percent levy on the owners of rural and urban estates, to be paid quarterly, with the first installment due on 30 September. In the Federal District, the amount of the tax would be deducted from the forced loan, if applicable. In addition, there were to be taxes on carriages, fuel, foreign liqueurs, silver, and gold; stores and warehouses had to pay a business tax, and professionals with a title were required to pay twenty-four pesos annually. All public employees, including clergy, would be assessed between 3 and 5 percent of their income, as would all dependencies such as mines, fields, and stores. In addition, the president assigned half the general income of the federal government to the fund.[37]

Despite the evident necessity to raise revenue, the populace was not prepared to pay higher taxes to the Guerrero government. After acrimonious debate, the law was revoked on 6 November, regardless of accumulating evidence concerning Spain's aggressive plans. On other emergency measures there was greater unanimity, and the president could act without endangering national unity. On 15 September he abolished slavery throughout the republic, although the regional government in San Antonio, Tejas, determined that the decree could not be published there without risking revolt by the immigrant planters. Guerrero also issued a declaration of amnesty for his old enemies, the participants in the Bravo revolt of January 1828, primarily Escoceses. The exiles would be allowed to return and reassume their posts, though the status of the few Spaniards among them remained unclear.[38] To make room for senior military promotions, on 19 September the president retired the last four inactive Spanish generals in the Mexican army: Negrete, Echávarri, Orbegoso, and Saravia. They were assigned pensions equal to their salaries, so long as they did not reside in enemy territory (and they did not).[39]

Regionalism resurfaced as an additional political problem in September 1829. A rebellion was brewing to the north and west of Mexico City, in the midst of the Spanish invasion. The federal government had to frustrate Jalisco's attempt to form a "league of states," to include San Luis Potosí, Zacatecas, Guanajuato, and Michoacán.[40]

The Spanish Surrender

While the president struggled to maintain national unity, Spaniards in both Havana and Madrid were actively planning the next stage of the reconquest. A Spanish fleet under Laborde was expected to bring 6,000–7,000 men to Tampico and another 8.000–10,000 soon left Cádiz to join the expedition. Reinforcements were not dispatched from Cuba, however, and Barradas and his troops were stranded on a deadly mosquito-infested beach in the rainy season, with dwindling supplies, surrounded by determined Mexican defenders. To make matters worse for both sides, a hurricane swept the Tampico area 9–11 September, destroying a number of houses and everything edible nearby.[41] The fighting that had occurred was costly but indecisive, and yellow fever ravaged the Spanish ranks.

In view of the difficulty of their situation, the leaders of the expedition resolved on 12 September to surrender to General Mier y Terán. On the next day, the Spanish troops moved to more salubrious inland towns to await their withdrawal, while two officers returned to Havana to arrange transport. Barradas agreed to pay the costs of maintaining his men in Mexico as well as their transfer to Cuba. The treaty signed by Mexican and Spanish officials guaranteed the lives and property of the invaders and committed the Spanish, on paper and without consultation with Havana or Madrid, to make no further attempts against Mexican sovereignty.[42] The Spaniards had suffered serious losses, primarily from disease. Of the 3,000 who landed, 85 were killed in battle, 130 were wounded, and 863 were incapacitated by yellow fever. Every building in Tampico was used as a hospital. Mexican deaths in action totaled at least 135, and many more must have been wounded or perished from yellow fever.[43]

On 29 September, six ships of the Spanish squadron arrived to pick up the first contingent of survivors. Naturally, Laborde was dissatisfied with the surrender agreement and spitefully refused to discuss resupplying his ships, even though Mier y Terán attempted to impress upon him the desperate condition of his men. The Mexican general recommended that this incident be used in future anti-Spanish propaganda, revealing to potential defectors the treatment that awaited them in Spanish ranks. At Tampico death was unrelenting. Almost three months after surrender the U.S. consul noted, "About

500 Spanish soldiers are still in Tampico, but the illness is so serious that 15 or 20 die each day." In the end, only 1,792 survivors were taken to Havana, mainly in three convoys during November and December 1829.[44]

While the public celebrated the victory, the administration was far from certain that the threat had passed. In the Californias, a localized pro-Spanish revolt materialized. On 12 November, Joaquín Solís rebelled for Spanish rule in Monterrey, California, with a small entourage. Solís, a rival of Governor Echeandía, was able to take the presidio of San Francisco without resistance. While attempting to return to Monterrey, however, he was arrested by the governor's men. The movement was supported by the missionaries, all of whom were Spaniards; Solís had requested a force of mission Indians to assist in the revolt.[45]

In Cuba, at first, Vives tried to dismiss rumors of the defeat at Tampico, but on 20 October he began to make arrangements for the survivors' evacuation. Twice Vives had requested more troops to send to Barradas, and it was not until 29 October, more than a month after the defeat, that Spain sent 1,000 men to serve in Cuba and another 1,000 for transfer to Mexico. Supplies had been wanting as well, and—too late—three resupply ships from Havana arrived at Tampico.[46] Havana now had to concentrate on the preparation of a new expeditionary force.

An Invasion That Lost Its Way

The brief conflict of 1829 had brought into being numerous measures affecting Mexico's Spaniards which, in the best of circumstances, would have created problems. Under a state of war, some Spanish residents lost their wealth and even their lives as the price of complicity. The *peninsulares*' dreams proved illusory but their enemies suffered even more. Barradas's invasion contributed to the fall of Guerrero in a way unforeseen by the court of Madrid. The threat from Spain did not end with the collapse of the Yorkinos, nor did the danger to independence inherent in the presence of Mexico's Spanish community. Bustamante was forced to prepare the defense of the republic while seeking to restore the nation's credit and complete the expulsion process.

Even after reports of new preparations appeared in *El Español*, in European periodicals, and by way of the Mexican representative in London, there remained skeptics in Mexico who dismissed the possibility of a second invasion. The official *El Gladiador* faithfully reported all that the government knew of invasion plans and, in June 1830, urged the pro-Guerrero rebels in the South to end their resistance, thereby freeing the federal army to prepare for the external enemy. The "radical" *El Atleta*, the opposition periodical, doubted the seriousness of Spanish invasion plans after the defeat suffered by Barradas. The editors claimed, as Suárez y Navarro and others would later, that military preparations were motivated solely by the regime's fear of revolution.[47] A stepped-up revolt threatened for two reasons: first, the radicals' hopes of restoring Yorkino government, and second, the loss of political liberties resulting from the repression unleashed by the vice-president against Guerrero's supporters. Rumors of invasion abounded in late 1829 and early 1830, but the defenders of the ousted Yorkinos saw this as mere subterfuge. Suárez y Navarro later argued that Spain was too preoccupied with events in Europe to have seriously contemplated a new invasion. Bourbon policy was made in France, he reasoned, and the French monarchy was in danger of being overthrown. His logic was correct if applied after July 1830, but not before. The rumors of an invasion were used in Mexico to disarm the opposition in San Luis Potosí, Guanajuato, Zacatecas, Michoacán, Veracruz, Mexico, and Jalisco—regions that were hostile to a government that seemed to threaten the prerogatives of the states. The administration stressed the need for unity, citing the Spanish threat as justification, but it would be an error to underestimate the ambitions and independence of action of Ferdinand VII. On occasions, even *El Atleta* recognized indications of a possible second Spanish expedition.[48]

Planning for a Second Invasion

Barradas's isolation did not mean that interest in the reconquest was lacking in Madrid. On the contrary, even as the expeditionaries wasted away in Tampico, a wealthy merchant, Juan Bautista de Iñigo, offered to finance an army of 8,000 men, complete with arms, supplies, transport, and pay for four months. On 25 August 1829, the king ordered an extensive study to determine the number and types of troops, possible plans, and embarkation points that would be most feasible.[49] Throughout October and November 1829, the Guerrero government received reports from reliable sources that additional expeditionary troops had left Spain. And yet the defeat of Barradas forced Guerrero to halt the collection of taxes for the special war fund.[50] This left the administration virtually without revenue, since the expulsion of the Spaniards, the war, and trade restrictions had devastated foreign commerce, cutting off the government's traditional source of revenue—import and export duties.

Guerrero was realistic about the persistance of the Spanish threat. The government took steps to prevent, or at least delay, further aggression from Cuba. Even before the invasion of Tampico, the president had decided to support a counterattack on Spain's overseas possessions and commerce on such a scale that Governor Vives had to take a more defensive posture. The task was assigned to the deputy, Col. Ignacio Basadre. As Guerrero's agent, he traveled to Haiti in an attempt to convince the intrepid Jean Pierre Boyer to enter the struggle for Cuban independence. Boyer had already unified Haiti and Santo Domingo in 1822, and France had recognized the independence of the island in 1825. The controversial aspects of Basadre's mission concerned his efforts to commission privately owned ships to inhibit Spanish trade and to raise an army of blacks and mulattos to invade Cuba. According to the U.S. consul at Veracruz, Basadre hoped to obtain arms and crew members in the United States. The British, who were opposed to the idea, claimed that Basadre had twenty blank corsair licenses signed by the president. Mexico hoped to launch an internal war in Cuba between the nonwhite population and the Spanish. Mexican foreign minister Bocanegra denied this, of course.[51]

Conservatives, Escoceses, and even many Yorkinos condemned the mission, claiming that Basadre was himself a Spaniard. The *Correo* also opposed it, but even Guerrero's critics had to admit that the affair would surely increase Vives's reluctance to send troops abroad. A strong supporter of the plan was Mexico's representative in London, Vicente Rocafuerte, who favored an alliance of Mexico, Colombia, and Santo Domingo to punish Cuba's colonial regime.[52] Captain General Vives reacted as the Mexicans desired. The frigate *Casilda*, destined for the Mexican invasion, was diverted to patrol the east coast of Cuba to avert any threat from Haiti. Every vessel proceeding from Haiti toward Cuba was halted and inspected, and the patents for piracy granted by Basadre did some damage to Spanish trade.[53] An offensive of this scale was insufficient to deter Madrid, however.

Soon Cuban authorities received new orders to step up planning the reconquest of "New Spain." Even before the defeat of Barradas, rumors circulated that the peninsula would send some 7,500 men to Cuba before the end of 1829. In October, the king again asked the captain general to report on forces available in Cuba for the reconquest, what was needed from Spain, and the best way to obtain political support. His interest was increased by offers of aid to finance the expedition, particularly from two Mexican exiles, Iñigo and Guadalupe Azpiroz. Formal negotiations began with the council of ministers and the minister of finance in October. Iñigo requested details of the plan, which was to include 8,000 men and 390 officers. It appears, however, that no agreement was reached, probably because the cost appeared to be much greater than the merchants had imagined.[54]

Aviraneta recognized that the Mexicans would not willingly support the restoration of Spanish rule and recommended, once again, that a force of 25,000 men would be needed to accomplish the task. Meetings in Havana took into account the defense needs of the island, which was already undergarrisoned after the formation of the first invasion force. On 13 December, a war plan was finally accepted. The scheme favored taking Yucatán at the outset. After the seizure of Mérida, incorporation of Campeche and Tabasco could follow, then Guatemala and Oaxaca. The final recommendation of Cuba's authorities was to retain the roughly 1,800 survivors recently transported from Tampico and to add them to the island's defense forces. The crown should send 25,000 men, with an additional 6,500 reserves. The troops could leave Spain at the end of 1830, and fighting ought to occur between April and the end of June, to avoid both winter winds and the summer's deadly mosquitoes. The cost of such an invasion was estimated at 15 million pesos.[55]

There was a social rationale behind Vives's plan. These regions of Mexico possessed an Indian majority, which, from the Spanish perspective, meant a "safe" population. Vives believed Yucatán could be seized with 9,500 men, the same number required for the defense of Cuba. Colonial officials now doubted that all of Mexico could be retaken, given the prevalence of anti-Spanish sentiment and the loss of *penisular* influence there, as evidenced by the expulsion even of Spaniards with Mexican families. Not only had eight years of independence weakened the criollos' ties with Spain, but Mexico had also gained allies and recognition from England, France, and the United States. Compromise seemed realistic.

The Spaniards did not know it, but in December 1829 the restoration of more conservative government under Bustamante and Alamán came at an important time for Mexico's shrinking Spanish community. The fall of the Yorkinos indicated that colonial society and its mentality had not completely disappeared. In Mexico City, monarchist plans were surreptitiously revived between January and March 1830. The French vice-consul, Laisne de Villeveque, represented the Duke of Parma as a possible pretender to a Mexican throne, and a French envoy contacted the Yorkino Zavala with a proposal to crown a member of the Orleans family. Even Alamán spoke with the British agent Pakenham concerning a British prince. When such discussions became public, Minister Polignac of France insisted that his diplomats desist, assuring the Spaniards that France would not interfere with Ferdinand's attempt to reconquer his former colony.[56] Great Britain, while opposing Spanish plans for reconquest, did not seek to divert Mexico from its republican path.

Madrid persisted in its attempts to muster forces for the reconquest, and the Mexican government was kept well posted on Spanish plans, albeit with some delay. Nations friendly to Mexico, particularly Great Britain, applied diplomatic pressure in an attempt to block these schemes. But it seemed that nothing could inhibit Ferdinand's attempt at restored colonial glory. Alamán's efforts to obtain a consensus on the Spanish threat responded to genuine Spanish plans. From Havana, in mid-January 1830, Vives and Pinillos clarified for the ministry of war financial and military recommendations the junta had sent to the crown. Pinillos reported that 3 million of the 15 million pesos required could be obtained in Cuba, although Vives doubted it, since he had been unable to raise funds for the defense of the island itself. Vives now believed Yucatán could be taken with just 6,000 Spaniards, but he reported that the region, in comparison with other Mexican provinces, was too poor to generate sufficient revenue to cover the cost of the expedition. The captain general was concerned that the invasion would seriously drain Cuba's income, already inadequate for its own needs, thus weakening her defenses.[57]

The extent of Mexico's threat to Cuba is difficult to assess. Alamán called a halt on 3 January to Basadre's attempt to foster a revolution in Cuba. However, the Spanish minister in the United States, Francisco Tacón, continued to consider Basadre dangerous. Tacón reported in April that the Mexican agent was still at the court of Boyer in Haiti, attempting to arrange a declaration of war against Spain or an alliance that would open Haiti's ports to the warships of Mexico and Colombia. Boyer had reinforced fortifications around Santo Domingo and was rumored to have 3,000 men prepared to invade Cuba.[58]

Meanwhile, exiles in France and Spain were convinced that the reconquest of Mexico was imminent. The Mexican agent in Bordeaux, Murphy, forwarded a lengthy list of *expulsos* who left France for Spain in December 1829 and January 1830.[59] And the British intensified their attempts to avert war. Addington, Britain's envoy in Spain, reported that 2,000–3,000 troops had already been sent to Cádiz and a line of warships and transports waited to take them to Havana.

His orders were to dissuade Ferdinand from attacking Mexico, since this could result in a counterattack on Cuba and a war that would involve France, England, and the United States. By March, however, Addington had concluded that the Spanish government was deaf to British diplomatic pressure. An expedition larger than Barradas's only awaited funds to be launched.[60] Accordingly, on 24 March 1830, the Napoles regiment left Cádiz and in May the first contingent, consisting of 2,000 men under Field Marshal Juan Bellido, arrived in Havana. They were immediately sent to the interior for training. In April Havana received the news that Gen. Juan Llauder would lead a new expedition consisting of 10,000 troops.[61]

Mexico's defenses were sadly lacking. The governor of Puebla reminded Bustamante that the coast from Cabo Rojo to the south was completely unprotected and that Spanish warships had been sighted there. In particular, the bar of Tuxpan needed fortification. Veracruz requested that its central plaza and fortress be prepared for attack. It was suggested that the felling of the forest between Altamira and Tampico be suspended, since the trees facilitated the defense of the region.[62] Local and state governments took whatever action they could, since militias were to be used for coastal defense. Tamaulipas attempted to raise funds locally, in February 1830, although first the problem of monetary scarcity caused by the forced loans of 1829 had to be overcome. Spanish-owned property would be expected to help pay for the war. A local decree required that "all monies, whether earned or inherited, which belonged to former employees of the Spanish government and were held by someone within the state, must be deposited with the state."[63] The funds were used to prepare for the invasion and their return was promised when the Spanish government recognized Mexico's independence.

An alternative invasion plan was prepared in March 1830, not by the Spanish, but by a Mexican official, José Antonio Mejía, secretary of the Mexican legation in the United States. Mejía was a friend of Guerrero and respected by the Yorkinos. He had served as secretary to Santa Anna during the campaign against Barradas and commanded a battalion at Tampico. Still, on 31 March he met privately with Spain's Minister Tacón in Baltimore. Mejía exhibited a plan of twenty-four points, which Tacón immediately forwarded to the Council of Ministers in Madrid. The strategy was ingenious. Eight thousand men should be concentrated in Havana and 2,000 soldiers would land at Soto de la Marina around 1 January 1831, announcing that they were the vanguard of a large army destined to land in the same place. Two weeks later, a second contingent of 2,000 men would land at Coatzacoalcos, far to the south of Veracruz. Responding to the attack, the government would divide its forces to fight these two contingents. Later the bulk of the invading army, some 4,000 men, would attack Antón Lizardi near Veracruz and march toward Mexico City. The contingents at Soto de la Marina and Coatzacoalcos would reembark and converge on Antón Lizardi. The fleet was to remain there to supply the army. But the Spanish government, in a cautious mood, rejected the plan; Point 20 would have given Mejía important information regarding the Spaniards' network of spies and informants in Mexico—very useful counterintelligence for the Mexican government.[64]

As preparation for war advanced, in April 1830 the efforts of foreign merchants and bankers to exert diplomatic pressure on Spain were stepped up. The Committee of the Mexican and South American Association, composed of British merchants, petitioned the cabinet in London to take firm steps to prevent Spain from regaining control of her ex-colonies. British bankers also tried to block Spanish ambitions, since not only Mexico but all the former colonies were deeply indebted to British banks. In May 1830, the British envoy Alexander Baring was able to report that Spain might consent to a truce "of 20 or 30 years." Alamán considered this inadequate, however, since any agreement would probably require readmission of the *expulsos* and the reopening of commerce with Spain as well as other concessions. This could only cause resentment so long as Mexico's independence was not recognized.[65]

By mid-April, the administration was ready to begin the collection of defense funds. Bustamante asked the governor of each state to invite "all landowners, government employees, and others to subscribe to maintain one or more soldiers with food and clothing." Alamán exhorted contributors, remonstrating, "If the city of Cádiz . . . has offered to equip and maintain 2,000 men until they are at the coasts of this republic, Mexican patriots cannot do less." The administration estimated the number of men needed to bring all military units up to full strength, and orders were dispatched to begin training immediately.[66] Local governments determined the wages of a soldier —for example, in Tamaulipas, a salary of 19 pesos, 6 reales a month for a cavalryman, and 10 pesos, 6 reales for an infantryman. To mount, clothe, and arm a cavalryman cost 50 pesos, while 28 pesos sufficed to clothe and arm an infantryman. In April and May 1830, the supply officers of each region began to collect funds. Militia in northeastern Mexico were confined to their districts and "vagabonds and idlers" from Nuevo León were forcibly enlisted.[67] Money for salaries would remain with state governments, but funds for arming and mounting the men were remitted to the federal treasury. Donations in kind were accepted and then sold, with the proceeds going to the treasury. Federal bureaucrats and politicans were generous contributors, and donations came from church groups, villages, merchants, officers, and corporations. The largest donor in Tamaulipas was Brig. Felipe de la Garza, who pledged to pay the total cost of equipping twenty-five cavalry, amounting to 1,269 pesos.[68]

Funds were received from April 1830 until February 1831, by which time collections had reached 19,478 pesos, 3 reales. The revenue was subsequently spent maintaining military installations along the coasts and the northern frontier. The governor of Nuevo León used 976 pesos to assist the families of a division that had left for Tampico. The final disbursements were made in January 1832, when Alamán authorized expenditures for the soldiers stationed at the presidio in Nuevo León.[69] The funds were not used against the southern rebels.

The towns and landowners of Mexico supported these measures in the belief that an invasion was imminent. The government received and published information that was, naturally, months behind events. As a result, Mexico was not aware until February 1831 of the changes in Ferdinand's plan caused by the revolution in France on 30 July 1830. One clue that a change might be under way was the disappearance in August of *El Español* in New Orleans.[70] This revealed a sudden reversal of official support from Spain for proinvasion propagandistic journalism.

Even after August, however, there were new rumors of Spanish invasions. One had the *gachupines* landing anew at Cabo Rojo, this time with 5,000 men. In September, *El Gladiador* published changes in the invasion plan, leaked before the French revolt:

Approximately 4,000 men will depart from various ports in Spain. These ships will rendezvous off the Canary Islands, where 2,000 men are already stationed. The troops will . . . proceed to Havana where they will join 8,000 chosen soldiers. These 14,000 men will form the expeditionary army whose commander will be the Marquís de las Amarillas, one of the best and most experienced generals in the Spanish army.[71]

Foreign diplomats and merchants still believed in summer 1830 that an invasion was inevitable. Pakenham professed amazement that Ferdinand should believe it possible to regain control of Mexico. The consul described for his government Mexican preparations for war, which took the form not of increasing the size of the army, nor of solving the economic problem, but rather, of "readying all the male citizens of the republic to fight in voluntary units." In July the members of the South American Association in Mexico asked, in light of the latest intelligence, how best to protect British lives and property. Great Britain claimed neutrality, but London hoped to detain the invasion through the efforts of its consul in Madrid, "for purely humanitarian reasons."[72] As late as July, then, the British still believed that invasion threatened.

The Final Outcome

It was not British pressure but rather the revolution in France that made Ferdinand VII too insecure on his throne to send troops abroad, forcing him to postpone indefinitely his plans for the ex-colonies. Events in France were precipitated by Charles X, who had tried to exercise control over the elected parliament and rule as an absolute monarch. In response, the Parisians barricaded the streets. After three days of revolt, the Bourbons were dethroned. Although a new king was named—Louis Philippe of the House of Orleans—in Madrid, Ferdinand, who ruled as an absolute monarch and confronted a liberal party of his own, was forced to look to his future in Europe. Ferdinand's profound change of heart can be seen in the sudden denigration that support and supporters of invasion plans encountered after 19 July.[73]

In February 1831 it became clear to the Mexicans that the expected second invasion would not take place. Subsequently, Spanish landowners regained the right to obtain all profits from their Mexican investments, and capital deposited with the government was returned.[74] These were the first steps of the long and painful process toward the restoration of equal treatment for Spaniards and Mexicans. But, first, *expulsos* who attempted to return to their adopted land would face two additonal expulsion attempts, in 1833–34, aimed at those whose exceptions in 1829 seemed invalid. Not until 1836, after the death of Ferdinand, did Spain finally recognize the independence of Mexico. And only then could Spanish residents feel secure.

10

The Exiles Attempt to Return, 1829–1832

THE *EXPULSOS* SOON launched a protracted effort to re-enter Mexico. By early 1832, the numbers arriving at the ports exceeded one-third of the *expulsos* of 1829 at New Orleans. According to ministry documents, 380 Spaniards entered Veracruz harbor between June 1830 and February 1832, and at least 175 (46.1 percent) were allowed to disembark. Various pretexts were employed by returnees, including exception by "acts of Congress" in ninety-two cases.[1] As a rule, the longer one delayed arrival, the greater chance of success, especially for those who claimed illness. Three crucial but questionable aspects of Bustamante's enforcement policy were, first, the respect shown for dubious U.S. citizenship papers; second, the notion that returnees who alleged illness should be examined by medical juntas; and, third, that those who possessed questionable certificates of exception issued by a chamber of Congress might remain until their cases were resolved. Each of these resulted in the reappearance of unpopular *gachupines* and a loss of credibility for the government.

First Efforts to Return

In December 1828, the issue of whether to admit Spaniards bearing U.S. citizenship papers arose at Campeche. Such documents were readily available at New Orleans. During the Victoria administration, *peninsulares* were not allowed to disembark. The question was raised anew at Ciudad Victoria in February 1829, under the Guerrero government. If a *gachupín* had been abroad when the 1829 law was passed, upon returning he might be granted a thirty-day pass to the Federal District to arrange his affairs, after which he was expected to depart. On 20 March 1829, Minister of Government Agustín Viezca forbade the Mexican consulate at New Orleans to allow Spaniards to embark without federal permission. It would be necessary to repeat these instructions frequently, however, for they deterred few returnees.[2]

The Spanish invasion in July 1829 created a special situation at Tampico. Just before the invasion, the port commander had permitted Spaniards holding exceptions to embark for foreign ports, though he was not certain they could be readmitted. President Guerrero decided that when passports anticipated returns, individuals should be allowed to disembark. In the midst of the invasion, Guerrero instructed port authorities to permit Spaniards arriving in ships of friendly nations to land, provided they reembarked on the same vessels.[3] The port commander also requested a congressional decision concerning Spaniards with citizenship in friendly or neutral nations. Eventually, in response to Mexico's urging, the U.S. secretary of state issued new regulations for citizenship in Louisiana. As late as 1832, however, "United States citizens" were still arriving from New Orleans—Spaniards who had resided there, or in Havana, for only the past three years.

The salaries of ex-officeholders who remained in New Orleans during the Barradas invasion and abjured suspicious behavior continued to be honored. Funds were delivered to their wives or representatives in Mexico, once the Bustamante regime had restored government revenues. Salary and reentry into Mexico was denied if an *expulso* had sailed to Cuba, even against his will. In December 1828, Francisco Martínez y Flores had the misfortune to land at Havana. Embarking anew for New Orleans, his second vessel touched at Tampico with supplies for Barradas's forces, and he was arrested by Mexican authorities. In February 1830, Bustamante allowed Martínez to consult the medical junta. Manuel María Giménez, an Escocés aide to Santa Anna, faced a similar fate. Though Giménez possessed a large Mexican family, he was expelled in 1829. Stormy seas forced his ship to Cuba, where he was imprisoned for his role in the independence movement and on suspicion that he might be a Mexican spy. Upon release, Giménez was expelled, only to arrive in New Orleans and confront suspicion again, now by Mexico's Yorkino consul, who thought him a Cuban spy. When the consul refused to forward his appeal to Mexico, Giménez embarked during the Barradas invasion to offer his services to Mexico. Santa Anna and ex-Deputy Cipriano Blanco, a Spaniard, aided Giménez, who became a Veracruz merchant.[4]

Touching at Havana could mean that even a *peninsular* whose name was on one of the congressional lists of exceptions would find reentry difficult, as Miguel José Bellido learned. And yet a "dangerous" Spanish merchant such as Luis Guevara could obtain congressional permission to resume his activities in Tampico, despite the warnings of the vice-consul at New Orleans. A *gachupín* with a poor record of loyalty to the cause of independence might enter, if his family had influence and tenacity. Even an *expulso* with anti-independence sentiments, like Jalapa merchant Bernabé Elías, could contemplate returning in December 1829. Such intentions on the part of other "dangerous" Spaniards led Mexican agents abroad to dispatch numerous warnings. Any *peninsular* who had become ill might be allowed to disembark at Veracruz in 1829–31, but returnees could not count on federal financial aid to reembark for New Orleans. *Expulsos* returning from South America could not land at Acapulco; only the north Pacific port of Guaymas welcomed them.[5]

Bustamante Policy in 1830

That the new regime allowed a number of Spanish exiles to return, there is no doubt. This was probably not a planned policy but rather the result of an enforcement that adhered to a literal interpretation of the 20 March 1829 law, seasoned by favoritism. The new regime also set aside funds to restore stranded Mexican families to their native land. As Bustamante policy evolved, pamphleteers who opposed the vice-president and favored Guerrero's rebel front in the south attacked the regime, labeling it the *padrino* of the *gachupines*. Charges were often inaccurate or exaggerated, like those of *El Atleta* in February 1830, that participants in Barradas's invasion were being admitted —the few cases that occurred involved defectors.[6]

In November 1829, Guerrero had ordered the designation of locations other than the fortress of Ulúa or the ship *Congreso*, to which returnees who lacked permission could be confined while their cases were resolved. It was decided to house them aboard the corvette *Libertad*. Costs mounted, and by late December funds were no longer available. Alamán and treasury minister Rafael Mangino decided to consult Congress, cautioning Veracruz officials to continue their compliance with the expulsion law.[7] *Expulso* embarkations at New Orleans grew in early 1830.

To stem the tide of "illegals," it was necessary to assure that only those with ministry of government passports issued after 20 March 1829 were allowed to disembark. The single exception included in the instructions of 23 February was provided in the expulsion law itself: illness enabled the *expulso* to consult a medical junta, even though he had already been expelled. This important proviso resulted in an ex post facto increase, in 1830–32, in Spaniards excepted. On the following day, when fifteen Spaniards arrived at Veracruz, only the two with federal passports were allowed to disembark.[8] But arrivals increased in March.

The inevitable political repercussions necessitated a remedy. On 3 March, Bustamante instructed the commanders of all border and coastal states that no Spaniard eligible for expulsion under the law of 20 March 1829 be permitted entry, except those granted passports by Guerrero during extraordinary powers. Bustamante insisted that his own administration had issued no such documents. He also ordered the port commanders to produce lists of all Spaniards who had entered the republic during the past year, specifying the authority granting their passports. Any returnee who lacked merit under these rules should be reembarked. The issue stirred such heat that the Veracruz congress voted in early March to re-expel within fifteen days any Spaniard who, having departed under an 1821 capitulation agreement or any expulsion law, had returned, with or without a passport. The bill also limited the stay of a *peninsular* in transit to fifteen days.[9] The act was probably unenforceable, since it is not mentioned in extant appeals.

As arrivals mounted in March, *El Atleta* speculated that this resulted from expectations of reconquest—one vessel brought thirty-four Spaniards. The real source of exile hopes was the probability of being judged to be ill by the medical junta at Veracruz. Some returnees were frustrated by instructions that allowed those claiming illness to disembark only for the time required to be cured, denying them permission to travel. The passengers were usually merchants, many of whom had obtained permission from the Guerrero government to sail for New Orleans in the summer of 1829, when anti-Spanish sentiment was at its peak. Col. Antonio García Moreno had left Mexico during the armed action of December 1828, with permission for two years, and returned in February 1830. García claimed his departure from New Orleans was hastened by the hostility of Spanish agents there who sought in vain to recruit him for the invasion. He was held at Veracruz for lack of a passport.[10]

The presence of a *peninsular* majority among the Veracruz *facultativos* gave rise to complaints from local authorities. Governor Sebastián Camacho received a secret report from the chief of Veracruz Department on 13 March that revealed what was transpiring. The policy of allowing ill Spaniards to land and consult the junta had been formalized on 23 February 1830. The governor decided that final judgment in each case should rest with the department chief, a responsibility the latter felt unqualified to accept. The chief believed that abuses would continue unless consultations were denied. One alternative was to change the composition of the *facultativos* (six Spaniards, one foreigner, and two Mexicans). Recently, another Spaniard had been added, due to a Mexican member's absence.[11] The chief's suggestions were not acted upon, ostensibly because of a shortage of medical practitioners.

During the first three months of 1830, responsibility for the returnees was shared by the ports' civil and military authorities. When the state military commander could not provide lists of disembarked Spaniards, as requested by Facio, the Veracruz departmental chief was called upon to do so. As a civil employee, the chief consulted the governor, hesitating to respond. Alamán agreed on 30 March that all matters related to the return of Spaniards should be handled by civil authorities. The issue reemerged in April, when Facio granted García Moreno permission to move to Jalapa, violating the order that prevented waiting Spaniards from passing to the interior. When queried, Alamán noted that since the colonel had indeed been excepted by Congress, a passport was issued. Facio was told to leave Spanish matters to civil authority in the future, and he agreed.[12]

The willingness of the Mexican vice-consul at New Orleans to issue permissions for return complicated matters. The consulate was cautioned on 23 February that without authorization from the ministry, no passports should be given to *expulsos*. Alamán insisted on 24 March that no *expulso* should return solely on the basis of a passport issued at New Orleans: once at Veracruz such returnees had to be reembarked. Bustamante insisted that "no passport, permission, or certificate of any kind whatsoever, except those for 'review' [by the *facultativos*], should be issued at New Orleans." Only returnees with valid passports issued by the federal government could disembark. Alamán had reminded the vice-consul on 1 June that no "certificates of good conduct" should be given, since the *expulsos* had the impression that these alone were sufficient to gain entry.[13]

Uncertainty persisted concerning whether Spaniards who had departed either before or after being excepted should be allowed to reenter. When Camacho raised this important matter, Alamán consulted Congress. Of five *expulsos* arriving at Veracruz on 7 March 1830, only one was permitted to disembark. A ship anchored on 10 March carrying ten returnees, three of whom had federal passports granted under extraordinary powers, and all were allowed to land. The seven undocumented men wished to be seen by the *facultativos*.

Camacho urged adoption of a general rule to prevent entry by those he considered of "no utility to the nation"—the "very poor and miserable." The governor suggested that a guard be posted from the moment of arrival on each vessel transporting *peninsulares*, obliging the captain to identify passengers lacking legal prerequisites for admission.[14] The government demurred.

By April the situation seemed hopelessly out of control. Spaniards came in increasing numbers, and existing regulations proved incapable of stemming the tide. On 3 April, fourteen *expulsos* arrived in two ships, one from New York. The returnees fell into three categories: men who claimed illness and wished to consult the *facultativos*, others whose passports were granted during extraordinary faculties, and those who claimed exception by Congress in 1829. Most bore documents of good conduct issued at New Orleans. Col. Santiago Moreno y Urrío, who had a valid passport, was among the passengers. The political attitudes of some returnees led the departmental chief to protest that the regulations of 23 February had opened the port to dangerous individuals and denied any remedy. Of those arriving on 13 March, only two remained in detention and they too were likely to go free. Men like "Barón and Menacho, whose hatred of the republic was current in New Orleans," had disembarked. The chief concluded that "the means of receiving Spaniards must be altered by new measures," otherwise the resulting scandal will be useful "for the enemies of the actual order of things."[15] The trend continued, as twenty-three *expulsos* arrived at Veracruz on 18 April.

The return of so many Spaniards created a furor among Guerrero's defenders. *El Atleta* demanded to know why, since Bustamante professed concern, had he not declared all passports issued under extraordinary faculties null and void? (It accepted the regime's assertions that this was a major source of arrivals.) And why had expulsions ceased, especially of those who were en route to the ports when the invasion occurred? And it asked: "Could these [returnees] be so dense as to expose themselves to a fruitless journey, seeing the discouragement of those who had been repulsed?" The editors suspected the government of giving "secret orders" that *gachupines* be welcomed. In response, the progovernment *El Gladiador* provided the official explanation: Spaniards were present because the 1829 law was passed "to take money from the rich" and because of the actions of a previous government that, together with the *facultativos*, had made a commerce of the affair.[16]

Spaniards who lacked funds could not be re-expelled without financial aid. Customs administrator Pablo Gomes Valdés reported that the majority of the returnees lacked money, and if their entry was blocked, ship captains refused to return them to New Orleans without payment. The poverty of returnees proved to be the greatest obstacle to compliance.[17] There could be no financial solution, unless Congress voted new funds for the transport of rejectees to New Orleans—an unlikely event, given the rebellion in the south and the threat of Spanish invasion.

Contradictions in federal policy were such that officials in Veracruz feared they might be blamed for the fiasco. A U.S. vessel arrived on 20 April with twenty-three Spaniards; fourteen held federal passports, seven brought only certificates of "good behavior," and two had nothing at all. Gomes and the departmental chief allowed them to land and consult the *facultativos* on the pretext of illness, though the chief noted that their "ills" were augmented by taking to sea. It was impossible to prevent these occurrences without accurate passenger lists, he insisted; nor could the returnees be made to post bonds while recuperating. Abuse could be eliminated only by denying disembarkation to those who lacked permission, except in cases of serious illness. Recovery should take place in a specified hospital, followed by reembarkation. Camacho agreed with the chief's recommendation and urged action, to save "the decorum of the supreme government."[18] But the vice-president was unwilling to apply this remedy.

Spaniards were returning to Pacific coast ports as well. In April ten *expulsos* disembarked at Guaymas, three of whom were returning from Chile. Local officials allowed them to remain under a regulation of 28 May 1828 that permitted *peninsulares* arriving on "friendly or neutral ships" to disembark with their goods, upon payment of the proper tax. The ministry considered their permanence a violation of the expulsion law and reprimanded the port authorities on 8 February 1831, some ten months after the fact, due to Guaymas's remoteness.[19]

As the 1830 epidemic season approached, Alamán sought to rescue Gulf port returnees from the threat of yellow fever. Transfers were authorized as far as the first healthy village. Upon learning that Spaniards had departed from Jalapa, he declared that, in future, federal passports would be required. On 19 May Bustamante alerted the commander at Perote fortress to guarantee that no returnees continued inland without a passport issued by the supreme government.[20]

In May, as rumors of a new invasion gained credence in New Orleans and Mexico, arrivals slacked considerably. Alamán contacted the vice-consul in New Orleans for a third time, insisting that no certificates accrediting good behavior be issued to returning *peninsu-lares*. The administration, now on the defensive, sought to shift the blame for the growing presence of Spaniards onto key Yorkinos associated with the last administration, accusing them anew of turning the expulsion into a source of illicit profit. Responding to charges by *El Atleta* that the government was selling passports, *El Gladiador* declared that the Yorkinos, and even President Victoria, had used the expulsion to enrich themselves, peddling exceptions through mechanisms such as the juntas of *facultativos*. And the Guerrero regime was worse, selling the passports that enabled so many to return to Mexico. The ministry reported finding a stack of blank passports signed by Guerrero. According to *El Gladiador*, under past administrations, deputies had accepted money from victims' families, promising exceptions, but some intermediaries had subsequently disavowed the proffered protection. When the families pressed their demands on the offending deputies, the Guerrero regime had allegedly issued the passports in question. And in 1830, according to the editors, there were "devious persons" still seeking passports for Spaniards who had paid in advance. Besieged by these "vendors of documents," the ministry had turned the requests over to Congress and promised resolution within two months.[21] The present government claimed (falsely) that returnees bearing such documents were being reembarked.

Camacho insisted that policy changes were required if the tide of returning Spaniards was to be halted. The chief reiterated his suggestions at the end of May, insisting that medical exams for the "gravely ill" should be conducted only on the pontoon. The governor added a new observation: if reason were to be introduced, Congress would have to modify the law, "reducing the prohibition to the unmarried, and permitting the return of those who had property and Mexican wives or children here, provided their political conduct had not been inconvenient, in the judgment of federal and state governments."[22] The political exigencies of the moment did not allow the regime to adopt this humane suggestion.

In June, Alamán was obliged to reinforce the vice-president's orders. A merchant, Manuel Balán, had disembarked on the pretext of illness and actually reached Mexico City without documents. Nine Spaniards landed on 23 June, most claiming illness, and were bonded by individual Mexicans. A defector from Barradas's forces turned up in San Luis Potosí, bearing a passport issued by General de la Garza. Congress still had not decided the fate of such individuals. In keeping with the trend, officials of the British-owned United Mexican Mining Company petitioned the ministry for the return of Narciso Anitua, expelled in 1828, and Alamán placed the matter before Congress.[23] Ministry circulars during summer 1830 revealed that the administration was resigned to the fact that Spaniards made the most of the medical exam opportunity. On 14 June, Camacho reminded the minister that *peninsulares* were still arriving without passports, hoping to be judged ill by the junta. Under existing orders, even those who lacked documents and wished to appeal their cases were permitted to land. Officials pleaded anew for a remedy, but no change was authorized.[24]

To stem the flow of returnees to the interior, the governors were instructed on 16 June to require all who lacked passports issued by the supreme government to return to the states through which they had entered for processing. A new policy was adopted at Veracruz: now, examinations by *facultativos* were conducted in the harbor, with a commissioner present, before landing. Then, if the junta judged the Spaniard to be ill, bond was posted. But the chief doubted that this would halt abuses; he would have preferred consignment of the "ill" to a hospital until they could be reembarked. Abuses in the examination system were "inevitable"' since, at this point, four of the eight *facultativos* were Spaniards.[25]

On 20 June, Camacho launched the idea of repatriating Mexican families abandoned at New Orleans. Numerous deaths among heads of families had left many dependents destitute, unable to pay passage home. He suggested that governors solicit contributions for the cause. The vice-president favored the idea, urging Camacho to head the campaign, which should be a popular humanitarian effort. "Patriotic juntas," established in each state to oversee independence celebrations on 16 September 1830, were to collect funds. Donations were deposited in the provincial general commissaries, then transferred to the Casa de Moneda, to be placed at the ministry of government's disposal. Funds came from every state; Yucatán donated 680 pesos, while Tamaulipas and Durango collected over 1,000 pesos each. Contributions were still arriving in November 1831.[26]

Alamán's efforts to define returnee policy and control the adverse reaction intensified in July 1830, as both sizable arrivals and attacks from the government's opponents persisted. A pamphlet entitled "Death to the Spaniards and Their Godfather the Government" appeared on 6 July, moving *El Gladiador* to counterattack. The pamphlet's author was exiled to the Californias and the printer imprisoned. But the increase in arrivals was unrelenting. When fifty-five Spaniards entered port on a single ship, Camacho desperately appealed for advice. Gervasio Rodríguez and many others had resided at Havana and, although some had proper passports, all were held aboard ship until Bustamante resolved the matter. The vice-president decided on 7 July that, since these Spaniards were "abusing Mexican hospitality," only those with congressional exceptions or the "bedridden" would be allowed to disembark. All others were to depart on the first ship weighing anchor.[27] One can imagine Spaniards taking to their bunks when this directive reached the port.

Camacho persisted, asserting that since returnees viewed internment in a local hospital with horror, the threat alone would discourage false appeals. The governor had pleaded with *facultativos* to observe the strictest legality, to no avail. He enlarged the junta and increased its Mexican members, to present more obstacles. Camacho also reported that three returnees had slipped out of Jalapa, bound for Puebla and Mexico City, possibly as spies. In response, on 8 July Bustamante granted the governor permission to designate the place where "recuperating" Spaniards should be kept. The vice-president was resolved to take action, since for so many to claim illness after embarking on a voyage seemed disingenuous. He ordered the removal of any *facultativo* whose conduct was suspicious. Camacho favored the remedy, noting that simply requiring new consultations had not sufficed. But the lack of alternate members for the Veracruz junta persisted. At Tampico, Customs Administrator Migoin also advocated a fixed place to hold returnees and an added complement of security. On 30 July three Spaniards who had been held aboard ship while awaiting departure fled to the interior. The vice-president agreed with Migoin, suggesting consultation with the military commander.[28]

The vice-president also ordered firm enforcement of the prohibition against disembarkation by anyone, Mexican or Spanish, who had willingly touched enemy soil. For having been at Havana, Antonio Valdez y Beltrán was restricted to the pontoon while his appeal was in process. His family had journeyed to meet him, but left disappointed.[29]

The governors of the littoral states were ordered, twice, on 24–25 July, to reembark all Spaniards who lacked a valid exception or a serious illness. These steps were required by "the law and the actual circumstances of the Republic." In response, the departmental chief at Orizaba returned six Spaniards from Córdoba and five from Cosamaloapan to Veracruz for embarkation. To assist with enforcement, Camacho relayed ten lists prepared by the departmental chief at Veracruz: between 29 September 1829 and 30 July 1830, 147 Spaniards had arrived in Veracruz harbor; 10 possessed exceptions and passports from the supreme government, 10 held passports granted under extraordinary faculties, 11 remained in Veracruz claiming exception by one of the chambers of Congress, 19 had moved elsewhere with similar exception, 36 claimed illness and remained at Veracruz, 30 were "ill" and had moved away, 13 were ordered from Jalapa to Veracruz, 9 had left the port without permission, just one was confined to the pontoon, and only 8 had returned to New Orleans.[30] Roughly 44.9 percent of returnees were "ill."

Spaniards continued to arrive in summer 1830 bearing the "permissions for voluntary departure" granted by the Victoria and Guerrero governments in 1828–29. In response to Camacho's repeated urging, Alamán drafted a new directive on 26 July: Spaniards who before 20 March 1829 had obtained temporary licenses to depart could not be readmitted on that basis alone, since the expulsion law did not provide for exception in such cases.[31] Arrivals finally slowed in August. The most protracted case concerned Esteban Toscano, an ex-official of the tobacco monopoly in San Luis Potosí who had favored Spain but relented, following the defeat of Barradas. The vice-consul at New Orleans warned of Toscano's alleged offer to serve Spain during the invasion, and Alamán instructed the port authorities that under no circumstances should Toscano be allowed to disembark. Though he claimed an exception granted by the Senate, Toscano's name was absent from the lists. On 23 August he was ordered to reembark, but three days later, after denying his offer of service to Spain, Toscano landed anew. Then, on 30 August, he was embarked once again. In mid-September his prospects brightened: Toscano submitted a new appeal and his son, Ricardo, a retired captain, represented him. In January 1831, the ministry consulted Congress. During May, Ricardo presented documents from New Orleans and Veracruz to disprove the treason charge and petitioned to have Toscano's salary restored. At last in June, the ministry reversed its ruling, allowing Toscano to remain in Mexico, and the treasury restored his salary.[32]

As late as August 1830, port officials lacked a complete list of the Spaniards excepted by the Senate in 1829—the most controversial of such documents. Since certificates of exception signed by Senate secretaries were so frequently presented at Veracruz, it was important to determine when each Spaniard was excepted. Camacho requested a copy. Alamán consulted the secretaries, noting that many of the claimants' names were absent from the published version, leading the authorities to force some Spaniards to reembark. He asked for an autographed copy of the final document. For the present, the administration ordered Camacho and port authorities to allow no *peninsular* to disembark if his name did not appear on one of the lists. When no Senate response was forthcoming by 6 February 1831, Alamán could only instruct the governors that claimants would simply have to await congressional resolution. The minister tried a new approach; he gave the secretaries of the chambers a list of those who had arrived with certificates of congressional exception, requesting that the names be checked against the original. He also asked, once again—apparently, without result—for resolution of the issue.[33] This reticence, especially in the Senate, suggests a cover-up, due to the expansion of "exceptions" after 21 April 1829.

Bustamante urged Camacho to prepare a list of Spaniards alleging infirmities who had disembarked before 27 August. The vice-president also recommended that indigent Spaniards ordered to re-embark should receive financial assistance from local authorities. The governor provided the names of ninety-six *peninsulares*, but said nothing about local monetary assistance.[34] In an effort to recapitulate policy and encourage uniform enforcement, summary instructions were circulated, on 11 September, to all relevant authorities. Facio urged military commanders to collaborate with the governors, "in order to avoid embarassing General Bustamante." Alamán summarized instructions currently in force to prevent excludable Spaniards from returning to Mexico: (1) no *peninsular* who arrived without a passport issued by the federal government after 20 March 1829 should be admitted; (2) exceptions conceded by the Guerrero government under extraordinary faculties or by the chambers of Congress were also acceptable; (3) returnees who bore a congressional document but whose names were absent from the published lists could not disembark; (4) all others could not land unless notoriously ill, as certified by a junta of *facultativos*; (5) in such cases, the individual might remain only until cured.[35] Alamán suspected that some of the documents of congressional exception were false. Attempts were under way to construct an accurate list. The minister called for reembarkation of all "illegal" Spaniards.

Alamán's instructions of 21 August were adhered to quite literally at Veracruz. When Domingo Urtetegui arrived bearing a Senate certificate and his name was not found in the lists, he was permitted to await congressional resolution. By late 1830, it was normal for Congress to inherit such cases, which gained time and enhanced the petitioner's chances of success. Some even sailed to Veracruz, began the process, then returned to New Orleans to await results. On 21 October, Lt. Col. José Alonso y Fernández, who claimed a Senate exception, appealed to Facio for permission to return plus back pay, in order to transport his family from the United States. Alonso's case was sent to the Senate, and he returned to New Orleans. Only those who possessed one of the controversial "documents of congressional exception" could do this, of course. In November, Col. José Joaquín de la Sota requested permission to return from Bayonne. Since he had not been excepted, his application was refused.[36]

Enforcement policy had evolved in 1830 from a narrow interpretation of the 1829 expulsion law to a generous tolerance of residence in coastal regions while appeals were placed before a Congress that hesitated to act. Free access to the medical juntas was granted with the distinct likelihood that infirmity would be verified. The law's original distinction between "temporary" and "permanent" illness was now absent from ministry correspondence. The assumption, no doubt, was that these were instances of "temporary" illness, in which case the law required reexamination. And yet the instructions said nothing about new consultations. It was clear from the directives of 1830 that the "ill" should be reembarked when cured, and yet no means of deciding when or financing transport was prescribed. This represented a fundamental flaw in Bustamante's enforcement policy.

In his annual report of January 1831, Alamán lamented the failure of Congress to act on a series of questions, the resolution of which could have altered enforcement outcome. Decisions were awaited concerning: (1) those who deserted Spanish ranks at Tampico or were crew members of the *Asia*; (2) individuals with citizenship in friendly nations, especially the United States; (3) *peninsulares* claiming exceptions from the chambers, though their names were absent from the lists; and (4) Frenchmen previously considered Spaniards. In addition, Alamán noted the numerous appeals for exception forwarded by state authorities that awaited resolution by Congress, and the tragic situation of Mexican families, many of whom were now orphaned, who had accompanied *expulsos* to New Orleans. He requested permission to use funds appropriated for colonization to resettle the latter in Mexico.[37]

The Fate of the "Exiled" Mexicans

Congress responded to the plight of families stranded abroad. On 14 January, the chamber of deputies authorized the expenditure of federal funds for resettlement. Deputy Bustamante noted that "even those who played an active role in that iniquitous [expulsion] law applauded this measure." The decree allowed the government to spend what was necessary of the 15,000 pesos provided for colonization in the law of 6 April 1830, to return impoverished Mexicans. Alamán began to implement the program on 26 January, sending instructions to Consul Francisco Martínez Pizarro in New Orleans, who was placed in charge. Passage was paid to the port nearest the individual's Mexican residence and for domestic transportation, with details to be worked out by Deputy Tornel. For those lacking means of support, colonization in Texas was available; settlers embarked for Matamoros, reporting to Mier y Terán to receive provisions. In January, Alamán sent instructions to all Mexican representatives abroad, then arranged in March for the treasury to forward 6,000 pesos to New Orleans for Lizardi Hermanos, the firm that provided initial funding. To cover these costs, Mangino assigned 80 percent of the import tax on ordinary cotton goods at Tampico.[38]

The first 73 beneficiaries embarked at New Orleans in July 1831, each receiving roughly twenty pesos for the voyage. Another group of 33 arrived in October and 45 more in December. At first, Veracruz customs officials denied aid to families with living fathers, but the minister ordered that all Mexicans, whether widowed or abandoned or not, should be assisted, including Mexicans at Bordeaux. In January 1832, Alamán revealed that 130 Mexicans had returned at a cost of 5,637 pesos. Extant documents raise the figure to 151. The process continued until at least 1840; later governments accepted responsibility under the law of 18 January 1831. During 1833–40 assistance was provided for María de la Luz Bulnes, Josefa Flores, María Antonia and Elena Ortiz, María Teadora Martínez, and two orphans.[39]

Bustamante's Policy in 1831

During 1831, *El Payo del Rosario* published at least ten satirical *folletos*, denouncing the growing presence of *gachupines*. In the new imagery, the Spaniards were no longer *coyotes* living among lambs but rather "cats" who had slipped in through the ports.[40] And yet the rate of arrivals declined in 1831, at least until December, when it increased anew. The consul at Bayonne noted in January that no Spaniards bound for Mexico had passed through during the past four months. As the number of *expulsos* in Europe declined, trade fell off as well. Some Spaniards who had departed voluntarily in January 1829, during the Acordada rebellion, applied in January 1831 for extensions of the "license" to remain abroad, in order to preserve return rights. The ministry concluded that no extension was needed—reentry simply required exception from the expulsion law. Among January's returnees who gained the right to remain, the military surgeon Francisco Merchante was unique. He had defected to the Mexican side at Tampico and served the wounded of both Mier y Terán and Barradas. Merchante was granted permission to reside at Tampico, but was separated from the battalion, under the *empleos* law of 10 May 1827.[41]

The old "Oaxaca problem" persisted in 1831—the tendency of officials there to drive Spaniards out of the state, regardless of documents or exceptions. Two Spaniards who were arbitrarily expelled in 1829 obtained permanent exceptions from the *facultativos* at Córdoba, in Veracruz State. Upon returning to Oaxaca, they were imprisoned in Santa María Chayuco and their documents confiscated. Following release local authorities refused to return their papers. In response to appeals, and with the support of Veracruz officials, Bustamante ordered the Oaxaca authorities to account for their actions.[42]

During 1831, wives often represented expelled husbands before the ministry. In cases of congressional exception, women appealed directly to the vice-president, urging that proper passports be issued. Since a federal passport was required after verification that a name appeared on a list, orders were sent to New Orleans to issue such a document. In February, as the rebel Guerrero was being executed on the Pacific coast, the ministry encountered daily wives who pleaded for favorable decisions concerning Senate "certificates." Alamán had recommended to Congress that, in each case, the reason for granting exception should be specified. This would have compromised illicit arrangements and led, no doubt, to congressional reticence. In these circumstances, no decision on appeals could be reached. Consequently, on 26 February Alamán instructed the consul at New Orleans that anyone bearing such a certificate whose name was not on one of the lists would be denied admission. He had recently complained of laxity at Tampico for admitting men who lacked proper documentation.[43]

Among February's returnees was José María Fagoaga, an ex-deputy and wealthy merchant, who found that his name was on the Senate lists. His brother Francisco, a criollo, was now governor of the Federal District. Under quite different circumstances, Pedro Rodríguez returned to the village of Zacapuastla, and was driven out of town by local citizens who petitioned the federal government to prevent him from remaining in Mexico. By now it was evident that even those who had resided in Havana would be readmitted, if their names were on one of the Senate lists. In late March, Camacho believed that the vice-president had ordered port authorities to deny entry to seven Spaniards who had resided in Havana. And yet, in April, when one of the seven, Ramón Fernández, arrived anew and was reembarked, Bustamante demanded to know why this had occurred when the victim's name was on a Senate list. Bustamante denied that any order had been sent, and insisted on Fernández's freedom. A chastised Camacho complied.[44]

The vice-president was soon faced with the presence of illegals in the capital itself. On 24 March, Alamán alerted Governor Fagoaga to a Puebla report that returnees were en route to Mexico City. He ordered a search for any who had illegally entered the Federal District. Fagoaga insisted on past compliance, but promised that enforcement would be redoubled. Alamán urged the port captain at Veracruz to keep the departmental chief current on all who disembarked, in order to prevent returnees from venturing into the interior.[45]

While returns slowed in April, old questions persisted. Camacho promised to apply the directive of 30 March, but he feared abuses would not cease unless returnees who had fled the coast were forced to return and a pecuniary penalty imposed, perhaps on the bondsmen. The ministry disagreed, considering it sufficient to have offenders returned by the governors. On 8 April, fifteen "U.S. citizens" arrived from New Orleans. Several had resided in enemy territory, and Camacho was determined to restrict them to the port. Alamán apprised Anthony Butler, the U.S. chargé, of the trend, urging that U.S. documents be granted less hastily. The ministry consulted the Chamber of Deputies anew, without result, and since the government "could not do otherwise," such claims continued to be recognized.[46] The nature of Louisiana "citizenship" was revealed by the U.S. vice-consul at Veracruz, Isaac Stone, who withheld protection. He noted that passports were issued by the governor of Louisiana, while citizenship certificates were made out by the New Orleans parish court or by a certain notary public. The same two persons witnessed nearly all documents and falsely swore that the Spaniards came as minors or were minors at the time the territory was incorporated into the United States. Some had inadvertently confessed to the consul that they paid three dubloons for the documents, "while others laughed when questioned." What most impressed Stone was that "not a soul of them can speak a word either of English or French and I know 'tis impossible for anyone to live there not to say 20 years—but 20 months without speaking some words of both."[47]

Charges surfaced in April that a payment was required for entry at Veracruz. *Voz de la Patria* printed a letter from the port contending that Spaniards who had "eight, ten, or more ounces" of gold at hand were allowed to disembark. The rest were held on the pontoon while

their Mexican families begged from door to door for funds to release
their men. The *facultativos* were accused of greed and, in all, some
eight to ten individuals were said to be living off this commerce. In
order to pass into the interior, a delay of a month was required, then
new payments were extracted before departure was permitted. This
was all the more distressing because yellow fever was abroad, increasing the human risk. The departmental chief protested the innocence
of all concerned, of course, but he noted that such assertions were
inevitable so long as the allegedly ill were allowed to disembark. He
recommended that in future, an elaborate series of steps be followed
to avoid the appearance of impropriety. Camacho agreed, but Bustamante ordered the simpler procedures to remain in force, due to
the lack of funds.[48]

The difficulty of shipping "rejectees" back to New Orleans persisted. A "full-time" transport vessel, the *Gral. Victoria*, plied the New
Orleans–Veracruz route in 1831, bringing Spanish returnees. In April
it arrived with fifteen *peninsulares*, and the captain, together with
the masters of the *Favorito* and *Flecha*, refused to take on board the
rejectees assigned by the port commander. These men, as usual, had
no funds for return passage. Orders of 7 July 1830 required officials
to return Spaniards to their original ships, but captains evaded this
by declaring a different destination. This forced officials to look for
other vessels, ad infinitum. On 14 May, Alamán consented that the
Veracruzana should not be forced to transport rejectees, since its alleged destination was Kingston, Jamaica. The "illegals" became wards
of the political authorities, to be held on the pontoon until another
ship sailed for New Orleans. The *Veracruzana* did indeed return to
New Orleans, once Alamán's instructions had arrived. The port captain, Francisco del Corral, repeatedly requested federal resolution
of the issue, without success. The captain of the *Gral. Victoria* was
particularly abusive, del Corral complained, to no avail.[49] Mexico City
was incapable of forcing captains to reembark indigents.

In response to difficulties of compliance, and public concern over
the return of so many *peninsulares*, Bustamante decided to review all
cases anew. On 23 April, Bustamante ordered governors and Mexican
consuls to collect from Spaniards all documents of exception granted
by Congress, or by the executive during extraordinary powers. These
should be forwarded to Mexico City and provisional protection
granted, while the ministry determined the legitimacy of each exception. Men with authentic documents would be permitted to remain
without further molestation, while any whose claims lacked legitimacy
would suffer "the penalties prescribed by law." Spaniards bearing

congressional certificates could land and proceed to the first healthy location while their claims were decided. The Federal District's *peninsulares* could deliver their documents to Fagoaga, while the "undocumented" should appear in person. In response to this directive, del Corral agreed to comply, but warned of a potential increase in the number of "exceptions."[50]

One result proved how many Spanish residents had certificates issued by congressional secretaries. Judging by the names on the published lists of 1829, there should have been 2,600 such "legitimate" certificates in Mexico, if all beneficiaries were present. Documents were still arriving as late as December. Apparently, at least 1,778 excepted Spaniards could no longer be accounted for; the ministry received just 921 certificates, of which 523 were still pending validation in 1832. My analysis of 511 documents which were never returned to their owners indicated that 426 (or 83.4 percent) were considered legitimate and 78 (16.6 percent) unacceptable. Some 182 individuals (or 42.7 percent of those "legitimately excepted") had settled in the Federal District; 59 (7 of whom were in prison) resided in the state of Puebla and 43 in Veracruz State. Only 11 *peninsulares* were reembarked, while 25 were considered ill, 23 "insufficiently documented," and 12 "temporarily present" in the ports.[51]

A partial explanation for the reduced number of certificates collected was revealed by the governor of Mexico State. Miguel Cervantes reported secretly to Alamán on 10 May that few Spaniards had appeared as directed, and yet he was certain that many had returned illegally, departing Veracruz without documents. There were three types of "illegals," according to Cervantes: (1) those who fled Veracruz without the governor's permission, (2) those who remained hidden within Mexico State, appearing only when it seemed safe, or (3) those who, having received temporary "medical" exceptions in 1829, had not appeared for reexamination. He believed that all these should be expelled, despite grave personal losses and large families who would be forced to depart. On 26 May, Cervantes appealed a third time for remedy, fearing that he would be accused of failing to enforce the expulsion law. The governor lamented congressional inaction, especially concerning whether the penalty for noncompliance should be applied by the executive or judicial branch. On 7 July, a new governor at Tlalpan, Melchor Múzquiz, learned of numerous Spaniards who had held documents of protection since 1829, pending receipt of travel funds. They still awaited federal assistance as late as 1834.[52]

Were the circulars of March and April merely an effort to maintain the appearance of strict enforcement, as the vice-president desired? In light of the obstacles to compliance, it seems more likely that the Bustamante government was legally correct in its enforcement—interpretations were logical and consistent and orders for strict observance were certainly frequent enough—but the regime was unwilling to engage in a campaign to undo the exceptions granted by Congress and the *facultativos*, or by the Guerrero administration. Bustamante and Alamán would be blamed for the consequences of policies set in motion by the Yorkino regime. The role of the "impartial" Senate was especially noteworthy—it supplied many of the exceptions that would embarass the vice-president. Of course, Senate documents were not always respected. Agustín Molinari, a former soldier, arrived in April with a Senate certificate. His name did not appear on the lists, and, moreover, he was accused of having served Spain. Facio proceeded against him "in accordance with the laws."[53] The fact that many Spaniards had large families was of special concern to some governors. The largest contingent of returnees in May numbered thirty-nine individuals, all of whom had Mexican families. On 6 May, Camacho appealed on behalf of these men, nine of whom were illiterate. Their only grounds for favor were their Mexican families, some with as many as seven children. The vice-president felt compelled to deny their petition, since the expulsion law did not permit such exceptions.[54]

A number of May returnees still used the ploy of citizenship "in the state of Louisiana," and, lacking congressional resolution, the ministry accepted such claims, while acknowledging their falsity. Six Spaniards arrived at Tampico with papers asserting residence in New Orleans since 1811 or 1812, when, in fact, they were *expulsos* from Tuxpan, Puebla, and Papantla. The case of Vicente Cerio, an 1829 *expulso*, was well documented by Puebla's Governor Juan Andrade.[55] Despite the anger of military officials, Camacho and Alamán continued to accept such claims.

The gap between the federal government's view of enforcement and that of the states became more obvious in June. It was clear that rules would have to change. This resulted, in part, from the circular of 23 April, which had called for collection of all documents of exception. Governor Jossef Rovirosa of Tabasco complied, noting that some thirteen returnees had stirred public resentment, while awaiting the opportune moment to bolt for the state capital. The departmental chief at Veracruz reported in June that the majority of those who remained did so, not as a result of exceptions, but rather "due to consideration granted by the authorities," or appeals pending for either exception or extension of time. For this reason, and because of the negative effect that document collection might have on individuals and commerce, the chief urged suspension or modification of instructions. Bustamante refused, ordering on 2 July that individuals be treated "in conformity with the law."[56]

But the rules did change. After 13 June, no Spaniard who lacked a passport issued by the Ministry of Government was permitted to disembark. Bustamante's concern was to avoid admitting any more who had settled in enemy territory, particularly the regular clergy. Seeking protection in another house of their order, regulars had emigrated to regions still under Spanish rule. In July, the vice-president authorized circulation of the instructions of 13 June to all officials involved in enforcement. The question of what should be done with those already at Veracruz would also be addressed. Camacho conveyed a new appeal from the Veracruz department chief on 22 July. Men could no longer be held on the pontoon due to a lack of guards. As a consequence, the chief and the port captain had reverted to holding the *peninsulares* on board ship, allowing only a few to come ashore each day to procure supplies. Camacho reiterated the impossibility of reembarking many Spaniards under existing instructions. The vice-president's response on 26 July repeated the directives of 13 June: Spaniards who lacked the requisites to land should remain on board ship, to be returned to their points of origin. Those who could should pay their own passage, while men lacking funds would have to be carried gratis. The rules had been made known in relevant foreign ports so that ships' captains might understand their obligations and act accordingly. Alamán repeated these instructions and cautioned port authorities to take care that those who went ashore in daylight were back on board by nightfall.[57]

The attempt to raise the stakes for the captains did not succeed. Camacho and the departmental chief reported on 14 October that reembarkation was still extremely difficult. Returnees continued to feign illness and, when this device was not employed, the majority still had no funds, and aid was unavailable. Funding for reembarkation was provided in a Senate accord currently pending in the lower house; in the meantime, Alamán could simply urge caution to assure that no one might enter the republic illicitly.[58] The fate of the insolvent remained unclear.

The wife of a frustrated returnee portrayed the agony of the human victims of Alamán's instructions in a letter of 10 August that illustrates the difficult position of the port authorities as well. "Margarita" described her desperate efforts on behalf of her husband. As a final resort, she approached Congress, succeeded in obtaining a certificate, and sent for "the man who was destined for [her]." But a shock awaited her; upon arriving, her husband was refused permission to land. Del Corral explained that he was acting on "confidential orders" which he received daily. In response, the disillusioned woman exclaimed: "Who today does not know that there are already on land many lacking exceptions, while others are denied the right of hospitality on orders of higher authority?" The wives will not give up, she insisted; "in the end justice will be served." As if to punctuate Margarita's protest against unequal treatment, the *expulso* Juan de la Puente arrived in Oaxaca in July bearing naturalization papers from the Grand Duchy of Baden and a passport granted at Bordeaux.[59]

By summer 1831, the state government of Puebla had repealed its local law of expulsion, and began accepting Spaniards whose documents were "legal." *Peninsulares* arrived at Puebla's port, Tuxpan, with family members and U.S. or French citizenship—the latter acquired from the French consul in New Orleans, Albin Hichel. Dr. Joaquín Prast arrived with his wife and a French passport on 23 July, as did the former first officer of artillery, Félix Solís, who was judged perpetually ill and settled in Puebla. On 13 August, Facio noted that Spaniards "who had never set foot in Mexico," were arriving with "documents of exception." Military authorities were cautioned to be alert for possible disembarkations at any point along the coasts and to cooperate with port commanders.[60]

By late July, the situation was critical; there were rumors of military revolt. Colonels Mariano Arista and Gabriel Durán broke with Bustamante and "petitioned" for the expulsion of excepted Spaniards. The governing coalition was fragmenting as regional variations developed over the *peninsular* presence. Congress, called into extraordinary session for a host of reasons, summoned the ministry to clarify steps taken to avoid rebellion. A virulent pamphlet appeared from the pen of "Payo del Rosario," entitled "If Bustamante is Responsible, As He Rose So Shall He Fall."[61] The Senate sought to resolve all questions concerning the legality of returnees in an accord forwarded to the Chamber of Deputies on 22 September. The measure, which the lower house did not approve, excepted nearly all who presented certificates signed by the secretaries of either chamber. It denied residency to any who (1) refused to swear allegiance to Mexican independence, (2) entered in violation of immigration law, (3) arrived with Barradas, or (4) attacked Mexico's independence, offering service to Spain. Beneficiaries were to deliver their certificates to the governors who would send them to the ministry for authentication. Congress would then have forwarded "authentic" copies of the April 1829 lists to the governors, and financial aid for reembarkation of the poor was authorized. Any official who obstructed implementation would lose his post.[62] The failure of the lower chamber to accept this solution left the administration as frustrated as ever.

While the new executive stand seemed harsh, it also changed things for those waiting aboard ship. Following repeated inquiries from port officials, permission to move inland came on 4 October, requiring that the governor approve the town and an address be reported. Only two groups were excluded: men who took part in the Barradas invasion, and Spanish "immigrants" who were refused landing rights under any circumstances.[63]

By October 1831, *expulsos* were returning with their families using a new pretext—the "impossibility" of supporting them in New Orleans. Alamán blamed defiant ship captains—who persisted, despite fines of up to 120 pesos, in bringing undocumented persons, ignoring orders that illegals be returned gratis. He was distressed to discover that the captain of the *Pearl* was a repeat offender who had neither been fined, nor forced to return any passenger. For the first time, Alamán claimed that the "laxity of port authorities" had caused him to be publicly denounced as responsible for the Spaniards' return.[64]

During 1831–32, a limited number of *expulsos* migrated to Spain, arriving through Bordeaux or Bayonne, and duly noted by Murphy or Despect, the Mexican agents. The most prominent exile to arrive at Bayonne in early 1832 was ex-General Pedro Celestino Negrete, who remained in France. Traffic was renewed to Mexico as well. During December 1831 and January 1832, four out of five ships leaving Bordeaux for Veracruz brought returning Spanish military officers and merchants. These men usually possessed French passports granted to "non-naturalized foreigners." In such cases—which were common in 1832—judicial inquiries were suggested to determine citizenship. If results were inconclusive, the Spaniard was to be reembarked, according to year-end instructions.[65]

The Spring 1832 Crisis in Bustamante Policy

Unlike earlier reports, Alamán's January 1832 annual message to Congress said nothing of the returnee issue. This seems peculiar, in light of extraordinary events transpiring at the port of Veracruz. In February, U.S. Vice-Consul John Cameron reported,

A great many Spanish subjects have arrived in this port within the last two
months–more than 300 [sic]. No obstacle has been thrown by the Government in the way of their free entry. During the last 10 days some
30 or 50 have arrived, all of whom Santa Anna has ordered to re-embark.
It is confidently said and believed that if he is successful, there will be a
second [sic] expulsion of Spaniards. They all, of this City, seem to look for
such a result.[66]

Two matters are notable in this curious report; the large numbers
said to be arriving and the sudden role of Santa Anna, who had
played no part in the returnee issue. The vice-consul may have over-
stated both the numbers and his case, but if he is even partially correct, the policies of Bustamante and Santa Anna now differed. Governor Múzquiz of Mexico State was also concerned about admissions.
In an undated letter penned in 1832, he demanded to know what
motives the government could have for disobeying existing laws
"without resort to the excuse that they may be bad or barbaric."[67]

The statistics reveal a great deal about enforcement effectiveness.
From June 1830 to 30 January 1832, some 380 arriving Spaniards
were noted at Veracruz (roughly 48 per month). Documents indicate
that 175 landed (22 per month) and 30 reembarked. While 92 possessed congressional certificates, 66 were judged "ill," and 30 claimed
U.S. citizenship. In all, 101 (nearly 13 per month) were allowed to
enter the country (26.6 percent of arrivals or 57.7 percent of those
who landed).[68] If this is typical for 1830–32, it would seem that few
who feigned illness actually succeeded in remaining. But reality in
this matter is elusive, and official reports may not reflect actual out-
comes. It is difficult to imagine so much hostility resulting from the
landing of 175 *gachupines* or the entry of 101. Since ship captains
refused to carry indigents to New Orleans, it is probable that most
of the 205 rejectees also remained in Mexico.

In spring 1832, a congressional grand jury launched an inquiry
into expulsion enforcement. Ministry records were requested, including all general orders. Alamán forwarded the latter on 25 April and
promised other pertinent materials as soon as a review could be completed. In addition, Congress sought to facilitate the deportation of
"suspicious foreigners." A decree of 22 February gave the executive
the authority to expel those "whose permanence is judged prejudicial
to the the public order, even when that person may have entered
. . . under regulations prescribed in the laws." Such an arrogation
of authority by the vice-president worried the British ambassador,
among others.[69] It was a tentative step toward a renewed expulsion
of *peninsulares*, which intensified in 1833.

The birth of that movement was signaled by the actions of military authorities at the Gulf ports in May 1832. Quite suddenly, Gen. Esteban Moctezuma, commandant at Tampico, adopted a rebellious posture and began, on his own, to enforce the 1829 expulsion law, which he interpreted as providing no exceptions for any person of Spanish birth. This included individuals claiming U.S. or British citizenship, which raised concerns among foreign agents. On 30 May, U.S. Consul George Robertson inquired whether U.S. citizens were to be included and what would be done about Spaniards' debts to North Americans. Moctezuma's reply revealed his hatred for the *peninsular* merchants, the majority of whom had been expelled by the law of 20 March 1829 and now possessed U.S. citizenship papers. By returning, he contended, they broke the law: "I cannot permit this"; the expulsion law did not speak of "citizen Spaniards" but, rather, of natives of the Spanish lands. "I have extended the law to all born Spaniards," he replied; "they are our common enemies, and our future peace demands . . . that we expel them from our soil." As for recovering debts, Moctezuma recommended the use of the courts and promised to support any ruling under "the military law that now exists here." Robertson was no enthusiastic defender of these "U.S. citizens." He noted in June that all but one of them were "men who have no interest in the United States." When Crawford, the British consul, asked why Tampico's Spanish-born British subjects were being expelled, Moctezuma replied in roughly the same terms, adding that nonfulfillment of the expulsion law was just one of many charges that could be brought against the Bustamante administration.[70] Moctezuma's rebellion was not eliminated.

The return of the Spaniards had now run its course, with only an occasional individual arriving during the next three years. The proexpulsion plot of Arista and Durán, renewed arrivals in 1832, the tension between the administration and key governors, and Moctezuma's arbitrary expulsion of Tampico's Spaniards, all indicated frustration over the enforcement of expulsion. They foreshadowed the resignation of the Bustamante government in August 1832 and the flight of its ministers into hiding. One result would be an effort in 1833 to expel "illegal" Spaniards under the 1829 law.

11

The Last Laws of Expulsion, 1833–1836

The expulsion of all Spaniards and their allies, without any exception whatsoever, is being heatedly discussed, because there are various persons who stand to gain . . . and it will surely occur, since one can appreciate at a glance the state of affairs here.

—Ex-Count of Peñasco, 1 April 1833

XENOPHOBIA WAS still at work in Mexico in 1832–33. In the missions of Alta California, controlled by Spanish friars, the process of secularization was begun with a congressional decree of 25 May 1832. Missions became parishes and the funds for their administration were "secularized," making them available for spoliation. At Tampico Moctezuma expelled the Spanish-born U.S. and British "citizens" on fifteen days' notice.[1] The Arista and Durán rebellion at Puebla gained strength, when Santa Anna and Moctezuma joined forces, depriving Bustamante of control over the major Atlantic ports and their revenue. Santa Anna marched on Puebla, where the loyalist General Calderón, like Mier y Terán in the north, asked for a truce. The result was a parley of contending parties near Puebla. Gómez Pedraza, Santa Anna, Miguel Ramos Arizpe, and Bernardo González Angulo met with the vice-president and his military staff on 21 December, hoping to end the civil conflict. The result, after two days, was the Plan of Zavaleta, which deposed Bustamante but preserved the federal system, called for new elections for state officials and federal deputies, and named Pedraza president, to serve out the remaining three months of the term he was elected to in 1828. Neither Pedraza, who exercised executive authority until 1 April 1833, nor the changeable Santa Anna favored a renewal of the expulsion. Pedraza had been drawn to the *expulso* community at Bordeaux during his own exile. But anti-Spanish activists believed the *gachupines* favored the Bustamante regime, and rebel supporters intended to hold the

184

peninsulares responsible if Santa Anna or any rebel leaders were assassinated.[2] And yet, despite the anti-*gachupín* rhetoric, in much of the nation returnees ran no greater risk under subsequent governments then they had in 1831.

The Third Federal Expulsion (16 January 1833)

As Pedraza took office on 3 January, he had to curb the entry of Spaniards and expel at least some "illegal" entrants. At the outset, Bernardo González Angulo, the new minister of government, requested from each of the chambers of Congress the official record for the day on which the lists of exceptions were produced. Antonio Mier, secretary of the Chamber of Deputies, forwarded the record for 15 April 1829. Mier acknowledged that the various secretaries "had given certificates of exception to many individuals, although they [were] not included in the list [published] on that day." Mier could not say whether this resulted from acts of the chamber or favoritism by the secretaries. An extra page had been inserted in the record of 15 April 1829, probably in February 1830, clearly a criminal act. The secretary believed that the chamber would remove the page, invalidating the "exceptions" it contained.[3]

When the Senate record for 21 April 1829 arrived, the secretary noted a similar trend—more exceptions had been "authorized" afterward and the total could not be ascertained. Secretary Alvio contended that certificates were granted partly to comply with congressional decrees of 10, 14, and 21 April 1829 extending the length of time for those whose cases were pending before Congress.[4] Clearly, an important distinction had been brushed aside: time extentions and exceptions were hardly equivalent. Record keeping was admittedly uneven, and the process went unrecorded.

The new administration was prepared to act, in response to the policy failures of the Bustamante era, without awaiting congressional agreement. On 16 January, Pedraza sought to reactivate the expulsion, but in a less harsh form. González Angulo justified the bill as congruent with the decree of 22 November 1832, which authorized the executive to "expedite passports and expel . . . any non-naturalized foreigner whose presence might be considered prejudicial to public order, even when the person had entered and become established in accordance with the law." Spaniards were defined as "non-naturalized foreigners" to make the case. Pedraza's decree was intended to complete the enforcement of the 1829 measure by reexpelling only unmarried *peninsulares* who had returned illegally.

The law satisfied Camacho's recommendation that *peninsulares* with Mexican families be tolerated. To minimize suspicion in the states, enforcement was delegated to the governors themselves. In order to remain, a Spaniard had to enjoy at least one of the following: (1) a legal exception, (2) marriage to a Mexican woman, living or deceased, with a dependent child (pending congressional resolution), or (3) citizenship or naturalization in a friendly nation, with a "letter of security" obtained from the ministry through a foreign representative. Governors were responsible for detecting dangerous *peninsulares* and recommending their expulsion. Full explanations were required for such actions, as well as monthly compliance reports. Spaniards who had established residence along the coast since 20 March 1829 could not remain there. Once again, the "ill" faced examination by the *facultativos*.[5]

Lists of exceptions by the chambers, the government (the ill), as citizens of friendly nations, or sons of Americans, were sent to each governor on 23 January, along with the law and instructions, and a description of citizenship papers recognized by friendly nations. The lists contained 2,706 names. Exceptions numbered as follows: permanent illness 1,491 (or 55 percent), temporary infirmity 664 (24.5 percent), by the Senate 453 (16.7 percent), by the deputies 73 (2.7 percent), under extraordinary faculties 14 (0.5 percent), and as sons of Americans 11 (0.4 percent).[6]

According to instructions, a Spaniard who was cured, and neither married to a Mexican or widowed with at least one child, faced expulsion. Now, a Spaniard with citizenship in a friendly nation could be expelled if his presence was considered prejudicial to public order. In the Federal District, all *peninsulars* had to appear before the local secretary of government, within fifteen days, presenting their 1829 exception documents. A married Spaniard was required to present the birth certificates of his wife and children, plus a marriage certificate, each authenticated by a scribe; while a widower should display his wife's burial document, certification from three neighbors, and a recommendation from the *regidor* (magistrate or alderman) of his sector attesting to his dependent Mexican children. A *peninsular* who claimed citizenship in a friendly nation should present the usual "letter of security," naturalization papers, authorized copies of the same, and a letter from his *regidor* evidencing employment. *Regidores* prepared a monthly report specifying whether Spaniards in their districts presented a danger to public order. The temporarily ill had to appear also, to obtain permission to be seen by the *facultativos*. Each Spaniard excepted due to marriage received a document that protected him until Congress resolved the matter. The circular reached most federal entities within the next two weeks, and was reprinted in Cuidad Victoria, Tamaulipas, for example, on 5 February for distribution to local authorities.[7]

Conservative periodicals attacked Pedraza's decree, charging that it violated amnesty provisions of the Plan of Zavaleta. The president defended the law, claiming that it was not a new expulsion but rather implementation of the 22 November 1832 decree requiring the executive to issue passports to dangerous foreigners. Suárez y Navarro erroneously believed that "fortunately for [the Spaniards], on this occasion the decree did not take effect," because other important matters distracted the parties. Previous authors have erred in following Suárez y Navarro.[8] Enforcement was attempted, but the results were quite uneven. The Spaniards, aware in January 1833 that under terms of the Zavaleta agreement a new government would emerge in less than three months, must have seen the wisdom of inaction until political affairs were sorted out.[9] Unlike previous expulsion measures, most enforcement decisions occurred at the state and territorial level, and it is there that we must look to judge compliance.

Enforcement of the January Decree in the Federal District

The Mexico City press publicized the names of Spaniards excepted from the 1829 law, as well as those who should be expelled, in the editors' view. Pressure to act would be considerable. But old problems persisted and the new administration soon faced the same dilemmas that had frustrated previous governments. The first difficulty was raised by Governor José Joaquín Herrera; he wisely urged the administration to decide in advance whether there would be funds to transport "illegal" Spaniards who had already received aid in 1829. Herrera hired four additional helpers for one month to assist in dispatching the documentary requirements of the decree. Pedraza authorized the temporary employees, but insisted that *expulsos* who had entered illegally should depart using "the resources with which they came."[10]

The new medical junta was functioning in the capital by 9 February, four evenings per week, with José María Hidalgo y Terán as its president. After 7 May, its chair was José María Martínez, and it met just two days a week. Initially, there was little response from the Spaniards and Pedraza asked González Angulo to verify that enforcement was initiated in the Federal District. Herrera had been active; he concurred that a fifteen-day deadline was an effective means of stimulating compliance. By mid-February, 617 Spaniards had done so in the capital. The governor's office worked "extraordinary hours," dedicating afternoons and evenings to classifying documents and arriving at proper decisions. The president recommended that *regidores* draw up lists of *peninsulares* residing in their districts, in order to determine who had not appeared. Among the 617 who had complied, 160 were noted in the exception lists published by the chambers, 135 cited the marriage exception, 110 awaited medical examination, 58 had perpetual illnesses, and just 6 possessed citizenship in friendly nations. Of the remainder, 82 had Senate certificates but their names were absent from the lists, 39 were temporarily ill, 33 had appeals pending, and 2 were born in Spanish territory of American parents.[11] In sum, 400 (64.8 percent) were clearly excepted, and many more would be judged ill.

In practice, men with questionable Senate certificates resorted to the *facultativos* for exceptions. In the Federal District the procedure was to appeal to the governor, who sent documents to the minister of government. On orders from the president, he in turn forwarded the appeal to the secretaries of the "president's private council," who recommended an appropriate resolution. Medical appeals were sent to the president of the medical junta. Any exception that might result was based solely upon the *facultativos'* decision—Senate certificates were neither returned nor cited in the final resolution.[12]

The president's private council performed this function until 1 April, when Congress reconvened. Weekly deliberations were published in *El Telégrafo*, with the intention, no doubt, of inspiring confidence in enforcement. At the meeting of 11 March, for example, two appeals were considered. Tirso Conde's questionable exception document was discussed, then sent to a commission established to treat such cases, "composed of Castro, Figueroa, and Yáñez." A second appeal, by Francisco Antonio Díaz Ordóñez, alleged the impossibility of his departure, and was also forwarded to the commission. Normally , after discussion the council voted; a majority was sufficient to recommend exception.[13]

The tradition of selecting *facultativos* in the order in which they appeared on a "guild" list was abandoned in mid-February, freeing the governors to select the meritorious. Herrera named new members on 19 February. The new governor's tolerance for persons with exceptional circumstances is illustrated in the case of Bernardo Copca, a Spanish immigrant of 1816. During the independence struggle, Copca had rescued José Ignacio Couto from the bishop's prison on the night before the patriot's scheduled execution. The only Spaniard elected to the second congress in 1823, Copca helped shape the Constitution of 1824. After the Acordada revolt, he fled to the United States, settling in Cincinnati, where his wife soon died. In January 1830, Copca and his Mexican daughter arrived in Veracruz, bearing a Senate certificate. Since his name was not on the published lists, he was admitted on a temporary basis. When his daughter died, he was threatened with expulsion by the law of 16 January, since he was neither married to a Mexican nor supporting a child. Copca appealed directly to his "old friends," González Angulo and Gómez Farías. The affair was extensively publicized in the official periodical, *El Telégrafo*, and on 2 March, Pedraza granted an exception, pending further congressional resolution.[14]

"Departure day" in the Federal District was 28 February; those with pending financial matters were granted an extra week. In any case, where appropriate, Herrera had been conceding an indefinite time extension, regardless of the type of appeal. The governor urged *regidores* and *alcaldes* (ward justices of the peace) to be vigilant, assuring that departures took place, "as required by the law of 20 March 1829"; after four years the thirty-day deadline was being reenacted. Herrera reminded local officials that Spaniards married to Mexicans or widowers with dependent children had received documents of protection for a specified time only, pending future congressional action. Anyone failing to appear before the authorities by 23 February, could be fined up to a hundred pesos and, failing payment, placed in the deputation prison for three to eight days. Fines were turned over to the hospice for the poor.[15]

After the deadline, Herrera broached the question of Spanish-born U.S. "citizens," forwarding for examination several documents granted in Louisiana. The president declared a change in policy, noting that one had to live in the United States for at least ten years to be eligible for citizenship; all but one of these claims should be rejected. Manuel del Castillo met the criteria, and on 16 April he was excepted from expulsion. González Angulo promised to notify Butler of the final determination in all such cases.[16]

The congressional sessions that began in April 1833 confronted unresolved aspects of the Spanish question. The status of suspended employees and the level of their salaries was raised in the Senate on 8 May. A bill that attempted to make the employee law of 10 May 1827 less costly to the treasury was considered. A clause limiting the income of suspended *peninsulares* to the level of retired employees gained unanimous approval. When Basadre attempted to except "those who had adhered to independence in March 1821, [and] had not acted in a manner that contradicted their adhesion to federal institutions," his effort was rebuffed.[17] Congress was placing limits on the administration's generosity.

Enforcement in the States

Under the January decree, the fate of Spaniards who had appeals pending with the federal government remained uncertain. The governor's authority in such cases was also unclear. When the question was raised at Jalapa in March, the president suggested that governors require a *peninsular* to justify his claim to exception, failing which he was obliged to depart. In Jalapa, Secretary of State José Díaz drew up instructions, and established a junta in each canton "to examine the exceptions and motives of each Spaniard living in the republic." As a result, Gregorio Calderón and Tomás Viella, who had been favored by the Senate, were expelled, since their names were absent from the lists.[18]

San Luis Potosí witnessed a vigorous revival of the anti-Spanish movement. It is not difficult to imagine Romero's vehement reaction to Pedraza's "lenient" January decree. The governor pointed to the new possibilities for exception it contained. Some Spaniards who had been temporarily excepted for physical impediment were now well. Others had been expelled and returned, some having obtained certificates of exception from the chambers. Since many of these men had families, they could take advantage of the new exception. In response, González Angulo, speaking for the president, curtly reiterated the new rules.[19] Romero ordered urban Spaniards to appear at the prefect's office, while those residing in outlying areas should go before the first *regidor* or *alcalde* of their locality. *Peninsulares* with exceptions were required to present proof, while those with no claim to exception should prepare to depart within the time allotted. Muro concluded that few Spaniards left their towns and villages, and then only to hide on haciendas and ranches, reemerging within a few months, when it seemed safe to do so. By Muro's own count, fifty-seven *peninsulares* complied in the state capital, of whom twenty-five were excepted and eighteen expelled, while fourteen suffered from temporary or permanent maladies.[20]

Pedraza was hardly in the presidential chair when the call for a new expulsion was sounded by two deputies at San Luis Potosí, José Antonio Barragán and Diego García. On 21 December 1832, they had proposed to the state congress an expulsion measure requiring all Spaniards to depart within thirty days, without exception.

Mexicans "linked" to *gachupines* were subject to expulsion as well, within twenty days. Mexican *expulsos* were to be selected by a committee of five individuals named by the state's executive, legislative, judicial, and militia authorities. Anyone obstructing enforcement would suffer expulsion on the same terms. The governor supported the effort, encouraging town councils to send favorable petitions to the state capital. Romero wrote to Pedraza pleading for a national law of the same sort. The bill did not prosper, however; a committee recommended that the matter be left to the next Congress.[21]

In the spring, authorities in San Luis Potosí set about designing new expulsion laws, both state and national. On 19 April, the local congress passed a draconian measure: all Spanish-born men had to leave the state within twenty days. A *peninsular* could apply to the congress, or in its absence, the permanent deputation, for exception. Only those who had contributed indisputably to the cause of liberty or the federal system, never having retreated from that commitment, and those who were absolutely physically impeded, need apply. The time spent traveling to the capital to initiate appeals would not count as part of the twenty days allowed for departure. Local Spanish military personnel, including those now in Mexico City, should all be expelled. Destinations were negotiable with federal authorities. Should it prove impossible for an *expulso* to conclude his affairs within twenty days, a delay could be prescribed, following verification of need. Anyone attempting to elude or frustrate the enforcement of the law would be punished. Families left behind would be "protected" as prescribed by the local constitutional congress in 1828. The governor expedited passports. *Peninsulares* in transit might remain for no more than thirty hours in a single location. And, finally, all the congresses of Mexico would be urged to pass similar measures.[22] Deputies Antonio Arce and José Velarde proposed such a bill to the federal Congress on 22 April, but it was too extreme to gain support.

Jalisco also attempted to eliminate its "Spanish problem" in 1833. First, on 17 April, a state law declared that Spaniards residing outside the republic could not own real property. Soon after, an expulsion decree was designed to apply to returnees since 1828, plus forty-one members of the local conservative party.[23] In other words, it was a *ley del caso*, a measure aimed at specific individuals.

The response in Yucatán was wholly different. Governor Lopes simply requested a ruling on the U.S. "citizens" who arrived from the north. González Angulo announced a new policy: if these men were recognized as citizens and given the required "letter of security" by the U.S. representative in Campeche, they should be allowed to remain. Lopes submitted the proper report, dividing the returnees into two categories: "U.S. citizens" and the "ill" who had consulted *facultativos*. All of the nine men listed were excepted from the 1829 expulsion, and the governor's decision to allow eighty days for the four "U.S. citizens" to obtain letters of security was approved.[24] It was not necessary to use the marriage exception.

In Zacatecas, Governor García responded by detailing the status of 117 men: of the 102 excepted, only five claimed foreign citizenship. The *facultativos* had not yet decided the fate of nine. Just five *peninsulares* lacked legal exceptions. From Chihuahua, on 6 July Governor José Ysidro Madero reported the presence of thirty-five Spaniards; twelve were "perpetually" ill, ten had certificates from the chambers, eight were temporarily ill, five had appeals pending, and just one was ordered to depart (and lacked the funds).[25]

A minimum of 886 Spaniards in ten states and the Federal District complied with the presidential decree of January 1833.[26] By my estimate, there were roughly 2,200 *peninsulares* in Mexico in December 1829. The difference between these two totals, some 1,300, reflects three factors at work: (1) the lack of reports from thirteen federal entities, including important states like Mexico, Jalisco, and Oaxaca, (2) understatement of the number in some major reporting states, resulting from Spanish noncompliance, and, possibly, (3) the absence of reports in the archives. A reliable total for all of Mexico following enforcement of the 1833 presidential decree is unobtainable. There were still between 1,000 and 2,000 Spaniards in Mexico, one-quarter of their number in 1827.

Why the new "liberality"? The concession of exceptions to married Spaniards responded to the campaign by abandoned wives and families, ongoing since 1828. Moreover, the threat of Spanish invasion had diminished, as had the *peninsular* community itself. Reviving expulsions through the 1829 law would attract renewed criticism from wives and families, despite the broadening of exceptions. A published appeal of 6 February to the Puebla legislature made the wives' case.[27] The principal reasons for concern were the danger of reviving attention to documents of exception and perpetuating the ban on reentry.

Enforcement Liberalization Under Gómez Farías

With the inauguration of President Santa Anna and Vice President Gómez Farías on 1 April, the approach to the Spanish question became more humane. Santa Anna retired to "Clove Spike," his hacienda near Jalapa, leaving day-to-day administration in the hands of

his able, liberal vice-president. The new government more than fulfilled the obligation assumed by Pedraza, to submit to Congress a
proposal legitimizing the expansion of exception categories in conformity with the January decree. The vice-president favored exceptions for five classes of *peninsulares*; those (1) with Mexican wives,
(2) supporting Mexican children, (3) widowed by Mexicans, (4) who
had served independence, or (5) who were crew members of the *Asia*
or the *Constant*. The appropriate measure was introduced into the
Chamber of Deputies on 18 April by Bernardo Gonzales. Gómez
Farías and Gonzales reasoned that "it was now necessary to provide
complete legality for the permanence and return of individuals who
obtained those documents [of exception] and, at the same time, to
comply with the dispositions of the . . . law." Moreover, Gonzales argued, "this proposal is adopted on a more just basis than was possible
when expediting the certificates." The expulsion of these individuals
would be more damaging to Mexicans than to the Spaniards themselves, when measured in terms of the well-being of families and the
economic utility of property.[28]

The federal government was unanimously supported by the Tabasco legislature. Governor Manuel Bueltas had recommended exceptions for all forty of Tabasco's Spaniards. On 6 May, deputies Hernández and Pérez proposed to the lower chamber that it grant these
men a blanket exception. They were all married and had resided
there since before 1821. Many had returned with Senate certificates
and others with nothing, simply because their families were in need.
Since, under the January decree, state authorities were free to except
married Spaniards, submission of a bill to the federal Congress now
seems superfluous. Clearly, the goal was to shield Tabascans from
future expulsion proposals.[29]

Ex-military Spaniards still drew salaries, adding to the drain on
the treasury. On 26 January, Pedraza had authorized Spaniards suspended by the law of 10 May 1827 to collect their salaries at payroll
offices or at military commissaries. The president had decided that
the Spanish crew of the *Asia* should not be molested, pending congressional resolution. With that goal in mind, a bill was submitted to the
Chamber of Deputies on 15 April, supported by Gómez Farías and
Minister of War Parres. Pedraza had also excepted Spanish military
men who favored independence and participated in the insurrections
of 1810 to 1821 under the January decree, pending congressional
resolution. All who qualified were to justify their claims before the
government, using service records and other evidence. In March,
Parres urged the president to take steps to prevent closure of the

naval academies at Córdoba and Tepic, which was likely if their directors were harassed. The authorities at Veracruz were determined to expel the director at Córdoba, even if it ended the school.[30] A federal decision was postponed.

A new issue required resolution in May—whether a Spaniard declared a citizen by a state legislature was subject to expulsion under the 1829 law. José Nandri of Durango was favored with such a decree, and the vice-president concluded that Nandri could not be expelled, a ruling that would not have been possible before 1833.[31]

If the government allowed many returnees to remain, and a skeptical public were to be pacified, a clear policy concerning disembarkations was required. On 7 May, the new minister of government, Carlos García, directed that returnees should be permitted to land, and their documents should be sent to the capital for verification. Authorities at the ports were instructed to assist customs administrators in this matter.[32] Clearly, the policy did not differ from Bustamante's in 1831, except that returnees would now come under the new, expanded rules of exception. At last, the wives and families had the government's ear.

While the Pedraza and Gómez Farías administrations were expanding possibilities for Spanish residence, the Chamber of Deputies' grand jury was building its case against officials of the Bustamante government. The central charge was instigating the assassination of Guerrero and several of his supporters. The "mishandling" of the expulsion was also at issue, and the grand jury pressed the ministry in April to provide all enforcement directives related to the 1829 expulsion. González Angulo found it difficult to pull the documents together, but assured the grand jury that copies would arrive in installments, as the entire collection was surveyed. Published trial proceedings, circulated by Bustamante's enemies, accused Alamán of "Permitting the introduction of a considerable number of [Spaniards], while hypocritically recommending vigilance in the matter." The formal charge was "infractions of the laws for the expulsion of Spaniards, permitting the introduction of many." Alamán and Facio stood accused of protecting Spaniards and a selection of expulsion documents was exhibited as evidence.[33]

Despite this "trial," it is clear that, although the 16 January executive decree revived the expulsion effort, the addition of grounds for protection—the "marriage" and "patriot" exceptions, revived from the 1827 expulsion law—made the majority of the *expulsos* eligible for residence in Mexico. It remained to be seen whether Congress and the public would accept these changes—instituted, ostensibly, as measures to strengthen enforcement of the 1829 expulsion law.

The Final Expulsion Laws (7 and 23 June 1833)

King Ferdinand's death in September 1833 fostered negotiations, but Mexican independence would not be recognized until 28 December 1836. Anti-Spanish tension persisted, and the government's generosity toward Spaniards probably contributed. Sánchez Espinosa wrote of his conviction that the political climate in Mexico City foretold another expulsion. Even Deputy Francisco Fagoaga, the brother of a prominent Spaniard, presented a bill in the chamber calling for the expulsion of all *gachupines*. On 5 June, the Querétaro legislature proposed a law for total expulsion, after the liberalized federal expulsion law of 23 April had been put into effect. A Chiapas bill was the first and only such measure to demand that Spanish women depart as well. It singled out for expulsion "citizens of whatsoever foreign power" and proscribed in perpetuity any who tried to return, "even if Spain should recognize independence." The Querétaro bill, introduced by Pablo Gudiño y Gómez and Julio Contreras, called for expulsion of all Spaniards within sixty days, excepting only those with "a notorious physical impediment," and demanding capital punishment for any *expulso* who attempted to return.[34] Neither of these extreme measures prospered.

The initiation of a new expulsion was avoided by a proclerical military revolt, led by Ignacio Escalada in Morelia on 26 May. It occurred during a cholera epidemic, which the gullible attributed to divine punishment brought on by the liberals in power. Santa Anna claimed on 30 May that, given the press of affairs of state, there had been no time to arrange an "appropriate measure" for the expulsion of Spaniards. His intention, he said, was to establish procedures assuring that no one was expelled unnecessarily. As if to demonstrate his moderation, in the same letter Santa Anna promised exception for one *peninsular* and readmission for another. The Spaniards were blamed for this rebellion too, even in official circles. On 1 June, Gabriel Durán rebelled at Tlalpan and Santa Anna was seized by his own troops when he marched there with Mariano Arista. According to his critics, Santa Anna was a willing victim who hoped to proclaim centralism and emerge as dictator. The "official" *Fénix* asserted that *gachupines* had paid Arista and Durán 5,000 pesos to assassinate Santa Anna. In response, Gómez Farías had many persons arrested, including the wealthy Spanish merchant, Antonio Alonso de Terán, to whom the treasury owed over one million pesos.[35]

Senate radicals seized the moment, seeking to promote a new expulsion while holding the *peninsulares* responsible for Santa Anna's "imprisonment." A law intended to save the government and resolve all pending "Spanish questions" was produced by Congress on 7 June 1833. The measure granted the regime "extraordinary faculties" for four months, in order to "re-establish order and consolidate federal institutions." It was to be applied only where rebellion threatened and in matters related to clergy, federal employees, and "illegal" Spaniards. Individuals could be exiled for a minimum of four years, or imprisoned, with Congress establishing time limits. What had been policy for some time gained legal sanction: Iturbide's "union" guarantee was ended and the notion that Spanish residents were simply "non-naturalized foreigners" substituted. Suspended *peninuslar* employees were reclassified as "retired," and their pensions limited by years of active service. The law would be used to expel two categories of *peninsulares*: those who had reentered with fraudulent Senate certificates, and all regular clergy previously excepted.[36]

The motives of the law's proponents were portrayed by the presidents of both chambers in an 8 June manifesto. José de Jesús Huerta and Joaquín Vargas accused the Spaniards of spreading fear that religion was threatened under liberal government and of responsibility in Guerrero's death and Santa Anna's capture. On 11 June, the Mexico City municipal government proposed to repress Spaniards who were accused of "fomenting discussions"—an unusual complaint from liberals. A commission urged the vice-president to order *peninsulares* to turn in their firearms, and to prohibit them from traveling on horseback, gathering in groups of three or more, venturing out after 10:00 P.M., or carrying arms in public. Penalties for violation ranged from 500 to 1,000 pesos, or from three to six months of public service. The commission also proposed to compile within three days a census of Spaniards in the Federal District. Mexicans were encouraged to report Spaniards who hid weapons.[37]

The frenzy reached its peak on 12 June when Congress considered a measure that would have imprisoned "the Spaniards and Americans notoriously disaffected from the federal system and enemies of the present regime," until Santa Anna was placed at liberty. *Gachupines* were to be held as hostages and, if Santa Anna came to harm, decapitated! Of course, the bill never became law. While such debates were publicly displayed, the Chamber of Deputies' committees of justice and public security were acting with moderation, considering exceptions for Pedro Haro, the brother-in-law of Judge Verde, and all Tabasco Spaniards.[38]

The third federal "expulsion" measure of 1833 was passed on 23 June, the famous Ley del Caso. Authority was granted to exile for six years fifty-one of the regime's enemies, the last of the Spanish regular clergy, and any who were found to be "in the same case" —hence the law's name. Two Spaniards, José Yermo and a medical doctor, Martínez Gutiérrez, in addition to the regular clergy, were included. The states were expected to implement measures of the same sort. Victims had three days to appear before the authorities, and those found hiding faced fines up to 1,000 pesos or imprisonment for six months or less. Officials obstructing enforcement would confront the same penalty; frontier and port authorities who did so risked their posts. An *expulso* who returned early faced reembarkation and permanent exile. The federal government reserved the right to decide the place of residence of anyone expelled by the states, and necessary funds were to be allocated to transport the indigent. An expelled government employee would be assigned up to two-thirds of salary, if he lacked property sufficient for his maintenance.[39]

Even under extraordinary powers in 1829, Guerrero was expressly prohibited from expelling Mexicans. The 1833 measure gave Gómez Farías the authority to exile any who opposed the regime. The vice-president immediately ordered the arrest of the remaining Spanish friars and confiscation of their property. The target was less the Spaniards per se than the foreign control and real estate of sectors of the church that were profoundly antiliberal. While the number of ecclesiastics had been declining, church property was on the increase, resulting in the growth of absentee landlordism.[40]

The friars of San Camilo and the Philippine missionaries were Spaniards, and, consequently, their property was especially vulnerable. Both convents in the capital had valuable holdings in Mexico State. A local law of 29 March 1833 had expropriated the missionaries' property and on 1 July the local congress declared San Camilo holdings to be state property as well. Not least among the Camilos' estates was the hacienda of Cuerámbaro in Guanajuato. On 2 August the vice-president authorized rapid sale of San Camilo convent's "goods and furnishings," and the whole was purchased by Cayetano Vigliete for 950 pesos. The vice-president took these measures under a grant of "extraordinary faculties" resulting from persistent rebellion in the *bajío*. The property of the Spanish Philippine missionaries was seized by federal authorities on 31 August. Because the expulsion laws had eliminated their order in Mexico, their holdings were in a state of abandonment. The hospices as well as rural and urban real estate, with all their contents and capital, became federal property, to be government administered. Justification was found in the fact that the estates had benefited regions still under Spanish rule.[41]

On 18 October, Bocanegra ordered the immediate sale of the temporal possessions, including real estate, of the Camilos and Filipinos.[42]

Spanish Ex-Employees: Their Posts and Salaries

The drain on the treasury forced the liberal government to confront the issue of salaried Spanish officeholders. On 29 July, all Spaniards who "possessed" public posts were reclassified as retired. Pensions ranged from one-third of salary after five years of service, to full salary after thirty years. These rules applied to Spanish ex-military men too, along with military regulations for retirement, with the exception that time in combat should not count double for any who fought against "independence or the Republic's liberty." Ecclesiastics in the Federal District or territories would receive one-third of their income, with the remainder going to their Mexican successors. Exception was made for those who had supported independence between 1810 and 1821, if they had neither subsequently reversed themselves nor opposed federalism. The crew of the *Asia* would continue to benefit, but with the limits set forth above, and Spanish-born generals were to be treated in the same terms.[43] Retired ex-employees would see their pensions adjusted downward accordingly.

In order to comply with the provisions of the 29 July decree, Gómez Farías ordered commanders to have subordinates specify their due, in terms of the decree, and send the service record of each at time of retirement for inspection. The vice-president also requested senior officials to provide opinions concerning the merits of each case. On 8 August, the requirements were set for establishing one's status under the 29 July decree. Office heads would determine the Spaniards' proper status and forward employment records to the ministry. In difficult cases, pay would be suspended until questions were resolved. Retired persons should forward authorized copies of their documents of retirement. The new rules took precedence over the 1830 regulations; once again it was stressed that the Spaniards were retired, not inactive employees.[44]

Two minor alterations occurred in October 1833 in the rights of *peninsulares* "possessing" public posts. The state of Mexico declared that a Spaniard holding an ecclesiastical sinecure should receive only one-third of his income, the rest reserved for the Mexican who filled his position. The state government claimed the right to name the new curates. Second, a federal decree of 26 October effectively retired the Spaniards who had formed a part of the military health branch. Military surgeons and professors of medicine had previously been excepted from the 10 May 1827 law, due to their technical skills.[45]

These arrangements prevailed until 21 March 1835, when, under the interim government of Gen. Miguel Barragán, the decree of 29 July 1833 was suspended. Barragán's more conservative regime reapplied the earlier law of 17 May 1828, restoring the rights of suspended Spanish employees and full salaries for posts they had not actually filled for the last eight years.[46]

The Pressure Persists

The spread of rebellion against the liberal government's anticlerical measures provided opportunities for the Spaniards to cultivate allies in a crusade for "religion and privileges." On 4 August 1833, accusations were launched against two *peninsulares*, Francisco de Paula Rubio and a certain Pumarejo. On 18 July, the vice-president had ordered all arms in the possession of Spaniards of the Federal District collected, under threat of a fine of 1,000 pesos or six months in prison for violators. The district government set twenty-four hours as the time limit for compliance and designated Col. Ignacio Yáñez as the responsible official.[47]

The push for renewed enforcement of the 20 March 1829 expulsion law came predominantly from the state of Mexico where numerous "illegals" were thought to live. The state legislature had begun to pressure the federal Congress and the governor in late March. On 2 September, a state congressional resolution urged the chambers to revise the lists of exceptions published in April 1829, and the federal and state executives to strictly comply with the 20 March 1829 law.[48] Governor García pressed the liberal government to actively enforce its own expulsion laws, which were aimed primarily at Spanish clergy.

Though the anti-*gachupín* mood persisted, federal enforcement followed the same "humane" track in 1833 that had characterized all post-Guerrero administrations for any except the clergy. A small number of Spaniards returned to Mexico, often settling in their original locations. The fate of Manuel Luna, a merchant of Guadalajara closely tied to British merchants, reveals the primacy of the governors in 1833. Anti-Spanish disturbances in June led to Luna's expulsion from the city, on charges of favoring the opposition. Pakenham took up his cause in Mexico City with limited success, and Luna was allowed to return to Guadalajara in September to wind up his affairs. The Oaxaca merchant Venancio Benito Muriel fared no better. Born in Spain but raised in New York, Muriel had immigrated to Mexico only in 1829, as a U.S. citizen, after the Mexico–United States treaty of friendship and commercial relations was signed. In 1833, Oaxaca passed another of its severe expulsion laws and, despite the protection due to foreign citizens, Muriel was expelled in October. Butler took up his cause in the capital. But on 29 October, the vice-president determined that, since the governor alleged the "danger" of Muriel's presence, it was not within federal authority to contradict the decision.[49]

Disappointed by uneven compliance, Herrera circulated new instructions in November, demanding expulsion of "illegal" Spaniards. He insisted that governors and state military commanders had joint responsibility for enforcement. In the remoteness of Upper California, the decree of 29 June arrived at a moment of social peace, following a period of conflict between the Spanish missionaries and non-Indian settlers. Echeandía was being replaced by a new governor, Figueroa. The Spanish friars there were, "with very few exceptions, advocates of Spanish interest and apologists of Spanish supremacy." Though never expelled, the padres were deprived of their missions, which became parishes controlled by the secular clergy. In Mexico State, proexpulsion sentiment was reflected in a law of 6 December that exiled for six years some fifty-three persons, drawn from a list of more than three hundred. Article 6 declared that "no Spaniard will be allowed to reside in the district of Cuernavaca and Hacienda of Jalmolonga." Violators were subject to expulsion within fifteen days. C. M. Bustamante noted that the task of enforcing the law was assigned to the vice-governor, Félix María Aburto, but that the "persecution" was mitigated by a Cuban, José María Heredia, a radical poet and deputy in the state congress.[50]

By December 1833, the federal government had adopted a tougher line on expulsion, as the fate of two upstanding Tampico Spaniards reveals. Informants had warned the administration that Mariano Cubí y Soler, a teacher and U.S. citizen, and Mateo López, a specialist in political economy, were dangerous men who should be expelled. The governor of Tamaulipas took strong exception to both the unfavorable testimony and the decision, and penned an eloquent appeal to the vice-president. The case of Cubí y Soler was unusually strong: he was a liberal and a conscientious professor who had founded a school which was much in demand—apparently the first in the region—and enjoyed strong support from the community. In addition, as a U.S. citizen, he might have been excepted. But Gómez Farías chose to ignore the governor's decision, insisting that since "no record of legal entry existed," the law must not be flouted. The military commander was ordered to expel the two.[51] The fact that the school would surely close merited no consideration in the ministry's response.

Enforcement in 1834

By late December 1833, many priests from Mexico, including Spaniards, were arriving at U.S. ports. In Mexico, the number of clergy fell from 1,726 in 1829, to 1,411 at the end of 1834. Spaniards represented only a part of a more general downward trend. The attack on Spanish clerics persisted into 1834: a law of 25 January reiterated the exile of fifty-one persons plus the Spanish regular clergy originally called for in the 23 June 1833 decree.[52] This fifth expulsion law amounted to an admission that enforcement in 1833 had not been complete. The two measures were not repealed until 27 February 1835, under General Barragán's centralist regime.

Merchants affected by the law would need time to settle their accounts; José María and Gabriel Yermo appealed to Congress on 27 January for four months' extension to arrange their affairs in Mexico and Puebla. The justice commission of the chamber of deputies rejected their petition in February, recommending appeal to the president. José María approached Congress anew, requesting six months for himself. The merchant Antonio Terán claimed illness, as usual, but lost important support in February. Governor Patricio Furlong of Puebla had believed Terán, then learned of deceit, and repented of ever having backed the appeal. "You were correct," the governor wrote to Gómez Farías, "do what you think just."[53]

By early 1834, some *peninsulares* expelled by local laws sought to reenter their states with federal documents. Andrés Palacio y Bringas, driven out of Querétaro by a local measure, had settled in the capital and gained exception from the federal law. In January he applied for a passport to return to Querétaro. Governor Tornel urged the vice-president to establish a policy for such cases, and Gómez Farías authorized a passport, in light of the federal exception. The expulsion of many *peninsulares* was still held up by lack of funding to complete the expulsion. Minister of Government Francisco María Lombardo asked Aburto for a detailed report, promising that money would be made available.[54]

In the remote regions of the north and west, anomalous situations were revealed in 1834. Several priests who should have been expelled under the law of 1829 were found residing in Sonora. Gómez Farías's policy in such cases was to order the violators marched to Mexico City where they would be judged—as Governor Múzquiz had recommended in 1831. In Sinaloa, Spaniards were encountered serving as federal employees and members of the militia in defiance of the *empleos* law; they too were ordered to the capital.[55]

The Gómez Farías regime frustrated the ambitions of certain *expulsos* who hoped to return from exile. Officials at the ports were alerted to watch for those claiming U.S. citizenship. In April, Governor Pedro Tames of Jalisco reported that José María Castaños y Aguirre was being held for reembarkation at Tepic. Castaños had entered through Tampico in January and recently obtained a letter of security from Butler for one year. The vice-president ordered his reembarkation, despite the U.S. citizenship claim and Butler's protection. Gómez Farías was more concerned than his predecessors about the political impact of having "U.S.-citizen Spaniards" in public view. His concerns were justified; an anti-*gachupín* riot had taken place in Celaya, Guanajuato, on 22 March and, in early April, a Spaniard, Fernández Aguado, was accused of inciting revolt in Veracruz. On 14 March, Herrera ordered port authorities to allow no returnee covered in the expulsion provisions of the 23 June law to disembark; once again, the government would attempt to hold ship captains responsible for infractions.[56]

Relief at Last:
Conservative Government and the Spaniards, 1834–1836

The regime's clash with the church hierarchy peaked on 29 March when Gómez Farías, confronting yet another attempted coup d'état, ordered the expulsion of Bishop Francisco Pablo Vázquez of Puebla, the last resident member of the hierarchy. The attempt was a fiasco; Vázquez evaded arrest and went into hiding. In response, Furlong decreed the expulsion from Puebla, within twenty-four hours, of twenty individuals, seven of whom were clerics. The crisis that ensued brought down the Gómez Farías government in May 1834. Santa Anna succumbed to the anguished cries of conservatives and removed his vice-president. He ended persecution of the church hierarchy, dismissed Congress, abolished the laws concerning ecclesiastical patronage, restored the authority of the fugitive bishops, and ended the banishment of individuals. The church-run university, closed by the liberals, reopened, and a thoroughly conservative government was put in place. On 2 May, before its abolition, the old Congress declared Santa Anna dictator, granting him the right "to make as many changes in the constitution of 1824 as he should think needful for the good of the nation, without the hindrances and delays which that instrument prescribed."[57] The pro-Santa Anna Plan of Cuernavaca, announced on 23 May 1834, spelled out a conservative agenda and called upon the president to act as dictator in order to effect it. *Peninsulares* could take heart from these events.

The advent of conservatism meant that no more laws of expulsion would be aimed at *gachupines*. Steps were immediately taken to invalidate the controversial decrees of the Gómez Farías era. On 2 May, the new government began to repeal the 23 June 1833 expulsion law. The income provisions of the decree, which had "retired" suspended Spanish employees, were modified on 9 May to invalidate payments to persons residing in enemy territory, then three days later the decree's expulsion provisions were repealed. Governors were instructed on 21 June that men who had not departed under the 1833 measure no longer need comply. In other words, the victims could safely come out of hiding. Two days later it was announced that those expelled under the law could return to their families, pending final resolution by Congress.[58]

Most revealing was a change in official attitudes concerning ex-military men who had served Spain during the reconquest effort. In May, Col. Diego Argüelles appealed from Bordeaux for permission to return. Using a new procedure for handling such cases, the minister of government, Francisco María Lombardo, passed the appeal to the minister of war for resolution. Lombardo was favorably inclined, noting the positive opinion of the Mexican envoy in France. But Herrera reminded his colleague that on 2 July 1831, Argüelles was discharged from service for desertion to Spanish ranks. Since he no longer possessed the *fuero militar,* his appeal would not pertain to the ministry of war. On 10 August, Santa Anna authorized Argüelles's return, in light of the colonel's "misery and illnesses." Lt. Col. Miguel de la Vega was excepted from the expulsion law of 1829 in March 1835. Another indicator of the new reality was the presence of Col. Joaquín Rea—the Spanish son-in-law of General Bravo—in the republic in August 1834.[59]

This did not mean that all Spaniards would be accepted and protected. *Peninsulares* considered dangerous by the new regime's definition would find themselves ordered to the ports. In September, Tornel secretly urged Lombardo to issue a passport to the Spaniard Mateo Llano, the editor of an opposition periodical, whom the adaptable Tornel found to be an "incorrigible" person with liberal pretensions. The government gave its approval and, though Llano appealed

for protection, he was arrested and expelled. Nor was nativist sentiment absent from the new conservative order. Mexican hostility to
foreign brokers threatened to deprive some *peninsulares* of their liveli-
hood. On 10 October, the governor of the Federal District decreed
new regulations outlawing broker activity by foreigners, but expressly
exempted "Spaniards who were in the republic in 1821." Such *peninsulares*, he declared, were "considered Mexicans." The governor's decree
treated all Spaniards arriving after 1821 as foreigners. The president
did not rebuke Tornel and, consequently, foreign merchants refused,
on 24 November, to provide a loan for Santa Anna.[60]

The new authorities in Mexico State also reconsidered their anticlerical and anti-Spanish legislation of 1833. On 15 October 1834,
the state government repealed the 29 March 1833 law concerning
the property of the Spanish religious, as well as the May laws "retir-
ing" public employees, and the 3 July expulsion law. In November,
at the national level, Gómez Farías's decree of 29 July 1833, which,
among other things, prohibited Spanish military men from receiving
double time towards retirement for campaigns served under the
Spanish flag, was modified in cases where the individual had later
rendered services to independence. The minister of war announced
on 29 October that back pay from November 1833 would accrue to
these men.[61]

During 1835, a second round of decrees sought to nullify the
laws of the Gómez Farías era. The new Congress pardoned all who
had committed political crimes between 27 September 1821 and 4
January 1835, excluding only "those not born in the republic who
had pronounced against the government since 1 May 1834." This
meant that Spaniards could now be politically active, so long as they
abjured conspiracy. A circular of 18 February declared that, in order
to restore fathers to their families, all political exiles could return
to the republic. The word *Spaniards* was not mentioned. A measure
of 27 February declared the 23 June 1833 decree "null in its origin," and restored ex-employee salary rights and standard calculations of career time. To consolidate the change, a decree of 21
March restored ex-employees' rights to those of 17 May 1828, while
the law of 22 May 1835 authorized the liquidation with bonds of the
"half salaries" assigned to these Spaniards on 12 September 1829.[62]

The new "official" periodical, *El Anteojo*, conveniently ignored
Santa Anna's past and blamed the expulsions on "extremists" who
pursued their goal "with notable damage to the laws and prejudice
to the nation." The editors remarked, "The permanance of the Spaniards among us was just, and they deserved to enjoy all the rights

and guarantees conceded to Mexicans." It was in this spirit that the government evolved toward centralism. A circular of 23 October set the basis for the new system: states would become departments, headed by elected governors and juntas. Henceforth, civil, criminal, and tax law would be uniform for the entire nation.[63]

As Spain drew nearer to recognizing Mexican independence, some Spaniards began to contemplate recovery of their old bureaucratic posts. The ministry forwarded to the congressional secretaries on 14 November 1835 an appeal for José González for reinstatement to a post in the tobacco monopoly. González believed, erroneously, that Spain had extended recognition—which would not occur until December 1836. Despite delays in recognition, the president recommended González's petition. A 29 January 1836 decree "provisionally" restored Spaniards' rights to positions that had not been abolished, at previous salaries. By order of the treasury minister, ex-employees were to apply for reinstatement through their department heads, providing evidence of past salary. Some *peninsulares* did regain official positions; in October 1839, the U.S. consul at Paral, Chihuahua, noted, "In this place the officers are all old Spaniards, and Centralists."[64]

Under the new policy of tolerance, exiled Spaniards in Europe could take ship for Mexico. The government declared anew in May 1835 that General Negrete could return, though he chose not to. In August, U.S. Consul Burrough at Veracruz complained that "foreigners" were arriving from France and Spain, with passports obtained from the Mexican consul in New York. They were admitted as U.S. citizens though Burrough refused to sign their passports. Eusebio García sailed from France in March 1836, bearing a letter of recommendation from Miguel Santa María, Mexico's representative, and despatches for the minister of government. His papers were routinely expedited at Veracruz, without reference to the expulsion law of 1829 or any decree or circular of 1833. When Ignacio Aloy disembarked at Veracruz in September 1836 with U.S. citizenship papers, the only concern of the central government was that passport regulations be adhered to. Aloy was only required to obtain the "letter of security" demanded of all foreign residents. The authorities were not blind to the potential hostility that returning Spaniards could generate, and they took steps to assure that formal requirements were fulfilled. When Lorenzo Serrano landed at Veracruz in October 1836, he was ordered to post a bond until he had proof of his marriage to a Mexican. Tornel verified Serrano's marital status and he was declared excepted by the law of 16 January 1833.[65]

New possibilities of entry led some Spanish emigrants to select Mexico as their destination in 1836. Acting President José Justo Corro sought to discourage this; on 26 October, two months prior to Spanish recognition, he prohibited disembarkation by any Spaniard who had not previously lived in the republic. To enter, a *peninsular* was required to possess a passport issued by the federal government and documents justifying his legal exception from the expulsion law of 1829.[66] Recognition of independence on 28 December 1836 brought with it the anticipated reconciliation, and permitted immigration to begin anew. At last, Spaniards could be guaranteed security of residence and freedom from prosecution. Just two days later, on 30 December, a conservative "constitution" was adopted, and Mexico embarked upon an era of restricted "democracy": suffrage was limited to males earning a minimum of 100 pesos per year, senators and the president were elected indirectly, and governors of departments were selected by the president from local lists.[67] After witnessing the "excesses" of popular government, by the late 1830s, persons of property favored limited representation, with property and income requirements for officeholders.

Eruptions of antigachupinism would still occur during periods of national crisis, foreign intervention, or civil strife. The alien merchant, whether Spanish or Chinese, was especially vulnerable at such times. In December 1861, for example, when Mexico's Gulf coast was besieged by the fleets of France, Spain, and England, and Spanish troops had occupied the port of Veracruz, the *peninsular* merchants of Tampico were expelled by General de la Garza. They were allowed to return in February 1862, after the Spanish marines had withdrawn.[68] In 1910–11, during the Revolution, Spaniards were expelled from Morelos, by Zapata, and Chihuahua, by Villa. As recently as 1929, a "subject of Tlalixcoyan" could call for the expropriation and expulsion of Spaniards, in response to an essay in praise of Spanish culture by José Vaconcelos.[69] And while in the late 1930s President Cárdenas welcomed the Spanish victims of the Franco regime, in more recent times Spaniards visiting Mexico were required to post bond guaranteeing their departure. The relationship between Mexican and Spaniard remains ambivalent. Perhaps this book can contribute to mutual tolerance by illustrating that persecution debilitates both sides. This constitutes one of the important lessons from Mexico's past.

Postscript

OUR PRINCIPAL task has been to examine the four national efforts to expel Mexico's Spanish-born male population occurring between 1827 and 1834. The interpretation was largely informed by voluminous archival records generated by the official nature of the purges. The executive and Congress oversaw these efforts (less so in the case of the two laws of 1833), and the minister of government became the principal figure who, under federalism, relied heavily upon the governors of the states and territories to assure compliance. In complex or controversial cases, the president usually made the final decision. Time limits for compliance and departure were set by the laws and the usual destination was New Orleans, since federal aid was authorized for the closest foreign port. To depart for Havana or Spain, or to touch at a port under Spanish domination, prejudiced not only one's "job ownership" rights but the possibility of return to Mexico in the future.

Behind the expulsion measures of 1827, 1829, and 1833 was a popular, national, anti-*gachupín* movement. To comprehend the seriousness of the anti-Spanish campaign, developments were examined not only at the federal level but in at least fourteen states where similar local movements gained momentum and anti-*peninsular* laws resulted. Numerous local and national revolts, plus a schism in Mexican Masonry were involved.

Passage of the laws was followed by countless dilemmas of enforcement—and contradictions between state and federal measures and policies. Under the constitution of 1824, citizenship was vested in the states. Radical federalists (state's rights advocates) would demand ever more stringent local laws to compensate for "loopholes" believed to exist in federal legislation. Spanish survivors of these efforts who resided in the states were veterans not only of the federal measures but, often, of an equal number of local laws as well. The result of a mass of hostile legislation was that roughly three-quarters of Mexico's *peninsular* community departed between 1827 and 1834.

On the eve of the first expulsion, the Spanish community numbered approximately 6,600 men, perhaps one-half of whom were

207

capitulados, veterans of the independence wars who had stayed on, married, and begun raising families, while engaging in humble occupations. The first federal law was aimed at the unmarried *capitulados*: they were seen as a potential fifth column during a Spanish invasion. The law was also directed at the *peninsular* clergy who, by definition, were unmarried; and, of course, at those considered dangerous. Excepted were those who were ill, had wives and children to support, had needed skills, or had served the cause of independence. Exemptions for so many categories facilitated abuse of the law, especially through favoritism toward friends, family members, or colleagues. The medical exemption opened the door for questionable professional judgments and bribes. So anxious were doctors and surgeons to join in these proceedings that rotational lists had to be drawn up by the guild itself to share the opportunities equitably. Many wealthy Spaniards found it possible to evade expulsion, while the poor majority—the enlisted men from the king's ranks during the wars—had fewer options. Article 9 made it possible to expel those considered dangerous, even if married. Federal authorities attempted to assure that governors who accused individuals under Article 9 could prove their cases and, as the months passed, it became more difficult to use its sweeping faculties. Both governors Tornel of the Federal District and Santa Anna of Veracruz stood accused of arbitrariness in expulsions and exceptions.

I estimated that at least 1,779 Spaniards were expelled in 1827–28, with 4,831 remaining by mid-1828. Former soldiers of Spain had suffered the most, followed by Spanish clerics, both regular and secular. Oaxaca and San Luis Potosí were zealous in their enforcement, while in Guanajuato, where Padre Hidalgo's followers had massacred hundreds of *gachupines* in 1810, the Spanish population was hardly molested—as if to atone for the excesses of the past. Mexico State, under Governor Zavala, saw only 5 percent of its *peninsulares* depart. Nationally, about 45 percent of the survivors were merchants.

The Montaño revolt, sponsored by Bravo and the Scottish party in December 1827, constituted a futile effort to prevent enforcement of the first federal law of expulsion. It was defeated by Yorkist leaders within the army. Those same Yorkinos would utilize Santa Anna's rebellion at Perote, and the Acordada revolt in December 1828, to take charge of a lame-duck Victoria government and prepare the way for a popular regime, headed by Guerrero—grand master of the Yorkino lodges. Santa Anna's rebellion at Perote revived the Spanish question—as a weapon to be used against the Victoria government and its minister of war, Gómez Pedraza, who had recently won indirect election (by state legislatures) for president. While Perote did not actually triumph, the rebels at the Acordada did, with the help of the poor of Mexico City. The Acordada uprising signaled the vigor of the anti-Spanish movement and the likelihood of a new, more severe law. The anti-*gachupín* tone of the revolt, and the looting of Mexico City's mercantile district, the Parián, resulted in the flight of a number of Spanish merchants who feared for their future in Mexico. Some also saw in emigration "with leave" a way of avoiding expulsion and thus stigmatization, which might make future return difficult or impossible.

Yorkist rule in 1829 produced a second general law of expulsion. A cooperative lower house overcame a hesitant Senate to present the Guerrero regime with a seemingly unyielding law. No longer would marriage, or services to independence, or special skills be acceptable sources of exception. And Congress claimed ultimate responsibility for decisions, implying that the ministry was to blame for the failures of 1828. In practice, Congress was anything but responsible. Not only did it fail to resolve any of the complex questions resulting from enforcement dilemmas, it proved to be the second most important source of exceptions. Influence was at work once again. Of the two houses, the Senate granted more favors, but the lower chamber, and even Yorkino deputies, provided at least forty-six exceptions. On 21 April 1829, Congress produced its lists of favored individuals. Since there was no general agreement on the names, the legal requirement of approval by both houses was unconstitutionally dispensed with, and, in practice, a Spaniard whose name appeared on one of the lists could remain in the republic or return from New Orleans or Bordeaux.

The *facultativos* provided even more exemptions. In Veracruz, in fact, the majority of the medical practitioners were *peninsulares*. As a result of their decisions, as well as those of the chambers, public wrath threatened to destabilize the regime. Tornel, the Yorkino governor of the Federal District, accused of favoring Spaniards in exchange for bribes, proved once again to be the most active enforcer of the general law. Of course, a result of the first expulsion had been to concentrate a great many uprooted *peninsulares* in the capital.

Guanajuato, and other states that had been lenient in 1828, compensated in 1829 by thorough enforcement of the new expulsion. Once again, the states passed their own expulsion laws, the most severe being San Luis Potosí and Oaxaca. In the latter, *expulsos* were allowed less than forty-eight hours to arrange their affairs, and the *facultativos* were unrelenting. The resort of the victims in such cases was, often, to attempt to find exception and refuge in Mexico City or in Veracruz State, where they might obtain a hearing.

As the five-month "official" period of enforcement ended in August 1829, Tornel was feuding—just as in June 1828—with the Ministry of Government over federally created "bureaucratic obstructions." These procedures had developed in the course of enforcement to prevent arbitrary behavior on the part of governors. The sole legal criterion for exception from expulsion was physical disability or illness, either temporary or permanent. In the former case, the *peninsular* was subjected to periodic reexamination by *facultativos*. Restoration of health resulted in expulsion. Any Spaniard who remained in Mexico was required to possess one of two documents: a "legitimate" certificate of exception from Congress, or a negative report from the medical junta. A market in both types of dispensations quickly developed.

Radical nativists soon noticed that prominent Spaniards, including notorious monarchists known to be hostile to independence, were still visible in Mexico City. An investigation of *facultativos* produced inconclusive results. Most *peninsulares* were excepted once again, but at least 1,090 arrived at New Orleans, most with passages paid by the federal government. The better-off usually sailed on to Bordeaux, where they continued their mercantile trade. Colonialists made for Havana, or Spain, where they were soon involved in hatching plans for the reconquest of "New Spain." Roughly 140 of the latter joined Barradas in his ill-fated reconquest attempt in 1829. Rich merchants, Spanish and Mexican, plied the court at Madrid with tales of easy conquest, tempting Ferdinand VII to pursue his dream of restored imperial glory.

In Mexico, by the summer of 1829, there were signs of a gradual return to the spirit of coexistence between Mexicans and Spaniards. Yorkino periodicals moderated their tone, influenced, in part, by the obvious suffering of Spaniards and their destitute Mexican families. The Yorkino party split along lines dictated by attitudes toward this second effort at expulsion, with the progovernment group convinced that enough had been accomplished, and the other outraged at the glaring exceptions. The crisis within the government party and Congress further weakened the Guerrero regime at a time when the treasury was nearing collapse and war threatened.

Ferdinand's ambition to reconquer his former colonies produced a number of naval actions in the course of the nineteenth century, but only one actual invasion, which prompted independent Mexico's first successful defense of its sovereignty. Close examination of the major plans of the colonist camp revealed a curious attempt to exploit social and racial divisions that had been major features of New Spain's society. The appeal did not succeed in undermining republican sentiment. The Spanish threat was real, not simply a charade concocted by a conservative government to mask its brutal domestic war against the supporters of the deposed Guerrero, and it continued to exist until the court at Madrid learned of the 1830 Paris revolt and decided to keep its military close to Madrid. Our interest is focused on the impact of such efforts upon the "Spanish question" in Mexico and the reality of the Spanish threat, which made preparations for a future invasion necessary. During much of 1830, Spain accumulated a sizable army of invasion in Cuba, and it made no secret of its aggressive intentions. Exiled Mexican and Spanish merchants were prepared to finance the effort.

By providing officers for the cause, the expulsions enhanced the external threat to Mexico's independence. The surrender of Barradas's forces at Tampico was owing to the failure of resupply, a yellow fever epidemic among the Spanish troops, and to the swift response of active and militia units. A number of the Mexican officers who fought at Tampico were Escoceses, men the Yorkinos had arbitrarily labeled monarchists. Mexico had defended herself, despite an empty treasury.

Resident *peninsulares* did not suffer unduly from this episode; the most serious retributive behavior was apparently limited to Tampico itself. The Guerrero government did not impose a harsher version of the expulsion, nor did exceptions cease. Some *expulsos* suffered the indignity of having to journey to Pacific ports, making the voyage to exile a lengthy one. A reticent Congress conceded "extraordinary powers" to the president, who used them with discretion. Guerrero even excepted fourteen Spaniards under this authority. Conservatives' later charges of arbitrary behavior seem wholly unjustified.

The opponents of expulsion and of the Yorkinos were able to act as a result of the fiscal crisis; when no solution emerged, the unpaid reserve army in the east marched on the capital in December 1829, abruptly ending "radical" government. It remained to be seen how the more conservative Liberals might implement the expulsion law. Minister Alamán chose to comply—confronted as he was by the threat of invasion sponsored by Spain. But Alamán's compliance was governed by the law in its most literal terms. The new regime and its supporters in Congress did not attack the law per se. The new government favored the return of Spaniards whose families had remained in Mexico, though this proved politically difficult and fiscally impossible in the short term. Bustamante and Alamán faced popular resistance to their policies and resorted to repressive actions in the face of a guerrilla threat in 1830–32. While Spanish plans for recon-quest were being implemented, the new regime put in place a system of voluntary contributions for coastal defense that elicited broad-based popular participation. Revenues generated in this cause were not used in the domestic conflict against the regime's enemies in the south.

The ministry issued more than 3,400 passports to Spaniards dur-ing 1829–32; perhaps as many as 1,200 departed. Approximately 2,090 were excepted from expulsion by alleged infirmities. The lists of the excepted, published in 1833, contained 2,699 names. Most of the survivors of 1829 sought refuge in three metropolitan areas: the capital, Puebla, and Guadalajara, as well as the port cities to which they had been sent by expulsion orders. A number who should have departed did not, for two reasons: first, funds to pay their passage were soon exhausted and, second, the Spanish invasion of July 1829 led to the evacuation from the Gulf coast of waiting *expulsos*.

The characteristics of the victims had changed: while the first law hit unmarried *capitulados* and clergy hardest, the second affected principally merchants and married Spaniards. The first two expul-sions, taken together, eliminated roughly half the 1827 Spanish com-munity: the 1827 law had expelled some 27 percent, and the 1829 measure exiled at least 29 percent of the survivors. The two laws also very nearly eliminated the Spanish regular orders. Capital flight was a serious problem, promoting the disappearance of specie from circulation. More than 3 million gold pesos arrived in Bordeaux, for example. Trade with Europe was temporarily interrupted as the ex-pulsions devastated merchant networks and cooled the demand for imports. Bankruptcies and bad debts were common. Tax revenue de-clined, since the system was heavily dependent upon import and ex-port levies. Foreign merchant houses took the place of Spanish family networks. Given the prevalence of voluntary emigration accompany-ing the purge, possibly no more than 2,200 *peninsulares* remained by 1830.

For some exiles, the only chance of return seemed to be successful reconquest. But whether they remained in New Orleans or attempted invasion of Tampico, many succumbed to the devastating fever epi-demic which swept through those areas in 1829–30. The *expulsos'* determination to return to Mexico was apparent from the outset, and the composition of the Bustamante government suggested new possibilities. Up to 400 chose to test the willingness of Bustamante and Alamán to allow reentry. As U.S. vessels began transporting returnees to Veracruz or Tampico, the administration confronted a crisis that, in time, proved to be its undoing. Initially, Alamán applied the 1829 law to the letter, refusing admission to those who lacked exceptions. But, as returnees began to present documents attesting to newly acquired U.S. citizenship (obtained in Louisiana), or certificates of exception provided by congressional secretaries, the minister was confronted with two profound dilemmas. In the case of the "U.S. citizens," Alamán protested to U.S. representatives the ease with which documents were obtained at New Orleans, but accepted the claims of the returnees. He did so even when U.S. consuls were not inclined to believe such individuals. Alamán found it necessary to probe the matter of congressional certificates. Congress was uncooperative, however, and the ministry was forced to conclude that many of the certificates were fraudulent. Eventually, it established a procedure that led to disembarkation for the Spaniards, and a period of waiting at or near the coast, while the validity of the congressional exceptions was examined in the capital. The lists of 21 April 1829 were searched to determine whether a returnee's name was present. But it soon became apparent that there were differing versions of the lists and when Alamán requested an "autographed copy," Congress balked. Clearly, "transactions" had taken place, and forthright responses to ministry inquiries would have risked their exposure.

What had occurred was quite simple. Wives, relatives, and agents of *expulsos* had exhausted all avenues in attempting to obtain exceptions for their Spaniards, even after their departure. Congress, especially the Senate, provided the most generous opportunity. The "final lists" of 21 April were not final at all. Names continued to be added and the lists multiplied. At least one attempt was made to insert new names into the original version. And someone began to distribute "certificates of exception" that could be sent to *expulsos* to enable them to return. The dilemma was whether these certificates should be recognized. The Bustamante administration rejected them and insisted upon re-embarkation, if the bearer's name was not on the original lists. In such cases, two options confronted the returnee: either return to New Orleans at his own expense (there were no government funds available), or join the many who claimed illness. Most chose the latter.

A number arrived without documents other than "letters of good conduct" obtained from the Mexican consulate. Once at the pontoon, they were prepared to claim illness, seeking an opportunity to be seen by Veracruz's notoriously lenient junta of *facultativos*, most of them Spaniards. Local authorities were convinced that they were favorably inclined towards the petitioners and that the only way to avoid abuses would be to confine the "ill" to what passed for a hospital —a tactic certain to drive many back to New Orleans. But Alamán and the vice-president would not accede to this measure, and even allowed the returnees to leave the ports to avoid the danger of fever. It was not long before returnees began appearing in the interior without documents, or with papers of dubious merit.

Popular wrath was stirred. The reappearance of *gachupines*, some of whom had been outspoken opponents of republican institutions, evoked a predictable response in Mexico's cities and villages. The Bustamante administration lost support partly because of popular conviction that they had openly connived for the Spaniards' return. What the documents reveal is not a conspiracy but, rather, the evolution of a fairly consistent policy that was strictly legal but quite generous in enabling Spaniards to take advantage of mechanisms (such as the juntas of *facultativos*) that developed in the law's wake. Perhaps the most questionable policy was to allow returnees to be seen anew by a medical junta. By implication, any "ill" Spaniard could take ship for a Mexican port and, having suffered through the voyage, be excepted, at least temporarily, from reexpulsion. Once word reached New Orleans (by return voyage), the floodgates were opened. Suspended government employees returned bearing certificates of good behavior (testifying to never having supported reconquest), hoping to retrieve their former salaries.

Popular passion seems to have exaggerated the number of returnees, but their visibility was sufficient to undermine confidence in the regime. Conspiracies were hatched, using the Spanish question as a motive, in addition to the administration's policy of assassinating its captured enemies in the guerrilla war of the south. In 1832, former government supporters joined the rebel ranks, and at Tampico, Moctezuma began to expel Spaniards anew, including merchants, all of whom claimed U.S. citizenship. When Santa Anna joined the rebellion, the demise of the Bustamante regime seemed assured. The resulting compromise, the Plan of Zavaleta, saved the federal system but ended the regime. The moderate Pedraza would serve out the final days of the presidential term to which he had been elected in 1828.

Between January and April 1833, the new president sought to resolve several aspects of the "Spanish question," including the matter of illegal returnees. González Angulo, the new minister of government, began by attempting to determine who possessed legal exceptions and halting returns based on false pretexts. A presidential decree of 16 January 1833 renewed the expulsion, but in a less harsh form. Now, the governors—not the executive or Congress—would be in charge of enforcement. The terms were set by Pedraza, however, and responded to the obvious need to deal humanely with the breakup of families, exacerbated by the 1829 measure. This third expulsion was aimed at unmarried Spaniards who had returned illegally. Married *peninsulares* with dependents in Mexico would be allowed to remain, legally or not. In addition, those with citizenship in friendly nations were safe for the moment. Governors could expel "dangerous" *gachupines*, but each case had to be justified to federal authorities.

What passed for original lists, dated 21 April 1829, were used by the governors in deciding the legitimacy of exceptions for the unmarried. The documents now contained precisely 2,706 names. Contemporaries sometimes assumed that this third law never took effect, clearly an oversimplification. In fact, it was not implemented everywhere, partly because many *peninsulares* preferred not to come forward, perhaps awaiting their fate under the government that would follow in April 1833. Obviously, only a small number of Spaniards were expelled under the 16 January decree, because, first of all, there were no funds to pay their passage. The limited available data—drawn primarily from the Federal District—suggest that at least two-thirds of the resident *peninsulares* were eligible for exception under the new law. Once again, many claimed illness.

To bolster public confidence in enforcement, governors were now allowed to overrule the medical guild in selecting the juntas of *facultativos*. In practice, a Spaniard who had served the cause of independence was granted exception. To eliminate the abuse of claiming U.S. citizenship, Gónzalez Angulo declared that ten years' residence in the United States was now required. When Congress opened sessions in April 1833, it began to limit the administration's generosity. One of its first acts was to demote suspended Spanish employees to retirees, lowering their salaries in accordance with time actually served. In another respect, federal policy was still restrictive: returnees continued to be barred. The returnee issue was still politically sensitive in early 1833.

Enforcement in the states varied according to the attitudes of local officials. San Luis Potosí still harbored considerable hostility, and its authorities pressured the federal Congress to consider a new law of expulsion. The 16 January decree displeased both the governor and the legislature. A harsh expulsion measure passed in San Luis Potosí

in April and efforts mounted, here and in other states, to obtain
a similar law at the national level. Jalisco, too, sought to eliminate
its Spaniards in 1833, passing a law that exiled not only *peninsulares*
but forty-one of the local government's Mexican opponents as well.
And Chiapas also demanded another round. An opposite response
came from Yucatán and Campeche, where local authorities worked
to gain exceptions for all Spanish residents. In liberal Zacatecas, 87.2
percent of the Spaniards were excepted under the 16 January measure.

   The inauguration of the Santa Anna–Gómez Farías government
in April 1833 resulted in greater flexibility on the Spanish question.
Santa Anna left the administration in the hands of his liberal vice-
president, whose real cause was to curb the secular wealth and political power of the church. Gómez Farías sent a measure to Congress
legitimizing the expanded exception categories put into practice by
Gómez Pedraza. Included in the ranks of the excepted were the married or widowed with Mexican children, those who served independence, or crew members of the Spanish naval vessels that had surrendered in 1821. In May, the new minister of government, García,
informed port authorities that returnees should be permitted to
land while their cases were resolved in Mexico City. This differed
from Bustamante policy of 1831 only in that the new possibilities
made exceptions easier to obtain. Not all political sectors approved
of such changes under the guise of renewed enforcement of the
1829 law. Public debate was soon under way concerning a new,
more drastic expulsion.

   While San Luis Potosí, Chiapas, and Querétaro pressed for a
tougher expulsion law, the Gómez Farías government launched its
anticlerical campaign, and—more telling perhaps—the country began to suffer a severe cholera epidemic. Both stirred crises of sufficient proportions to distract even the most avid hispanophobe. Conservatives seized the moment to rebel. Under the circumstance, no
new policy initiative was forthcoming. In fact, the movement for centralism began to gather strength. Spaniards could take renewed hope
in the prospect and their enemies claimed to see the *gachupín's* nefari-
ous hand at work in the rebellion. The administration obtained a
law on 7 June 1833 granting the executive "extraordinary faculties"
for four months. Exile of individuals was permitted, in order to "save
federal institutions," and Spaniards were now designated "non-
naturalized foreigners." Suspended employees were officially declared to be retired, formalizing the Pedraza decree. The 7 June mea-

sure was the first of two laws that launched a fourth and final expulsion effort. It resulted in an attempt to expel two categories of *peninsulares*: returnees with illegal certificates of exception, and all remaining Spanish regular clergy.

The momentum came from Congress and the governments of the Federal District and several states. Spaniards' civil liberties were sharply curtailed in the capital. Behind the scenes, however, congressional committees were still authorizing exceptions for qualified *peninsulares*. A law of 23 June 1833, the second such measure, had a greater impact, however. The famous Ley del Caso ordered the expulsion of fifty-one enemies of the regime and the Spanish regular clergy as a whole, plus anyone found to be "in the same case." The Spanish friars were arrested and their property confiscated, to be sold at public auction. Two religious orders were particularly affected, since they were entirely Spanish—the Philippine missionaries and the San Camilos.

The issue of the rights of suspended government employees begged resolution as well. By a decree of 29 July 1833, they were limited to either one-third or two-thirds of former salaries, unless they had actually served thirty years or more. Spanish military officers could not count their combat time in Spanish service as double time toward retirement, unless they later served independence and had not "regressed" since 1821.

Despite these measures, calls for a renewed expulsion continued. Increasingly, the push came from Mexico State, which unwillingly harbored a large number of illegals. In self-defense, some *peninsulares* joined in the evolving conspiracy to abolish federalism. But despite pressure, federal authorities continued recent policies deriving from the new rules broadening exceptions. In addition, returnees continued to trickle in, spreading out across Mexico. To defend itself, the Gómez Farías government, when pressed, gave way to the will of state governors, refusing through much of 1833 to override local decisions. In the case of "U.S. citizens," the vice-president failed to defend their legitimacy. The numbers claiming such citizenship had declined sharply, perhaps as a result of the ruse's ineffectiveness. In December, Gómez Farías occasionally felt compelled to adopt a tougher line on expulsion, defying some state governors. For the first time, federal military authorities were given a role in the expulsion process, as the vice-president became more sensitive to the presence of "dangerous Spaniards," who lacked liberal ideals. The anticlerical campaign was well advanced and had reduced the number of secular clergy more rapidly than that of regulars. Spanish friars represented only a fraction of the general decline.

In late 1833, fewer local expulsion measures were passed and these were limited in their application. Expulsion enforcement could hardly proceed in 1834, for lack of funds. Nevertheless, in a fifth effort, a law of 25 January reiterated the expulsion measure of the previous June. Spaniards were discovered in the remote north who had not complied with the law of 1829, and they were marched to Mexico City to stand trial. Orders went out to the ports to prohibit the disembarkation of any who returned bearing U.S. citizenship papers. The regime sealed its own fate in March 1834, however, by ordering the expulsion of a Mexican, the late resident bishop. The failure of the attempt sparked new expulsions of Mexicans in Puebla, and the government was undermined by its own zeal. Santa Anna was moved by the call of conservatives to reestablish a regime that respected the traditional rights of the church. The general responded in May, dismissing Congress and overturning its laws, including those that affected the *peninsulares*. Santa Anna became dictator, urged on by the Plan of Cuernavaca, which set the conservative agenda that eventually terminated the first Federal Republic. Mexico's Spaniards took heart.

Between May 1834 and December 1836, when Spain finally recognized Mexican independence, the plight of resident *peninsulares* eased considerably. The 23 June expulsion measure was revoked by Santa Anna, as were the pension provisions that had adversely affected suspended employees. Spanish merchants hesitated to trust the new government, however, so long as Santa Anna was in charge. The January and June 1833 expulsion laws were repealed in February 1835 under interim President Barragán, as centralism was being constructed. Even Gómez Farías's "retiree" provisions were eliminated on 21 March, when Barragán ordered the traditional rules reinstated. By November, all of the Gómez Farías measures, apart from the exceptions granted to married Spaniards, had been repealed, including those affecting Spanish friars. Illegal Spaniards could safely come out of hiding. Even ex-military *gachupines* who had served the reconquest effort found that they could safely return to Mexico. The notion of a "dangerous" Spaniard, remained, however—now redefined as one who represented a liberal threat to this government—and such individuals could be ousted. Nativism was not entirely absent from the new regime, but did not reach the point of advocating expulsion crusades.

During 1835, the Barragán government was engaged in an effort to bury the controversies that had divided Mexicans. For the opposition, the Spaniards had been replaced by Santa Anna himself, and his "serviles," as the source of national threat. *Peninsulares* could participate in political life anew, so long as they abjured conspiracy. Spanish merchants exiled in Europe began to return. Even *expulsos* with questionable U.S. citizenship papers were admitted, despite the refusal of the U.S. consul at Veracruz to recognize their documents. These developments provoked little opposition among the Mexican public. The change may have resulted, in part, from the abandonment of reconquest rhetoric in Spain since the death of Ferdinand VII in 1833 and the discussions between Mexican and Spanish representatives leading to recognition of Mexican independence. Certainly, the establishment of de facto centralism helped silence authorities in the new departments (which replaced the states).

A striking change occurred in January 1836: a law provisionally restored the rights of Spaniards to occupy previously held government posts. Throughout that year, *expulsos* and exiles returned seemingly at will. Only routine passport regulations were observed. Clearly, in practice, former Spanish residents were now considered entitled to Mexican residence. The generous provisions of the Pedraza and Gómez Farías expulsion laws facilitated the process. The trend unintentionally encouraged new Spanish immigration in 1836 until discouraged by the Corro government in October, at least until independence was recognized on 28 December 1836.

Reconciliation followed recognition and coincided with Mexico's adoption of a new conservative constitution that restricted officeholding and suffrage to males enjoying the prescribed income. The Spaniards gained security in a Mexico that was no longer an unfettered popular democracy. From 1836 to the present, the relationship between Mexican and Spaniard has been amicable, except in times of national crisis, when *peninsular* immigrants have been singled out as scapegoats. At other times, Spaniards were welcomed with proverbial Mexican generosity, such as occurred during the contrasting eras of Porfirio Díaz and Lázaro Cárdenas. Since its twentieth-century revolution—with the notable exception of the years immediately following the Spanish Civil War—Mexico has attempted to restrict the influx of Spaniards. But immigration was not abolished entirely, and, indeed, *peninsulares* have continued to arrive. Mexicans and Spaniards are reconciled to coexistence, but the past has not been completely overcome. The *gachupín* as merchant is still an unpopular figure, and difficult times tend to revive old hostilities. We may hope that Mexicans will not forget that the Spaniards among them are an essential part of the cultural variety that is Mexico. With a concerted effort by both sides, the burden of history can be overcome.

Notes
Bibliography
Index

Notes

Introduction

1. See Flores Caballero, *La contrarrevolución [Counterrevolutión*, trans. Rodríguez O.].
2. Reyes Heroles, *El liberalismo mexicano* 2:63–64.
3. Hamill, *The Hidalgo Revolt*; Anna, *The Fall of Royal Government in Mexico City*.

Chapter 1. The Origins of the First Attempt at Expulsion

1. For greater detail, see Sims, *La expulsión*.
2. Ortiz de Ayala, *Resumen de la estadística del imperio mexicano*, cited in Sierra, *El nacimiento de Mexico*, p. 115; Navarro y Noriega, *Catálogo de los curatos y misiones*, p. 13, cited in Flores Caballero, *La contrarrevolución*, p. 17.
3. Alamán, *Historia de Méjico* 2:106–07.
4. Sierra, *El nacimiento de México*, p. 120; Flores Caballero, *La contrarrevolución*, p. 17.
5. See "The Spaniards and the Iturbidean Empire," in Sims, "The Expulsion," pp. 57–101.
6. "Informe sobre la existencia de logias masónicas," in Zavala, *Juicio imparcial*, pp. 10–11; Alpuche to Bishop Guerra, New Orleans, 6 Jan. 1836, in Gurría Lacroix, *Monografías históricas*, p. 109.
7. Ibar, *Regeneración política*, pp. 1–8; Poinsett to Clay, Mexico City, 8 Dec. 1827, Smith Papers.
8. Zavala, *Ensayo histórico* 2:10.
9. Gómez Pedraza, *Manifiesto*, pp. 41–42.
10. Ward, *Mexico* 2:489.
11. Data compiled from lists and reports in AGN, Ramo de Expulsión, legs. 1–27, and Ramo de Gobernación, legs. 65–68, 74–77, 83–84, 88–89, 93–94, 97, 134, 144, 169, 1,367, 1,553, 1,662, 1,940, 1,991, 2,064.
12. Senate, session of 12 Nov. 1827, *El Aguila Mexicana*, 19 Nov. 1827, pp. 1–2.
13. Sims, "Las clases económicas y la dicotomía criollo."
14. Dublán and Lozano, eds., *Legislación Mexicana* 2:12.
15. Minister of Treasury Esteva, *Memoria* (1828), in *Guía de Hacienda*, pp. 63–64.

16. Sims, *La expulsión*, p. 59, table 6; Bustamante, *Continuación*, p. 107.

17. Englehardt, *Santa Barbara Mission*, pp. 139–40.

18. Sims, *La expulsión*, pp. 63–64, table 7.

19. Aviraneta, *Mis memorias íntimas*, pp. 56–65; Manning, *Early Diplomatic Relations*, p. 350.

20. Sims, *La expulsión*, pp. 68–76.

21. Pakenham to Dudley, Mexico City, 16 Aug. 1827, FO 50/35.

22. Sims, *La expulsión*, pp. 84–86, tables 8-9.

23. AGN, Ramo de Gobernación, leg. 66, exps. 5, 8-13, fols. 1-369.

24. Poinsett to Guerrero, Mexico City, 28 Oct. 1827, in Rippy, *Joel Roberts Poinsett*, p. 126; Guerrero to Poinsett, Jalapa, 1 Nov. 1827, Smith Papers; Poinsett to Clay, Mexico City, 10 Nov. 1827, in Manning, *Early Diplomatic Relations*, pp. 351-52; *El Aguila*, 27 Nov. 1827.

25. *El Aguila*, 22 Sept. 1827, pp. 2-3.

26. AGN, Ramo de Gobernación, leg. 66, exp. 11, fols. 1–70; Archivo Histórico Militar, exp. XI/481.3/394, fols. 1–153, cited in *Guía del Archivo Histórico Militar* 1:54; Bustamante, *Continuación*, pp. 117–20; Suárez y Navarro, *Historia de México* 1:88.

27. Espinosa de los Monteros to governor of Chihuahua, Mexico City, 1 Sept. 1827, AGN, Ramo de Expulsión, leg. 13, vol 29, exp. 28b, fol. 35.

28. *El Aguila*, 22 Sept. 1827, pp. 2–3; Pakenham to Dudley, Mexico City, 23 Sept. 1827, FO 50/35.

29. Chamber of Deputies, session of 4 Sept. 1827, *El Aguila*, 6 Sept. 1827, p. 1.

30. "Suplemento No. 340," *El Aguila*, 6 Dec. 1827, pp. 1-2; bando, Oaxaca, 24 Nov. 1827, *El Baratillo* (Puebla), 8 Dec. 1827, p. 304.

31. Sims, *La expulsión*, pp. 126–27, table 10.

32. Ibid., p. 131ff.

33. "Suplemento al No. 1193," *El Oriente* (Jalapa), pp. 1–2; Welsh to O'Gorman, Veracruz, 11 Dec. 1827, FO 203/17; British Merchants of Mexico City to Pakenham, Mexico City, 17 Dec. 1827, in FO 50/36.

34. Sims, *La expulsión*, tables 11–13, pp. 137, 140–41, 143.

35. Arrillaga, comp., *Recopilación de leyes* 1:100–03.

36. Pedraza, *Manifiesto*, pp. 47-48; Tornel, *Breve reseña histórica*, p. 178.

37. Poinsett to Clay, Mexico City, 9 Jan. 1828, Smith Papers; Bustamante, Diary, 21 Dec. 1827; *Voz de la Patria*, 15 May 1830, p. 7; Alamán, *Méjico* 5:772; Tornel, *Breve reseña histórica*, p. 179.

38. Facio, "Memoria," Paris, 1 Apr. 1835, in Tornel, *Breve reseña histórica*, p. 197.

39. Bustamante, Diary, 2 Jan. 1828.

40. "Iniciativa del honorable congreso de la Unión," Jalapa, 7 Jan. 1828; "Proclama," Jalapa, 7 Jan. 1828; Peña to Barragán, Jalapa, 6 Jan. 1828, *El Oriente*, 9 Jan. 1828, pp. 1-4.

41. Sims, *La expulsión*, pp. 270–73, appendix VI.

Chapter 2. Results of the First Expulsion

1. Cuevas, *Porvenir de México*, pp. 277–78.
2. Arrillaga, comp., *Recopilación de leyes* 1:103–07.
3. Marginalia dated 21 May, Esteva to oficial mayor (government), Mexico City, 21 Jan. 1828, AGN, Ramo de Expulsión, leg. 8, tom. 19, exp. 25, fol. 1; marginalia dated 12 Nov., leg. 18, tom. 39, exp. 4, fols. 24–32.
4. Zavala to oficial mayor (government), Tlalpan, 30 Jan. 1828, and oficial mayor (government) to Zavala, Mexico City, 15 Mar. 1828, leg. 13, tom. 29, exp. 28a, fols. 3, 49.
5. Sims, *La expulsión*, p. 182, n. 42; Bustamante, Diary, 12 and 21 Mar. 1828.
6. Tornel, *Breve reseña histórica*, pp. 284–85.
7. AGN, Ramo de Gobernación, leg. 75, exp. 12, fol. 1; Arrillaga, comp., *Recopilación de leyes* 1:81.
8. Senate, session of 29 Mar. 1828, *El Aguila*, 27 May 1828, p. 1.
9. *El Aguila*, 20 Mar. 1828, p. 3.
10. Tornel to oficial mayor (government), Mexico City, 23 Feb. 1828, AGN, Ramo de Gobernación, leg. 66, exp. 14, fol. 3; *El Aguila*, 16 mar. 1828, p. 4; Pedraza to Cañedo, Mexico City, 21 Mar. 1828, AGN, Ramo de Expulsión, leg. 9, tom. 21, exp. 39, fol. 9.
11. Vives to de Pinillos, Havana, 16 Jan. 1828, in Franco, *Documentos para la historia de México*, p. 345.
12. Engelhardt, *The Missions* 3:267–68; Engelhardt, *Santa Barbara*, pp. 140–41.
13. Cañedo to Gonzales Cabotrano, Mexico City, 18 April 1828, AGN, Ramo de Expulsión, leg. 5, tom. 12, exp. 18, fol. 41.
14. Pedraza to Cañedo, Mexico City, 24 Apr. 1828, leg. 2, tom. 6, exp. 71, fols. 1–2; Cañedo to Santa Anna, Mexico City, 30 Apr. 1828, leg. 5, tom. 11, exp. 16, fol. 8.
15. AGN, Ramo de Gobernación, leg. 75, exp. 12, fol. 2; ibid., exp. 17, fol. 1; Arrillaga, comp., *Recopilación de leyes* 1:97–99; Pakenham to Dudley, Mexico City, 28 May 1828, FO 50/42.
16. Cañedo to Santa Anna, Mexico City, 6 and 21 May 1828, AGN, Ramo de Expulsión, leg. 2, tom. 6, exp. 76, fols. 2, 4.
17. Arrillaga, comp., *Recopilación de leyes* 1:194–95; *El Sol*, 1 June 1828; Cañedo to Santa Anna, Mexico City, 24 May 1828, and Cañedo to Lopes, Mexico City, 20 June 1828, AGN, Ramo de Gobernación, leg. 75, exp. 11, fols. 1–2.
18. AGN, Ramo de Expulsión, leg. 2, tom. 6, exp. 72, fol. 1; "Noticias Nacionales," *El Aguila*, 7 June 1828, p. 3.
19. Bustamante, Diary, 29 May 1828; Tornel to Cañedo, Mexico City, 14 June 1828, AGN, Ramo de Expulsión, leg. 9, tom. 22, exp. 66, fols. 2–3; ibid., exp. 67, fols. 5, 16.

20. Tornel to Cañedo, Mexico City, 23 June 1828, AGN, Ramo de Expulsión, leg. 9, tom. 22, exp. 56, fol. 1.

21. Bustamante, Diary, 2 July 1828; Tornel, *Breve reseña histórica*, pp. 284–85.

22. AGN, Ramo de Expulsión, leg. 2, tom. 6, exp. 73, fols. 1–3; Arrillaga, comp., *Recopilación de leyes* 1:204-06.

23. Ibid., 3:491–95; *El Aguila*, 26 April 1828, p. 2.

24. Chamber of Deputies, session of 28 Apr. 1828, *El Aguila*, 18 May 1828, p. 2.

25. Bustamante, Diary, 17 May 1828.

26. Chamber of Deputies, session of 19 Apr. 1828, *El Aguila*, 2 July 1828, p. 1.

27. Bustamante, Diary, 11 June 1828; Pakenham to Dudley, Mexico City, 2 July 1828, FO 50/44; Barreiro to Reyes Veramendi, Guadalajara, 4 July 1828, Hernández y Dávalos Papers, HD 19-3.4596.

28. Bancroft, *History of Arizona and New Mexico*, p. 314.

29. The statistical analysis in this section is the result of a meticulous tabulation and refinement of raw data pertaining to the expulsion of 1827-28 from lists and reports in AGN, Ramo de Expulsión. Space limitations prohibit citation of individual manuscripts.

30. *Expedientes* concerning such cases are scattered throughout AGN, Ramo de Expulsión.

31. Flores Caballero, *La contrarrevolución*, pp. 136, 154.

32. Ward, *Mexico* 2:474.; extracts of twenty-five relevant reports, in *Las relaciones franco-mexicanas*, ed. Weckmann, 1:78–156.

33. Data derived by combining figures in Minister of Justice and Ecclesiastical Affairs, *Memoria, 1827*, table 8; ibid., *1828*, tables 6, 11; ibid., *1829*, tables 9, 21; Sims, *La expulsión*, pp. 237–41, tables 28–31.

34. Merchants of Veracruz to Pakenham, Veracruz, 11 Dec. 1827, FO 50/36; "Párrafo traducido de una carta escrita en Méjico en 15 de julio por un negociante inglés a su socio residente en Veracruz," *El Aguila*, 12 Sept. 1828, pp. 1–2.

35. Sims, *La expulsión*, p. 247, tables 34–35; Romero, *Mexico and the United States*, pp. 139, 145; Lerdo de Tejada, *Comercio exterior de México*, table 36.

36. Sims, *La expulsión*, pp. 248–50, tables 36–39; Lerdo de Tejada, *Comercio exterior de México*, tables 33–35, 38, 41; Romero, *Mexico and the United States*, pp. 155, 173; Humphreys, *British Consular Reports*, appendix 1, pp. 346–49.

37. Report by Martin, Mexico City, 30 Nov. 1827, in *Correspondencia diplomática*, ed. Torre Villar, 1:59–60; Bustamante, *Voz de la Patria*, 18 Jan. 1829, p. 1; *Correo de la Federación*, 12 Feb. 1829, p. 1, in Flores Caballero, *La contrarrevolución*, pp. 146–47.

38. Figures in twenty-five reports, extracted in *Las relaciones franco-*

mexicanas, ed. Weckmann, 1:78–156; Bustamante, *Diary*, 6 July 1828; Howe, *The Mining Guild of New Spain*, p. 45.
   39. Ward, *Mexico* 2:489.
   40. Ibid., 1:297–303; Costeloe, "The Administration," p. 21.
   41. Niles, *History of South America*, pp. 194–95; Hale, *Mexican Liberalism*, p. 115.

Chapter 3. Anti-Gachupinism and the Rebellion of 1828

   1. *Cardillo de las Mujeres* attacked Mexican women who had married Spaniards.
   2. *Correo de la Federación*, 29 Dec. 1828, pp. 2–3; Mateos, *Historia de la masonería* 1:35.
   3. Zamaçois, *Historia de Méjico* 12:29–30.
   4. Olavarría y Ferrari, *México independiente* 4:194; Zavala, *Ensayo histórico* 2:125.
   5. *El Aguila*, 2 Sept. 1828, p. 1; Cuevas, *Porvenir de México*, p. 284.
   6. Minister of the Treasury, *Memoria, 1828*.
   7. Beginning in 1828, the correspondence of the British and U.S. consuls are full of analyses of these activities (García Papers, D61, no. 4).
   8. *El Aguila*, 17 Sept. 1828, p. 4; Tornel, "Pronunciamiento de Perote," p. 11; Castillo Negrete, *México en el siglo XIX* 18:192–96.
   9. Dublán and Lozano, comps., *Legislación Mexicana* 2:79–80.
   10. *El Sol*, 2 Oct. 1828, p. 7,634.
   11. *El Aguila*, 25 Sept. 1828, p. 4.
   12. *El Aguila*, 27 Sept. 1828, p. 3.
   13. "El Amigo de la Constitución" to the editors, *El Aguila*, 30 Sept. 1828, p. 2; Zavala to the editors, *El Aguila*, 4 Oct. 1828, p. 4.
   14. Poinsett to Clay, Mexico City, 25 Sept. 1828, Smith Papers.
   15. *El Aguila*, 5 Oct. 1828, pp. 3–4.
   16. *Correo de la Federación*, 4 Nov. 1828; *El Aguila*, 5 Nov. 1828, p. 4.
   17. Sprague, *Vicente Guerrero*, pp. 75–76.
   18. Castillo Negrete, *México en el siglo XIX* 18:209–13.
   19. Sprague, *Vicente Guerrero*, pp. 75–76.
   20. Prieto, *Memorias de mis tiempos* 1:32; Bustamante, *Voz de la Patria*, 10 July 1830, p. 7; ibid., 17 July 1829, p. 4; Zavala, *Ensayo histórico* 2:243; Zavala, *Juicio imparcial*, p. 19; Zerecero, *Memorias*, p. 109.
   21. *Correo de la Federación*, 1 Dec. 1828, p. 3; Bustamante, *Voz de la Patria*, 8 July 1829, pp. 2–3.
   22. "Declaration, proposed by Col. Santiago García, General in Chief of the Army, to be Made to the Government on the Expulsion of Spaniards," 20 Nov. 1828, FO 50/49; Zavala, *Juicio imparcial*, p. 19; Zavala, *Ensayo histórico* 2:243; Alamán, *Méjico* 5:777–78; Bustamante, *Voz de la Patria*, 8 July 1829, pp. 2–3; Flores Caballero, *La contrarrevolución*, p. 143.

23. Poinsett to Clay, Mexico City, 10 Dec. 1828, Smith Papers; Bustamante, *Voz de la Patria*, 8 July 1829, pp. 2–3; Arrillaga, ed., *Recopilación de leyes* 1:276–77.

24. *Correo de la Federación*, 1 Dec. 1828, p. 3.

25. Bustamante, *Voz de la Patria*, 8 July 1829, pp. 2–3.

26. Bustamante, Diary, 4 Dec. 1828.

27. "Manifiesto de la diputación permanente de Jalisco, de 6 enero de 1829," with the Yorkino response in notes, *Correo de la Federación*, 23 Jan. 1829, pp. 1–3.

28. Prieto, *Memorias de mis tiempos*, pp. 33–34; Zavala, *Juicio imparcial*, p. 19; Poinsett to Clay, Mexico City, 10 Mar. 1829, Smith Papers.

29. Suárez y Navarro, *Historia de México* 1:129–30.

30. Zavala, *Juicio imparcial*, pp. 19–20.

31. O'Gorman to Foreign Office, Mexico City, 19 Dec. 1828, FO 50/49; *Correo de la Federación*, 30 July 1829; Zavala, *Juicio imparcial*, pp. 19–20.

32. Robertson to Clay, Tampico, 19 Dec. 1828, U.S. Consular Correspondence, microcopy 241; Bustamante, Diary, *passim*.

33. Suárez y Navarro, *Historia de México* 1:414.

34. O'Gorman to Foreign Office, Mexico City, 19 Dec. 1828, FO 50/49; Martin to Ministère des Affaires Étrangères, Mexico City, 19 Dec. 1828, in *Correspondencia diplomática*, ed. Torre Villar, 1:69–70.

35. Poinsett to Clay, Mexico City, 10 Mar. 1829, Smith Papers; *Poinsett Papers* 18:16–17; 21:71ff., in Rippy, *Joel Roberts Poinsett*, pp. 127–28.

36. Pakenham to Earl of Aberdeen, Mexico City, 8 Jan. 1829, FO 50/53; Bancroft, *History of Mexico* 5:61.

37. *Correo de la Federación*, 23 Jan. 1829, pp. 1–3; Bustamante, *Continuación*, pp. 205–06.

38. Olavarría y Ferrari, *México independiente*, p. 190; Pakenham to Earl of Aberdeen, 8 Jan. 1829, FO 50/53; Carrión, *Historia de la ciudad de Puebla* 2:262.

39. "Acta, del ejército pronunciado en la capital del Distrito Federal," Mexico City, 15 Dec. 1829, FO 50/49.

40. Pedraza, *Manifiesto*, pp. 85–86.

41. Carrión, *Historia de la ciudad de Puebla* 2:262; Olavarría y Ferrari, *México independiente*, p. 190.

42. Bustamante, *Continuación*, pp. 221–22.

43. "Pronunciamiento de Juan J. Codallos," *Correo de la Federación*, 21 Jan. 1829, p. 2.

44. "Acuerdo," *Correo de la Federación*, 23 Jan. 1829, p. 1.

45. Bustamante, *Continuación*, pp. 221–22; Taylor to Clay, Veracruz, 28 Dec. 1828, U.S. Consular Correspondence, microcopy 183; *Correo de la Federación*, 25 Feb. 1829, p. 2.

46. De Aguado to Espino, Toluca, 2 Jan. 1829, and Espino to comandante militar, Toluca, 1 Jan. 1829, in Díaz-Thomé, "Cartas al general Vicente Gue-

rrero," pp. 419–21; "Acta sobre las Milicias Cívicas de Toluca," 1 Jan. 1829, ibid.

47. Petition from Zacapu, Michoacán, 7 Dec. 1828, in *Correo de la Federación*, 28 Dec. 1828, p. 3.

48. *Correo de la Federación*, 31 Dec. 1828, p. 3.

49. Political chief of Sombrerete to governor of Zacatecas, Sombrerete, 12 Jan. 1829, *Correo de la Federación*, 26 Jan. 1829, p. 2.

50. Arrillaga, comp., *Recopilación de leyes* 2:2.

51. Cáceres to Guerrero, Mexico City, 7 Jan. 1829, in Díaz-Thomé, "Cartas al general Vicente Guerrero," pp. 431–32; *Correo de la Federación*, 18 Jan. 1829, p. 4; ibid., 19 Jan. 1829, p. 4.

Chapter 4. The Defeat of the "Impartial" Senators

1. Bustamante, *Continuación*, p. 224.

2. Minister of Government, *Memoria, 1829*, pp. 9–11.

3. Minister of Justice and Ecclesiastical Affairs, *Memoria, 1829*, p. 22.

4. *Correo de la Federación*, 3 Jan. 1829, p. 4; Chamber of Deputies, session of 2 Jan. 1829, *Correo de la Federación*, 9 Jan. 1829, pp. 1–2; Mateos, ed., *Historia parlamentaria*.

5. Senate, session of 5 Jan. 1829, *Correo de la Federación*, 13 Jan. 1829, p. 1.

6. "México 6 enero de 1829," *Correo de la Federación*, 6 Jan. 1829, p. 1.

7. "Noticias Nacionales. Díctamen," *Correo de la Federación*, 10 Jan. 1829, pp. 1–2.

8. "Proclama del coronel D. Gordiano Guzmán en el estado de Xalisco," *Correo de la Federación*, 9 Jan. 1829, p. 2.

9. "Varios patriotas de la Acordada" to the editors, *Correo de la Federación*, 10 Jan. 1829, p. 3; Arrillaga, comp., *Recopilación de leyes* 2:6–7.

10. Chamber of Deputies, session of 14 Jan. 1829, *Correo de la Federación*, 9 Feb. 1829, p. 1.

11. Bustamante, *Voz de la Patria* 4:1–8.

12. Secretaries of the Chamber of Deputies to Cañedo, "Ejecutivo," and Cañedo to secretaries of the Chambers, Mexico City, 14 Jan 1829, AGN, Ramo de Expulsión, leg. 22 3/4, tom. 55, exp. 83, fols. 6–7.

13. *Correo de la Federación*, 27 Feb. 1829, p. 1; ibid., 18 Feb. 1829, pp. 1–2.

14. *Correo de la Federación*, 23 Feb. 1829, p. 1.

15. Chamber of Deputies, session of 17 Jan. 1829, *Correo de la Federación*, 24 Feb. 1829, p. 1; ibid., 28 Feb. 1829, p. 1.

16. "Varios ciudadanos" to the editors, "México 28 enero de 1829," *Correo*

de la Federación, 18 Jan. 1829, pp. 2–3; and editorial, ibid., 19 Jan. 1829, p. 3.

17. Chamber of Deputies, session of 20 Jan. 1829, *Correo de la Federación*, 2 Mar. 1829, p. 1.

18. Ibid.

19. Esteva to Guerrero, [no location], 21 Jan. 1829, in Díaz-Thomé, "Cartas al general Vicente Guerrero," pp. 458–59.

20. Chamber of Deputies, session of 23 Jan. 1829, *Correo de la Federación*, 7 Mar. 1829, p. 1.

21. Pakenham to Cañedo, Mexico City, 23 Jan. 1829; Bocanegra to Pakenham, Mexico City, 4 Feb. 1829, FO 50/53.

22. Chamber of Deputies, session of 27 Jan. 1829, *Correo de la Federación*, 11 Mar. 1829, p. 1.

23. "México 27 de enero de 1829," *Correo de la Federación*, 27 Jan. 1829, p. 3; Pakenham to Earl of Aberdeen, Mexico City, 31 Jan. 1829, FO 50/53; Bustamante, *Voz de la Patria* 4:5–6; "México 30 de enero de 1829," *Correo de la Federación*, 30 Jan. 1829, p. 4; "Varios Cronologistas" to the editors, *Correo de la Federación*, 31 Jan. 1829, p. 2; ibid., 1 Feb. 1829, p. 3.

24. "México 31 de enero de 1829," *Correo de la Federación*, 31 Jan. 1829, p. 3; Pakenham to Earl of Aberdeen, Mexico City, 31 Jan. 1829, FO 50/53.

25. Chamber of Deputies, sessions of 5–6 Feb. 1829, *Correo de la Federación*, 10 Mar. 1829, p. 1; ibid., 19 Mar. 1829, p. 1; ibid., 21 Mar. 1829, p. 1.

26. Ibid.

27. Almonte, "Proyecto de ley presentado a la cámara de diputados," *Correo de la Federación*, 19 Feb. 1829, p. 3.

28. Alamán, *Méjico* 5:779–80; Arrangoiz, *México desde 1808* 2:191–92; Zamaçois, *Méjico* 11:707–08; Arista to Guerrero, Jalapa, 5 Feb. 1829, in Díaz-Thomé, "Cartas al general Vicente Guerrero," pp. 93–94; Valadés, *Alamán*, p. 230.

29. "Noticias Nacionales," *Correo de la Federación*, 11 Feb. 1829, pp. 1–2; "Jalapa 25 de febrero," *Correo de la Federación*, 6 Mar. 1829, p. 3.

30. Coromina, ed., *Recopilación de leyes . . . de Michoacán* 3:123, 141–42; "Morelia," *Correo de la Federación*, 25 Feb. 1829, pp. 1–2; ibid., 21 Mar. 1829, p. 3.

31. "Querétaro febrero 15 de 1829," *Correo de la Federación*, 21 Feb. 1829, pp. 2–3.

32. *Correo de la Federación*, 26 Feb. 1829, p. 3.

33. Secretaría de Gobierno del Distrito Federal, "Prevenciones que deberán observar los piquetes de las garitas," *Correo de la Federación*, 20 Feb. 1829, p. 3; "Dictamen de la comisión de hacienda del Escmo. Ayuntamiento de México, para la destrucción del Parián," *Correo de la Federación*, 21 Feb. 1829, p. 4.

34. Senate, session of 6 Feb. 1829, *Correo de la Federación*, 6 Mar. 1829, p. 1; Coronel to Bocanegra, Mexico City, 9 Feb. 1829, and Bocanegra to

Coronel, Mexico City, 10 Feb. 1829, AGN Ramo de Expulsión, leg. 22 3/4, tom. 55, exp. 103, fols. 1–4.

35. Espinosa de los Monteros to Bocanegra, Mexico City, 18 Feb. 1829, and Bocanegra to the governors of eight federal entities, Mexico City, 20 Feb. 1829, AGN, Ramo de Expulsión, leg. 22 3/4, tom. 55, exp. 101, fols. 23–24, 26.

36. "Noticias Nacionales," *Correo de la Federación*, 24 Feb. 1829, pp. 2–4.

37. Senate, session of 25 Feb. 1829, *Correo de la Federación*, 9 Apr. 1829, p. 1.

38. Senate, session of 26 Feb. 1829, *Correo de la Federación*, 9 Apr. 1829, p. 1.

39. Senate, session of 27 Feb. 1829, *Correo de la Federación*, 15 Apr. 1829, pp. 1–3.

40. "Varios mexicanos" to the editors, *Correo de la Federación*, 2 Mar. 1829, p. 3.

41. Senate, session of [2] Mar. 1829, *Correo de la Federación*, 16 Apr. 1829, p. 1.

42. Senate, session of 3 Mar. 1829, *Correo de la Federación*, 18 Apr. 1829, pp. 1–2; ibid., 5 Mar. 1829, p. 3.

43. Ibid.; Pakenham to Earl of Aberdeen, Mexico City, 4 Mar. 1829, FO 50/53.

44. Senate, session of 5 Mar. 1829, *Correo de la Federación*, 21 Apr. 1829, p. 1.

45. Senate, session of 6 Mar. 1829, *Correo de la Federación*, 21 Apr. 1829, p. 1; session of 10 Mar. 1829, ibid., 30 Apr. 1829, p. 1.

46. "Comunicados. Querétaro Marzo 2 de 1829, *Correo de la Federación*, 9 Mar. 1829, pp. 2–3; "Noticias Nacionales," *Correo de la Federación*, 8 Mar. 1829, p. 2.

47. Senate, session of 9 Mar. 1829, *Correo de la Federación*, 25 Apr. 1829, p. 1.

48. Senate, session of 10 Mar. 1829, *Correo de la Federación*, 30 Apr. 1829, p. 1.

49. Bustamante, in *Voz de la Patria*, 21 Aug. 1830, p. 6, and *Continuación*, pp. 233–34; Chamber of Deputies, session of 13 Mar. 1829, *Correo de la Federación*, 27 Apr. 1829, pp. 1–2.

50. Senate, session of 14 Mar. 1829, *Correo de la Federación*, 4 May 1829, p. 1; Bustamante, *Continuación*, p. 234.

51. Senate, session of 16 Mar. 1829, *Correo de la Federación*, 5 May 1829, p. 1; session of 17 Mar. 1829, ibid., 13 May 1829, p. 1; Bustamante, *Voz de la Patria*, 25 Aug. 1830, pp. 1–3.

52. Arrillaga, comp., *Recopilación de leyes* 2:44.

53. Chamber of Deputies, session of 18 Mar. 1829, *Correo de la Federación*, 4 May 1829, p. 1; Bustamante, *Continuación*, pp. 234–37.

54. AGN, Ramo de Expulsión, leg. 15, tom. 33, exp. 26; Dublán and Lozano, comps., *Legislación mexicana* 2:98–99.

55. Ibar, *Muerte Política*; Bustamante, *Voz de la Patria*, 8 Apr. 1829, p.
8; *Correo de la Federación*, 18 Apr. 1829, pp. 3–4; Montes de Oca to Bocanegra,
Guanajuato, 18 and 21 Mar. 1829, and Bocanegra to Montes de Oca, Mexico
City, 21 Mar. 1829, AGN, Ramo de Expulsión, leg 22 3/4, tom. 55, exp. 97,
fols. 1–3.; Marmolejo, *Efemeridades Guanajuatenses* 3:204.
    56. Dublán and Lozano, comps., *Legislación mexicana* 2:98–99.
    57. Minister of Government, *Memoria, 1830*, p. 26; *Correo de la Federación*,
5 Feb. 1829, p. 4.
    58. Reyes Heroles, *El liberalismo mexicano* 2:69–70.

Chapter 5. From Expulsions to Exceptions

    1. AGN, Ramo de Expulsión, leg. 18, tom. 39, exp. 1; "Ayuntamiento
de México. Sesión del día 24 de marzo de 1829," *Correo de la Federación*, 5
Apr. 1829, p. 2; "Interior. Oaxaca marzo 29 de 1829, *Correo de la Federación*,
15 Apr. 1829, pp. 2–3; "Veracruz marzo 26 de 1829," *Correo de la Federación*,
7 Apr. 1829, p. 3; López to Guerrero, Guadalajara, 31 Mar. 1829, in Díaz-
Thomé, "Cartas al general Vicente Guerrero," pp. 114–15; Prieto Papers,
wallet 19, no. 4; Bancroft, *History of California* 3:96–97; Hutchinson, *Frontier
Settlement*, pp. 136–37.
    2. Prieto Papers, wallet 19, no. 4; Arce to Bocanegra, Chihuahua, 7
Apr. 1829, AGN, Ramo de Expulsión, leg. 18, tom. 39, exp. 1, fols. 2, 4.
    3. Bustamante, *Continuación*, pp. 238–41; Alamán, *Méjico* 5:780;
Sprague, *Guerrero*, p. 78.
    4. "México 28 de marzo de 1829," *Correo de la Federación*, 28 Mar. 1829,
p. 3; "Un practicante patriota" to the editors, *Correo de la Federación*, 24 Apr.
1829, p. 3.
    5. *El Patriota* (Puebla), 15 Apr. 1829, in *Correo de la Federación*, 26 Apr.
1829, p. 2.
    6. AGN, Ramo de Gobernación, leg. 93, exp. 5, fols. 23–30; AHMA,
Orozco Papers, leg. 66, xvi; petition from wives of Campeche to the president,
AGN, Ramo de Expulsión, leg. 12, tom. 27, exp. 24, fols. 3–11; Lopes to
Bocanegra, Mérida, 14 May 1829, ibid., fol. 1; Bocanegra to Lopes, Mexico
City, 15 June 1829, ibid., fol. 2.
    7. Tornel to Bocanegra, Mexico City, 21 Mar. 1829, AGN, Ramo de
Gobernación, leg. 74, exp. 5, fols. 1, 3.
    8. Bocanegra to Tornel, Mexico City, 24 Mar. 1829, ibid., fol. 2.
    9. Bocanegra to secretaries of Chamber of Deputies, Mexico City, 24
Mar. 1829; four letters between Tornel and Bocanegra, Mexico City, 24 and
29 Mar., 3 and 7 Apr., 1829, ibid., fols. 3–7.
    10. Arrillaga preferred not to reproduce it (Recopilación de leyes 2:55);
Bustamante, *Continuación*, p. 238.
    11. Zavala, *Venganza*, pp. 25–26; Bustamante, *Voz de la Patria*, 4 Sept.
1830, p. 1, and *Continuación*, pp. 241–42.
    12. Tornel to Bocanegra, "Ejecutivo," Mexico City, 15 Apr. 1829, and

Bocanegra to Tornel, Mexico City, 15 Apr. 1829, AGN, Ramo de Gobernación, leg. 74, exp. 5, fols. 8–9.

13. Tornel to Bocanegra, Mexico City, 19 Apr. 1829, ibid., fol. 10.

14. Ibid.; Bocanegra to Ioronel, Mexico City, 20 Apr. 1829, ibid., fol. 11.

15. Seven letters between Tornel and Bocanegra, Mexico City, 20 Apr. 2–July 1829, AGN, Ramo de Gobernación, leg. 1, exp. 5, fols. 12–20.

16. Bustamante, *Continuación*, pp. 241–42.

17. Tornel to Bocanegra, "Muy ejecutivo," Mexico City, 21 Apr. 1829 (two letters), AGN, Ramo de Gobernación, leg. 74, exp. 5, fols. 21–22; a daily notice was published in the *Correo de la Federación*, 22–25 Apr. 1829, p. 4.

18. Tornel to Bocanegra, Mexico City, 23 Apr. 1829, and Bocanegra to Zavala, Mexico City, 25 Apr. 1829, AGN, Ramo de Gobernación, leg. 74, exp. 5, fols. 32–33.

19. Tornel to Bocanegra, Mexico City, 21 Apr. 1829, AGN, Ramo de Expulsión, leg. 18, tom. 39, exp. 2, fols. 9–10, and AGN, Ramo de Gobernación, leg. 93, exp. 5, fols. 2–14.

20. Tornel to Bocanegra, Mexico City, 21 Apr. 1829, AGN, Ramo de Gobernación, leg. 93, exp. 5, fols. 2–14.

21. *Correo de la Federación*, 24–26 Apr. 1829, p. 4.

22. Bocanegra to secretaries of Congress, Mexico City, 15 Apr. 1829, AGN, Ramo de Gobernación, leg. 74, exp. 4.

23. Santa Anna to Bocanegra, Jalapa, 2 Apr. 1829, and Bocanegra to Santa Anna, Mexico City, 15 Apr. 1829, AGN, Ramo de Expulsión, leg. 18, tom. 40, exp. 17, fols. 2–3.

24. Santa Anna to Bocanegra, Jalapa, 25 Apr. 1829, ibid.

25. Sotomayor to Bocanegra, Tlalpan, 22 Apr. 1829, Bocanegra to Zavala, Mexico City, 27 Apr. 1829; Zavala to Bocanegra, Mexico City, 21 Apr. 1829, AGN, Ramo de Expulsión, leg. 22 3/4, tom. 55, exp. 82, fols. 1–2; ibid., leg. 18, tom. 40, exp. 10, fols. 9–10.

26. Zavala to Bocanegra, Mexico City, 3 and 14 Apr. 1829, Bocanegra to Zavala, Mexico City, 8 Apr. 1829, Bocanegra to Sotomayor, Mexico City, 22 Apr. 1829, AGN, Ramo de Expulsión, leg. 22 3/4, tom. 55, exp. 19, fols. 2–5.

27. Flores Caballero, *La contrarrevolución*, p. 151; Bocanegra, *Memorias* 2:9–10; Bustamante, *Continuación*, pp. 239–40.

28. Circular to state governors and political chiefs of the territories, 18 Apr. 1829, AGN, Ramo de Expulsión, leg. 23, tom. 57, exp. 65, fol. 12.

29. Micheltorina to Guerrero, Oaxaca, 22 Apr. 1829, ibid., fols. 135–37.

30. Bocanegra to Pakenham, Mexico City, 21 Apr. 1829, Bocanegra to Poinsett, Mexico City, 21 Apr. and 8 May 1829, Bocanegra to David, Mexico City, 21 Apr. 1829, Poinsett to Bocanegra, Mexico City, 23 Apr. 1829, *Resguardo* for Pedro Mont, 10 Aug. 1829, AGN, Ramo de Expulsión, leg. 23, tom. 57, exp. 65, fols. 22–23; ibid., exp. 66, fols. 3–5; Pakenham to Bocanegra, Mexico City, 23 Apr. 1829, FO 50/54.

31. Bocanegra to the secretaries of Congress, Mexico City, 25 Apr. 1829, AGN, Ramo de Expulsión, leg. 18, tom. 39, exp. 2, fols. 3, 11.

32. "México 26 de abril de 1829," *Correo de la Federación*, 26 Apr. 1829, p. 3.

33. AGN, Ramo de Gobernación, leg. 74, exp. 3.

34. *Correo de la Federación*, 9 Apr. 1829, p. 4; ibid., 10 Apr. 1829, p. 4.

35. The *expediente* includes cases for 1829–31: AGN, Ramo de Expulsión, leg 18, tom. 39, exp. 9, fols. 1–156, esp. 20, 31, 41.

36. AGN, Ramo de Justicia Eclesiástica, tom. 84-B, exp. 28, fols. 105–22, in Flores Caballero, *La contrarrevolución*, p. 151.

37. Bustamante, *Continuación*, pp. 237, 246.

38. Bocanegra to Febles, Mexico City, 7, 8, 10 Apr. 1829, AGN, Ramo de Expulsión, leg. 18, tom. 40, exp. 10, fols. 32–73; ibid., leg. 23, tom. 57, exp. 63, fol. 11.

39. "Lista de los expedientes que están en poder de esta junta hasta el 27 de abril de 1829," marginalia in ibid., fols. 82–84; *Correo de la Federación*, 1 May 1829, p. 4.

40. "Lista de españoles a quiénes no ha satisfecho la tesorería general," AGN, Ramo de Expulsión, leg. 22 3/4, tom. 54, exp. 63, fols. 7–10.

41. AGN, Ramo de Gobernación, leg. 74, exp. 2; Arrillaga, comp., *Recopilación de leyes* 2:61–62.

Chapter 6. Two Distinct Modes of Compliance

1. Chamber of Deputies, session of 21 Mar. 1829, *Correo de la Federación*, 7 May 1829, p. 1.

2. "Consultas que se han hecho a las cámaras," AGN, Ramo de Expulsión, leg. 23, tom. 57, exp. 56, fols. 2, 5.

3. "Consulta a la Cámara de Diputados," 7 Apr. 1829, AGN, Ramo de Gobernación, leg. 74, exp. 4.

4. Cañedo to Bocanegra, Guadalajara, 30 Mar. 1829, submitted to the deputies 15 Apr. 1829, ibid.

5. Secretaries of the Chamber of Deputies to Bocanegra, Mexico City, 8 Apr. 1829, AGN, Ramo de Expulsión, leg. 18, tom. 39, exp. 5, fol. 53.

6. Bocanegra to secretaries of Chamber of Deputies, Mexico City, 10 Apr. 1829, ibid., fol. 55.

7. Bustamante, *Voz de la Patria*, 1 Sept. 1830, pp. 1–4, and *Continuación*, pp. 239–40.

8. "Consulta a la Cámara de Diputados," 9 Apr. 1829, AGN, Ramo de Gobernación, leg. 74, exp. 4.

9. "México 10 de abril del 1829," *Correo de la Federación*, 10 Apr. 1829, p. 3.

10. "Veracruz abril 19," *Correo de la Federación*, 30 Apr. 1829, p. 3; Chamber of Deputies, session of 11 Apr. 1829, *Correo de la Federación*, 19 May

1829, p. 1; Bustamante, *Voz de la Patria*, 13 Apr. 1829, p. 5, and ibid., 22 Apr. 1829, p. 4.

11. *Correo de la Federación*, 19 May 1829, p. 1; Bustamante, in *Voz de la Patria*, 22 Apr. 1829, pp. 5–6.

12. Senate, session of 14 Apr. 1829, *Correo de la Federación*, 8 June 1829, pp. 1–2.

13. Chamber of Deputies, session of 15 Apr. 1829, *Correo de la Federación*, 20 May 1829, p. 2; Secretaries of Congress to Bocanegra, Mexico City, 15 Apr. 1829, AGN, Ramo de Expulsión, leg. 18, tom. 40, exp. 20, fol. 2; Bustamante, *Continuación*, p. 240.

14. Bustamante, *Continuación*, p. 239; *Correo de la Federación*, 20 May 1829, p. 2.

15. Bocanegra to secretaries of the Senate, Mexico City, 18 Apr. 1829, AGN, Ramo de Expulsión, leg. 18, tom. 40, exp. 20, fol. 3.

16. Bocanegra to the president of the Senate, Mexico City, 18 Apr. 1829, and Pacheco Leal to Bocanegra, Mexico City, 18 Apr. 1829, ibid., fols. 4–5.

17. Bustamante, *Continuación*, p. 240; "Iniciativa de la honorable legislatura de Puebla," *Correo de la Federación*, 22 Apr. 1829, p. 2.

18. AGN, Ramo de Expulsión, leg. 15, tom. 33, exp. 28, fol. 11; Arrillaga, comp., *Recopilación de leyes* 2:60; Dublán and Lozano, comps., *Legislación mexicana* 5:15–16; Prieto papers, wallet 19, no. 5.

19. Secretaries of the Senate to Bocanegra, Mexico City, 25 and 29 Apr. 1829, AGN, Ramo de Expulsión, leg. 15, tom. 33, exp. 28, fols. 4, 8; leg. 23, tom. 57, exp. 52, fol. 7.

20. Pakenham to Earl of Aberdeen, Mexico City, 3 May 1829, FO 50/54.

21. Lana to Bocanegra, Tuxtla, 12 May 1829, AGN, Ramo de Expulsión, leg. 23, tom. 57, exp. 52, fol. 8.

22. Bocanegra to Lana, Mexico City, 29 May 1829, ibid., fol. 9.

23. Ibid., fol. 7; ibid., leg. 15, tom. 33, exp. 28, fols. 5–10b; *El Telégrafo*, 11 and 17 Feb. 1833, *passim*.

24. Archivo del Estado de Oaxaca, leg. 1,863, unnumbered.

25. "Oaxaca, Lista de los españoles calificados hasta la fecha en esta capital," 31 Mar. 1829, *El Oaxaqueño Libre*, and *Correo de la Federación*, 15 Apr. 1829, p. 3.

26. Muro, *Historia de San Luis Potosí* 1:494–95; Velázquez, *Historia de San Luis Potosí* 3:161.

27. Muro, *Historia de San Luis Potosí* 1:493.

28. AGN, Ramo de Expulsión, leg. 15, tom. 32, exp. 13, fol. 37.

29. *Colección de los decretos . . . Puebla* 3:39–40; Zavala, *Memoria, 1829*, *passim*.

30. Alamán, *Méjico* 5:780–81; Navarro y Rodrigo, *Vida de Agustín de Iturbide*, p. 197.

31. Arrillaga, comp., *Recopilación de leyes* 2:70; Arrangoiz, *México desde 1808* 2:194; Galos to Murphy, Bordeaux, 20 July 1820, extracted in *Las relaciones franco-mexicanas*, ed. Weckmann, 1:182; Iturribarría to Bocanegra,

Oaxaca, 8 May 1829, AGN, Ramo de Expulsión, leg. 23, tom. 58, exp. 70, fol. 1; Tornel to Bocanegra, Mexico City, 29 July 1829, ibid., leg. 18, tom. 39, exp. 4, fol. 39; Bocanegra to Tornel, 1 Aug. 1829, ibid., leg. 18, tom. 39, exp. 4, fol. 41; Circular, Minister of Relaciones, 2 May 1829, leg. 23, tom. 57, exp. 43, fol. 9.

32. Alamán, *Méjico* 5:780–81; Arrangoiz, *México desde 1808* 2:192–93; AGN, Ramo de Expulsión, leg. 18, tom. 39, exp. 5, fol. 3.

33. Arista to Guerrero, Jalapa, 26 Mar. 1829, in Díaz-Thomé, "Cartas al general Vicente Guerrero," pp. 106–07; *El Telégrafo*, 12 Feb. 1833, p. 2.

34. Sprague, *Guerrero*, p. 48.

35. "Lista de los españoles eceptuados en uso de las facultades estraordinarias en el año de 1829," *El Telégrafo*, 17 Feb. 1833, p. 2; AGN, Ramo de Expulsión, leg. 18, tom. 39, exp. 5, fols. 13, 31; Allende to Guerrero, San Miguel de Allende, 13 Apr. 1829, in Díaz-Thomé, "Cartas al general Vicente Guerrero," pp. 125–26.

36. AGN, Ramo de Expulsión, leg. 18, tom. 39, exp. 5, fol. 29; Arrillaga, "Apuntes de los servicios que he prestado a la independencia," Salce Arredondo Papers, HD 20-1.4622; *El Telégrafo*, 17 Feb. 1833, p. 2.

37. Nine representatives from Yucatán in the two chambers to Bocanegra and Guerrero, Mexico City, 9 Apr. 1829, AGN, Ramo de Expulsión, leg. 12, tom. 27, exp. 22, fols. 5, 7; Bocanegra to Lopes, Mexico City, 11 Apr. 1829, ibid., fol. 6.

38. Note from the ministry of government, 2 Apr. 1829, AGN, Ramo de Gobernación, leg, 83, exp. 60, fol. 1.

39. Pasaporte a Benito de la Serna para salir por el puerto de Veracruz, San Luis Potosí, 9 July 1828, Hernández y Dávalos Papers, HD 19-3.4597; ibid., 6 Apr. 1829, HD 10-1.4627.

40. Ladrón de Guevara to Bocanegra, Jalapa, 14 July 1828, resubmitted 20 Apr. 1829, AGN, Ramo de Expulsión, leg. 17, tom. 36, exp. 24, fol. 20.

41. Summarized in AGN, Ramo de Expulsión, leg. 18, tom. 39, exp. 5, fol. 107.

42. Ibid., fols. 69–98.

43. AGN, Ramo de Expulsión, leg. 15, tom. 33, exp. 25, fol. 12.

44. AGN, Ramo de Expulsión, leg. 18, tom. 39, exp. 5, fols. 51–56; *El Telégrafo*, 11 Feb. 1833, p. 1.

45. "Petición al Ayuntamiento de Monte Morelos," Nuevo León, 22 Apr. 1829, AGN, Ramo de Expulsión, leg. 21, tom. 45, exp. 4, fols. 6–7; "El desagradecido" to the editors, *Correo de la Federación*, 29 June 1829, p. 1; [seventy-two persons] to the editors, ibid., pp. 1–2.

46. Sánchez Espinosa to Conejo, Jalapa, 24 Apr. 1829, Sánchez Espinosa Papers, García wallet 215.

47. Severo to Pedro Arana, Puebla, 24 Apr. 1829, Jalapa, 30 Apr. 1829, Veracruz, 16 May 1829, and Arana to Severo, Mexico City, 28 Apr. 1829, and n.d., AGN, Ramo de Expulsión, leg. 13, tom. 28, exp. 8, fols. 4–14.

48. Sánchez Espinosa to Guerrero, Mexico City, 26 Apr. 1829, AGN, Ramo de Expulsión, leg. 18, tom. 39, exp. 3, fols. 67–71.

49. "México 29 abril de 1829," *Correo de la Federación*, 29 Apr. 1829, p. 3.

50. Bocanegra to Tornel, Mexico City, 5 May 1829, and Tornel to Bocanegra, Mexico City, 9 May 1829, AGN, Ramo de Expulsión, leg. 18, tom. 39, exp. 3, fols. 66, 72.

51. Tornel to Bocanegra, Mexico City, 11 May 1829, ibid., fol. 76.

52. Ibid.; Tornel to Bocanegra, Mexico City, 21 May and 17 June 1829, ibid., fols. 2, 77–78, 80–81. The four notebooks were entitled, "Los testimonios de lo actuado sobre la averiguación de ecepciones de Españoles formado por el Juez de letras Pedro Galindo."

53. Ibid., fols. 5–30, table I.

54. Tornel to Bocanegra, Mexico City, 27 Apr. 1829; Bocanegra to Tornel, Mexico City, 29 Apr. 1829, AGN, Ramo de Gobernación, leg. 74, exp. 5, fols. 23–24.

55. See the report of 22 Aug. 1829, AGN, Ramo de Expulsión, leg. 4, tom. 9, exp. 10, fols. 5–9.

56. Tornel to Bocanegra, Mexico City, 29 Apr. 1829, AGN, Ramo de Gobernación, leg. 74, exp. 5, fol. 25.

57. Arrillaga, comp., *Recopilación de leyes* 2:71–73; Bocanegra to Tornel, Mexico City, 2 and 8 May 1829, Tornel to Bocanegra, Mexico City, 5 and 9 May 1829, ibid., fols. 26, 28–29, 31.

58. Tornel to Bocanegra, Mexico City, 27 Apr. 1829, Bocanegra to Tornel, Mexico City, 2 May 1829, ibid., fols. 25–26.

59. *Correo de la Federación*, 8 May 1829, p. 3; Tornel to Lozano, "Ejecutivo," Mexico City, 6 May 1829; ibid., 9 May 1829, p. 3.

60. Report from Tornel to Bocanegra, 22 May 1829, AGN, Ramo de Expulsión, leg. 18, tom. 39, exp. 2, fol. 18.

61. Tornel to Bocanegra, "Ejecutivo," Mexico City, 22 June 1829, Bocanegra to Tornel, Mexico City, 27 June 1829, AGN, Ramo de Gobernación, leg. 74, exp. 5, fols. 34–35.

62. Tornel to Bocanegra, Mexico City, 25 June 1829, Bocanegra to Tornel, Mexico City, 27 June 1829, ibid., fols. 36–37.

63. Moctezuma to Bocanegra, Mexico City, 28 June 1829, AGN, Ramo de Expulsión, leg. 15, tom. 32, exp. 12, fol. 14.

64. Adame to Guerrero, Chapultepec, 10 July 1829, Hernández de Guerrero Papers.

65. Tornel to Bocanegra, Mexico City, 1 July 1829, AGN, Ramo de Gobernación, leg. 74, exp. 5, fols. 38–40; *Correo de la Federación*, 5 July 1829, p. 4.

66. Marginalia, Tornel to Bocanegra, Mexico City, 29 Sept. 1829, AGN, Ramo de Gobernación, leg. 74, exp. 5.

67. Tornel to Bocanegra, Mexico City, 21 Aug. 1829, AGN, Ramo de Expulsión, leg. 18, tom. 39, exp. 2, fol. 23.

68. "Lista de los españoles esceptuados por el senado el 21 de abril del presente año, de la ley de 20 de marzo último, que dejaron de ir puestos en la relación remitida al poder ejecutivo el 22 del mismo," Mexico City, 25 Apr. 1829, AGN, Ramo de Expulsion, leg. 23, tom. 57, exp. 52, fols. 6–7; Prieto Papers, wallet 19, no. 12.

69. *Correo de la Federación*, 24 Apr. 1829, p. 3; Berduzco to the editors, ibid., 27 Apr. 1829, p. 3.

70. *Correo de la Federación*, 26 Apr. 1829, p. 3; ibid., 3 May 1829, pp. 2–3; Decrees, Articles, etc., 1,823–38, García wallet 110.

71. Argüelles to Bocanegra, Mexico City, 1 May 1829; Bocanegra to the council of government of Veracruz State, Mexico City, 5 May 1829, Bocanegra to Santa Anna, Mexico City, 5 May 1829, Santa Anna to Bocanegra, Jalapa, 8 May, 1829, AGN, Ramo de Expulsión, leg. 18, tom. 40, exp. 25, fols. 2–5.

72. *Correo de la Federación*, 5 May 1829, p. 3; ibid., 15 May 1829, p. 4.

73. *Correo de la Federación*, 9 May 1829, p. 3.

74. Bustamante, *Continuación*, pp. 247–48; "México 22 de abril de 1829," *Correo de la Federación*, 22 Apr. 1829, pp. 3–4; ibid., 19 May 1829, p. 3.

75. "Consultas a la cámara de diputados sobre algunas dudas," Bocanegra to secretaries of the chambers, Mexico City, 16 May 1829, AGN, Ramo de Gobernación, leg. 74, exp. 4.

76. Ibid.

77. Bustamante, in *Voz de la Patria*, 22 May 1829, p. 1–6.

78. *Correo de la Federación*, 23 May 1829, pp. 2–3; Castillón, ed., *Informes y manifiestos*, vol. 3.

Chapter 7. From Exceptions to Coexistence

1. AGN, Ramo de Expulsión, leg. 23, tom. 57, exp. 43, fol. 9; AGN, Ramo de Gobernación, leg. 144, exp. 30, fol. 1; Arrillaga, comp., *Recopilación de leyes* 2:70; Bocanegra to Pakenham, Mexico City, 2 May 1829, Pakenham to Bocanegra, Mexico City, 23 Apr. 1829, FO 50/54.

2. Pakenham to Earl of Aberdeen, Mexico City, 3 May 1829, ibid.

3. Arrillaga, comp., *Recopilación de leyes* 2:69–70; "Lista de los españoles que han debuelto los viáticos," 22 Aug. 1829, AGN, Ramo de Expulsión, leg. 4, tom. 9, [no exp.].

4. Extract, AGN, Ramo de Expulsión, leg. 18, tom. 40, exp. 11, fols. 2–6.

5. *Para Rayo* (Chiapas), 21 May 1829, p. 1; Bocanegra to Sotomayor, Mexico City, 27 May 1829, AGN, Ramo de Expulsión, leg. 22 3/4, tom. 55, exp. 82, fol. 19; ibid., leg. 24, tom. 61, exp. 43, fol. 19; Arrillaga, comp., *Recopilación de leyes* 2:157–58.

6. Zavala to Bocanegra, Mexico City, 6 July 1829; Bocanegra to Sotomayor, Mexico City, 11 July 1829; Múzquiz to Bocanegra, Tlalpan, 7

July 1831; Aburto to Lombardo, Tlalpan, 14 Jan. 1834, AGN, Ramo de Expulsión, leg. 22 3/4, tom. 55, exp. 82, fols. 6–9.

7. Cañedo to Bocanegra, Guadalajara, 6 May 1829, Bocanegra to Cañedo, Mexico City, 20 May 1829, AGN, Ramo de Expulsión, leg. 18, tom. 40, exp. 26, fols. 1–2.

8. Bocanegra to Cañedo, Mexico City, 6 May 1829; Herrera to Bocanegra, Mexico City, 22 May and 11 June 1829, AGN, Ramo de Expulsión, leg. 23, tom. 57, exp. 68, fols. 2–3, 11.

9. AGN, Ramo de Gobernación, leg. 144, exp. 29, fol. 1.

10. Bocanegra to secretaries of the chambers, Mexico City, 22 May 1829, AGN, Ramo de Expulsión, leg. 18, tom. 39, exp. 2, fols. 1, 3, 19.

11. "México 27 de mayo de 1829," *Correo de la Federación*, 27 May 1829, pp. 2–3; "México 30 de mayo de 1829," ibid., 30 May 1829, pp. 2–3; ibid., 1 July 1829, p. 3.

12. Santa Anna to Bocanegra, Veracruz, 11 June 1829, Bocanegra to Santa Anna, Mexico City, 17 June 1829, AGN, Ramo de Expulsión, leg. 17, tom. 37, exp. 34, fols. 1–2.

13. Bocanegra to Cañedo, Mexico City, 18 July 1829, Bocanegra to Zavala, Mexico City, 5 Aug. 1829, AGN, Ramo de Expulsión, leg. 19, tom. 42, exp. 25, fols. 1, 14.

14. By my calculations, the Spanish community in 1827 numbered 6,610—declining to about 4,831 after the first expulsion.

15. *El Telégrafo*, 17 Feb. 1833, p. 2.

16. *Correo de la Federación*, 12 and 19 May 1829, p. 4; Salce Arredondo Papers, wallet 6, no. 32; "Cesantes y Pensionistas," [Governor of Michoacán], *Memoria*, 7 Aug. 1829.

17. Argüelles to Bocanegra, Jalapa, 24 Nov. 1829, AGN, Ramo de Expulsión, leg. 17, tom. 38, exp. 74, fol. 1.

18. Gil y Sáenz, *Historia de Tabasco*, pp. 243–45.

19. Ponce de León, *Reseñas históricas*, pp. 209–11.

20. Bancroft, *History of California* 3:52, 96–97; Hittel, *History of California* 2:87–88.

21. Taylor to Clay, Veracruz, 1 July 1829, U.S. Consular Correspondence, microcopy 183; Galos to Murphy, Bordeaux, 30 July 1829, extracted in *Las relaciones franco-mexicanas*, ed. Weckmann, 1:183; Report of accounting office of general commisary at Veracruz, 8 July 1829, AGN, Ramo de Expulsión, leg. 8, tom. 19, exp. 46, fols. 21–24; *Noticioso*, 3 May 1829, *Correo de la Federación*, 13 May 1829, p. 2.

22. Zálazar to Ramírez, New Orleans, 17 July 1829, in Suárez y Navarro, *Historia de México* 1:419; Zamaçois, *Méjico* 11:710–11; seven letters between Lopes, Bocanegra, and Zavala, 27 June–23 Sept. 1829, and 18 July 1829 (two letters), AGN, Ramo de Expulsión, leg. 18, tom. 39, exp. 6, fols. 2–11; ibid., exp. 7, fols. 2–4; ibid., exp. 8, fols. 4–5.

23. *Correo de la Federación*, 10 Oct. 1829, p. 4.

24. Alamán, *Méjico* 5:785–87.

25. Ibid., 5:782–83; Suárez y Navarro, *Historia de México* 1:425; González de Cossío, *Xalapa*, p. 73; Zavala, *Juicio imparcial*, pp. 23–24; *Proceso instructivo*, pp. 133–35; Alamán, *Méjico* 5:782–83.

26. Bustamante, *Continuación*, pp. 283–86, 297.

27. A. I., "Victoria de Tampico, No. 3," García Papers, D 64, vol. 4, no. 5, pp. 2–3; Mier y Terán to Bustamante, Pueblo Viejo, Hernández y Dávalos Papers, HD 20-3.4745; Santa Anna to Guerrero, Jalapa, 29 Oct. 1829, in Díaz-Thomé, "Cartas al general Vicente Guerrero," pp. 257–58.

28. Muñoz, *Antonio López de Santa Anna*, p. 94; Santa Anna to Guerrero, Jalapa, 12 Nov. 1829, in Díaz-Thomé, "Cartas al general Vicente Guerrero," pp. 291–92.

29. Salce Arredondo Papers, wallet 6; Bustamante to Guerrero, 27 Nov. 1829, in Díaz-Thomé, "Cartas al general Vicente Guerrero," p. 293.

30. Muñoz, *Antonio López de Santa Anna*, pp. 95–96; Rippy, *Joel Roberts Poinsett*, p. 129; Zavala, *Juicio imparcial*, p. 10, n. (a).

31. Alamán, *Méjico* 5:783–84; Muñoz, *Antonio López de Santa Anna*, pp. 95–96; Salce Arredondo Papers, wallet 6, no. 70.

32. Mier y Terán to Alamán, Tampico, 2 Jan. 1830, García Salinas Papers.

33. Bustamante, "La patria ya se salvó y su remedio es seguro," pp. 6–7; Alamán, "Este si está mas picante que el del señor Bustamante," p. 7.

34. Minister of Government, *Memoria: 1830*, pp. 10, 24; Alamán, *Méjico* 5:787–88.

35. *El Atleta* and *El Gladiador*, 13 Apr.–2 May 1830.

36. Arrillaga, comp., *Recopilación de leyes* 3:43, 67; 11:496.

37. Mangino to Alamán, Mexico City, 30 Mar. 1830; Facio to Alamán, Mexico City, 23 Aug. 1830; Alamán to Mangino, Mexico City, 3 Sept. 1830, AGN, Ramo de Expulsión, leg. 22, tom. 48, exp. 20, fol. 1; ibid., exp. 33, fols. 1, 3; *El Gladiador*, 18 May 1830, pp. 213–14.

38. "Solicitudes pendientes de Españoles," AGN, Ramo de Expulsión, leg. 1, tom. 3, exp. 57.

39. Facio to Alamán, Mexico City, 20 Jan. 1830, Alamán to commandant general of Mexico, 6 Sept. [1829], Cervantes to Alamán, Tlalpan, 20 July 1830, Alamán to Cervantes and Facio, Mexico City, 24 July 1830, Alamán to Cervantes, Mexico City, 9 July 1830, Múzquiz to Alamán, Tlalpan, 30 July 1830, Alamán to governor of Federal District, Mexico City, 30 Oct. 1830, Camacho to Alamán, Jalapa, 8 Apr. 1831, Alamán to Camacho, Mexico City, 15 Apr. 1831, AGN, Ramo de Expulsión, leg. 22, tom. 48, exp. 28, fols. 1–4; ibid., exp. 26, fols. 31–38; ibid., leg. 23, tom. 57, exp. 47, fols. 2, 5.

40. *Colección de los decretos . . . Jalisco*, pp. 76, 231.

41. Pèrez de Lebrija to Alamán, Mexico City, 9 Feb. 1830, Alamán to Pérez de Lebrija, Mexico City, 17 Feb. 1830, AGN, Ramo de Expulsión, leg. 23, tom. 56, exp. 17, fols. 1–2.

42. Montes de Oca to Alamán, Guanajuato, 8 Mar. 1830, Alamán to Montes de Oca, Mexico City, 13 Mar. 1830, AGN, Ramo de Expulsión, leg. 11, tom. 25, exp. 4, fols. 1–2.

43. Montes de Oca to Alamán, Guanajuato, 3 May, 23 July, and 10 Oct. 1830, Alamán to Montes de Oca, Mexico City, 3 Feb. 1831, AGN, Ramo de Expulsión, leg. 11, tom. 25, exp. 3, fols. 1–4.

44. Salce Arredondo Papers, wallet 7, no. 56; Prieto Papers, wallet 19, nos. 19, 25, 74.

45. Secretary of State, Chihuahua, *Memoria, 1830*, p. 19.

46. Hittell, *History of California* 2:126.

47. Ibid., 2:154; Hutchinson, *Frontier Settlement*, pp. 136–37.

48. Hittell, *History of California* 2:130; Bancroft, *History of California* 3:401.

Chapter 8. The Impact of the 1829–1831 Expulsion

1. AGN, Ramo de Expulsión, legs. 3, 5, 8, 9; "Entradas y salidas de embarcaciones," *Correo de la Federación*, 1 Jan.–20 Mar. 1829.

2. Exceptions rise from 2,090 to 2,699 when the two chambers' lists are tabulated (see table 8).

3. AGN, Ramo de Expulsión, leg. 15, tom. 33, exp. 22.

4. AGN, Ramo de Expulsión, leg. 15, tom. 32, exp. 8; ibid., tom. 33, exp. 18.

5. AGN, Ramo de Expulsión, leg. 15, tom. 33, exps. 17, 23; "Lista de los profesores de medicina y cirugía," *Correo de la Federación*, 1 June 1829, p. 4; U.S., Bureau of Customs, microcopy 259, rolls 7–8.

6 AGN, Ramo de Expulsión, leg. 15, 17, 22 3/4, 23; AGN, Ramo de Gobernación, leg. 1,662, *passim*; Minister of Justice and Ecclesiastical Affairs, *Memoria, 1830*, table 3.

7. AGN, Ramo de Expulsión, leg. 4, tom. 9, exp. 10; ibid., leg. 15, tom. 32, exp. 8; ibid., leg. 15, tom. 33, exps. 18, 24–25.

8. Minister of Government, *Memoria, 1830*, p. 26; Viesca to Bocanegra, Saltillo, 30 Oct. 1829; AGN, Ramo de Expulsión, leg. 22 3/4, tom. 55, exp. 55.

9. Bustamante, *Continuación*, p. 236.

10. Letters from Galos to Murphy, Bordeaux, 20 Mar.–14 Sept. 1829, in *Las relaciones franco-mexicanas*, ed. Weckmann, 1:156–84.

11. Ibid., 1:180–95; Alamán, *Méjico* 5:780; Ward, *Mexico* 1:ix, 2:489, *passim*.

12. Fifteen reports, Galos to Murphy, Bordeaux, 27 Feb.–14 Sept. 1829, extracted in *Las relaciones franco-mexicanas*, ed. Weckmann, 1:180–95.

13. Cañedo to Murphy, Mexico City, 18 Dec. 1828, ibid., 1:155–56.

14. Howe, *The Mining Guild of New Spain*, pp. 45, 458–59.

15. Lerdo de Tejada, *Comercio exterior de México*, tables 38, 41; Romero, *Mexico and the United States*, pp. 139, 145.

16. Romero's totals are slightly lower (p. 145); Lerdo de Tejada, *Comercio exterior de México*, tables 36, 43.

17. Lerdo de Tejada, *Comercio exterior de México*, tables 36, 43; Romero, *Mexico and the United States*, p. 139, table 1.

18. See Bernecker, *Industrie und Aussenhandel*.

19. Taylor to Clay, Veracruz, 1 July 1829, U.S., Consular Correspondence, microcopy 183.

Chapter 9. Spain Attempts Reconquest, 1829–1830

1. Reports of Pablo Obregón, Washington, D.C., *Correspondencia de la legación de México en Estados Unidos*, pp. 63–102.

2. Murphy to Cañedo, "Reservadísimo," Paris, 5 Jan. 1828; Cañedo to Murphy, Mexico City, 18 Dec. 1829, extracted in *Las relaciones franco-mexicanas*, ed. Weckmann, 1:155–56; AGN, Ramo de Expulsión, leg. 4, tom. 9, exp. 10, fols. 68, 71; *Correo de la Federación*, 25 Oct. 1829, p. 4; Rocafuerte to Cañedo, London, 24 Mar. 1829, in Bosch García, *Problemas diplomáticos*, p. 142.

3. Aviraneta, *Mis memorias íntimas*, pp. 120–21; Bustamante, *Voz de la Patria*, 24 Nov. 1830, pp. 3–4; Despect to Murphy, Bayonne, 24 Nov. 1830, extracted in *Las relaciones franco-mexicanas*, ed. Weckmann, 1:156; "Veracruz 26 de junio de 1829," *Correo de la Federación*, 8 July 1829, p. 2; *El Aguila*, 16 Aug. 1828, pp. 1–2.

4. Taylor to Clay, Veracruz, 21 Mar. 1829, in U.S., Consular Correspondence, microcopy 183; Franco, ed., *Documentos*, pp. 398–400; Suárez y Navarro, *Historia de México* 1:414–24; Francisco de Paula [Tamariz] to Guerrero, Veracruz, 11 Apr. 1829, in Díaz-Thomé, "Cartas al general Vicente Guerrero," pp. 122–24.

5. Delgado, *España y México* 1:443–44; *Boletín del Archivo Nacional* (Havana) 56:44–112.

6. Franco, *Política continental*, pp. 403–04; Aviraneta, *Mis memorias íntimas*, pp. 155–56, 249–68, appendix 1; Pizarro Martínez to Camacho, New Orleans, 13 Apr. 1828, in Chávez Orozco, comp., *Un esfuerzo de México*, pp. 182–84.

7. Delgado, *España y México* 3:127–48 and appendix, doc. 26, pp. 438–39; Havana, Archivo Nacional, Asuntos Políticos, leg. 34, no. 1, in *Documentos*, ed. Franco, pp. xcv–xcvi.

8. Aviraneta, *Mis memorias íntimas*, pp. 144–55; Basadre to Viezca, New York, 27 Dec. 1829, in Chávez Orozco, comp., *Un esfuerzo de México*, pp. 201–02.

9. "Memoria sobre el estado actual del Reyno de Mégico y modo de pacificarlo," in Delgado, *España y México* 1:400–05, 441; Franco, ed., *Documentos*, p. xcv.

10. "México 4 de mayo de 1829," *Correo de la Federación*, 4 May 1829, p. 3; ibid., 11 July 1829, p. 1.

11. Aviraneta, *Mis memorias íntimas*, pp. 167–72.

12. Zambrano to Vives, Madrid, 20 July 1829, in *Documentos*, ed. Franco, p. 416.

13. Moctezuma to Bocanegra, Mexico City, 3 Jan. 1829; Bocanegra to Lopes, Mexico City, 7 Jan. 1829, AGN, Ramo de Gobernación, leg. 75.

14. Cuevas, *Porvenir de México*, pp. 327–28.

15. Montenegro to Guerrero, New Orleans, 16 and 18 June 1829, in Díaz-Thomé, "Cartas al general Vicente Guerrero," pp. 331–35.

16. Suárez y Navarro, *Historia de México* 1:138; *El Sol* reappeared on 1 July 1829; Zavala, *Juicio imparcial*, p. 24; A. I., "La Victoria de Tampico . . . núm. 2," García Papers, D 64, vol. 4, no. 2, p. 4; Cuevas, *Porvenir de México*, p. 329.

17. Trens, ed. *Historia de Veracruz* 3:670–71; Santa Anna to Guerrero, Veracruz, 15 July 1829, in Díaz-Thomé, "Cartas al general Vicente Guerrero," p. 272; "Campeche 15 de julio de 1829," *Correo de la Federación*, 28 July 1829, p. 1; Mediaville to Aviraneta Havana, 14 Aug. 1829, in "Aviraneta," *Boletín del Archivo Nacional* (Havana) 56:109.

18. Tampico's Spaniards fled by sea on 4 July 1829, FO 50/54; Moctezuma to Bocanegra, Mexico City, 24 July 1829, AGN, Ramo de Expulsión, leg. 18, tom. 39, exp. 9, fol. 43; memoirs of participants tend to confirm the estimate of Jacobo de la Pezuela, *Historia de la isla de Cuba*, in Franco, *Política continental*, p. 408; Lerdo de Tejada, *Apuntes históricos* 2:341; Mier y Terán to Moctezuma, Pueblo Viejo, 12 Dec. 1829, in Suárez y Navarro, *Historia de México* 1:160–61.

19. Suárez y Navarro, *Historia de México* 1:224–25; Bustamante, *Continuación*, p. 275; Poinsett to Van Buren, Mexico City, 11 Nov. 1829, U.S., Correspondence of Ministers in Mexico.

20. "Proclama del Exmo. Sr. Presidente con motivo de la espedición Española," 2 Aug. 1829, Anaya Papers; Welsh to Pakenham, Veracruz, 8 Aug. 1829, FO 50/55; Poinsett to Van Buren, Mexico City, 9 Aug. 1829, U.S., Correspondence of Ministers in Mexico; Díaz-Thomé, "Cartas al general Vicente Guerrero," *passim*.

21. Zavala, *Venganza de la colonia*, p. 34; *Correo de la Federación*, 2 Aug. 1829, pp. 1–2; Suárez y Navarro, *Historia de México* 1:142–43; Olavarría y Ferrari, *México independiente*, p. 195; FO 50/55; Cuevas, *Porvenir de México*, p. 328.

22. Poinsett to Van Buren, Mexico City, 9 Aug. 1829, U.S., Correspondence of Ministers in Mexico; Zavala, *Venganza de la colonia*, pp. 42–43; Bustamante, *Voz de la Patria*, 3 aug. 1829, pp. 7–8.

23. Amador, *Bosquejo histórico de Zacatecas* 2:355; *Correo de la Federación*, 17 Aug. 1829, pp. 2–3.

24. *Correo de la Federación*, 22 Aug. 1829, p. 1; ibid., 26 Aug. 1829, p. 1.

25. Ibid., 22 Aug. 1829, p. 1; Poinsett to Van Buren, Mexico City, 9 Aug. 1829, U.S., Correspondence of Ministers in Mexico.

26. Welsh to Pakenham, Veracruz, 5 Aug. 1829, FO 50/55; Bancroft, *His-*

tory of the North Mexican States 2:93–94; Muro, *Historia de San Luis Potosí* 1:528–29.

27. Arrillaga, comp., *Recopilación de leyes* 2:205; Dublán and Lozano, comps., *Legislación mexicana* 2:150–51; Franco, ed., *Documentos*, p. xcvi; *Correo de la Federación*, 19 Aug. 1829, pp. 1–3.

28. Sims, *La reconquista*, p. 91.

29. Bocanegra, *Memorias* 2:81–82; Bocanegra to Poinsett, Mexico City, 29 July 1829, Poinsett to Bocanegra, Mexico City, 31 July 1829, U.S., Correspondence of Ministers to Mexico; "Españoles emigrados de México que han tomado partido en La Habana contra la República," *Correo de la Federación*, 18 Aug. 1829, p. 2.

30. Bocanegra, *Memorias*, 2:92–93; Bustamante, *Continuación*, pp. 277–78.

31. *Colección de los decretos . . . de Jalisco*, p. 66; Muro, *Historia de San Luis Potosí* 1:494–95 1:494–95; Velázquez, *Historia de San Luis Potosí* 3:161.

32. Chamber of Deputies, session of 7 Aug. 1829, *Correo de la Federación*, 13 Aug. 1829, p. 1; Arrillaga, comp., *Recopilación de leyes* 2:194–95.

33. Bustamante, *Continuación*, pp. 276, 280; Bancroft, *History of Mexico* 5:73. The vote was 31–18.

34. "México 3 de septiembre de 1829," *Correo de la Federación*, 3 Sept. 1829, p. 3; Bocanegra to Tornel, Mexico City, 3 Sept. 1829, AGN, Ramo de Gobernación, leg. 1540, exp. 5, fol. 2; *El Sol*, 4 Sept. 1829; Dublán and Lozano, comps., *Legislación mexicana* 2:156.

35. "Resumen de las diez listas," in departmental chief to governor of Veracruz, Veracruz, 28 July 1830, AGN, Ramo de Expulsión, leg. 23, tom. 57, exp. 42, fol. 6; *El Gladiador*, 11 May 1830, pp. 183–84.

36. Bustamante, *Continuación*, p. 290; Zamçois, *Méjico* 11:807; Arrillaga, comp., *Recopilación de leyes* 2:271.

37. Salgado to Bocanegra, Mexico City, 18 Dec. 1829, AGN, Ramo de Expulsión, leg. 23, tom. 57, exp. 43, fol. 4; Arrillaga, comp., *Recopilación de leyes* 2:205, 214–24; FO 50/57.

38. Note in Arrillaga, comp., *Recopilación de leyes* 2:224; Bancroft, *History of Mexico* 5:79–80; Barker, *Mexico and Texas*, pp. 54–56, 78–86; Prieto Papers, wallet 19, no. 75; AGN, Ramo de Gobernación, leg. 87, exp. 3.

39. Galván Rivera, comp., *Colección de órdenes y decretos* 5:159–60; Arrillaga, comp., *Recopilación de leyes* 2:231.

40. Bustamante, *Continuación*, p. 291; 'México 24 de septiembre de 1829," *Correo de la Federación*, 24 Sept. 1829, p. 3; Bocanegra, *Memorias* 2:39.

41. Report of 11 Aug. 1829, *El Boletín Oficial*, no. 2, in FO 50/54; Alamán, *Méjico* 5:782.

42. Hernández y Dávalos Papers, HD 20-2,47410; Prieto Papers, wallet 6, no. 51 and wallet 19, no. 73; Lerdo de Tejada, *Apuntes históricos* 2:318.

43. Sims, *La reconquista*, p. 118, table.

44. Batres to Comodoro, Sevilla to Comandante, Mier y Terán to Sevilla,

Pueblo Viejo, 30 Sept. 1829; Sevilla to Mier y Terán, Pueblo Viejo, 1 Oct. 1829, *El Boletín Oficial*, no. 31, in FO 50/54b; Pakenham to Earl of Aberdeen, Mexico City, 30 Sept. 1829, FO 50/54; Robertson to Van Buren, Tampico, 4 Dec. 1829, in U.S., Consular Correspondence, microcopy 241; Mier y Terán to Moctezuma, Pueblo Viejo, 12 Dec. 1829, in Suárez y Navarro, *Historia de México* 1:160, n. 1; Lerdo de Tejada, *Apuntes históricos* 2:341.

45. Hittel, *California* 2:108–12; Bancroft, *History of California* 3:84, n.

46. Vives to intendent of the army, Havana, 1 Mar. 1830; Count of Villanueva to Vives, Havana, 2 Mar. 1830, in *Documentos*, ed. Franco, pp. 493–94; Viesca to Poinsett, Federal District, 10 Nov. 1829, Poinsett to Van Buren, Mexico City, 11 Nov. 1829, in U.S., Correspondence of Ministers to Mexico.

47. *El Atleta*, 11, 17, and 24 Mar. 1830, pp. 327, 355, 380; *El Gladiador*, 3 Mar. 1830.

48. Suárez y Navarro, *Historia de México* 1:195; *El Gladiador*, 19 June 1830, pp. 337–40, in Flores Caballero, *La contrarrevolución*, p. 168.

49. Delgado, *España y México* 3:444–45, appendix, doc. 28; Franco, ed., *Documentos*, pp. 417–18.

50. Arrillaga, comp., *Recopilación de leyes* 2:224.

51. Taylor to Van Buren, Veracruz, 19 Sept. 1829, in U.S., Consular Correspondence, microcopy 183; Pakenham to Earl of Aberdeen, Mexico City, 16 Nov. 1829 (two letters), in FO 50/55; Zamaçois, *Méjico* 12:19.

52. Arrangoiz, *México* 2:196; *La Verdad Desnuda*, 16 Mar. 1833, p. 2; Bocanegra, *Memorias* 2:42–43.

53. Suárez y Navarro, *Historia de México* 1:166–68.

54. Flores Caballero, *La contrarrevolución*, p. 162; Cuartel general de Jalapa, 8 Oct. 1829, *Correo de la Federación*, 14 Oct. 1829, p. 1; Delgado, *España y México* 1:441–42; Iñigo to minister of the treasury, Madrid, 16 Oct. 1829, ibid., p. 447.

55. Aviraneta, "Memoria," in "Aviraneta," *Boletín del Archivo Nacional* (Havana) 61:70–73; "Acta," 22 Nov. and 13 Dec. 1829, in *Documentos*, ed. Franco, pp. xcvii, 434–90.

56. Pakenham to Earl of Aberdeen, 25 Mar. 1830, FO 50/55, in Rippy, *Joel Roberts Poinsett*, pp. 129–30; Zavala, *Ensayo histórico* 2:248; marginalia by Polignac, Villeveque to his father, Mexico City, 24 Jan. 1830, in *Correspondencia diplomática*, ed. Torre Villar, 1:82.

57. Vives to minister of war, Havana, 15 Jan. 1830, in *Documentos*, ed. Franco, pp. 491–93.

58. Pakenham to Earl of Aberdeen, Mexico City, 30 Jan. 1830, FO 50/55; Franco, *Política continental*, pp. 416–20.

59. List in *Las relaciones franco-mexicanas*, ed. Weckmann, 1:156.

60. Addington to Foreign Office, Madrid, 10, 17, 18 Feb. and 3 Mar. 1830, Pakenham to Foreign Office, Mexico City, 20 Feb. 1830, Earl of Aberdeen to Pakenham, London, 20 Feb. 1830, FO 50/64; Delgado, *España y México* 1:150.

61. Franco, *Política continental*, p. 423; Delgado, *España y México* 1:450; *Documentos*, ed. Franco, pp. xcviii–xccix.

62. These *consultas* constitute hundreds of manuscripts in AGN, Ramo de Expulsión, leg. 21, tom. 45, exp. 35; ibid., leg. 21, tom. 46, exps. 39, 40, 44, 45.

63. Salce Arredondo Papers, wallet 7, nos. 23, 29; Prieto Papers, wallet 19, no. 11.

64. Delgado, *España y México* 1:380–91; "Proyecto para la reconquista y posesión del Reyno de Nueva España," ibid., 3:289–94, summarized in 1:467–68.

65. Committee to Foreign Office, London, 19 Apr. 1830; Pakenham to Earl of Aberdeen, Mexico City, 7 May 1830, FO 50/60, 64.

66. AGN, Ramo de Expulsión, leg. 21, tom. 45, exp. 36, fols. 1–10.

67. Circulars, Ciudad Victoria, 7 May 1830, and Tamaulipas, 11 May 1830, Prieto Papers, wallet 19, nos. 30, 31; Nuevo León Imprints, no. 262; Salce Arredondo, wallet 7, no. 94, original in AGN, Ramo de Expulsión, leg. 21, tom. 46, exp. 37, fols. 1–89.

68. Prieto Papers, wallet 19, no. 32.

69. Report, AGN, Ramo de Expulsión, leg. 21, tom. 47, exp. 1, fols. 1–43; governor of Nuevo León to Alamán, Monterrey, ibid., leg. 21, tom. 47, exp. 2, fols. 1–15; Alamán to governor of Nuevo León, Mexico City, 8 Feb. 1830, ibid., exp. 9, fol. 20.

70. "Noticias Estrangeras," *El Gladiador*, 27 Aug. 1830, p. 613.

71. "Madrid 20 de mayo," *El Gladiador*, 4 Sept. 1830, p. 645.

72. Pakenham to Earl of Aberdeen, Mexico City, 10 June 1830, Thompson to Earl of Aberdeen, London, 8 July 1830, Earl of Aberdeen to Pakenham, London, 24 July 1830, FO 50/59, 61, 64.

73. Secretary of Council of Ministers to minister of treasury, Madrid, 19 July 1830, in Delgado, *España y México* 1:449–50.

74. "Nota," in Arrillaga, comp., *Recopilación de leyes* 10:186.

Chapter 10. The Exiles Attempt to Return, 1829–1832

1. Reports, port commander at Veracruz, AGN, Ramo de Expulsión, leg. 23, tom. 60, exp. 119, fols. 1–151.

2. Bocanegra to secretaries of Chamber of Deputies, Mexico City, 16 Apr. 1829, AGN, Ramo de Expulsión, leg. 18, tom. 39, exp. 9, fols. 4–5; two letters between governor of Tabasco and Bocanegra, 7 Dec. 1828 and 12 Jan. 1829, ibid., leg. 23, tom. 57, exp. 58, fols. 2–5; two letters between govenor of Tamaulipas and Bocanegra, 16 Feb. 1829 and 16 Mar. 1829, ibid., leg. 22 3/4, tom. 55, exp. 98, fols. 1–2; Bocanegra to vice-consul at New Orleans, Mexico City, 20 Mar. 1829; Alamán to vice-consul at New Orleans, Mexico City, 1 June 1830, leg. 22, tom. 48, exp. 17, fols. 1–4.

3. AGN, Ramo de Expulsión, leg. 22, tom. 48, exps. 21, 24; ibid.,

leg. 18, tom. 39, exp. 9, fol. 43; ibid., leg. 25, tom. 64, exp. 38, fols. 24–25.

4. Moctezuma to Bocanegra, Mexico City, 24 July 1829, Bocanegra to Moctezuma, Mexico City, 1 Aug. 1829, AGN, Ramo de Expulsión, leg. 18, tom. 39, exp. 9, fols. 43–44; files, Lt. Col. Manuel María Leyton, ibid., leg. 22, tom. 48, exp. 44, fols. 1–16; Francisco Martínez y Flores, ibid., leg. 20, tom. 44, exp. 12, fol. 29; Giménez, *Memorias*, pp. 37–58.

5. Files, Miguel José Bellido, AGN, Ramo de Expulsión, leg. 23, tom. 56, exp. 38; Luis Guevara, ibid., leg. 23, tom. 56, exp. 39; Francisco Ramírez and Mauricio Villegas, ibid., leg. 22, tom. 48, exp. 21; Francisco Casasús, ibid., leg. 12, tom. 26, exp. 3, fols. 8–9; central commissioner of war and marine to Bocanegra, Mexico City, 14 Apr. 1829, ibid., leg. 20, tom. 44, exp. 12, fols. 1–4.

6. Chávez Orozco, comp., *Un esfuerzo de México*, pp. 196–98; Rivera Cambas, *Historia . . . de Jalapa* 2:591; Radin, ed., *Catalogue*, "Supplement," p. 594; *El Atleta*, 26 Feb. 1830, p. 355.

7. File, Bernardo Copca, AGN, Ramo de Expulsión, leg. 20, tom. 44, exp. 12, fol. 26; Argüelles to Alamán, Jalapa, 30 Jan. 1830, Alamán to Argüelles, Mexico City, 6 Feb. 1830, Mangino to Alamán, Mexico City, 10 Feb. 1830, ibid., leg. 22, tom. 48, exp. 23, fols. 1–3.

8. Ibid., leg. 4, tom. 1, exp. 10; ibid., leg. 22, tom. 48, exp. 22, fols. 2–3; ibid., leg. 22, tom. 48, exp. 22, fols. 1–4; lists of returnees, 24 and 27 Feb. 1830, *El Atleta*, 10 Mar. 1830, p. 322.

9. Arrillaga, comp., *Recopilación de leyes* 3:108–09; "Jalapa 3 [and 4] de marzo de 1830," *El Atleta*, 10 Mar. 1830, pp. 321–22.

10. "Veracruz 17 de marzo de 1830," *El Atleta*, 23 Mar. 1830, p. 376; ibid., 24 Mar. 1830, p. 381; case summaries, seven merchants who went to New Orleans "with permission" in August 1829, AGN, Ramo de Expulsión, leg. 20, tom. 44, exp. 15, fol. 1; summary, Col. Antonio García Moreno, ibid., leg. 20, tom. 44, exp. 13, fol. 2.

11. Camacho to Alamán, Jalapa, 15 Mar. 1830, AGN, Ramo de Expulsión, leg. 22, tom. 48, exp. 27, fols. 8–9.

12. Marginalia, Camacho to Alamán, Jalapa, 20 Mar. 1830, AGN, Ramo de Expulsión, leg. 22, tom. 48, exp. 27, fols. 3–5; six letters between minister of government and minister of war, ibid., leg. 22, tom. 48, exp. 39, fols. 1–9.

13. Alamán to vice-consul in New Orleans, Mexico City, 24 Mar. and 1 June 1830, AGN, Ramo de Expulsión, leg. 22, tom. 48, exp. 17, fols. 1, 4.

14. Alamán to Camacho, Mexico City, 24 Mar. 1830, AGN, Ramo de Expulsión, leg. 22, tom. 48, exp. 27, fol. 7; ibid., leg. 23, tom. 56, exp. 5; Camacho to Alamán, Jalapa, 28 Mar. 1830, ibid., leg. 22, tom. 48, exp. 27, fols. 10–14.

15. Camacho to Alamán, 5 Apr. 1830 (two letters), AGN, Ramo de Expulsión, leg. 22, tom. 48, exp. 27, fols. 15–16; ibid., leg. 23, tom. 57, exp. 43, fols. 5–7; ibid., leg. 22, tom. 56, *passim*.

16. "México 10 de abril de 1830," *El Atleta*, 10 Apr. 1830, pp. 448–49;

ibid., 11 Apr. 1830, p. 453; *El Gladiador*, 18 Apr. 1830, p. 88; ibid., 11 May 1830, p. 182, in Flores Caballero, *La contrarrevolución*, p. 168.

17. Maritime administrator to Alamán, Veracruz, 21 Apr. 1830, AGN, Ramo de Expulsión, leg. 23, tom. 56, exp. 3, fol. 1; Taylor to Van Buren, Veracruz, 26 Apr. 1830, U.S., Consular Correspondence, microcopy 183.

18. Camacho to Alamán, Jalapa, 22 Apr. 1830, AGN, Ramo de Expulsión, leg. 22, tom. 48, exp. 27, fols. 17–18, 21.

19. Returnees, Guaymas, AGN, Ramo de Expulsión, leg. 18, tom. 39, exp. 9, fol. 124.

20. Alamán to governors of Veracruz and Tabasco, Mexico City, 28 Apr. 1830, Alamán to Facio, Mexico City, 19 May 1830, Alamán to Camacho, Mexico City, 19 May 1830, AGN, Ramo de Expulsión, leg. 22, tom. 48, exp. 41, fols. 1–3; Facio to Alamán, Mexico City, 9 July 1830, ibid., leg. 23, tom. 57, exp. 45, fol. 1.

21. Taylor to Van Buren, Veracruz, 16 May 1830, U.S., Consular Correspondence, microcopy 183; Alamán to vice-consul at New Orldeans, Mexico City, 22 May 1830, AGN, Ramo de Expulsión, leg. 22, tom. 48, exp. 17, fol. 5; *El Gladiador*, 11 May 1830, pp. 183–84.

22. Camacho to Alamán, Jalapa, 31 May 1830, AGN, Ramo de Expulsión, leg. 23, tom. 56, exp. 9, fols. 1–2.

23. Files, Manuel Balán, AGN, Ramo de Expulsión, leg. 23, tom. 56, exp. 19; José Antonio Gómez, AGN, Ramo de Gobernación, leg. 1662; Pakenham to Earl of Aberdeen, Mexico City, 10 June 1830, FO 50/61.

24. Camacho to Alamán, Jalapa, 14 June 1830, Alamán to Camacho, Mexico City, 26 June 1830, AGN, Ramo de Expulsión, leg. 22, tom. 48, exp. 27, fols. 1–2.

25. AGN, Ramo de Expulsión, leg. 1, tom. 1, exp. 6; Camacho to Alamán, Jalapa, 18 June 1830, AGN, Ramo de Expulsión, leg. 23, tom. 56, exp. 11, fols. 1–2.

26. AGN, Ramo de Expulsión, leg. 22, tom. 48, exp. 41, fols. 1–17.

27. Camacho to Alamán, Jalapa, 1 July 1830, circular, 7 July 1830, Alamán to Camacho, Mexico City, 10 July 1830, AGN, Ramo de Expulsión, leg. 22, tom. 48, exp. 35, fols. 1–4; *El Gladiador*, 8 July 1830, pp. 413–14; ibid., 9 July 1830, pp. 415–16; ibid., 10 July 1830, p. 424.

28. AGN, Ramo de Expulsión, leg. 23 tom. 60, exp. 119, fols. 12–16, 29; Migoin to Alamán, Tampico, 31 July 1830, Alamán to Migoin, 17 Aug. 1830, ibid., leg. 22, tom. 48, exp. 25, fols. 1–2

29. Camacho to Alamán, Jalapa, 10 July 1830, Alamán to Camacho, Mexico City, 16 July 1830, certificate of good conduct, 24 May 1830, AGN, Ramo de Expulsión, leg. 22, tom. 48, exp. 34, fols. 1–4.

30. AGN, Ramo de Expulsión, leg. 1, tom. 1, exp. 7; lists, Cosamaloapan, Córdoba, and Orizaba, Veracruz, AGN, Ramo de Expulsión, leg. 23, tom. 57, exp. 42, fols. 7–10; summary of ten lists, ibid., fols. 5–6; Camacho to Alamán, Jalapa, 14 June 1830, Alamán to Camacho, Mexico City, 26 July 1830, AGN, Ramo de Expulsión, leg. 22, tom. 48, exp. 27, fols. 1–2.

31. Summary of Toscano's case, 27 July 1831, AGN, Ramo de Expulsión, leg. 22, tom. 48, exp. 24.

32. Camacho to Alamán, Jalapa, 10 Aug. 1830, Alamán to Camacho, Mexico City, 21 Aug. 1830, Alamán to secretaries of the Senate, 30 Aug. 1830, AGN, Ramo de Expulsión, leg. 24, tom. 61, exp. 1, fols. 1–4.

33. Summary of consultations, 1829–31, AGN, Ramo de Expulsión, leg. 23, tom. 57, exp. 56, fols. 2, 5; Alamán to Camacho, Mexico City, 31 Aug. 1830, Alamán to Veracruz administrator of customs, Mexico City, 31 Aug. 1830, ibid., leg. 23, tom. 57, exp. 42, fols. 3–4; AGN, Ramo de Expulsión, leg. 1, tom. 1, exp. 8; Arrillaga, comp., *Recopilación de leyes*, 3:423–24.

34. Arrillaga, comp., *Recopilación de leyes* 3:434–36; AGN, Ramo de Expulsión, leg. 23, tom. 58, exp. 74, fols. 4–5.

35. File, Domingo Urtetegui, AGN, Ramo de Gobernación, leg. 1662.

36. Files, José Alonso y Fernández and Col. José Joaquín de la Sota, AGN, Ramo de Expulsión, leg. 18, tom. 39, exp. 9.

37. Minister of government, *Memoria, 1831*, pp. 15–18.

38. Bustamante, *Continuación* 3:443; Galván Rivera, comp., *Colección de órdenes y decretos* 6:14; Alamán to Martínez Pizarro, Mexico City, 26 Jan. and 2 Apr. 1831, Alamán to Lizardi Hermanos, Mexico City, 26 Jan. and 16 Apr. 1831, Alamán to Tornel, Mexico City, 26 Jan. 1831, Alamán to Mangino, Mexico City, 26 Jan., 7 Feb., and 17 May 1831, Mangino to Alamán, 7 Feb. 1831, AGN, Ramo de Expulsión, leg. 23, tom. 59, exp. 109, fols. 1–9, 14, 17, 20.

39. Alamán to Martínez Pizarro, Mexico City, 5 Aug. 1831, Alamán to Lebrija, Mexico City, 31 Aug. 1831, Lebrija to Alamán, Veracruz, 7 Dec. 1831, Alamán to Mangino, Mexico City, 31 Dec. 1831, 13 Jan. and 14 Apr. 1832, minister of government to minister of treasury, Mexico City, 26 Mar. 1833, 27 July 1835, 9 Mar. 1836, and 9 Nov. 1840; minister of government to consul at New Orleans, 7 Mar. 1834, AGN, Ramo de Expulsión, leg. 23, tom. 59, exp. 109, fols. 68–69, 84, 91–92, 98, 101; lists of returning Mexicans, 14 July and 14 Oct. 1831, ibid., fols. 33–34, 42–43, 49, 58, 73, 75, 77, 79; minister of government, *Memoria, 1832*, p. 11.

40. Radin, ed., *Catalogue*, "Supplement," pp. 214 ff.

41. Despect to Murphy, Bayonne, 4 Jan. 1831, extracted in *Las relaciones franco-mexicanas*, ed. Weckmann, 1:245; files, Manuel Peláez, Matías Martín de Aguirre, and Francisco Merchante, AGN, Ramo de Expulsión, leg. 18, tom. 39, exp. 9.

42. "Extracto," AGN, Ramo de Expulsión, leg. 13, tom. 29, exp. 27, fols. 11–12.

43. AGN, Ramo de Expulsión, leg. 23, tom. 59, exp. 98; Senate certificate cases, ibid., leg. 24, tom. 61, exps. 4–16; Alamán to Tampico customs administrator, Mexico City, 16 Feb. 1831, ibid., leg. 23, tom. 60, exp. 121, fol. 1; Alamán to Martínez Pizarro, Mexico City, 26 Feb. 1831, leg. 24, tom. 61, exp. 28, fol. 2.

44. "List of Havana residents to be reembarked," 24 Mar. 1831, Lemus

to del Corral, Jalapa, 30 Mar. 1831, Alamán to del Corral, Mexico City, 27 Apr. 1831, Camacho to Alamán, Jalapa, 30 Apr. 1831, del Corral to Alamán, Veracruz, 4 May 1831, AGN, Ramo de Expulsión, leg. 24, tom. 61, exp. 48, fols. 1–3, 5, 7; report, Veracruz, ibid., leg. 23, tom. 59, exp. 119, fol. 87; file, Pedro Rodríguez, ibid., leg. 23, tom. 56, exp. 20.

45. Alamán to Fagoaga, Mexico City, 24 Mar. 1831, Alamán to Facio, Mexico City, 24 Mar. 1831, Fagoaga to Alamán, Mexico City, 29 Mar. 1831, Alamán to del Corral, Mexico City, 16 Apr. 1831, AGN, Ramo de Expulsión, leg. 23, tom. 60, exp. 120, fols. 4, 6, 10; Arrillaga, comp., *Recopilación de leyes* 4:223–24.

46. Camacho to Alamán, Jalapa, 4 and 8 Apr. 1831, marginalia, Camacho to Alamán, Jalapa, 10 May 1831, Alamán to Butler, Mexico City, 18 Apr. 1831, Alamán to Camacho, Mexico City, 15 Apr. 1831, Alamán to Chamber secretaries, Mexico City, 15 Apr. 1831, AGN, Ramo de Gobernación, leg. 144, exp. 30, fols. 1–7; AGN, Ramo de Expulsión, leg. 23, tom. 56, exp. 36, fol. 6.

47. Stone to Van Buren, Veracruz, 28 Apr. 1831, U.S., Consular Correspondence, microcopy 183.

48. Bustamante, *Voz de la Patria*, 20 Apr. 1831, pp. 7–8; Camacho to Alamán, Jalapa, 18 June 1831, Alamán to Camacho, Mexico City, 2 July 1831, AGN, Ramo de Expulsión, leg. 23, tom. 59, exp. 108, fols. 22, 26–27.

49. Alamán to Lebrija, Mexico City, 7 July 1831, del Corral to Alamán, Veracruz, 20 Apr., 18 May, and 20 June 1831, Alamán to del Corral, Mexico City, 14 May and 14 July 1831, Alamán to Camacho, Mexico City, 14 May and 14 July 1831, Camacho to Alamán, Jalapa, 27 May 1831, AGN, Ramo de Expulsión, leg. 21, tom. 45, exp. 29, fols. 1–2; ibid., leg. 23, tom. 56, exp. 36, fol. 5; ibid., leg. 23, tom. 56, exp. 26, fol. 1; ibid., leg. 23, tom. 60, exp. 111, fols. 12–13, 18–19.

50. Lists, circulars of 23 Apr. 1831, AGN, Ramo de Expulsión, leg. 23, tom. 57, exps. 51, 53–54; ibid., leg. 23, tom. 58, exp. 81–83, 85–93; ibid., leg. 24, tom. 61, exps. 32, 34; ibid., leg. 24, tom. 62, exp. 58; ibid., leg. 27, tom. 69, exp. 1; del Corral to Alamán, Veracruz, 30 Apr. 1831, ibid., leg. 23, tom. 56, exp. 2, fol. 1; Arrillaga, comp., *Recopilación de leyes* 4:244–51.

51. Lists, *El Telégrafo*, 11 and 17 Feb. 1833, *passim*.

52. Cervantes to Alamán, "Resrvado," Tlalpan, 10, 18, and 26 May 1831, AGN, Ramo de Expulsión, leg. 21, tom. 45, exp. 30, fol. 1; ibid., leg. 21, tom. 45, exp. 31, fols. 1–2; ibid., leg. 21, tom. 45, exp. 33, fols. 1–2; Múzquiz to Alamán, Tlalpan, 7 July 1831, leg. 22 3/4, tom. 55, exp. 82, fol. 8.

53. Flores Caballero, *La contrarrevolución*, pp. 170–71; Alamán to Facio, Mexico City, 6 Apr. 1831, AGN, Ramo de Expulsión, leg. 23, tom. 60, exp. 117, fol. 2.

54. Alamán to Camacho, Mexico City, 14 May 1831, AGN, Ramo de Expulsión, leg. 23, tom. 60, exp. 111, fol. 22.

55. Files, six "U.S. citizen" Spaniards, AGN, Ramo de Expulsión, leg.

23, tom. 56, exp. 20; ibid., leg. 20, tom. 44, exp. 28, fols. 1, 4–5; ibid., leg. 21, tom. 45, exp. 26, fols. 1, 4.

56. Rubirosa to Alamán, San Juan Bautista, 4 June 1831, AGN, Ramo de Expulsión, leg. 27, tom. 69, exp. 39, fol. 1; Camacho to Alamán, "Reservado," Jalapa, 18 June 1831, Alamán to Camacho, Mexico City, 2 July 1831, ibid., leg. 23, tom. 58, exp. 80, fols. 4–6.

57. Alamán to customs administrators and port captains, Mexico City, 13 June 1831, AGN, Ramo de Expulsión, leg. 23, tom. 58, exp. 75, fols. 12–14; Camacho to Alamán, Jalapa, 22 July 1831 (two letters), Alamán to Camacho, Mexico City, 29 July 1831 (two letters), ibid., leg. 23, tom. 59, exp. 108, fols. 4, 6–9, 11; Murphy to Lunyt, 29 Sept. 1831, extracted in *Las relaciones franco-mexicanas*, ed. Weckmann, 1:246.

58. Camacho to Alamán, Jalapa, 14 Oct. 1831, AGN, Ramo de Expulsión, leg. 23, tom. 59, exp. 108, fol. 10.

59. López to Alamán, Oaxaca, 12 July 1831, AGN, Ramo de Expulsión, leg. 23, tom. 56, exp. 24, fols. 8–10; Bustamante, *Voz de la Patria*, 10 Aug. 1831, pp. 7–8.

60. File, Félix Solís, AGN, Ramo de Expulsión, leg. 18, tom. 39, exp. 9, fols. 154, 156; Andrade to Alamán, Puebla, 10 Aug. 1831, Alamán to Andrade, Mexico City, 10 Oct. 1831, ibid., leg. 23, tom. 57, exp. 53a, fols. 1–4, 14–16; Arrillaga, comp., *Recopilación de leyes* 4:439–40.

61. Bustamante, *Continuación* 4:20–21.

62. Aviles to Gonzáles Angulo, 15 Jan. 1833, AGN, Ramo de Expulsión, leg. 25, tom. 64, exp. 38, fol. 33; Senate accord, 22 Sept. 1831, ibid., fol. 34.

63. AGN, Ramo de Expulsión, leg. 23, tom. 57, exp. 59, fol. 10.

64. Martínez Pizarro to Alamán, New Orleans, 14 Oct. 1831, Alamán to Martínez Pizarro, Mexico City, 23 Nov. 1831, Alamán to customs administrators at Matamoros and Veracruz, Mexico City, 23 Nov. 1831, AGN Ramo de Expulsión, leg. 23, tom. 57, exp. 59, fols. 59–60, 63, 71.

65. Reports, Veracruz, AGN, Ramo de Expulsión, leg. 23, tom. 60, exp. 119, fols. 139–51; Alamán to Camacho, Mexico City, 21 Jan. 1832, leg. 24, tom. 62, exp. 67, fol. 2; Despect to Murphy, Bayonne, 1 Dec. 1831, 2 Jan. and 2 Feb. 1832, extracted in *Las relaciones franco-mexicanas*, ed. Weckmann, 1:236.

66. Cameron to Jackson, Veracruz, 2 Feb. 1832, U.S., Consular Correspondence, microcopy 183.

67. Múzquiz to Alamán, Tlalpan (n.d., 1832), AGN, Ramo de Expulsión, leg. 24, tom. 62, exp. 62, fol. 1.

68. Analysis of Veracruz reports, AGN, Ramo de Expulsión, leg. 23, tom. 60, exp. 119, fols. 1–151.

69. Alamán to president of Chamber of Deputies' grand jury, Mexico City, 25 Apr. 1832, AGN, Ramo de Expulsión, leg. 23, tom. 57, exp. 56, fol. 4; ibid., leg. 25, tom. 64, exp. 38, fol. 21; Galván Rivera, comp., *Colección*

de órdenes y decretos 6:78; Packenham to Palmerston, 9 Mar. 1832, FO 50/71.
70. Robertson to Moctezuma, Tampico, 30 May 1832, Moctezuma to Robertson, Tampico, 9 June 1832, Robertson to Livingston, Tampico, 9 June 1832, U.S., Consular Correspondence, microcopy 241; Moctezuma to Crawford, Tampico, 6 June 1832, FO 50/77.

Chapter 11. The Last Laws of Expulsion, 1833–1836

1. Hittell, *History of California* 2:181–83; Crawford to Bidwell, Tampico, 3 July 1832, FO 50/77.
2. Bustamante, *Continuación* 4:133; "Si asesinan a Santa Anna no quedara un gachupín" (Mexico City, 1833), cited in Flores Caballero, *La contrarrevolución*, p. 171; Suárez y Navarro, *Historia de México* 1:370–71; Arrangoiz, *México* 2:221.
3. Chamber of Deputies, session of 15 Apr. 1829, in Mier y Terán to González Angulo, Mexico City, 4 Jan. 1833, AGN, Ramo de Expulsión, leg. 25, tom. 64, exp. 38, fol. 26.
4. "Decretos que se han dado relativos a la ley de espulsión de españoles," in Alvio to González Angulo, Mexico City, 5 Jan. 1833, AGN, Ramo de Expulsión, leg. 25, tom. 64, exp. 38, fols. 27, 32–34.
5. Suárez y Navarro, *Historia de México* 1:369–70; Flores Caballero, *La contrarrevolución*, p. 173; AGN, Ramo de Expulsión, leg. 25, tom. 64, exp. 38, fols. 16–18; Dublán and Lozano, comps., *Legislación mexicana* 2:476–78.
6. See Dublán's and Lozano's version of the lists, ibid., pp. 477–78, n. 1.
7. Ibid., pp. 477–78; blank forms in AGN, Ramo de Gobernación, leg. 169; Suárez y Navarro, *Historia de México* 1:370–71; Olavarría y Ferrari, *México independiente*, p. 309.
8. *El Telégrafo*, 21 Dec. 1833–17 Feb. 1834; Bocanegra, *Memorias* 2:374; Arrangoiz, *México* 2:214, 221–22; Zamaçois, *Méjico* 12:9; Flores Caballero, *La contrarrevolución*, p. 173.
9. Flores Caballero, *La contrarrevolución*, p. 173.
10. *El Fénix de la Libertad* 31 Jan. and 11 Feb. 1833; Herrera to González Angulo, Tlalpan, 24 Jan. 1833; González Angulo to Herrera, Mexico City, 26 Jan. 1833, AGN, Ramo de Expulsión, leg. 25, tom. 64, exp. 33b, fols. 1–2.
11. "Avisos," *El Telégrafo*, 9 Feb. 1833, p. 4; ibid., 7 May 1833, p. 4; González Angulo to Herrera, Mexico City, 11 and 18 Feb. 1833, Herrera to González Angulo, Tlalpan, 15 Feb. 1833, "Estado que manifiesta," AGN, Ramo de Gobernación, leg. 134, exp. 7, fols. 2–4.
12. González Angulo to Herrera, Mexico City, 15 Feb. 1833, AGN, Ramo de Expulsión, leg. 25, tom. 63, exp. 2.
13. "Parte Oficial. Consejo Privado," *El Telégrafo*, 16 Mar. 1833, p. 4; ibid., 28 Mar. 1833, p. 1.

14. González Angulo to Herrera, Mexico City, 15 Feb. 1833, Herrera to González Angulo, Tlalpan, 19 Feb. 1833, AGN, Ramo de Expulsión, leg. 25, tom. 64, exp. 32, fols. 1–2; *El Telégrafo*, 5 Mar. 1833, pp. 2–3; ibid., 9 Mar. 1833, p. 1.

15. Dublán and Lozano, comps., *Legislación mexicana* 2:489.

16. Marginalia, González Angulo to Herrera, Mexico City and Tlalpan, 28 Feb. 1833 (two letters), 4 Mar. and 16 Apr. 1833, AGN, Ramo de Goberación, leg. 134, exps. 10–11; González Angulo to Butler, Mexico City, 28 Mar. 1833, U.S., Correspondence of Ministers in Mexico.

17. Senate, session of 8 May 1833, *El Telégrafo*, 5 June 1833, p. 1.

18. González Angulo to Tuille y Moreno, Mexico City, 20 Mar. 1833, AGN, Ramo de Gobernación, leg. 134, exp. 24, fol. 2; Rivera Cambas, *Historia . . . de Jalapa* 3:134–35.

19. Romero to González Angulo, San Luis Potosí, 16 Feb. 1833, González Angulo to Romero, Mexico City, 2 Mar. 1833, AGN, Ramo de Gobernción, leg. 134, exp. 20, fols. 8–9.

20. Muro, *Historia de San Luis Potosí* 2:65.

21. Ibid., 2:63–65; Velázquez, *Historia de San Luis Potosí* 3:176; Hernández y Dávalos Papers, HD 22.4841.

22. Hernández y Dávalos Papers, HD 22.4856.

23. Ibid., HD 22.4857; Chamber of Deputies, session of 30 Apr. 1833, *El Telégrafo*, 15 May 1833, p. 1; Pérez Verdia, *Historia . . . de Jalisco* 2:265–70, 341–42.

24. Lopes to González Angulo, Mérida, 25 Jan. 1833, González Angulo to Lopes, Mexico City, 19 Feb. and 16 Apr. 1833, Lopes, "Nota circunstanciada," 28 Mar. 1833, AGN, Ramo de Expulsión, leg. 25, tom. 64, exp. 33a, fols. 1–2; ibid., leg. 12, tom. 26, exp. 1, fols. 1–3.

25. Lists, García to García, Zacatecas, 17 May 1833; lists, Madero to García, Chihuahua, 6 July 1833, AGN, Ramo de Expulsión, leg. 26, tom. 65, exp. 8, fols. 2–3, ibid., leg. 26, tom. 65, exp. 15, fols. 14–15; Hernández y Dávalos Papers, HD 22.4859.

26. Voluminous lists and reports, AGN, Ramo de Expulsión, legs. 25, 26, 27, toms. 63–65, 67–68, 71.

27. AHMA, Orozco Papers, leg. 66, xvi, "Papeles contra la Ley de espulsión," no. 2.

28. González Angulo to secretaries of the Chamber of Deputies, Mexico City, 18 Apr. 1833, AGN, Ramo de Expulsión, leg. 25, tom. 64, exp. 30, fol. 1; Hernández y Dávalos Papers, HD 22.4855; Senate, session of 22 Apr. 1833, *El Telégrafo*, 7 May 1833, p. 1.

29. Marginalia, 4 June 1833, Hernández y Dávalos Papers, HD 22.4859.

30. Arrillaga, comp., *Recopilación de leyes* 5:327–28; Dublán and Lozano, comps., *Legislación mexicana* 2:489–91; Arrangoiz, *México* 2:215; Zamaçois, *Méjico* 12:10–11; AGN, Ramo de Expulsión, leg. 25, tom. 64, exp. 37, fol. 1; ibid., leg. 25, tom. 64, exp. 44, fols. 1–2; Parres to González Angulo, Mexico City, 27 Mar. 1833; AGN, Ramo de Gobernación, leg. 134, exp. 24, fol. 1.

31. Herrera to García, Tlalpan, 9 May 1833, García to Herrera, Mexico City, 13 May 1833, AGN, Ramo de Gobernación, leg. 134, exp. 4, fols. 1–2.
32. AGN, Ramo de Expulsión, leg. 25, tom. 64, exp. 45, fol. 2; Arrillaga, comp., *Recopilación de leyes* 6:147.
33. González Angulo to president of Chamber of Deputies' grand jury, Mexico City, 23 Apr. 1833, AGN, Ramo de Expulsión, leg. 23, tom. 57, exp. 56, fol. 3; *Proceso instructivo formado por la sección de gran jurado*, pp. 5–6, 63, 69, 237.
34. Sánchez Espinosa to [unknown], [Mexico City], 1 Apr. 1833, Sánchez Espinosa Papers; Chamber of Deputies, session of 9 Apr. 1833, *El Fénix de la Liberdad*, 11 Apr. 1833, in Costeloe, *La primera república*, p. 377; Hernández y Dávalos Papers, HD 22.4860, 22.4871.
35. Santa Anna to Echeverría, Veracruz, 30 May 1833, Riva Palacio Papers, no. 232; Calcott, *Church and State in Mexico*, p. 90; Bustamante, *Continuación* 4:174, 176, 182; *El Fénix de la Liberdad*, 9 June 1833, in Costeloe, *La primera república*, p. 389.
36. Galván Rivera, *Colección de órdenes y decretos* 7:54; Alamán, *Méjico* 5:793; Zamaçois, *México* 12:31–32.
37. "Los representantes de la Nación mexicana a sus conciudadanos," in *Informes y manifiestos*, ed. Castillón, 3:124–25; Gómez Farías Papers, 146, F44B.
38. Bustamante, *Continuación* 4:177; Alamán, *Méjico* 5:793; Zamaçois, *México* 12:30–31; marginalia, 18 June 1833, Hernández y Dávalos Papers, HD 22.4855.
39. Arrillaga, comp., *Recopilación de leyes* 7:129–30.
40. Bustamante, *Continuación* 4:182–85, 187; Galarza, *The Roman Catholic Church*, p. 90; Calcott, *Church and State in Mexico*, p. 66.
41. *Colección de decretos y órdenes del primer congreso constituyente* 4:261–62; Mariano Ortiz de la Peña, "Proclama a la nación," Cuernavaca, 4 July 1833, Gómez Farías Papers, 87, F44A; Galván Rivera, comp., *Colección de órdenes y decretos* 7:159, 167, 177–78, 186.
42. Galván Rivera, comp., *Colección de órdenes y decretos* 7:165–66.
43. Hernández y Dávalos Papers, HD 22.4879; *El Telégrafo*, 1 Aug. 1833, p. 1; Arrillaga, comp., *Recopilación de leyes* 7:223–24.
44. Arrillaga, comp., *Recopilación de leyes* 8:1, 10, 53–60.
45. Ibid., 8:126–27, 563; *Colección de decretos y órdenes del congreso constituyente del estado . . . de México* 2:271–72.
46. Prieto Papers, wallet 23, no. 5; Tamaulipas Imprints, no. 64.
47. *El Telégrafo*, 4 Aug. 1833, p. 3; Dublán and Lozano, comps., *Legislación mexicana* 2:540.
48. Solorzano and Aburto to García, Mexico City, 9 Sept. 1833, García to secretaries of Congress, Mexico City, 19 Sept. 1833, AGN, Ramo de Expulsión, leg. 25, tom. 64, exp. 41, fols. 1–2; Hernández y Dávalos Papers, HD 22.4927.
49. Barron to O'Gorman, Tepic, 27 Sept. 1833, O'Gorman to Bidwell,

Mexico City, 31 Oct. 1833, FO 50/80b; García to Butler, Mexico City, 29 Oct. 1833, U.S. Correspondence of Ministers in Mexico; Sánchez de Tagle to Gómez Farías, [no location], 24 Oct. 1833, Gómez Farías Papers, 211, F44B.

50. Arrillaga, comp., *Recopilación de leyes* 8:143–44; Hittell, *California* 2:266; Bustamante, *Continuación* 4:247–49; *Colección de decretos y órdenes del congreso constituyente del estado . . . de México* 2:276–77.

51. Fernández to Lombardo, Ciudad Victoria, 29 Dec. 1833, Lombardo to Fernández, Mexico City, 14 Jan. 1834, AGN, Ramo de Expulsión, leg. 25, tom. 63, exp. 1, fols. 1, 4, 5–8.

52. *Nile's Weekly Register* (Baltimore), 21 Dec. 1833, in Calcott, *Church and State in Mexico*, p. 96; Minister of Justice, *Memoria, 1834*, p. 70; Tornel to Lombardo, Mexico City, 8 Jan. 1834, Lombardo to Tornel, Mexico City, 6 Feb. 1834, AGN, Ramo de Expulsión, leg. 27, tom. 71, exp. 2, fols. 1, 7.

53. Aburto to Lombardo, Toluca, 14 Jan. 1834, Lombardo to Aburto, Mexico City, 7 Feb. 1834, AGN, Ramo de Expulsión, leg. 22 3/4, tom. 55, exp. 82, fols. 9–10; Arrillaga, comp., *Recopilación de leyes* 9:35–36.

54. Hernández y Dávalos Papers, HD 22.4934; Furlong to Gómez Farías, Puebla, 5 Feb. 1834, Gómez Farías Papers, 245, F45.

55. Barragán to Lombardo, Mexico City, 11 Feb. 1834; Quintana Roo to Lombardo, Mexico City, 24 Feb. 1834, AGN, Ramo de Expulsión, leg. 27, tom. 71, exp. 3, fols. 1, 1a, 1b.

56. Tames to Lombardo, Guadalajara, 9 Apr. 1834, "letter of security" signed by Butler, 19 Apr. 1834, Lombardo to Tames, Mexico City, 21 Apr. 1834, AGN, Ramo de Expulsión, leg. 27, tom. 71, exp. 12, fols. 1–3; Apolo to Gómez Farías, Veracruz, 6 Apr. 1834, Gómez Farías Papers, 284, F45; Esteva to Alamán, Veracruz, 22 Mar. 1834, in Alamán, *Obras* 4:259–60; Arrillaga, comp., *Recopilación de leyes* 9:79–80.

57. Furlong to Gómez Farías, Puebla, 31 Mar. and 5 Apr. 1834, Gómez Farías Papers, 282, 284, F45; Gómez Farías to Furlong, 29 Mar. 1834, in Calcott, *Church and State in Mexico*, pp. 96, 101–02; *Colección de los decretos . . . de Puebla* 3:145, Arrangoiz, *México* 2:229–31; Zamaçois, *Méjico* 12:45–46.

58. Arrillaga, comp., *Recopilación de leyes* 7:290–92; 9:241–42, 279–81.

59. Ibid., 10:91; Anaya to Rea, [no location], 20 Aug. 1834, Anaya Papers; Lombardo to Herrera, 26 May 1834, Herrera to Lombardo, 26 July 1834, Lombardo to Mexican minister to France, 10 Aug. 1834, AGN, Ramo de Expulsión, leg. 27, tom. 71, exp. 9, fols. 2–4.

60. Tornel to Lombardo, "Reservado," Mexico City, 13 and 25 Sept. 1834, Lombardo to Tornel, Mexico City, 13 and 23 Sept. 1834, AGN, Ramo de Expulsión, leg. 27, tom. 71, exp. 7, fols. 1–4; *El Tiempo*, 10 Oct. 1834, pp. 398–99, in Parrott to Forsyth, Mexico City, 20 Oct. 1834, Parrott to Forsyth, Mexico City, 24 Nov. 1834, U.S., Consular Correspondence, microcopy 296.

61. *Colección de decretos y órdenes del congreso constituyente del estado . . . de México* 1:261–62; Arrillaga, comp., *Recopilación de leyes* 9:558–59.

62. Arrillaga, comp., *Recopilación de leyes* 10:68–70, 80, 107–08;

"Pronunciamiento," Gen. Juan Alvarez, 23 Mar. 1835, Prieto Papers, D61, vol. 2, no. 9; Nuevo León Imprints, NL 541.

63. Arrillaga, comp., *Recopilación de leyes* 10:186–87, 197.

64. Burrough to Forsyth, Veracruz, 6 Aug. 1835, U.S., Consular Correspondence, microcopy 183; *El Anteojo*, 12 Aug. 1835, p. 3; *Diario del Gobierno*, 3 Nov. 1835, p. 2; Bravo Ugarte, *México independiente*, pp. 68–71.

65. Arrillaga, comp., *Recopilación de leyes* 11:234–35; Davis to Jones, Paral, 17 Oct. 1839, U.S., Correspondence of Ministers in Mexico; Salce Arredondo Papers, wallet 10, no. 45; Ortiz Monasterio to secretaries of Congress, Mexico City, 14 Nov. 1835, Santa María to Muñoz y Muñoz, Madrid, 15 Jan. 1836, Muñoz y Muñoz to Ortiz Monasterio, Jalapa, 19 Mar. 1836; Ortiz Monasterio to Muñoz y Muñoz, Mexico City, 29 Mar. 1836, AGN, Ramo de Expulsión, leg. 4, tom. 9, exp. 10, fol. 55; ibid., leg. 27, tom. 71, exp. 19, fols. 1–3.

66. Tornel to Ortiz Monasterio, Mexico City, 14 Oct. 1836, AGN, Ramo de Expulsión, leg. 27, tom. 71, exp. 17, fol. 3; ibid., leg. 27, tom. 71, exp. 20, fol. 1.

67. "He Who Visited You in Alpolleca" to Gómez Farías, [no location], 4 Sept. 1836, in Calcott, *Church and State in Mexico*, pp. 101, 106–07; Zamaçois, *Méjico* 12:102–03.

68. Chase to secretary of state, Tampico, 4 Feb. and 12 May 1862, U.S., Consular Correspondence, microcopy 241.

69. Vasconcelos, *México y España*.

Bibliography

Archival Materials

Guanajuato: Archivo del Estado de Guanajuato
London: Public Record Office, Foreign Office: Diplomatic Correspondence, Mexico, F.O. 50, 97, 203 (FO)
Mexico City
    Archivo de ex-Ayuntamiento
        Ramo de Historia en General, tomo 1256–3
    Archivo General de la Nación (AGN)
        Ramo de Expulsión de Españoles, 71 tomos
        Ramo de Gobernación, 25 legajos
    Archivo Histórico del Museo de Antropología: Papeles sueltos de Gómez Orozco, Papeles varios, legajo 66 (AHMA)
    Secretaría de Relaciones Interiores y Exteriores: Serie Primera, Expulsiones 1823–81, caja 1 (SRIE)
Oaxaca: Archivo del Estado de Oaxaca, legajo 1863
Seville: Archivo de Indias, legajo 1564
Washington, D.C.
    U.S. Bureau of Customs: Lists of Passengers of Ships Arriving at New Orleans, microcopy 259, rolls 7–8
    U.S. Department of State
        Despatches of U.S. Consuls in Campeche, microcopy 286
        Despatches of U.S. Ministers in Mexico, microcopy 97
        Despatches of U.S. Consuls in Mexico City, microcopy 296
        Despatches of U.S. Consuls in Tampico, microcopy 241
        Despatches of U.S. Consuls in Veracruz, microcopy 183

Manuscript Collections

Lucas Alamán Papers. University of Texas Nettie Lee Benson Latin American Collection (UTLAC)
Juan Pablo Anaya Papers. UTLAC
Carlos María Bustamante Diary. UTLAC
Carlos García Papers. UTLAC
Francisco García Salinas Papers. UTLAC
Valentín Gómez Farías Papers. UTLAC

Vicente Guerrero Papers. UTLAC
Hernández y Dávalos Papers. UTLAC
María Guadalupe Hernández de Guerrero Papers. UTLAC
Nuevo León Imprints, 1802–1913. UTLAC
Alejandro Prieto Papers. UTLAC
Guillermo Prieto Papers. UTLAC
Mariano Riva Palacio Papers. UTLAC
Pablo Salce Arredondo Papers. UTLAC
José Sanchez Espinosa Papers. UTLAC
Antonio López de Santa Anna Papers. UTLAC
Justin H. Smith Papers. UTLAC
Sutro Collection. California State Library, San Francisco
Tamaulipas Imprints. UTLAC
Decrees, Articles, etc., 1823–38. UTLAC

Newspapers

Baltimore: *Nile's Weekly Register*
Cádiz: *Redactor General*
Chiapas: *Para Rayo*
Jalapa: *El Oriente*
Madrid: *Gazeta de Madrid*
Mexico City

El Aguila Mexicana	*El Gladiador*
El Amigo del Pueblo	*El Observador de la República*
El Anteojo	*Mexicana*
El Atleta	*Registro Oficial*
El Boletín	*Repertorio Mexicanao*
El Boletín Oficial	*El Sol*
Cardillo de las Mujeres	*El Telégrafo*
Correo de la Federación	*La Verdad Desnuda*
El Fénix de la Liberdad	*Voz de la Patria*
Gazeta Diaria de México	

New Orleans: *Mercantile Advertiser*
Oaxaca: *El Oaxaqueño Libre*
Puebla
    El Baratillo
    El Amigo de la Verdad
Veracruz: *El Censor*

Printed Materials: Primary Sources

A. I. "La victoria de Tampico desengaña a muchos bobos. Núm. 2." Mexico City, 1829.

Alamán, Lucas. *Historia de Méjico.* 5 vols. Mexico City: Editorial Jus, 1942.

———. "Este si está mas picante que el del señor Bustamante, . . . No. 4." Mexico City, 1830.

———. *Obras de Lucas Alamán: Documentos diversos (inéditos y muy raros).* Ed. Rafael Aguayo Spencer. 4 vols. Mexico City: Editorial Jus, 1945–47.

Arrillaga, Basilio José, comp. *Recopilación de leyes, decretos, bandos, reglamentos, circulares, y providencias de los supremos poderes y otras autoridades de la república mexicana.* 17 vols. Mexico City: Imprenta de J. M. Fernández de Lara, 1834–50.

Aviraneta e Ibargoyen, Eugenio de. *Mis memorias íntimas ó apuntes para la historia de los últimos sucesos ocurridos en la emancipación de la Nueva España (1825–1829).* Mexico City: Moderna librería religiosa de J. L. Vallejo, 1906.

———. "Memoria sobre el estado actual del Reyno de Méjico y modo de pacificarlo." Havana, February 1828.

"Aviraneta en el Archivo Nacional." *Boletín del Archivo Nacional* (Havana) 56:44–112.

Bocanegra, José María. "Causas que se han seguido y terminado contra los comprendidos en la conspiración llamada del Padre Arenas." Mexico City, 1828.

———. *Memorias para la historia de México independiente, 1822–1846.* 2 vols. Mexico City: Imprenta del gobierno federal, 1892–97.

Bustamante, Carlos María. *Continuación del cuadro histórico de la revolución mexicana.* Vols. 1–3. Mexico City: Biblioteca Nacional, 1953–54. Vol. 4. Mexico City: Instituto Nacional de Antropología e Historia, 1963.

———. *Continuación del cuadro histórico. História de los gobiernos de los generales Guadalupe Victoria, Vicente Guerrero y Anastacio Bustamante.* 2d ed. Mexico City, 1954.

———. *Diario histórico de México, 1822–1823.* Ed. Elías Amador. Zacatecas: J. Ortega, 1896.

———. "La patria y se salvó y su remedio es seguro." Mexico City, 1830.

Castillón, J. A., ed. *Informes y manifiestos de los poderes ejecutivo y legislativo de 1821 a 1904.* 3 vols. Mexico City: Imprenta del gobierno federal, 1905.

Castillo Negrete, Emilio del. *México en el siglo XIX.* 26 vols. Mexico City, 1875–92.

Chávez Orozco, Luis, ed. *El comercio exterior y la expulsión de los españoles.* Vol. 2 of *Colección de documentos para la historia del comercio exterior de Mexico.* 2d ser. Mexico City: Banco Nacional de Comercio Exterior, 1966.

———. *Un esfuerzo de México por la independencia de Cuba.* Vol. 32 of *Archivo Histórico Diplomático Mexicano.* Mexico City: Secretaría de Relaciones Exteriores, 1930.

Colección de decretos y órdenes del congreso constituyente del estado libre y soberano de Mexico. 2 vols. Toluca, 1848–50.

Colección de decretos y órdenes del honorable congreso constituyente del estado libre de Jalisco desde su instalación en 14 de septiembre de 1823 hasta 24 de enero de 1824 en que cesó. Guadalajara, 1826.

Colección de los decretos y ordenes más importantes que espidió el congreso constituyente del estado de Puebla en los años de 1824–25, 1826–28, 1830–31. 3 vols. Puebla: Imprenta del gobierno, 1827–34.

Colección de decretos y órdenes del primer congreso constituyente de México. 8 vols. Tlalpan and Toluca, 1827–28.

Colección de los decretos y órdenes del Tercer Congreso Constitucional del estado libre de Jalisco. Guadalajara, 1832.

Coromina, Amador, ed. *Recopilación de leyes, decretos, reglamentos y circulares expedidos en el estado de Michoacán*. 9 vols. Morelia: Imprenta de los hijos de I. Arango, 1886–1919.

Díaz-Thomé, Hugo. "Cartas al general Vicente Guerrero." *Boletín del Archivo General de la Nacion* 21 (1950): 419–32; 22 (1951): 122–24, 274–337.

Dublán, Manuel, and José María Lozano, eds. *Legislación Mexicana; ó colección completa de las disposiciones legislativas expedidas desde la independencia de la República*. 34 vols. Mexico City: Imprenta del Comercio, 1876–1904.

Franco, José Luciano. *Documentos para la historia de México existentes en el Archivo Nacional de Cuba*. Publicaciones del Archivo Nacional de Cuba, no. 53. Havana: Archivo Nacional, 1961.

Galván Rivera, Mariano, ed. *Colección de órdenes y decretos de la Soberana junta provisional gubernativa y soberanos Congresos generales de la Nación Mexicana*. 8 vols. Mexico City: Imprenta de Galván á cargo de M. Arévalo, 1829–40.

Giménez, Manuel María. *Memorias del Coronel Manuel María Giménez, Ayudante de Campo del General Santa Anna, 1798–1878*. Mexico City: 1911.

Gómez Pedraza, Manuel. *Manifiesto que Manuel Gómez Pedraza, Ciudadano de la República de Méjico, dedica á sus compatriotas, ó sea una reseña de su vida pública*. New Orleans and Guadalajara: Oficina de Brambila, 1831.

[Governor of Chihuahua]. *Memoria (1829)*. Chihuahua, 1829.

[Governor of Guanajuato]. *Memoria (1829)*. Guanajuato, 1829.

[Governor of Mexico]. *Memoria (1829)*. Toluca, 1829.

[Governor of Michoacán]. *Memoria (1829)*. Valladolid, 1829.

Guía del Archivo Histórico Militar de México. Vol. 1. Mexico City: Secretaría de Defensa Nacional, 1948.

Guía de Hacienda de la República Mexicana. Mexico City, 1825–28.

Humphreys, R. A., ed. *British Consular Reports on the Trade and Politics of Latin America, 1824–1826*. London: Offices of the Royal Historical Society, 1940.

Ibar, Francisco. *Muerte política de la República Mexicana ó Cuadro histórico de los sucesos políticos acaecidos en la República desde el 4 de diciembre de 1828 hasta el 23 de agosto de 1829* (pamphlet series). Mexico City: Imprenta á cargo del Sr. Tomás Uribe y Alcalde, 1829.

———. *Regeneración política de la República Mexicana ó Cuadro Histórico de los sucesos políticos acaecidos en ella desde el 23 de diciembre de 1829 hasta el 19 de junio de 1830* (pamphlet series). Mexico City: Imprenta de la Calle Cerrada de Jesús, 1830.

Mateos, Juan A. *Historia parlamentaria de los congresos mexicanos.* 10 vols. Mexico City: Imprenta de J. V. Villada, 1877–1912.

[Minister of Government]. *Memoria.* 13 vols. Mexico City, 1823–35.

[Minister of Justice and Ecclesiastical Affairs]. *Memoria.* 14 vols. Mexico City, 1822–35.

[Minister of the Treasury]. *Memoria.* 11 vols. Mexico City, 1825–35.

[Minister of War]. *Memoria.* 13 vols. Mexico City, 1823–35.

Navarro y Noriega, Fernando. *Catálogo de los curatos y misiones de la Nueva España, seguido de la Memoria sobre la población del reino de Nueva España (primer tercio del siglo XIX).* Mexico City: Instituto Mexicano de Investigaciones Histórico-jurídicas, 1943.

Obregón, Pablo. *Correspondencia de la legación de México en los Estados Unidos.* Vol. 32 of *Archivo Histórico Diplomático Mexicano.* 2d ser. Mexico City: Secretaría de Relaciones Exteriores, 1930.

Ortiz de Ayala, Tadeo. *Resumen de la estadística del Imperio Mexicano.* Mexico City: Imprenta de Doña Herculana del Villar y socios, 1822.

Prieto, Guillermo. *Memorias de mis tiempos.* Puebla: Editorial José M. Cajica, Jr., 1970.

Proceso instructivo formado por la sección del Gran jurado de la Cámara de Diputados del Congreso general, en averiguación de los delitos de que fueron acusados los ex-ministros d. Lucas Alamán, d. Rafael Mangino, d. José Antonio Facio y d. José Ignacio Espinosa. Mexico City: Impreso por I. Cumplido, 1833.

Radin, Paul, ed. *Catalogue of the Mexican Pamphlets in the Sutro Collections, 1623–1888.* 14 vols. and "Supplement." San Francisco: California State Library, 1939–40, mimeographed.

Secretary of State, Chihuahua. *Memoria (1830).* Chihuahua City, 1830.

Tornel y Mendívil, José María. *Breve reseña histórica de los acontecimientos más notables de la nación mexicana, desde el año de 1821 hasta nuestros días.* Mexico City: Imprenta de Cumplido, 1852.

———. "Manifiestacion del c. José María Tornel: Exposición de los hechos y motivos de la carrera del autor." Mexico City, 1833.

———. *Pronunciamiento de Perote por el General Antonio López de Sta. Anna, y sucesos de su campaña hasta la derogación de la ley que lo proscribió.* Mexico City: Imprenta del Aguila, 1829.

Torre Villar, Ernesto de la, ed. *Correspondencia diplomática franco-mexicana (1808–1839).* 2 vols. Mexico City: El Colegio de México, 1957.

Ward, H. G. *Mexico in 1827.* 2 vols. London: Henry Colburn, 1828.

Weckmann, Luis, ed. *Las relaciones franco mexicanas (1823–1867).* 2 vols. Mexico City: Secretaría de Relaciones Exteriores, 1961–62.

Zavala, Lorenzo de. *Ensayo histórico de las revoluciones de Méjico desde 1808 hasta 1830.* 2 vols. Paris: Imprimerie de P. Dupont et G. Laguionie, 1831.

———. "Juicio imparcial sobre los acontecimentos de México en 1828 y 1829." Mexico City: Oficina de Galván á cargo de M. Arévalo, 1830.

———. *Venganza de la colonia*. Mexico City: Empresas Editoriales, 1950.

Zerécero, Anastacio. *Memorias para la historia de las revoluciones en México*. Mexico City: Imprenta del gobierno, á cargo de J. M. Sandoval, 1869.

Secondary Sources

Amador, Elías. *Bosquejo histórico de Zacatecas*. Vol. 2. Zacatecas: Talleres Tipográficos "Pedroza," 1943.

Anna, Timothy E. *The Fall of Royal Government in Mexico City*. Lincoln: University of Nebraska Press, 1978.

Arrangoiz, Francisco de Paula. *México desde 1808 hasta 1867*. 4 vols. Madrid: D. A. Pérez Dubrull, 1871–72.

Bancroft, Hubert Howe. *History of Arizona and New Mexico, 1530–1888*. San Francisco: A. L. Bancroft, 1889.

———. *History of California*. 7 vols. San Francisco: A. L. Bancroft, 1886.

———. *History of Mexico*. 6 vols. San Francisco: A. L. Bancroft, 1883–88.

———. *History of the North American States and Texas*. 2 vols. San Francisco: A. L. Bancroft, 1889.

Barker, Eugene C. *Mexico and Texas, 1821–1835*. New York: Russell & Russell, 1965.

Bernecker, Walter L. *Industrie und Aussenhandel. Zur politischen Ökonomie Mexikos im 19. Jahrhundert*. Forschungen Lateinamerika. Vol. 13. Saarbrücken: Verlag breitenbach Publishers, 1987.

Bosch García, Carlos. *Problemas diplomáticos del México independiente*. Mexico City: El Colegio de México, 1947.

Bravo Ugarte, José. *México independiente*. Barcelona: Salvat Editores, 1959.

Calcott, Wilfred H. *Church and State in Mexico, 1822–1857*. Durham, N.C.: Duke University Press, 1926.

Carreño, Alberto María. *Los españoles en el México independiente. Un siglo de beneficencia (1842–1942)*. Mexico City: Imprenta M. L. Sánchez, 1942.

Carrión, Antonio. *Historia de la ciudad de las Puebla de los Angeles*. 2 vols. Puebla: Tip. de las Escuelas salesianas de artes y oficios, 1896–1900.

Corbitt, Duvon C. "Immigration in Cuba." *Hispanic American Historical Review* 22(1942): 280–308.

Costeloe, Michael P. "The Administration, Collection, and Distribution of Tithes in the Archbishopric of Mexico, 1800–1860." *The Americas* 23 (July 1966): 3–27.

———. *La primera república federal de México (1824–1835)*. Mexico City: Fondo de Cultura Económica, 1975.

Cuevas, Luis G. *El Porvenir de México, ó juicio sobre su estado político en 1821 y 1851*. Mexico City: Editorial Jus, 1954.

Delgado, Jaime. *España y México en el siglo XIX*. 3 vols. Madrid: Instituto Gonzalo Fernández de Oveido, 1950.

Englehardt, Zephryin, O.F.M. *The Missions and Missionaries of California*. 4 vols. San Francisco: J. H. Barry Co., 1912–15.

———. *Santa Barbara Mission*. San Francisco: J. H. Barry Co., 1923.

Flores Caballero, Romeo. *La contrarrevolución en la independencia: Los españoles en la vida política, social, y económica de México (1804–1838)*. Mexico City: El Colegio de México, 1969.

———. *Counterrevolution in Mexico. The Role of the Spaniards in the Independence of Mexico, 1804–38*. Lincoln: University of Nebraska Press, 1974.

Franco, José L. *Política continental americana de España en Cuba, 1812–1830*. Havana: Archivo Nacional, 1947.

Galarza, Ernesto. *The Roman Catholic Church as a Factor in the Political and Social History of Mexico*. Sacramento, Calif.: Capital Press, 1928.

Gil y Sáenz, Manuel. *Compendio histórico, geográfico y estadístico del estado de Tabasco*. San Juan Bautista: Consejo Editorial del gobierno del estado de Tabasco, 1872.

González de Cossío, Francisco. *Xalapa: Breve reseña histórica*. Mexico City: Talleres Gráficos de la Nación, 1957.

Green, Stanley C. *The Mexican Republic: The First Decade, 1823–1832*. Pittsburgh, Pa.: University of Pittsburgh Press, 1987.

Gurría Lacroix, Jorge. *Monografías históricas sobre Tabasco*. Mexico City: Edición del Instituto de Historia, 1952.

Hale, Charles. *Mexican Liberalism in the Age of Mora 1821–1853*. New Haven, Conn.: Yale University Press, 1968.

Hamill, Hugh M. *The Hidalgo Revolt. Prelude to Mexican Independence*. Gainesville: University of Florida Press, 1966.

Hittell, Theodore H. *History of California*. 2 vols. San Francisco: Pacific Press & Occidental Publishing House, 1885.

Howe, Walter P. *The Mining Guild of New Spain and Its Tribunal General, 1770–1821*. Cambridge, Mass.: Harvard University Press, 1949.

Hutchinson, C. Alan. *Frontier Settlement in Mexican California: The Híjar Padrés Colony and Its Origins, 1763–1835*. New Haven, Conn.: Yale University Press, 1969.

Lerdo de Tejada, Miguel M. *Apuntes históricos de la heróica ciudad de Veracruz*. 3 vols. Mexico City: Secretaría de Educación Pública, 1940.

———. *Comercio exterior de México desde la Conquista hasta hoy*. 2d ed. Mexico City: Banco Nacional de Comercio Exterior, 1967.

Manning, William R. *Early Diplomatic Relations Between the United States and Mexico*. Baltimore: Johns Hopkins Press, 1916.

Marmolejo, Lucio. *Efemeridades guanajuatenses, ó datos para formar la historia de la ciudad de Guanajuato*. 4 vols. Guanajuato: Imprenta del Colegio de artes y oficios á cargo de Francisco Rodríguez, 1883.

Meade, Joaquín. *Biografías veracruzanas. José Ignacio Esteva*. Vol. 12 of

Memorias de la Academia Mexicana de la Historia (Mexico City, 1953), pp. 17–90, 145–84, 241–76, 307–38.

Muñoz, Rafael F. *Antonio López de Santa Anna*. Mexico City: México Nuevo, 1937.

Muro, Manuel. *Historia de San Luis Potosí*. 3 vols. San Luis Potosí: Imprenta de M. Esquivel y cía., 1910.

Navarro y Rodrigo, Carlos. *Vida de Agustín de Iturbide*. Madrid: Editorial América, 1919.

Niles, John Milton. *History of South America and Mexico*. 2d ed. Hartford, Conn.: H. Huntington, 1839.

Olavarría y Ferrari, Enrique. *México independiente 1821–1855*. Vol. 4 of *México a través de los siglos*, ed. Vicente Riva Palacio. Mexico City: Ballesca y Compañía; Barcelona: Espasa y Compañía, 1888–89.

Pérez Verdía, Luis. *Historia particular del estado de Jalisco*. 3 vols. Guadalajara: Gráfica, 1952.

Pezuela, Jacobo de la. *Historia de la isla de Cuba*. 4 vols. Madrid: 1868–78.

Ponce de León, José María. *Reseñas históricas del estado de Chihuahua*. 2d ed. Chihuahua: Imprenta del gobierno, 1910.

Potash, Robert A. *El Banco de Avío de México. El fomento de la industria, 1821–1846*. Mexico City: Fondo de Cultura Económica, 1959.

Reyes Heroles, Jesús. *El liberalismo mexicano*. 3 vols. Mexico City: Universidad Autónoma de México, 1957–61.

Rippy, J. Fred. *Joel Roberts Poinsett, Versatile American*. Durham, N.C.: Duke University Press, 1935.

Rivera Cambas, Manuel. *Historia antigua y moderna de Jalapa y de las revoluciones del estado de Veracruz*. 5 vols. Mexico City: Imprenta de I. Cumplido, 1869–71.

Romero, Matías. *Mexico and the United States; a Study of Subjects Affecting Their Political, Commercial and Social Relations, Made with a View to Their Promotion*. New York and London: J. P. Putnam's Sons, 1898.

Sánchez Lamego, Miguel A. *La invasión española de 1829*. Mexico City: Editorial Jus, 1971.

Sierra, Catalina. *El nacimiento de México*. Mexico City: Universidad Autónoma de México, 1960.

Sims, Harold. "Las clases económicas y la dicotomía criollo-peninsular en Durango, 1827." *Historia Mexicana* 20 (1971): 539–62.

———. *Descolonización en México: El conflito entre mexicanos y españoles (1821–1831)*. Mexico City: Fondo de Cultura Económica, 1982.

———. "Los exiliados españoles de México en 1829." *Historia Mexicana* 119 (January–March 1981): 390–414.

———. *La expulsión de los españoles de México (1821–1828)*. Mexico City: Fondo de Cultura Económica, 1974.

———. "The Expulsion of the Spaniards from Mexico, 1827–1828." Ph.D. diss., University of Florida, 1968.

————. *La reconquista de México: La historia de los atentados españoles, 1821–1830.* Mexico City: Fondo de Cultura Económica, 1984.

Sprague, William Forrest. *Vicente Guerrero, Mexican Liberator; A Study in Patriotism.* Chicago: R. R. Donnelley & Sons, 1939.

Suárez y Navarro, Juan. *Historia de México y del General Antonio López de Santa Anna.* 2 vols. Mexico City: Imprenta de Ignacio Cumplido, 1850–51.

Tenenbaum, Barbara. *The Politics of Penury, Debts and Taxes in Mexico, 1821–1856.* Albuquerque: University of New Mexico Press, 1986.

Trens, Manuel B. M. *Historia de Veracruz.* Jalapa: Jalapa-Enríquez, 1948.

Valadés, José C. *Alamán, estadista e historiador.* Mexico City: Antigua Librería Robredo, J. Porrúa e hijos, 1838.

————. *Orígines de la república mexicana.* Mexico City: Editores Mexicanos Unidos, 1965.

Vasconcelos, José. *México y España; opiniones de . . . sobre el libelo de un sujeto de Tlalixcoyán, pidiendo el saqueo y la expulsión de los españoles.* 4th ed. Mexico City: Imp. M. León Sánchez, 1929.

Velázquez, Primo Feliciano. *Historia de San Luis Potosí.* 4 vols. Mexico City: Sociedad Mexicana de Geografía y Estadística, 1947.

Vergès, J. M. Miguel I. *La diplomacia española en México (1822–1823).* Mexico City: El Colegio de México, 1956.

Ynsfran, Pablo Max. "Catálogo del Archivo de Don Lucas Alamán que se conserva en la Universidad de Texas, Austin." *Historia Mexicana* 4 (1954): 281–316, 431–76.

————. *Catálogo de los manuscritos del Archivo de Don Valentín Gómez Farías obrantes en la Universidad de Texas, Colección Latinoamericana.* Mexico City: Editorial Jus, 1968.

Zamaçois, Niceto. *Historia de Méjico desde sus tiempos más remotos hasta nuestros días.* 23 vols. Barcelona: J. F. Parres y co., 1878–88.

Index

267

Pitt Latin American Series

COLE BLASIER, EDITOR

ARGENTINA

Argentina in the Twentieth Century
David Rock, Editor

Argentina: Political Culture and Instability
Susan Calvert and Peter Calvert

Discreet Partners: Argentina and the USSR Since 1917
Aldo César Vacs

Juan Perón and the Reshaping of Argentina
Frederick C. Turner and José Enrique Miguens, Editors

The Life, Music, and Times of Carlos Gardel
Simon Collier

The Political Economy of Argentina, 1946–1983
Guido di Tella and Rudiger Dornbusch, Editors

BRAZIL

External Constraints on Economic Policy in Brazil, 1889–1930
Winston Fritsch

The Film Industry in Brazil: Culture and the State
Randal Johnson

The Manipulation of Consent: The State and Working-Class Consciousness in Brazil
Youssef Cohen

The Politics of Social Security in Brazil
James M. Malloy

Urban Politics in Brazil: The Rise of Populism, 1925–1945
Michael L. Conniff

COLOMBIA

Gaitán of Colombia: A Political Biography
Richard E. Sharpless

Roads to Reason: Transportation, Administration, and Rationality in Colombia
Richard E. Hartwig

CUBA

Cuba Between Empires, 1878–1902
Louis A. Pérez, Jr.

Cuba in the World
Cole Blasier and Carmelo Mesa-Lago, Editors

Cuba Under the Platt Amendment, 1902–1934
Louis A. Pérez, Jr.

Cuban Studies, Vols. 16–20
Carmelo Mesa-Lago, Editor

Intervention, Revolution, and Politics in Cuba, 1913–1921
Louis A. Pérez, Jr.